FAITH AND ORDER:
THE RECONCILIATION OF LAW AND RELIGION

EMORY UNIVERSITY
STUDIES IN LAW AND RELIGION

General Editor: John Witte, Jr., Emory University

Theology of Law and Authority in the
English Reformation
By Joan Lockwood O'Donovan

Political Order and the Plural Structure of Society
Edited by James W. Skillen & Rockne M. McCarthy

Faith and Order:
The Reconciliation of Law and Religion
By Harold J. Berman

FAITH AND ORDER:
THE RECONCILIATION OF LAW AND RELIGION

Harold J. Berman

Scholars Press
Atlanta, Georgia

EMORY UNIVERSITY
STUDIES IN LAW AND RELIGION

Faith and Order
The Reconciliation of Law and Religion

by
Harold J. Berman

Library of Congress Cataloging in Publication Data
Berman, Harold Joseph, 1918–
   Faith and order: the reconciliation of law and religion/ by
Harold J. Berman.
      p. cm. — (Emory University studies in law and religion; no. 3)
   Includes index.
   ISBN 1–55540–852–4 (hard). — ISBN 1–55540–853–2
   1. Religion and law. 2. Law. I. Title. II. Series.
BL65.L33B47 1993
340'.1—dc20   93–20362
                                                 CIP

Published by Scholars Press
for
Emory University

To Ruth

CONTENTS

PREFACE

Most of the essays published in this book were first presented as talks to various university audiences of faculty and students or to groups of specialists in various academic disciplines—principally legal scholars, historians, sociologists, philosophers, theologians, and political scientists. Others were written for publication in various scholarly journals. One was written more than fifty years ago for a seminar in legal history at the London School of Economics and is published here for the first time. The justification for collecting them in a book is that despite the diverse topics which they address they all have a common underlying theme: that the legal order of a society, that is, the formal institutions, structures, rules, and procedures by which it is regulated, is intrinsically connected with fundamental beliefs concerning the ultimate meaning of life and the ultimate purpose of history, that is, with religious faith.

The need to elaborate this thesis in a variety of different contexts arises from the fact that most people today—at least in the academic world—see only a remote connection between legal institutions and religious beliefs. Exceptions are sometimes made for what have come to be called "family values," but in general religion has come increasingly to be treated, during the past two generations, as solely a private matter, "what the individual does with his own solitariness" (in Alfred North Whitehead's definition), while law has come increasingly to be treated as solely a public matter, a matter of social policy.

There are, to be sure, some people in the academic world, and many in what may be called the real world, who connect law with religion by emphasizing the link which both have with morality. On the theoretical level, it is argued that law is based ultimately on certain moral principles (contracts should be kept, crimes should be punished, civil rights should be protected and civil wrongs should be remedied, trials should be fair, and, in general, justice should be done), and that morality, in turn, including legal morality, is based ultimately on religion. A related, though different, argument is made by some religious moralists, namely, that society has a duty to enact laws prohibiting conduct which violates their religious morality. I do not, however, address these themes, except indirectly, and must therefore warn those who see in morality the only connection, or the basic connection, between law and religion that they may be disappointed by this book. It is not only, and not primarily, about legal and religious morality. It is primarily about what I have called the religious dimension of law and the legal dimension of religion. It is about the dynamics of the interaction between these two great forces, which may be said to constitute the outer and the inner aspects of social life.

Some readers will wish that more had been said here about the tensions between these two forces. Indeed, the tensions need to be preserved if law is to be saved from new forms of theocracy that would legislate religious dogmas, and religion from new forms of politicization that would co-opt it for secular purposes. The existence of such tensions is, in fact, presupposed in our federal and state constitutions, which, by guaranteeing the free exercise of religion and prohibiting an establishment of religion, protect both our religious and our political liberties.

It is not, however, the task of this book to explore in depth the tensions between law and religion, about which much has been written by others. My task is rather to show that despite those tensions the two stand in a dialectical relationship with each other and cannot maintain their vitality independently of each other. At the highest level, surely, the just and the holy are one, and our sense of each rests partly on our sense of the other. It is necessary to say this because the conventional wisdom has separated them to the point of disaster.

The danger that faces us today, in contrast with earlier times, is, I believe, not the danger of excessive sanctification of law or excessive legalization of religion; it is not a crisis of their excessive integration but rather a crisis of their excessive fragmentation. We are threatened more by contempt for law than by worship of it, and more by skepticism regarding the ultimate meaning and purpose of life and of history than by some great all-embracing totalitarian eschatology. Emphasis on the dualism of church and state, spiritual and secular, faith and order, religion and law, makes sense as an answer to monistic claims of the total state or of the total church. In the West today, however, we are threatened more by anarchy than by dictatorship and more by apathy and decadence than by fanaticism. That, at least, is my starting-point in addressing various aspects of the interrelationship of law and religion.

The first chapter of the book is an anthropological introduction which argues that, in all societies, law, in the broadest sense, shares with religion, in the broadest sense, certain elements, namely, ritual, tradition, authority, and universality—elements, or values, that protect law from degenerating into legalism. This introductory chapter offers definitions of law and religion which set the stage for subsequent analysis of various specific aspects of both.

In Part I historical themes are addressed, including the importance of religious belief and ecclesiastical legal institutions in the formation of the Western legal tradition in the twelfth to fifteenth centuries, the impact of Lutheranism on Western legal philosophy in the sixteenth century, English Puritan influences on the development of the principle of absolute obligation for breach of contract in the seventeenth century, and religious sources and implications of the constitutional protection of religious freedom in the United States viewed in a historical perspective.

In Part II sociological and philosophical themes are addressed, including an analysis of philosophical fallacies implicit in Max Weber's sociology of law as well as in contemporary debates between adherents of individualist and communitarian theories of law. The argument that both sociology of law and social theory generally have suffered from a failure to recognize the religious dimension of law is developed further in the next chapter in the context of the emergence in the latter half of the twentieth century of a new brand of sociology, called sociology of the world system. Here both the roles of law and of religion have been addressed, if at all, in negative terms, as obstacles to global unification, whereas the more striking fact is the emergence of a large body of world common law and also of a movement toward rapprochement among the world's great religions. Finally, Part II closes with a chapter ana-lyzing the three major schools of legal philosophy, namely, natural-law theory, legal positivism, and historical jurisprudence, arguing that it is history that determines whether we emphasize the source of law in morality (natural-law theory) or the source of law in politics (positivism). The thesis is advanced that through historical jurisprudence the truths in natural-law theory can be integrated with the truths in positivism.

Part III addresses theological themes, including Biblical concepts of the relation of law to love as well as differences between "academic" and Judaic-

Christian modes of scholarship and the prophetic tasks of law and religion in the development, for the first time in the history of mankind, of a global economy and a global culture. The crisis of American legal education is discussed in this context.

Finally, Part IV addresses problems of religion and law in Russia—chiefly in Soviet Russia, but also to some extent in pre-Soviet and post-Soviet Russia. It is argued that Russian experience has much to teach us concerning the nature of legal systems and the nature of belief-systems as well as the nature of the interaction of the one with the other.

A book such as this, whose chapters were written during a period of over fifty years, could not have come into existence without the inspiration, intellectual nourishment, and support of literally hundreds of teachers, colleagues, students, and friends, not to mention the practical assistance of secretaries, librarians, editors, and publishers. Under the circumstances, the author may be forgiven for acknowledging the help of only a few who worked assiduously in producing the present edition: Nancy Knaak and Marie Warren, who typed the manuscript; John Salatti, who checked the footnotes and brought them into proper order; Bruce Frohnen and Charles J. Reid, who gave valuable editorial suggestions; and—above all—my friend and colleague John Witte, Director of the Law and Religion Program of Emory University, whose idea it was to produce this volume and who worked tirelessly to give it the shape that it has finally taken. Professor Witte not only coauthored one of the chapters of this book but also gave valuable assistance and advice in the preparation of many others.

> Harold J. Berman
> Atlanta, Georgia
> January 11, 1993

╼╾ **1** ╼╾

INTRODUCTION:
RELIGIOUS DIMENSIONS OF LAW*

W estern man is undergoing an integrity crisis—the kind of crisis that many individual men and women experience in their early fifties when they ask themselves with utmost seriousness, and often in panic, what their lives have stood for and where they are headed. Now we are asking that question not only as individuals but as nations and as groups within nations. Our whole culture seems to be facing the possibility of a kind of nervous breakdown.[1]

---

* Reprinted from *The Interaction of Law and Religion* (Nashville, Tennessee, 1974), comprising the Lowell Lectures on Theology, delivered at Boston University in 1971.

[1] The phrase "integrity crisis" is derived from the writings of Erik Erikson; it is less well known than his phrase "identity crisis," perhaps because the latter phrase relates to the transition from youth to adulthood, which is open and notorious, whereas the former relates to the "closure" of the whole life cycle, about which there is apt to be more secrecy and more embarrassment. Erikson speaks of "the despair of the knowledge that a limited life is coming to a conscious conclusion." He describes in the following terms the integrity needed to balance such despair:

> It is the ego's accrued assurance of its proclivity for order and meaning. It is a post-narcissistic love of the human ego—not of the self—as an experience which conveys some world order and spiritual sense, no matter how dearly paid for. It is the acceptance of one's one and only life cycle as something that had to be and that, by necessity, permitted of no substitutions: it thus means a new and a different love of one's parents. It is a comradeship with the ordering ways of distant times and different pursuits, as expressed in the simple products and sayings of such times and pursuits. Although aware of the relativity of all the various life

- 1 -

One major symptom of this threatened breakdown is the massive loss of confidence in law—not only on the part of law-consumers but also on the part of law-makers and law-distributors. A second major symptom is the massive loss of confidence in religion—again, not only on the part of those who (at least at funerals and weddings) sit in the pews of our churches and synagogues, but also on the part of those who occupy the pulpits.

Historians will tell us that in every generation the complaint is made that people are losing their religious faith and their respect for law. And it may also be true that there are more churchgoing, law-abiding Europeans and Americans today than there were in previous periods of history. Yet the symptoms of an integrity crisis are unmistakable. Among the earliest signs were those given after the First World War by artists and poets and novelists—men like Picasso and Joyce—whose work revealed that traditional conceptions of space and time and even of language itself were disintegrating, cracking up. Then came the intellectual upheavals of the 1930s when social scientists told us that the traditional social, political, and economic structures had lost their validity. Europe was torn by new revolutionary mythologies, while America withdrew herself. Ironically, the Second World War gave the nations of the West a temporary lift; we found that we were, after all, capable of collective action and of personal sacrifice for traditional common goals. This spirit was artificially maintained for a time after the war, especially by the campaign against communism. But since the late 1950s we have increasingly experienced a sense of futility and a premonition of doom, the most visible signs of which are the progressive demoralization of the cities, the deep frustration of a significant portion of the youth, and the incapacity of the nations to act decisively in the interests of peace either at home or abroad.

What makes this an integrity crisis rather than some other kind of crisis is precisely its relation to the loss of confidence in religion and in law. In the centuries prior to World War I religion and law—especially in America— were the patrimony of our collective life. They embodied our sense of

---

styles which have given meaning to human striving, the possessor of integrity is ready to defend the dignity of his own life style against all physical and economic threats. For he knows that an individual life is the accidental coincidence of but one life cycle with but one segment of history; and that for him all human integrity stands or falls with the one style of integrity of which he partakes. The style of integrity developed by his culture or civilization thus becomes the "patrimony of his soul." . . . Before this final solution, death loses its sting.

Erik H. Erikson, *Childhood and Society* (New York, 1963), 268; Erik H. Erikson, *Insight and Responsibility* (New York, 1964), 134. This is not the place to develop the idea that whole societies may undergo stages of development analogous to stages in the life cycle of an individual person.

common purpose and our sense of social order and social justice—"the style of integrity" (in Erikson's words) "developed by [our] . . . civilization."[2] Our disillusionment with formal religion and with formal law is thus symptomatic of a deeper loss of confidence in fundamental religious and legal values, a decline of belief in and commitment to any kind of transcendent reality that gives life meaning, and a decline of belief in and commitment to any structures and processes that provide social order and social justice. Torn by doubt concerning the reality of those values that sustained us in the past, we come face to face with the prospect of death itself.

How are we to explain our disillusionment with law and with religion? There are, of course, many causes. One of them, I believe, is the too radical separation of one from the other. That in turn is partly the result of our failure to make the right connections between formal legal and religious systems, on the one hand, and the underlying legal and religious values to which I have referred, on the other. Both the law schools and the schools of theology bear their share of responsibility for the narrowness and the rigidity of our thought on these matters.

If we see law in dictionary terms merely as a structure or "body" of rules laid down by political authorities, and similarly see religion merely as a system of beliefs and practices relating to the supernatural, the two seem connected with each other only very distantly or in only a few rather narrow and specific respects. But in reality both are much more than that. Law is not only a body of rules; it is people legislating, adjudicating, administering, negotiating—it is a living process of allocating rights and duties and thereby resolving conflicts and creating channels of cooperation. Religion is not only a set of doctrines and exercises; it is people manifesting a collective concern for the ultimate meaning and purpose of life—it is a shared intuition of and commitment to transcendent values. Law helps to give society the structure, the *Gestalt*, it needs to maintain inner cohesion; law fights against anarchy. Religion helps to give society the faith it needs to face the future; religion fights against decadence.[3]

---

[2] Erikson, *Childhood and Society*, 268.

[3] Cf. Eugen F. Rosenstock-Huessy, *Speech and Reality* (Norwich, VT, 1970), 12ff. Some readers may at this point want more precise definitions of law and religion. The author begs their indulgence: in a sense, this volume is a search for the right definitions of these two terms. However, it may be helpful at the outset to emphasize several points in explanation of this paragraph. First, I view law not only as a social but also as a psychological phenomenon: it involves the sense of social order, the sense of rights and duties, the sense of the just, which is felt by individual members of society, and not only the society's collective system of regulation. Second, I view religion not only as a psychological phenomenon but also as a social phenomenon: it involves a society's collective concern with transcendent values, and not only the individual's personal beliefs. Both law and reli-

These are two dimensions of social relations—as well as of human nature—which are in tension with each other: law through its stability limits the future; religion through its sense of the holy challenges all existing social structures. Yet each is also a dimension of the other. A society's belief in the ultimate transcendent purpose will certainly be manifested in its processes of social ordering, and its processes of social ordering will likewise be manifested in its sense of an ultimate purpose. Indeed, in some societies (ancient Israel, for example) the law, the Torah, is the religion. But even in those societies which make a sharp distinction between law and religion, the two need each other—law to give religion its social dimension and religion to give law its spirit and direction as well as the sanctity it needs to command respect. Where they are divorced from each other, law tends to degenerate into legalism and religion into religiosity.

In this introduction, I shall speak chiefly about the dependence of law upon religion.

Anthropological studies confirm that in all cultures law shares with religion four elements: ritual, tradition, authority, and universality.[4] In every

---

gion are thus to be seen as dimensions both of human nature and of social relations. Third, I avoid the question whether religion necessarily involves a belief in a divine being or beings. Instead, I treat as religion those sets of beliefs and practices which give to any persons or things or forces—whether or not they are expressly considered divine—the same kinds of devotion and attribute to them the same kinds of powers that are usually given and attributed to God or to gods in conventional deistic religions. For example, Soviet schoolchildren are taught to say: "Lenin lived. Lenin lives. Lenin will live." This we would call an expression of a religious faith, even though the same Soviet schoolchildren are taught to be atheists and antireligious.

The statement that religion "is people manifesting a collective concern for the ultimate meaning and purpose of life—it is a shared intuition of, and commitment to, transcendent values" is not intended as a comprehensive definition of religion but rather as an indication of its central aspects. There are other aspects, such as the inner life of the solitary mystic, but I believe that these are ultimately dependent on the collective faith. Also it is possible to find contrasts and tensions between "ultimate" and "transcendent," between "meaning" and "values," and between "concern" and "intuition" or "commitment;" yet for present purposes I believe that these terms should be seen as complementary rather than contradictory to each other. Readers who wish to grapple further with problems of definition of the scope of the concept of religion may consult such works as Rem B. Edwards, *Reason and Religion: An Introduction to the Philosophy of Religion* (New York, 1972), Roland Robertson, *The Sociological Interpretation of Religion* (Oxford, 1970), and Peter L. Berger, *The Sacred Canopy: Elements of a Sociological Theory of Religion* (New York, 1967). Of these, the last is closest to my way of thinking, especially in that it avoids the tendency of many to reduce religion to metaphysics or to morals or to both.

[4] Cf. Huston Smith, *The Religions of Man* (New York, 1958), 90-92, where ritual, tradition, and authority are listed among six aspects of religion which "appear so regularly as to suggest that their need is rooted in man's very makeup to an extent that no religion which proposes to speak to mankind at large can expect to elude them indefinitely." A fourth element listed by Smith is "the concept of God's sovereignty and grace;" for this I

society these four elements, as I shall try to show, symbolize man's effort to reach out to a truth beyond himself. They thus connect the legal order of any given society to that society's beliefs in an ultimate, transcendent reality. At the same time, these four elements give sanctity to legal values and thereby reinforce people's legal emotions: the sense of rights and duties, the claim to an impartial hearing, the aversion to inconsistency in the application of rules, the desire for equality of treatment, the very feeling of fidelity to law and its correlative, the abhorrence of illegality. Such emotions, which are an indispensable foundation of every legal order, cannot obtain sufficient nourishment from a purely utilitarian ethic. They require the sustenance of a belief in their inherent and ultimate rightness. The prevailing concept in contemporary Western societies that law is primarily an instrument for effectuating the policies of those who are in control is, in the long run, self-defeating. By thinking of law solely in terms of its efficiency, we rob it of that very efficiency. By failing to give enough attention to its religious dimensions, we deprive it of its capacity to do justice and possibly even its capacity to survive.

The Secular-Rational Model.—A heavy burden of proof rests on one who asserts that not only in past eras of our own history and not only in non-Western cultures but also in modern, technologically advanced countries of the West, including the United States today, religious elements play an indispensable part in the effective working of the law.

The conventional wisdom is the opposite: that although law in most cultures may have originally been derived from religion and although during certain eras such as the Catholic Middle Ages or the age of Puritanism our own law may have contained religious elements, these have been gradually purged away during the past two centuries so that today there is almost nothing left of them; and further, that modern law is to be explained solely in instrumental terms, that is, as a consciously elaborated means of accomplishing specific political, economic, and social policies.

---

have substituted the concept of universality, since I include among religions world faiths that purport not to recognize the existence of God. Smith's other two aspects of all world religions are speculation (in the sense of metaphysical wondering) and mystery (in the sense of the occult and the uncanny).

See also Roscoe Pound, "*Law and Religion*," *Rice Institute Pamphlet* 27 (April, 1940), where authority and universality are treated as ideas which religion has contributed to law. However, Pound treats religion as one of the competing sources of the received ideals of a given legal system rather than as a necessary dimension of law.

Most anthropological studies dealing with the relation of law to religion in primitive societies define religion too narrowly for our purposes, confining its meaning to supernaturalism and magic.

Contemporary social science characterizes modern law by the words "secular" and "rational."[5] The alleged secularism of law is linked with the decline of the belief in either a divine law or a divinely inspired natural law. The law of the modern state, it is said, is not a reflection of any sense of ultimate meaning and purpose in life; instead, its tasks are finite, material, impersonal—to get things done, to make people act in certain ways.

This concept of the secular character of law is closely linked with the concept of its rationality, in the special sense in which that word has come to be used by social scientists. The lawmaker, in inducing people to act in certain ways, appeals to their capacity to calculate the consequences of their conduct, to measure their own and others' interests, to value rewards and punishments. Thus legal man, like his brother economic man, is conceived as one who uses his head and suppresses his dreams, his convictions, his passions, his concern with ultimate purposes. At the same time, the legal system as a whole, like the economic system, is seen as a huge, complex machine—a bureaucracy (in Max Weber's definition)—in which individual units perform specific roles according to specific incentives and instructions, independently of the purposes of the whole enterprise.

The contrast between this conception of law and the conception of religion that goes with it has recently been expressed by Professor Thomas Franck of New York University. Law, he writes, in contrast to religion "has . . . become undisguisedly a pragmatic human process. It is made by men, and it lays no claim to divine origin or eternal validity." This leads Professor Franck to the view that a judge, in reaching a decision, is not propounding a truth but is rather experimenting in the solution of a problem, and if his decision is reversed by a higher court or if it is subsequently overruled, that does not mean it was wrong but only that it was, or became in the course of time, unsatisfactory. Having broken away from religion, Franck states, law is now characterized by "existential relativism." Indeed, it is now generally recognized "that no judicial decision is ever 'final', that the law both follows the event (is not eternal or certain) and is made by man (is not divine or True)."[6]

On the other hand, Franck recognizes that to proclaim this philosophy too loudly may involve a certain cost in popular respect for legality. The legal system is apt to become "more open to challenge and less likely to inspire unquestioning mass loyalty." I would go one step further and ask what it is that inspires not unquestioning mass loyalty to law but simply a general

---

[5] See Max Weber, *On Law in Economy and Society*, ed. Max Rheinstein (Cambridge, MA, 1954), 224-283.

[6] Thomas M. Franck, *The Structure of Impartiality: Examining the Riddle of One Law in a Fragmented World* (New York, 1968), 62, 68-69.

willingness to obey it at all. If law is merely an experiment, and if judicial decisions are only hunches, why should individuals or groups of people observe those legal rules or commands that do not conform to their interests?

The answer usually given by adherents of the instrumental theory is that people generally observe the law because they fear the coercive sanctions which will otherwise be imposed by the law-enforcing authority. This answer has never been satisfactory. As psychological studies have now demonstrated, far more important than coercion in securing obedience to rules are such factors as trust, fairness, credibility, and affiliation.[7] It is precisely when law is trusted and therefore does not require coercive sanctions that it is efficient; one who rules by law is not compelled to be present everywhere with his police force. Today this point has been proved in a negative way by the fact that in our cities that branch of law in which the sanctions are most severe— namely, the criminal law—has been powerless to create fear where it has failed to create respect by other means. Today everyone knows that no amount of force which the police are capable of exerting can stop urban crime. In the last analysis, what deters crime is the tradition of being law-abiding, and this in turn depends upon a deeply or passionately held conviction that law is not only an instrument of secular policy but also part of the ultimate purpose and meaning of life.

Law itself, in all societies, encourages the belief in its own sanctity. It puts forward its claim to obedience in ways that appeal not only to the material, impersonal, finite, rational interests of the people who are asked to observe it but also to their faith in a truth, a justice, that transcends social utility—in ways, that is, that do not fit the image of secularism and instrumentalism presented by the prevailing theory. Even Joseph Stalin had to reintroduce into

---

[7] The Swiss psychologist Jean Piaget pioneered studies of the moral development of children showing the importance of cognitive, as contrasted with coercive, factors. See Jean Piaget, *The Moral Judgment of the Child* (New York, 1932). More recently Lawrence Kohlberg has built on Piaget's work, demonstrating the universality of sequential modes of thought about rights, obedience, justice. Cf. Lawrence Kohlberg and Elliot Turiel, eds., *Research in Moralization: The Cognitive-Developmental Approach* (New York, 1972). See also Derek Wright, *The Psychology of Moral Behavior* (Baltimore, MD, 1971). Cross-cultural psychological studies by June L. Tapp, influenced by the theories of Piaget and Kohlberg, emphasize the importance of the factors listed in the text—affiliation, credibility, fairness, and trust—in children's development of principles for evaluating right and wrong and for perfecting a sense of law and justice. Cf. June L. Tapp and Felice J. Levine, "Persuasion to Virtue: A Preliminary Statement," *Law and Society Review* 4 (1970): 565, 576-581; June L. Tapp, ed., "Socialization, the Law, and Society," *Journal of Social Issues* 27 (1971): 1-16, 65-92. Erik H. Erikson, in his essay in the symposium "Identity and the Life Cycle," *Psychological Issues* (1959), discusses the importance of trust and affiliation in developing notions of law and justice; later works of Erikson also stress these factors. Cf. Erikson, *Insight and Responsibility* (New York, 1964).

Soviet law elements which would make his people believe in its inherent rightness—emotional elements, sacred elements; for otherwise the persuasiveness of Soviet law would have totally vanished, and even Stalin could not rule solely by threat of force. Though he unleashed all his terror against potential enemies, he invoked "socialist legality" as a source of support among the rank and file of the people, and in the name of "socialist legality" and "stability of laws" he attempted to restore the dignity of the Soviet courts and the sacredness of the duties and rights of Soviet citizens.[8]

Similarly, the idea that law is wholly existential, wholly relative to circumstances of time and place, that it cannot be measured by standards of truth or of rightness but only by standards of workability, that it "lays no claim to divine origin or eternal validity,"[9] is also self-defeating. It is tenable in the classroom but not in the courtroom or in the legislature. Judicial decisions or statutes that purport to be merely hunches or experiments lack the credibility upon which observance of law ultimately depends—observance not only by "the masses" but by all of us, and especially by judges and lawmakers.

Once in 1947 when the late Thurman Arnold, who as a teacher and writer carried the theory called "legal realism" to the point of genuine cynicism, was urging upon a class at Yale Law School his view that judges decide solely according to their prejudices, a student interrupted to ask whether when Arnold himself was on the bench he did the same. Arnold paused before answering; one had the impression that he was transforming himself from Mr. Hyde to Dr. Jekyll as the professor in him yielded to the judge. He replied, "Well, we can sit here in the classroom and dissect the conduct of judges, but when you put on those black robes and you sit on a raised platform, and you are addressed as 'Your Honor', you *have* to believe that you are acting according to some objective standard."[10]

Common Elements of Law and Religion.—The secular-rational model neglects the importance of certain elements of law which transcend rationality, and especially of those elements which law shares with religion. This neglect is connected with the fallacy of viewing law primarily as a body of rules and of underestimating the context in which rules are enunciated. Once

---

[8] See Harold J. Berman, *Justice in the USSR: An Interpretation of Soviet Law*, 2d ed. (Cambridge, MA, 1963), 46-65. See also chapters 20 and 22 herein.

[9] Franck, *The Structure of Impartiality*, 62.

[10] This incident is reported from memory, the author having been a student in Professor/Judge Arnold's class at the time. The same ambivalence toward legal ritual and legal myths is reflected in Arnold's two major works, Thurman Arnold, *The Symbols of Government* (New York, 1935) and Thurman Arnold, *Folklore of Capitalism* (New York, 1937).

law is understood as an active, living human process, then it is seen to involve—just as religion involves—man's whole being, including his dreams, his passions, his ultimate concerns.

The principal ways in which law channels and communicates transrational values are fourfold: first, through *ritual*, that is, ceremonial procedures which symbolize the object:vity of law; second, through *tradition*, that is language and practices handed down from the past which symbolize the ongoingness of law; third, through *authority*, that is, the reliance upon written or spoken sources of law which are considered to be decisive in themselves and which symbolize the binding power of law; and fourth, through *universality*, that is, the claim to embody universally valid concepts or insights which symbolize the law's connection with an all-embracing truth. These four elements—ritual, tradition, authority, and universality—are present in all legal systems, just as they are present in all religions. They provide the context in which in every society (though in some, of course, to a lesser extent than in others) legal rules are enunciated and from which those rules derive their legitimacy.

It is striking that Thurman Arnold, in the episode which I have related, stressed the effect upon himself, as a judge, of the symbols of office—the robes, the furniture of the courtroom, the rhetoric of respect. Such symbols are supposed to impress not only the judge, but also other participants in the proceeding, and indeed the society as a whole, with the fact that one charged with the dread responsibility of adjudication should put aside his personal idiosyncrasies and personal prejudices, his *pre*judgments. Similarly, the jurors, the lawyers, the parties, the witnesses, and all others involved in a trial, are given their respective roles by the ceremonious opening ("Oyez! Oyez!" with all rising), the strict order of appearance, the oaths, the forms of address, and the dozens of other rituals that mark the play. This is no free-for-all in which everyone "is himself." On the contrary, each participant subjects his own personality to the requirements of the legal process. Thus the great ideals of legal justice are dramatized: objectivity, impartiality, consistency, equality, fairness. As the English say, justice must not only be done, it must also be *seen* to be done. This does not mean that unless it is seen it will not be accepted; it means that unless it is seen it is not justice. In Marshall McLuhan's famous phrase, "the medium is the message."

The rituals of law (including those of legislation, administration, and negotiation, as well as of adjudication) like the rituals of religion are a solemn dramatization of deeply felt values. In both law and religion the dramatization is needed not only to reflect those values, not only to make manifest the intellectual belief that they are values that are useful to society, but also to induce an emotional belief *in* them as a part of the ultimate meaning of life. More than that, the values have no existence, no meaning, outside the process of their dramatization. By virtue of their symbolization in judicial, legislative, and other rituals, the ideals of legal justice come into being not primarily as matters of utility but rather as matters of sanctity, not primarily as ideals but rather as shared emotions: a common sense of rights, a common sense of duties, a demand for fair hearing, an aversion to inconsistency, a passion for equality of treatment, an abhorrence of illegality, and a commitment to legality.

Moral philosophers attribute beliefs concerning justice to man's capacity to reason, but we are speaking here of something different, namely, man's emotions; and we are speaking not of his moral emotions but more specifically of his legal emotions.[11] Justice Holmes once wrote that even a dog knows the difference between being stumbled over and being kicked. We would add that even a dog becomes upset if his master rewards him one minute and punishes him the next for the same thing. The rituals of law symbolize (bring into being) the fundamental postulate of all legal systems, even the most rudimentary, that like cases should be decided alike: they raise that postulate from a matter of intellectual perception and moral duty to a matter of collective faith. It is no overstatement, therefore, to speak of fidelity or faithfulness to law. This is essentially the same kind of dramatic response to the sacred, to the ultimate purpose of life, that is characteristic of religious faith. Law, like religion, originates in celebration and loses its vitality when it ceases to celebrate.[12]

---

11 Among the "moral feelings" or "moral sentiments," John Rawls, following Kant, includes guilt, shame, remorse, indignation, resentment, and the like; he classifies love, friendship, trust, and the like as "natural feelings," or natural attitudes. See John Rawls, *A Theory of Justice* (Cambridge, MA, 1971), 479-490. But surely moral feelings include not only negative but also positive feelings—such as innocence, pride, satisfaction, thankfulness, and others. Also there are feelings of cooperation, sharing, solidarity, and reciprocity, which must be classified as (at least partly) moral. But, apart from the Kantian and post-Kantian range of moral and natural feelings, there are also legal feelings, such as the feeling of entitlement, the feeling of violation of rights, the feeling of legal obligation, the feeling that like cases should be decided alike, the satisfaction of a fair hearing, and others. A pioneer in the study of such legal emotions was the prerevolutionary Russian-Polish jurist Leon Petrazhitskii. See Leon Petrazhitskii, *Law and Morality*, trans. H. Babb, with an introduction by Nicholas S. Timasheff (Cambridge, MA, 1955).

12 Although there is a burgeoning literature on the role of celebration and play in social life generally, surprisingly little has been written about their role in the legal process. However, Johan Huizinga's pioneering book, *Homo Ludens: A Study of the Play Element in Culture* (Boston, 1955), contains a short chapter on "Play and Law," focusing chiefly on the elements of contest (*agon*) in trial procedure in archaic law. Huizinga writes: "The winning as such is, for the archaic mind, proof of truth and rightness." Ibid., 81. The ordeal, the wager, the vow, and various forms of potlatch are among the examples given by

Law also shares with religion its emphasis on tradition and authority. All legal systems claim that their validity rests in part on continuity with the past, and all preserve such continuity in legal language and legal practices. In Western legal systems, as in Western religions, the historical sense of ongoingness is comparatively very strong, so that even drastic changes are often consciously explained as necessary to preserve and carry forward concepts and principles handed down from the past. But in other cultures as well, the drive for consistency leads to some sense of continuity with the past. The Moslem khadi has a reputation to preserve and will not judge differently each

---

Huizinga of the play element in law. He writes: "In Rome, too, any and every means of undoing the other party in a lawsuit was held as licit for a long time. The parties draped themselves in mourning, sighed, sobbed, loudly invoked the common weal, packed the court with witnesses and clients to make the proceedings more impressive. In short, they did everything we do today." Ibid., 87.

The importance of celebration in social life is reaffirmed in Harvey Cox, *The Feast of Fools: A Theological Essay on Festivity and Fantasy* (Cambridge, MA, 1969), which, however, unfortunately omits consideration of legal ceremonies, perhaps because it is primarily concerned with less solemn and less structured forms of celebration. However, the distinction between spontaneous festive play (frolic, fantasy, etc.) and structured games—a distinction which some writers have charged Huizinga with failing to make—can easily be overdrawn. The cardinal point is that the game, whether or not structured, is played for its own sake, as an end in itself.

Just as philosophers of ritual have written little about law, so philosophers of law have written little about ritual, except occasionally to discuss its utility, or lack thereof, in facilitating the aims of a legal system. Thus Lon L. Fuller stresses the communicative function of ritual in signaling and clarifying interactional expectancies. See Lon L. Fuller, "Human Interaction and the Law," *The American Journal of Jurisprudence* 14 (1969): 6ff. From another point of view, Charles Fried has written of trial procedure as a dramatization of principles of justice. Criminal procedure, in particular, he writes, is

> expressive of [the] relation of trust and respect for the accused, for his victim, and for all potential participants in the criminal process. When the accused is presented as an equal of the accuser, his stature as a member of the community is dramatically affirmed. Moreover, there is dramatically affirmed the community's commitment to the principle of justice as superior to material advantage. In a sense every rational action is a dramatization of its principle; procedure, however, bears a particularly close affinity to drama and to ritual. Legal procedure might well be classed as a moral ritual or a ritual of justice.

Charles Fried, *Anatomy of Values: Problems of Personal and Social Choice* (Cambridge, MA, 1970), 129-132. This comes close to saying that ritual is an essential element of law (or at least of "legal procedure")—part of its basic reality, and not merely a means to other legal ends. Yet the passage also suggests that the basic reality of any legal (or other rational) action is to be found in "its principle," of which the action is a (mere) dramatization. The point being made in the text is that principle and action are one: in opposition to Platonic concepts, we assert that all legal speech is, in part, a ritual, and that the meaning of the ritual is to be found in itself—in its context—and not in some preexisting idea or principle which it embodies.

time. Even the Greek oracles were supposed to reflect a hidden consistency. The law need not be eternal, but it also must not be arbitrary, and therefore it must change by reinterpreting what has been done before. The traditional aspect of law, its sense of ongoingness, cannot be explained in purely secular and rational terms, since it embodies man's concept of time, which itself it bound up with the transrational and with religion.[13]

Similarly, the law need not be revealed in the sense of written by God on tablets of stone (indeed, there are few such reported cases); yet the law is invariably appealed to, when parties are in dispute, as though someone in authority once embodied it in a constitution or statute or precedent or custom or learned book or some other authoritative source. In most political, economic, or social experience of a nonlegal nature (say, an election campaign or an industrial program or a family crisis or a neighborhood feud), people feel free to propose new courses of action based solely on utility; but if a legal question is posed, alternative solutions are almost invariably debated in terms of rules and decisions laid down by those in authority. Of course, the power to interpret the rules and decisions is also the power to remake them. Nevertheless, we say that the court is "bound" by the statute; the legislature is "bound" by the Constitution; even the framers of the Constitution felt themselves to be "bound" by a "higher law." They made it, but they did not make it out of whole cloth.

Except in cultures where law and religion are not differentiated, the specific rituals, traditions, and authorities of the law are not generally the same as the rituals, traditions, and authorities of religion, although they may overlap to some extent. Nor are the emotional responses which they induce the same, although they may overlap to some extent. The legal emotions differ from the ecstasy or sense of grace or anxiety or fear of damnation that

---

[13] That time itself is a religious category has been demonstrated in Mircea Eliade's studies of the antithesis between archaic time, which, being based on a religion of periodic redemption, is cyclical and unhistorical, and Judaic-Christian time, which is progressive (historical), continuous, and irreversible, being based on a religion of ultimate redemption at the end. Cf. Mircea Eliade, *Cosmos and History: The Myth of the Eternal Return*, trans. W. Trask (New York, 1959). Eliade mentions (ibid., 31-32) as "too well known for us to insist upon" the fact that "human justice, which is founded upon the idea of 'law', has a celestial and transcendent model in the cosmic norms (*tao, artha rta tsedek, themis*, etc.)." In archaic or traditional societies (as Eliade calls them), human law is viewed as a repetition of a divine or cosmic justice which first occurred in mythical time, that is, at the extratemporal instant of the beginning, whereas in the monotheistic revelation of Judaism, Moses received the law at a certain place and at a certain date and it is replenished by interpretation from time to time. See ibid., 105.

Soren Kierkegaard and Rudolf Otto attributed to the "idea of the Holy."[14] Nevertheless, legal emotions share with religious emotions the same sense of "givenness," the same reverence, the same urgency. In secular religions the givenness, the sanctity, may be attached to the state rather than to God, or to the court, or to the party, or to the people.

Also there is the same potentiality for abuse of ritual, tradition, and authority in law as in religion. Here the chief danger is that symbols needed to reflect and induce commitment to higher values may become objects of reverence for their own sake, ends in themselves, rather than "outward and visible signs of an inward invisible grace." In religion this is called magic and idolatry. In law it is called procedural formalism—as in trial by ordeal or by battle or by ritual oaths. The whole history of Western law from the twelfth century on has been marked by efforts, by no means always successful, to break away from the domination of such formalism. The secularists and the rationalists would have us escape from magic and idolatry and formalism by entirely rejecting emotional commitment to legal values, together with the ritual, tradition, and authority which reflect and induce them. They would rely wholly on an intellectual commitment to law as a useful instrument of policy in promoting the finite, material interests of individuals and groups in society and would disparage efforts to ground logic and policy in an emotional commitment to law as an integral part of the ultimate meaning of life, with the "penumbra of mystery" (as Reinhold Niebuhr has put it) which "surrounds every realm of meaning."[15] What I am urging is that law will not survive such a desiccation, such a draining of its emotional vitality. On the contrary, law and religion stand or fall together; and if we wish law to stand, we shall have to give new life to the essentially religious commitments that give it its ritual, its tradition, and its authority—just as we shall have to give new life to the social, and hence the legal, dimensions of religious faith.

The fourth major commitment which law shares with religion is the belief in the universality of the concepts and insights which it embodies. Such a belief should be distinguished from the theory of natural law, which may be wholly independent of religion. Indeed, a secular and rational theory of natural law is not only entirely possible but is the most widespread form which current natural-law theory takes. The morality inherent in law itself, the principles of justice which are implicit in the very concept of adherence to general rules, may be perceived by moral philosophers without reference to

---

14 Cf. Soren Kierkegaard, *Fear and Trembling*, trans. R. Payne (Oxford, 1939). Rudolf Otto, *The Idea of the Holy*, trans. J. Harvey (New York, 1958).

15 Reinhold Niebuhr, "Faith as the Sense of Meaning in Human Existence," *Christianity and Crisis* 26 (1966): 127.

religious values or religious insights. Also, anthropologists are able to show by empirical observation that no society tolerates indiscriminate lying, stealing, or violence within the in-group, and indeed, the last six of the Ten Commandments, which require respect for parents and prohibit killing, adultery, stealing, perjury, and fraud, have some counterpart in every known culture. In fact, many natural law theorists consider a religious explanation of law to be superstitious and dangerous. Such theorists are able to demonstrate by reason and observation alone that basic legal values and principles correspond to human nature and to the requirements of a social order. Contracts should be kept; injuries should be compensated; one who represents another should act in good faith; punishment should not be disproportionate to the crime. These and a host of other principles reflect what reason tells us is morally right and what in virtually all societies is proclaimed to be legally binding.

It was the Greeks who taught us this kind of thinking. It was they who first translated religion into philosophy. Since Plato we have not needed the gods to tell us what virtue is; we can discover it by using our minds. So, at least, we have said, although as Christopher Dawson has shown, the Greek secularization of philosophy also involved a deification of reason. Today we are no longer so convinced that thought can be as "pure" as the philosophers have assumed.[16] We have learned that when the mind tries to operate wholly independently, when it pretends to stand wholly outside the reality it observes, it breaks down and becomes skeptical even of itself.

On a more pragmatic level, the trouble with a purely intellectual or philosophical analysis of morality is that the very inquiry, by its exclusive rationality, tends to frustrate the realization of the virtues it proclaims. The intellect is satisfied, but the emotions, without which decisive actions cannot be taken, are deliberately put aside. Therefore all legal systems require not only that we recognize the proclaimed legal virtues with our intellect but also that we become committed to them with our whole being. And so it is by a religious emotion, a leap of faith, that we attach to the ideals and principles of law the dimension of universality. To say, for example, that it is against human nature to tolerate indiscriminate stealing and that every society condemns and punishes certain kinds of taking of another's property is not the same thing as to say that there is an all-embracing moral reality, a purpose in the universe,

---

[16] Christopher Dawson, *Religion and Culture* (New York, 1948), 154-155: "The secularization of law in Greece was like the secularization of philosophy. If they were rationalized, reason itself was divinized, and the lawgiver and the philosopher never entirely lost their sacred and prophetic character." See also Eric A. Havelock, *Preface to Plato* (Cambridge, MA, 1953).

which stealing offends. And when a society loses its capacity to say *that*—when it rests its law of property and of crime solely on its rational perception of human nature and of social necessity and not also on its religious commitment to universal values—then it is in grave danger of losing the capacity to protect property and to condemn and punish stealing.

The Revitalization of Law.—But is there not a serious danger that an emphasis on the law's commitment to universal truths will serve to deify existing social structures and thus to bring us to idolatry by another route? Must not the prophetic aspect of religion and the tension between law and love, law and faith, law and grace, be preserved for the sake of the integrity of religion, whatever may be the consequences for law? And are not the consequences for law, too, apt to be disastrous if law is not only respected but also sanctified?

These are questions which take us beyond the scope of this chapter. However, there is one aspect of them that has to be dealt with immediately, or everything said thus far will be misunderstood. It is *not* to be supposed that since law is failing to communicate its values to large numbers of people in the urban ghettos, in the new youth culture, in the peace movement, and elsewhere, therefore we should set about simply to manipulate its rituals, traditions, and concepts of authority and universality, leaving the underlying social, economic, and political structure unchanged. It is *not* suggested that the way to overcome our integrity crisis is to prop up the legitimacy of the old legal system with various religious devices plus a return to the Puritan ethic.

On the contrary, a recognition of the dialectical interdependence of law and religion leads us in the opposite direction—in the direction of fundamental social, economic, and political change and of new legal solutions for the acute problems confronting us: unemployment, racial conflict, crime, pollution, corruption, international conflict, war. But in order to find new *legal* solutions to such problems we must give new vitality to law—for law as it now presents itself, shorn of its mystique and its authority and its role in the grand design of the universe, is too weak a reed to support the demands we place upon it. In many areas of American life law reform will not work because law will not work—until it finds rituals that effectively communicate its objectivity, until it recovers its relationship to universal truths concerning the purpose of life itself.

Let me give a few practical examples. The breakdown in administration of criminal law is perhaps the most striking. Our press as well as our scholarly literature has been full of accounts of the grotesque and humiliating character of our system of detention prior to trial, our system of disposition of cases by negotiation between the prosecutor and the accused, and our prison system. We seem to he reliving the times of Charles Dickens. There is no easy way out of this morass; nevertheless, an understanding of the religious dimensions of law can show the direction to be taken. We need new forms of investigation, new forms of hearing, and new forms of custody which will dramatize humaneness and sympathy in the treatment of offenders, on the one hand, and, on the other hand, indignation both at their offenses and at the conditions which produce the offenses. It is not enough to remove the usual criminal sanctions of imprisonment or fines for so-called "crimes without victims" (drunkenness, drug abuse, prostitution, gambling, homosexuality), thereby releasing a very large amount of the time and energy of the police, the courts, and the detention agencies. This is advocated by the experts, and to a considerable extent it should be done; but it is only half the solution. The other half is to devise new legal procedures both inside and outside the criminal courts—new liturgies, if you will—for dealing with cases of persons who engage in such conduct (to the extent that it is antisocial), including new ways of enlisting the participation of the community—of psychiatrists, social workers, and clergy, and also of family, friends, neighbors, and fellow workers—before, during, and after the case is heard. To speak of "decriminalization" of the law, as some do, is misleading. To speak of offenders as "ill persons," as some do, is also misleading. We must find ways of hearing such cases and treating such persons humanely and creatively while at the same time expressing society's condemnation, not of them as persons, but of their conduct and of the conditions underlying their conduct. This, indeed, is in our religious tradition; and it makes sense.[17]

---

[17] It is a cardinal principle of the Western religious tradition (both in its Christian and its Judaic aspects) to "hate the sin but love the sinner." Unfortunately, that principle is often violated—on the one hand, by those whose sympathetic concern for the criminal undermines their indignation at the criminal act, and on the other hand, by those whose indignation at the criminal act undermines their sympathetic concern for the person who committed it.

The main reason criminal sanctions should be removed from many types of so-called victimless crimes is that the absence of a complainant makes it very difficult to obtain evidence sufficient to convict, and this in turn leads to police abuses in obtaining evidence and to police corruption. The other argument often made—that the offenses in question should not be criminally punishable because they are merely acts of personal immorality—simply assumes that they do not also harm society. In principle, no act should be made criminally punishable unless it is both wrongful (immoral) and harmful to society (antisocial). Today opinions differ regarding both the moral and the social aspects of homosexuality, but none would deny that the other offenses listed—excessive drinking, drug abuse, prostitution, and gambling—should be subject to some form of public control, which inevitably also means some kind of criminal sanction for violating such control.

Another example is that of political crimes. We need new forms of proceedings, new rituals, for dealing with cases like those in recent times of the Chicago Seven where the defendants seek to use the courtroom as a platform for proclaiming their political views.[18] One clue to what is possible in such cases was provided in the case of the Catonsville Nine, an anti-war group accused of burning some hundreds of draft cards. The judge permitted the trial to be conducted in a relatively informal way. The defendants, who included the priests Daniel and Philip Berrigan, had ample opportunity to express their motives, with which the judge and the prosecuting attorney were sympathetic. Yet the illegal actions were condemned.[19] Thus the trial served a larger purpose than putting guilty persons in prison. All trials should be educational, not vindictive. It is better to delay the proceedings than to bind or gag or ridicule a defendant. It is better that he go free than that the court—to paraphrase Holmes—should do an ignoble thing. A trial should provide a catharsis, not a new assault upon our dignity. It should dramatize, not caricature, the values implicit in the legal process.

We also need new forms of procedure in many types of civil cases. New types of family courts are needed to deal with problems of family disorganization. In the area of automobile accidents, nonjudicial agencies should determine the amount of damages, thus avoiding the travesty of leaving it to a jury to determine the extent of the plaintiff's losses, including his pain and suffering; but at the same time new procedures should also be devised in automobile cases to expose and condemn negligent driving as well as defects in our automobile technology. Once again, the law should not settle for convenience only; it should insist on educating the legal emotions of all who are involved—the parties, the spectators, the public.

Nevertheless, the crimes in question—which we must continually remember constitute the bulk of the crimes committed in the United States in our time and are at the root of organized crime and of police corruption—are significantly different from "crimes against the person" (homicide, rape, assault and battery, etc.) and "crimes against property" (burglary, larceny, embezzlement, etc.). A crime such as gambling or prostitution or drug abuse usually involves no desire to cause harm and no consciousness of moral wrongdoing, but rather a defiance of orthodox community values. It is partly for this reason that it is important to involve a wide circle of people other than law enforcement officials in the treatment of such misconduct. Thus far, however, except for the important role of social workers (in which the United States has been the pioneer and the outstanding example), little has been done to bring about such community involvement.

[18] See Mark L. Levine, George C. McNamee, and Daniel Greenberg, eds., *The Tales of Hoffman* (New York, 1970), an abridgment of the trial of the Chicago Seven, with an introduction by Dwight Macdonald.

[19] See Daniel Berrigan, *The Trial of the Catonsville Nine* (Boston, 1970).

Apart from the adjudicative process, we need new forms of proceedings in local and state government in order to revitalize branches of law relating to public education, pollution, welfare, low-cost housing, fair employment practices, and other like matters. Here the community itself can begin to create the new quality of life that many of our youth have rightly demanded. But new forms, new rituals, are needed to channel popular participation in creative rather than destructive ways. One important reform that has been undertaken in many places is the establishment of the office of Complaint Commissioner (the so-called Ombudsman), who will effectively investigate and act on citizens' complaints. A second, more general suggestion is to establish procedures for encouraging the expression of popular sentiment—"town meeting" types of procedures—without permitting domination by too vocal minorities.

Ultimately, broader participation of the public in the processes of the law is an important key to its revitalization. People must feel that it is their law, or they will not respect it. But they will only have that feeling when the law, through its rituals and traditions and through its authority and its universality, touches and evokes their sense of the whole of life, their sense of ultimate purpose, their sense of the sacred. At the end of the First World War, Max Weber charged that "the fate of our times is characterized by rationalization and intellectualization and, above all, by the 'disenchantment of the world'."[20] It is true that many branches of our law have suffered from such a disenchantment, though often without benefit of much rationalization or intellectualization. But despite all our disillusionment, it is wrong to suppose that America is without faith. The faith of America is expressed above all in participation itself, in the sense of people in local communities and groups, all over the country, acting somehow together. This is the heritage of Puritan congregationalism, on the one hand, and of the social and religious experience of ethnic immigrant communities on the other. It would be tragic if America's tradition of participation were allowed to die. Even in the raw, ugly context of the modern city, we have a chance to bring back into public life "the ultimate and most sublime values" which Weber said had "retreated" either into

---

[20] Max Weber, "Science as a Vocation," in Hans H. Gerth and C. Wright Mills, eds. and trans., *From Max Weber: Essays in Sociology* (New York, 1958), 155-156. Weber added: "It is not accidental . . . that today only within the smallest and [most] intimate circles, in personal human situations, in *pianissimo*, that something is pulsating that corresponds to the prophetic *pneuma* which in former times swept through the great communities like a firebrand, welding them together." Although he seemed to deplore this disenchantment, Weber nevertheless rejected any role for the intellectual in attempting to change it other than the role of maintaining "plain intellectual integrity" and of meeting "the demands of the day." Ultimately Hitler took over.

mystical experience or into intimate personal relations,[21] by enlisting people of all kinds, and in large numbers, in the processes of law enforcement, in new types of parajudicial proceedings, in local and state administration, and in many other areas of public life.

We have considered religion and law in the broadest possible terms—religion as man's sense of the holy, law as man's sense of the just—recognizing that in all societies, though in widely varying ways, law draws on the sense of the holy partly in order to commit people emotionally to the sense of the just. This is true among the Barotse tribesmen of Africa, where witchcraft stands behind legal custom and mediation as a kind of last resort. It was true in another way in traditional China, where law was seen as a necessary evil but was nevertheless dialectically related to Confucian gentility and politeness as well as to neo-Confucian ancestor worship and emperor worship. The interdependence of the sense of the holy and the sense of the just was true also of Soviet Russia, where the law proclaimed that socialist property is sacred and where socialist eschatology—the coming of a communist utopia—was an important factor in the development of legal institutions and of legal doctrine. It is true of the United States, where not only traditional Christianity and Judaism but also the secular religion of the American way of life give sanctity to basic legal norms and procedures; indeed, in few other legal systems does one find such explicit reliance on divine guidance and divine sanctions and so great a reverence for constitutional appeals to universal standards of justice.[22]

By emphasizing the interaction of law and religion we may come to see them not just as two somewhat related social institutions, but as two dialectically interdependent dimensions—perhaps the two major dimensions—of the social life of man.

---

[21] Ibid.

[22] Cf. Robert N. Bellah, "Civil Religion in America," in William G. McLoughlin and Robert N. Bellah, eds., *Religion in America* (Boston, 1968). Bellah traces the idea of civil religion (the phrase itself is Rousseau's) to the Founding Fathers. He writes that "from the earliest years of the republic" we have had "a collection of beliefs, symbols, and rituals with respect to sacred things and institutionalized in a collectivity. This religion—there seems no other word for it—while not antithetical to and indeed sharing much in common with Christianity, was neither sectarian nor in any specific sense Christian"—though at first the society itself "was overwhelmingly Christian." Ibid., 10. "Behind the civil religion at every point lie Biblical archetypes: Exodus, Chosen People, Promised Land, New Jerusalem, Sacrificial Death and Rebirth. But it is also genuinely American and genuinely new. It has its own prophets and its own martyrs, its own sacred events and sacred places, its own solemn rituals and symbols. It is concerned that America be a society as perfectly in accord with the will of God as men can make it, and a light to all the nations." Ibid., 20.

Taken alone, so broad a concept may obscure the tensions that exist between law and religion in given historical situations. That is, of course, the danger of an anthropological approach—that it tends to view culture as an integrated, harmonious whole. Some anthropologists writing on religion treat virtually everything in the culture they are writing about as religion; and similarly, some anthropologists writing on law treat virtually everything in the culture they are writing about as law.

Despite this danger, I believe we must start with an anthropological perspective on law and religion—a perspective which takes into account the fact that in all known cultures there has been an interaction of legal and religious values. In a sense everything is religion; and in a sense, everything is law—just as everything is time and everything is space. Man is everywhere and always confronting an unknown future, and for that he needs faith in a truth beyond himself, or else the community will decline, will decay, will fall backward. Similarly, man is everywhere and always confronting social conflict, and for that he needs legal institutions, or else the community will dissolve, will break apart. These two dimensions of life are in tension—yet neither can be fulfilled without the other. Law without faith degenerates into legalism; this indeed is what is happening today in many parts of America and of the Western world. Faith without law degenerates into religiosity. We must begin with these basic cross-cultural truths if we are to succeed in understanding what history requires of us here and now.

Part One

HISTORICAL THEMES

⤳ 2 ⤳

WHY THE HISTORY OF WESTERN LAW
IS NOT WRITTEN*

T he title of this chapter is adapted, of course, from Maitland's famous
Inaugural Lecture, "Why the History of English Law is not Written."
Maitland said that "there are vast provinces [of English legal history] that lie
unreclaimed, not outlying provinces but the very heart of the country,"[1]
including "the evolution of the great elementary conceptions, ownership,
possession, contract, tort and the like."[2]

The history of English law has not been written, Maitland said, first and
foremost "because of the traditional isolation of the study of English law from
every other study,"[3] especially its isolation from the study of other legal
systems. "History involves comparison," he wrote, "and the English lawyer
who knew nothing and cared nothing for any system but his own hardly came

---

* Reprinted from *University of Illinois Law Review* (1984): 511-520. Delivered as the
General Address at the Annual Meeting of the American Society for Legal History, October
23, 1982. The principal themes of this Address and much of the language were subsequently included in Harold J. Berman, *Law and Revolution: The Formation of the Western
Legal Tradition* (Cambridge, MA, 1983).

[1] "Why the History of English Law is not Written," in F.W. Maitland, *The Collected
Papers of Frederic William Maitland: Downing Professor of the Laws of England*, ed. H.A.L.
Fisher (Cambridge, 1911), 1: 484.

[2] Ibid.

[3] Ibid., 487.

in sight of the idea of legal history."[4] "English lawyers," he stated, "have for the last six centuries exaggerated the uniqueness of our legal history. . . . I know just enough to say this with confidence, that there are great masses of medieval law very comparable with our own; a little knowledge of them would send us to our Year Books with new vigour and new intelligence."[5]

These statements were made almost a century ago. Since then some of the "provinces" of English legal history have been reclaimed. Yet the complaint remains valid—and even more so with regard to American legal history. Without a knowledge of "foreign law" (as Maitland called it—actually such law is less "foreign" than he thought), we cannot "come within sight" of the "idea" of legal history.[6]

Blackstone, more than a century before Maitland, recognized that English law had many features that were "very comparable" with features of other European legal systems, and further, that England was itself governed, in part, by some of the same bodies of law that prevailed elsewhere in Europe. Blackstone discussed briefly, at the beginning of the *Commentaries*,[7] the following kinds of law then prevailing in England: natural law, divine law, the law of nations, Roman law (by which the universities were governed), ecclesiastical law (in the church courts), the law merchant—as well as the English common law, local customary law, statutory law, and equity. Implicit in this catalogue was a view of history that transcended the nation, a view of overlapping histories: the history of Christianity and Judaism, the history of Greece, the history of Rome, the history of the church, local history, national history, international history, and more.

Notwithstanding his conservatism, Blackstone saw England as part of a larger world. He saw that the law merchant, although traditionally not part of the English *common* law, was nevertheless part of English law as a whole, as it was part of French and German and Italian law. It was European law. Similarly, the canon law of the Church of Rome prior to the Reformation was as much English law as it was Italian or German or French law. Canon law was no more foreign to England than the Internal Revenue Code of the United States is foreign to Massachusetts or Missouri.

It is the tragedy of "scientific" history that it was invented in the nineteenth century, in the heyday of nationalism. From Ranke on, history was to be an objective study of "how things actually happened." It was simply taken

---

[4] Ibid., 488.

[5] Ibid., 490.

[6] Ibid., 488.

[7] William Blackstone, *Commentaries on the Laws of England* (Oxford, 1765; repr. ed., London, 1966), 1: 38-92.

for granted, however, that "what happened" was chiefly what happened in, or to, the nation. History was to be primarily national history, and more than that, it was to emphasize those elements that distinguish the nation's history from that of other nations. This was a hidden ideological bias of scientific history, which had important repercussions on the study of law. Not only in England and America but also in France, Germany, and elsewhere, it contributed to the virtual exclusion from the law curriculum, or at least the strict isolation, of canon law, the law merchant, the law of nations, military law, and other branches of Western law that transcend national legal systems. Natural law was relegated to philosophy, and divine law to theology.

The narrowness of legal historiography has been due not only to its nationalist ideology but also to its positivist presuppositions. It was presupposed that law is primarily, if not exclusively, a manifestation of the will, that is, the policies, of lawmaking authorities, namely, the legislative, administrative, and judicial branches of the state. Law, it was thought, cannot exist without the state, and since there was no European state, there was no European, or Western, law. Neglected in this jurisprudence were other sources of law, such as custom, equity, and tradition. Neglected also were such shaping factors as legal language, legal scholarship, and legal science. There is, to be sure, no European state—at least there was none prior to the formation of the European Economic Community; yet European countries share a host of common legal values, legal concepts, and legal institutions. There is a Western legal tradition. As Edmund Burke said, the laws of every European country are "[a]t bottom . . . all the same," being "derived from the same sources."[8]

What are the principal features of the Western legal tradition? What are the characteristic elements that give it its structure and its dynamic? I would list the following ten elements, each of which may be traced to the great transformation of Europe that took place in the late eleventh and the twelfth centuries:

First, a relatively sharp distinction is made in the Western legal tradition between legal institutions and other types of institutions. Law has a certain character of its own, a relative autonomy; it is disembedded from religion, politics, morality, and custom, although it is, of course, influenced by them.

Second, in the Western legal tradition the administration of legal institutions is entrusted to a special corps of people, called lawyers or jurists, who engage in legal activities on a professional basis as a more or less full-time occupation.

---

8 Edmund Burke, "Three Letters on the Proposals for Peace with the Regicide Directory of France, 1796, Letter 1," in Edmund Burke, *Works* (Boston, 1939), 4: 399.

Third, legal professionals are specially trained in a discrete body of higher learning identified as legal learning, with its own professional literature and its own professional schools or other places of training.

Fourth, the body of legal learning in which legal specialists are trained is supposed to have a strong effect on the legal institutions; the legal learning conceptualizes and systematizes the law, with the result that the law is seen to contain within itself a legal science, a meta-law, by which it can be both analyzed and evaluated.

These first four elements of the Western legal tradition—the relative autonomy of law, its professional character, its learned character and its scientific character—had been features also of classical and post-classical Roman law. They were not present to any substantial extent, however, in the legal order that prevailed among the Germanic (including Anglo-Saxon) peoples of Western Europe prior to the eleventh century. Germanic law was almost completely fused with political and religious life and with custom and morality. There were, of course, laws, but there was no professional corps of lawyers or judges, no corps of professional legal scholars, no legal literature, and no developed legal science.

The church also, prior to the eleventh century, lacked an autonomous, systematized body of law and a developed legal profession. Canon law was fused with theology. While there were some local collections of canons, and also local penitentials,[9] there was little else that could be called a literature of canon law. The very phrase "canon law" (*jus canonicum*) was rarely if ever used. It was the revolutionary upheaval of 1075-1122, traditionally called the Investiture Struggle or the Gregorian Reform, and more recently the Papal Revolution, which, by freeing the clergy from imperial, royal, and baronial domination and by creating a strong papal monarchy within the Western church, laid the foundation for the rediscovery of the Roman texts of Justinian; for the creation of the first European university, at Bologna, to train jurists and to create a science of law; and for the emergence of separate ecclesiastical and secular jurisdictions as well as separate ecclesiastical and secular legal institutions. The church, which was the first modern state, needed a modern legal system to regulate its internal relations as well as its relations with the newly secularized polities. Those polities, in turn, needed modern legal systems for similar reasons.

The fifth characteristic of the Western legal tradition was not present in the older Roman law of Justinian; it is, I believe, uniquely Western. It is the

---

[9] See John T. McNeill and Helena M. Gamer, *Medieval Handbooks of Penance: A Translation of the Principal Libri Poenitentiales and Selections from Related Documents* (New York, 1938).

conception of law as a coherent whole, an integrated system, a "body." Using the twelfth-century scholastic technique of reconciling contradictions and deriving general concepts from rules and cases, Western jurists were able to coordinate and integrate the chaotic mass of rules and concepts that constituted the older Roman legal texts. They converted those texts into a *corpus juris*—a phrase that was not known to Justinian. The same technique made it possible for Gratian to write his *Concordance of Discordant Canons*,[10] which was the first comprehensive legal treatise, the first systematic analysis of an entire body of law, ever written.

The Western concept of a body or system of law carries with it a sixth characteristic of the Western legal tradition, namely, the belief in the ongoing character of law, its capacity for growth over generations and centuries. This belief, too, seems to be uniquely Western. Each generation consciously develops the legal institutions handed down by its forebears. The body of law is thought to contain a built-in mechanism for organic change.

Seventh, the growth of law in the West is thought to have an internal logic. Changes are not only adaptations of the old to the new but are also part of a pattern of changes. The process of development is subject to certain regularities and, at least in hindsight, seems to reflect an inner necessity. Changes proceed by reinterpretation of the past to meet present and future needs. This is the myth, the faith. The law is not merely ongoing; it has a history.

Eighth, the historicity of law is linked with the belief in its supremacy over the political authorities. It is thought that law, at least in some respects, transcends politics; it binds the state itself. This belief also goes back to the late eleventh and the twelfth centuries and to the separation of the ecclesiastical from the secular power. The secular authorities, it was then argued, may make law, but they may not make it arbitrarily, and until they have lawfully remade it, they are to be bound by it. Similarly, the ecclesiastical authorities may not overstep the bounds of their lawmaking authority, and may not violate their lawmaking authority, without challenge from the secular sword.

Ninth, perhaps the most distinctive characteristic of the Western legal tradition is that diverse jurisdictions and diverse legal systems co-exist and compete within the same community. This characteristic originated in the late eleventh century with the church's establishment of an "external forum," a hierarchy of ecclesiastical courts, with exclusive jurisdiction in some matters and concurrent jurisdiction in others. Laymen, though governed generally by secular law, were also subject to ecclesiastical law, and to the

---

10 Gratian's treatise, also called the *Decretum Gratiani*, was written in about 1140. In a modern edition it fills over 1400 pages. See "Decretum Magistri Gratiani," in *Corpus Iuris Canonici*, ed. Emil A. Friedberg (Leipzig, 1879), 1: 1-1435.

jurisdiction of ecclesiastical courts, in matters of marriage and family relations, inheritance, spiritual crimes, contract relations where faith was pledged, and a number of other important matters. Conversely, the clergy, though governed generally by canon law, were also subject to secular law, and to the jurisdiction of secular courts, with respect to certain crimes, certain property disputes, and related matters. Secular law consisted of various competing types, including royal law, feudal (lord-vassal) law, manorial (lord-peasant) law, urban law, and mercantile law, each with its own jurisdiction. Throughout Europe, the same person might be subject to the ecclesiastical courts in one type of case, the king's court in another, his lord's court in a third, the manorial court in a fourth, a town court in a fifth, and a merchant's court in a sixth.

The pluralism of Western law was a source of legal sophistication and of legal growth. It was also a source of freedom. A serf might run to the town court for protection against his master. A vassal might run to the king's court for protection against his lord. A cleric might run to the ecclesiastical court for protection against the king.

Finally, a tenth characteristic of the Western legal tradition is the tension that has existed between its ideals and its realities, between its dynamic qualities and its stability, and between its transcendence and its immanence. These tensions have periodically led to the violent overthrow of legal systems by revolution. Nevertheless, the legal tradition, which is bigger than any of the legal systems that comprise it, eventually survived and, indeed, was renewed by such revolutions.

Six great revolutions have punctuated the organic development of Western legal institutions: the Papal Revolution of 1075-1122; the German Revolution—that is, the Lutheran Reformation in Germany—of 1517-55; the English Revolution of 1640-89; the American Revolution which began in 1776; the French Revolution, which began in 1789; and the Russian Revolution, which began in 1917.

These revolutions represent great explosions that occurred when a legal system proved too rigid to adapt to new conditions and was perceived to have betrayed its ultimate purpose and mission. Each revolution marked a fundamental, rapid, violent, and lasting change in the social system as a whole. Each sought legitimacy in a fundamental law, a remote past, and an apocalyptic future. Each took more than one generation to establish roots. Each eventually produced a new system of law, which embodied some of the major purposes of the revolution, and which changed the Western legal tradition but ultimately remained within that tradition.

Clearly, the Papal Revolution may be called Western, but one might ask whether the national revolutions since the sixteenth century can be properly characterized in the same way. The legal system that emerged from the Papal Revolution—the new canon law of Gratian and the papal decretals, culminating in the decrees of the Fourth Lateran Council in 1215—was a transnational body of law. But is it proper to characterize the law of the German principalities after the Lutheran Reformation, or the law of England after 1689, as in some sense transnational, or European?

Two points support an affirmative answer to this question. First, all the national revolutions since the sixteenth century—except the American—were directed in part against the Roman Catholic Church or, in Russia, the Orthodox Church, and all of them transferred large portions of the transnational canon law from the church to the national state.

Second, all the great national revolutions of the West were Western in nature; that is, each was partially prepared in other countries and each had repercussions in other countries. Before breaking out in Germany, the Protestant Reformation was prepared by Wycliffe in England, by Hus in Bohemia, and by active reform movements in every country of Europe. The Puritan movement in England was based on the earlier teachings of the French-Swiss reformer John Calvin and had close ties with Calvinist movements in Holland and elsewhere on the Continent. The Enlightenment of the eighteenth century was, of course, an all-Western phenomenon, which formed the ideological basis not only of the American and French Revolutions but also of agitation for radical change in England and elsewhere. The Russian Revolution was born in the international communist movement founded by two Germans; its roots lay in the Paris Commune of 1870.

Similarly, these national revolutions had enormous repercussions throughout the Western world. Lutheranism contributed to the rise of absolute monarchies supported by a strong civil service. This form of government eventually appeared in England, France, and other non-Lutheran countries. A century later, English Puritanism contributed to the development of parliamentary supremacy and constitutional monarchy in England, and in the late 1600s and early 1700s, somewhat similar developments took place in various other European countries. After the French and American Revolutions subsided, England reformed its political process in a democratic direction, enlarging the electorate to include some of the middle classes. After the Russian Revolution subsided, "socialist" or "new deal" governments appeared in Western Europe and the United States.

Also in criminal and civil law, the great national Revolutions had important consequences that extended beyond national boundaries. Lutheran concepts of the Christian conscience influenced the protection of individual contract and property rights in many Western countries. The English Puritans laid the foundations for a more independent judiciary, trial by jury, and increased civil rights—not only in England but eventually in other countries of the West as well. The codification of French law after the French Revolution stimulated the movement for codification throughout Europe and in the United States. The development of socialist law in the Soviet Union affected the socialization of various aspects of law in many other countries.

All the various national systems of law in the West have certain important features in common. All share some basic modes of categorization. For example, all strike a balance between legislation and adjudication and, in adjudication, between statute law and case law. All make a sharp division between criminal and civil law. In all, crimes are analyzed (as they were first analyzed by Abelard in the early twelfth century[11]) in terms of act, intent or negligence, causation, duty and similar concepts. In all, civil obligations are divided, either expressly or implicitly, into contract, delict (tort), or unjust enrichment (quasi-contract).

Behind these and other common analytical categories lie common policies and common values—above all, a common concept of legality. In the 1930s, for instance, a statute of National Socialist Germany, which made criminally punishable any act that "deserves punishment according to sound popular feeling (*gesundes Volksgefühl*)"[12] was generally viewed as a violation of the traditional Western concept of legality, and the Permanent Court of International Justice struck down a similar law of the Free City of Danzig, based on the German statute, as contrary to the rule of law (*Rechtsstaat*).[13]

A history of Western law would reveal not only the origin and development of common concepts, but also the interconnections among the various legal systems that have prevailed in the West. For example, in the twelfth century, which Maitland called "a legal century," one may see a broad range of legal activity throughout the West within a period of fifty or sixty years. Within the church, the first major series of papal decretals appeared,[14] as well

---

[11] See Peter Abelard's *Ethics*, ed. David E. Luscombe (Oxford, 1971), 38-49, 55.

[12] Law of June 28, 1935, Reichsgesetzblatt 1935 (No. 70), Teil I, art. 12, at 839. The statute also provided: "If there is no specific penal law directly applicable to the act it shall be punished under the statute whose fundamental conception most nearly applies." Ibid.

[13] 1935, P.C.I.J. Ser. A No. 13.

[14] Papal decretals were, in many instances, holdings in decided cases, that is, rules of law which were the necessary implications of papal decisions. Pope Alexander III (1159-81), a famous jurist and a former pupil of Gratian, issued 700 decretals which have been preserved, in addition to others which have not been preserved.

as the first major treatise on canon law—Gratian's.[15] Developments in secular law included the first major treatise on royal law—Glanvill[16]—as well as the first major royal legislation: the Assizes of Ariano of Roger II,[17] the peace statutes of Frederick Barbarossa,[18] and the possessory assizes of Henry II.[19] In addition, the first major collections of urban law developed in various Italian, Flemish, German, and other cities,[20] and the first major writings on feudal law appeared.[21] Certain basic concepts and principles run throughout all of these twelfth-century firsts. One example is the concept of seisin, *saisina*, and the principle of novel disseisin, namely, that one who has been recently disseised is to be restored without reference to right of ownership. The study of these interconnections is not a matter of comparative legal history, but rather a matter of the legal history of a single civilization.

To say that the history of Western law has not been written is not to say that it has been wholly neglected. Distinguished scholars such as Heinrich Mitteis[22] and John P. Dawson[23] have written brilliant works comparing legal institutions of various countries of Europe in their historical development. The challenge laid down by Paul Koschaker just after World War II, in his *Europa und das römische Recht*,[24] to restore the historical unity of European law against nationalist barbarism, has not gone without response. Especially among Italian and German historians there has been a movement toward the "Europeanization" of legal history. The Western dimensions of our law are also being studied by some of the younger American legal historians.

Yet, for the most part scholars study each country's legal system independently. Consequently, the mutual interaction of the legal institutions and the

---

15 See Gratian, "Decretum Magistri Gratiani."

16 *The Treatise on the Laws and Customs of the Realm of England Commonly Called Glanvill*, ed. G.D.G. Hall (London, 1965).

17 The text of the Assizes of Ariano (1140) is reproduced in Francesco Brandileone, *Il diritto romano nelle leggi normanne e sveve del regno di sicilia* (Rome, 1884).

18 Barbarossa's peace statutes of 1152 and 1158 as well as his Peace Writ against Arsonists of 1186 may be found in Lorenz Weinrich, *Quellen zur Deutschen Verfassungs-, Wirtschafts-, und Sozialgeschichte bis 1250* (Darmstadt, 1977), 166-167.

19 F.W. Maitland, *The Forms of Action at Common Law: A Course of Lectures by F.W. Maitland* (Cambridge, 1965) remains the best short introduction to Henry II's law-making and its subsequent significance.

20 See Berman, *Law and Revolution*, 357-403.

21 Ibid., 295-315.

22 See Heinrich Mitteis, *The State in the Middle Ages: A Comparative Constitutional History of Feudal Europe*, trans. H. Orton (Amsterdam, 1975).

23 See John P. Dawson, *The Oracles of the Law* (Ann Arbor, MI, 1968).

24 The third edition of this work was published in Munich and Berlin in 1958. It remains untranslated into English.

legal thought of the various polities of the West have barely been explored. Above all, English and American legal history have been isolated; indeed, they have often been isolated even from each other.

It is, once again, the old story of the blind men and the elephant. Historians of each country have a firm grasp on the leg, or the trunk, or the tail, or an ear. They may, to be sure, make no claim to understand the whole animal. But how can one understand a part without understanding what it is a part of?

Why, then, is the whole not studied more frequently as a whole? Some easy answers have been given. It is said: "there is no time to study the law of more than one country," "it requires too much training, too many skills," or "there is no demand for work in comparative legal history." However, more complex reasons may also be suggested.

Many legal historians prefer to be nationalistic because they tend to accept the belief-system—the ideology—of the national revolutions, and especially the belief-system of the revolution or revolutions to which the historian's own country looks for its origins. Such historians do not wish to seek the sources of their own beliefs in the pre-Protestant, pre-humanist, pre-nationalist, pre-individualist, pre-capitalist era of Western history, when the Western legal tradition was first formed. They view the period prior to the sixteenth century as a period of feudalism, to which they feel alien, and they think of it as the Middle Ages rather than as the beginning of the modern era. English legal historians, on the other hand, may identify themselves much more affirmatively with medieval English law, viewing it as the source of the English common law that triumphed over its rivals in the seventeenth century. By the same token, however, they may be quite unhappy to be told that the first modern Western legal system was the canon law of the Roman Catholic Church, and that all royal legal systems in Europe including the English, first developed in rivalry with and in emulation of the canon law.

Also, many legal historians are unwilling to trace legal institutions to their political, economic, social, and ideological (which in Western history chiefly means religious) sources. They are especially unwilling to trace the sources of legal evolution to the upheavals of political revolution. The interaction of revolution and evolution has not captured the imagination of legal historians. They prefer to trace the origins of laws to earlier laws.

The need for a broader and longer view of legal history derives from the predicament in which the Western legal tradition finds itself in the twentieth and twenty-first centuries. Our law has become uprooted; it is no longer viewed as founded in a universal reality. Furthermore, the West itself is in danger of losing its identity, and no longer believes either in its future or in its past. Nationalist legal historiography is incapable of providing an under-standing of the basic changes that have taken place in the various Western legal systems in the past or the direction in which they are now moving. We must therefore retrace the steps by which our entire legal tradition has come to its present predicament, beginning with its origins and proceeding in the widest possible context.

─── ⚮ 3 ⚭ ───

THE RELIGIOUS FOUNDATIONS
OF WESTERN LAW*

The Western legal tradition, like Western civilization as a whole, is undergoing in the twentieth century a crisis greater than any other in its history, since it is a crisis generated not only from within Western experience but also from without. From within, social, economic, and political transformations of unprecedented magnitude have put a tremendous strain upon traditional legal institutions and legal values in virtually all countries of the West. Yet there have been other periods of revolutionary upheaval in previous centuries, and we have somehow survived them. What is new is the confrontation with non-Western civilizations and non-Western philosophies. In the past, Western man has confidently carried his law with him throughout the world. The world today, however, is more suspicious than ever before of Western "legalism." Eastern man and Southern man offer other alternatives. The West itself has come to doubt the universal validity of its vision of law—its validity for non-Western cultures. What used to seem "natural" now seems only "Western," and often it seems obsolete even for the West.

  * Reprinted from Catholic University Law Review 24 (1975): 490-508. Delivered as the Tenth Annual Pope John XXIII Lecture on October 25, 1974, at the Catholic University of America Law School. The text remains substantially as delivered. The principal themes and much of the language were subsequently included in Harold J. Berman, Law and Revolution: The Formation of the Western Legal Tradition (Cambridge, MA, 1983).

We shall not understand the dimensions of the crisis of the Western legal tradition unless we are willing to view that tradition in large historical perspective. It is said that a drowning man may see his whole life flash before him. Perhaps that is an unconscious, desperate effort to find the resources within himself to escape from his predicament. While this article does not propose to recount the whole life history of the drowning Western legal tradition, it will attempt to recall the circumstances under which it first came into being, in order to identify the foundations on which it rests. It seems that this is a necessary first step in assessing the predicament in which we now find ourselves.

To speak of historical origins is, of course, risky. Wherever one starts in the past, one can find still earlier beginnings. Nevertheless, I am prepared to argue that the history of law is *not* a "seamless web," there *are* seams; there are new things under the sun, and the starting point is not necessarily arbitrary. More particularly, it can be shown that there was a time—less than 900 years ago—when what we know today as *legal systems* did not exist among the peoples who lived in what we today call Europe; and that in the late eleventh, twelfth, and thirteenth centuries legal systems were created first within the Roman Catholic Church and then within the various kingdoms of the West which shared power with the Church.

By the term "legal systems," I mean something narrower and more specific than a "legal order." There was, of course, a legal order in every society of the West prior to the late eleventh and twelfth centuries, in the sense that there were legally constituted authorities which applied law. Indeed, we know of no time in the history of the peoples of Europe when there was not a legal order in that sense: the earliest written records of their history are collections of laws, and Tacitus, writing in the first and second centuries A.D., describes Germanic assemblies acting as courts. In addition, the Church from very early times had declared laws and had established procedures for deciding cases.[1] Nevertheless, the legal rules and procedures which were applied in the various legal orders of Europe, both secular and ecclesiastical, in the period after the decline of the Roman Empire and prior to the late eleventh and twelfth centuries, were largely undifferentiated from social custom and from political and religious institutions generally. No one had attempted to organize the prevailing laws and legal institutions into a distinct structure. Very little of the law was in writing. There was no professional judiciary, no professional class of lawyers, no professional legal literature. Law was not consciously systematized. There was no independent, integrated body of legal

---

[1] For a useful short treatment of the history of church law prior to the eleventh century, see Robert C. Mortimer, *Western Canon Law* (Berkeley, CA, 1953), 1-37.

principles and procedures clearly differentiated from other processes of social organization and consciously articulated by a corps of persons specially trained for that task.

Then about the year 1100, for reasons which I shall try to explain, the first modern law school was founded in the town of Bologna in Northern Italy. Students came from all over Europe—thousands of them each year—to study law as a distinct and coherent body of knowledge, a science, separate from politics and separate from religion.

Law was studied—but what law? Not, at first, the unstructured, unsystematic customary laws and legal institutions of the Germanic tribes and kingdoms, nor, at first, the unstructured, unsystematic laws of the Church, which were at that time wholly interwoven with theology, liturgy, rhetoric, and morals. Curious as it may sound to modern ears, the law that was first taught and studied at Bologna, and later at the other universities that sprang up throughout the West, was the law contained in an ancient manuscript which had come to light in a library in the Italian town of Pisa near the end of the eleventh century. The manuscript contained the enormous collection of legal materials which had been compiled under the Roman Emperor Justinian at Constantinople in about 534 A.D., almost six centuries earlier.[2]

Roman law had, of course, at one time prevailed in the Western Roman Empire as well as the Eastern. In 476, however, the last of the Western Emperors was deposed; and even before then, Roman civilization had been superseded in the West by the primitive, tribal civilization of the Goths, the Vandals, the Franks, the Saxons, and other Germanic peoples. Between the sixth and tenth centuries, Roman law barely survived in the West, although it continued to flourish in the Eastern Empire. Vestiges of it remained in the tradition of the Western Church and of Western rulers, and some of its rules and concepts survived in the customary law of the peoples of (what we call today) France and Italy; but generally speaking, Roman law as such had no practical validity in Western Europe when Justinian's work was rediscovered in Italy, and the memory of it had only recently been revived.

---

[2] The manuscript consisted of four parts: (1) the Code (*Codex*), comprising twelve books of ordinances and decisions of the Roman Emperors before Justinian; (2) the Novels (*Novellae*), containing the laws promulgated by Emperor Justinian himself; (3) the Institutes (*Institutiones*), a short textbook designed as an introduction for beginning law students; and (4) the Digest (*Digestum*), whose 50 books contain a multitude of extracts from the opinions of Roman jurists on a wide variety of legal questions. In a modern English translation, the Code takes up 1,034 pages, the Novels 562 pages, the Institutes 173 pages, and the Digest 2,734 pages. Samuel P. Scott ed., *The Civil Law* (Cincinnati, OH, 1932).

Thus it was the body of law, the legal system, of a remote civilization, as recorded in a large set of books, that formed the object of Europe's first systematic legal studies. That earlier law was venerated as an ideal law, a body of legal ideas, taken as a perfect system; current legal problems, previously unclassified and inchoate, eventually came to be analyzed in its terms and judged by its standards.

The conception of legal science, of law as a body of knowledge found in authoritative books, is a major and indispensable part of Western law, that is, of the Western legal tradition, which encompasses diverse legal orders and diverse legal systems. A second major ingredient is the method of analysis which was applied to the ancient texts, a method which in modern times has been called, somewhat disparagingly, "scholasticism."[3] At Bologna the scholastic method was applied in law—as it was then applied in theology—to analyze and synthesize authoritative texts, to identify contradictions and reconcile them by applying criteria for judging which doctrines were of universal validity and which were of only relative validity. In law as in theology, the written text as a whole—the "body of civil law" (*corpus juris civilis*), as it then came to be called—was accepted as a sacred embodiment of human reason, but the techniques of reconciliation of contradictions gave the medieval jurists considerable freedom to limit or expand the scope of the concepts and rules laid down in the text. For example, they were able to establish general criteria by which to test the validity of a rule of customary law, such as the duration of the custom, its universality, its reasonableness, etc. The significance of this is apparent when one considers that until the twelfth century most law in Europe was customary law. Most legal rules were binding not because they had been promulgated by political or ecclesiastical authorities, but because they were customs practiced by the political or ecclesiastical community. Now for the first time custom lost its sanctity. A custom might be binding or it might not.

The scholastic method also led to the construction of legal systems out of the preexisting diverse and contradictory customs and laws. The techniques of harmonizing contradictions—expressed in the title of the first systematic legal treatise ever produced in the West, Gratian's *Concordance of Discordant*

---

[3] The scholastic method, developed in the early 1100s in theology and law, presupposes the absolute authority of certain books, which are to be comprehended as containing an integrated and complete body of doctrine. Paradoxically, however, it also presupposes that there may be both gaps and contradictions within the text. Its primary task is the summation of the text, the closing of gaps within it, and the resolution of the contradictions. The method is dialectical, in that it seeks reconciliation of opposites. See Guido Le Bras, "Canon Law," in Charles G. Crump and Ernest F. Jacob, eds., *The Legacy of the Middle Ages* (Oxford, 1926), 321, 325-326.

Canons, written in about the year 1140—coupled with the belief in an ideal "body of law," made it possible to begin to synthesize first canon law (*corpus juris canonici*) and ultimately royal and feudal law as well.

A third major ingredient of the Western legal tradition is the context in which the scholastic method was applied to the books of Roman law, namely, the context of the university. The universities of Europe, which were founded in the twelfth century and thereafter, brought together legal scholars—teachers and students—from many countries;[4] brought them in contact not only with each other but also with teachers and students of other disciplines, which were now for the first time also identified as separate branches of scholarship, namely, theology, philosophy, and medicine, and made of them a guild or, as we would say today, a profession. Thus the European universities gave to the study of law both a transnational character and a professional character, distinct from theology and philosophy, and this in turn helped to give the law itself a transnational and distinctive vocabulary and method. The graduates of the university law schools went back to their own countries, or moved to other countries, where they served as ecclesiastical or lay judges, practicing lawyers, legal advisers to ecclesiastical, royal, and city authorities and to lords of manors, and administrative officials of various kinds in both Church and State. To the extent that they were involved in canon law, they could use their university training directly, since canon law came to be taught in the universities alongside Roman law; to the extent that they were concerned with secular law, they applied to it the vocabulary and the method of the Roman and canon law which they had studied.

The fact that law was taught as a university discipline, the fact that it was considered to be transnational in character, and indeed a branch of universal

---

[4] David Knowles, *The Evolution of Medieval Thought* (New York, 1962), 80-81. Knowles writes:

> For 300 years, from 1050 to 1350, and above all in the century between 1070 and 1170, the whole of educated Western Europe formed a single undifferentiated cultural unit. In the lands between Edinburgh and Palermo, Mainz or Lund and Toledo, a man of any city or village might go for education to any school, and become a prelate or an official in any church, court or university (when there existed) from north to south, from east to west. . . . In this period a high proportion of the most celebrated writers, thinkers, and administrators gained greatest fame and accomplished the most significant part of their life's work far from the land of their birth and boyhood. Moreover, [in their writing] there is not a single characteristic of language, style or thought to tell us whence they sprang. . . . [O]n the level of literature and thought there was one stock of words, forms, and thoughts from which all drew and in which all shared on an equality. If we possessed the written works without their authors' names we should not be able to assign them to any country or people.

knowledge, made it inevitable that legal doctrines would be criticized and evaluated in the light of general truths, and not merely studied as a craft or technique. Even apart from the university, the Church had long taught that there is a natural law and a moral law by which all human law was to be tested and judged; but the university jurists added the concept of an ideal human law; the Roman law of Justinian's books, which—together with the Bible, the writings of the Church Fathers, the decrees of Church councils and popes, the writings of Aristotle, and other sacred texts—provided basic legal principles and standards for criticizing and evaluating legal rules and institutions. These inspired writings of the past, and not what any lawgiver might say or do, provided the ultimate criteria of legality.

Thus far the discussion has centered on what might be called generally the "style" of the Western legal tradition during its formative era. Let me turn for a moment to the historic events which produced that style at that time, for thereby we shall understand better what might be called the "content" of the tradition.

The rediscovery of the lawbooks of Justinian at the end of the eleventh century was not an accident. They had been diligently searched for in the libraries of Italy by supporters of the papacy in its struggle for the independence of the Church from secular authority, and possibly also by supporters of the emperor in his resistance to the papal party. For each side believed that Roman law would support its claims to supremacy.

Moreover, the systematic study of Roman law which was undertaken after the books of Justinian were rediscovered, and the consequent construction of a new legal science and of new bodies of ecclesiastical and secular law, were a response to the new situation which came into existence during and after that struggle between the ecclesiastical and the secular powers. Historians have traditionally referred to this period by the rather tame title, "The Investiture Contest"; however, it is coming more and more to be recognized as a genuine revolution in the modern sense, the Papal Revolution, which established the modern form of the Western Church and its relation to the secular authority.[5] The essence of that revolution was that it established the Church as a visible, corporate, legal structure, standing opposite the visible, corporate, legal structures of the secular authorities. Therefore, each side, the ecclesiastical and the

---

[5] The view that the *Dictates* of Pope Gregory VII and the Investiture Contest constituted a fundamental break in the historical continuity of the Church, and was the first of the Great Revolutions of Western history, was pioneered by Eugen Rosenstock-Huessy. See Eugen F. Rosenstock-Huessy, *Die europäischen Revolutionen* (Stuttgart, 1951); Eugen F. Rosenstock-Huessy, *Die Europäischen Revolutionen und der Charakter der Nationen* (Jena, 1931). See also Eugen F. Rosenstock-Huessy, *The Driving Power of Western Civilization: The Christian Revolution of the Middle Ages* (Boston, 1949).

secular, needed its own system of law to maintain its own internal cohesion and both sides needed a common legal tradition to maintain the balance between them.

With our modern ideas of the separateness of ecclesiastical and secular institutions—ideas which date precisely from the period of the Papal Revolution—it is hard to realize that prior to the latter part of the eleventh century the Church was conceived not as a separate institution at all but rather as the whole Christian people, *populus Christianus,* governed both by secular and priestly rulers (*regnum* and *sacerdotium*). Moreover, the *regnum* controlled the *sacerdotium.* Charlemagne himself in 794, six years before he consented to be crowned emperor by the pope, called a church council at Frankfurt at which he promulgated important changes in theological doctrine and ecclesiastical law. Some historians argue that Pope Leo III made Charlemagne the emperor, but it is more nearly true to say that Charlemagne made Leo pope; and in 813 Charlemagne crowned his own son emperor without benefit of any clergy whatever.[6] In fact, later emperors required the pope on his election to swear an oath of loyalty to the emperor. Of the twenty-five popes who held office in the century prior to 1059 (when a Church synod for the first time prohibited lay investiture, that is, appointment of priests), twelve were directly appointed by emperors and five were dismissed by emperors. Moreover, it was not only the German emperors who controlled bishops within their domain. The other rulers of Western Christendom did the same. In 1067 William the Conqueror issued a decree asserting that the king has the power to determine whether or not a pope should be acknowledged by the Church in Normandy and England, that the king makes ecclesiastical law through Church synods convened by him, and that the king has a veto power over ecclesiastical penalties imposed on his barons and officials.

Even more significant than imperial control over the papacy was the dispersal of authority within the Church among bishops and priests, each of whom was appointed by his respective king or feudal lord. The bishop of Rome was only first among equals. His permission was not generally required for appointment of other bishops or priests, nor was he empowered by cannon law to annul decisions taken by them.

In 1075, however, Pope Gregory VII, in his famous *Dictatus Papae* (*Dictates of the Pope*), proclaimed the legal supremacy of the pope over all Christians and the legal supremacy of the Church, under the pope, over all

---

[6] See Francois L. Ganshof, *The Imperial Coronation of Charlemagne* (Glasgow, 1971).

secular rulers.[7] Popes, he said, could depose emperors—and he proceeded to depose Emperor Henry IV. Moreover, Gregory proclaimed that all bishops and other clergy were to be appointed by the pope and were to be subordinate ultimately to him and not to secular authorities. Thus, the independence of the Church also meant the centralization of authority within the Church.

How was the papacy to make good its claims? How was it to exercise the universal jurisdiction it asserted? One important part of the answers to these questions lay in the potential role of law as a source of authority and as a means of control.[8] In his *Dictates* Pope Gregory declared that the bishop of Rome alone has the power to make new laws, and that the most important cases of every church may be appealed to the papal curia. Indeed, the use of the phrase "papal curia" to refer specifically to a court of law, rather than to the entire papal household, dates from this time.

Many of the rulers of Europe, and many of the bishops and other clergy, refused to accept the Papal Revolution; civil war raged in Europe for forty-five years, from 1077 to 1122, before the "contest" was resolved—by compromise. Separate but equal jurisdictions were carved out for the secular and spiritual realms. In England the matter was not settled until almost fifty years later when Thomas Becket suffered martyrdom at the hands of Henry II in order to prevent a return to royal supremacy over the Church.

In the century after the end of the Investiture Contest the Western Church, under the papacy, elaborated a new system of law, the modern canon law. As already indicated, ecclesiastical law has previously consisted as much of theological doctrines and liturgy as of law in the technical sense. Occasionally, collections had been made of "canons" derived from sacred writings, decisions of church councils and of leading bishops, laws of Christian emperors and Kings concerning the Church, Penitentials describing various sins and the penalties to be attached to them, and various other writings. These collections were usually arranged chronologically or under a very loose classification of topics, and none of them had more than regional significance. But after the Papal Revolution something new was created: a *system* of canon law, distinct from liturgy, distinct from rhetoric and morals, a system which utilized the newly rediscovered Roman law for much of its

---

[7] Cf. Yves Congar, "The Historical Development of Authority in the Church: Points for Christian Reflection," in John M. Todd, ed., *Problems of Authority: An Anglo-French Symposium* (Baltimore, 1962), 119, 139 ("One is actually obeying God when one obeys his representative.").

[8] Gregory purported to find legal authority, in the modern sense, for every one of the revolutionary provisions in the *Dictates*. See Augustin Fliche, *La Réforme Grégorienne* (Louvain, 1924).

vocabulary and legal doctrine and the newly invented scholastic method for its technique of harmonizing contradictory texts into a whole body.

In addition, this new legal system, binding throughout Western Christendom, was conceived as a dynamic system, developing in time. More specifically, the newly proclaimed power of the pope to make new laws—to legislate—introduced into Western law for the first time the concept that law may be, and must be, continually replenished, continually renewed. Prior to the twelfth century, legislation, whether by popes or kings, was a rare thing, and was usually disguised as the reaffirmation of older custom. This now changed, first in the Church and then in the kingdoms of Europe. The first four Lateran Councils from 1123 to 1215 issued hundreds of new laws, and in addition the popes issued their own laws in the form of decretals; more than 700 decretals remain from the twenty-two-year reign of Pope Alexander III (1159-81), and five major systematic collections of decretals were prepared during the eighteen year reign of Pope Innocent III (1198-1216).[9] In 1234 there appeared the first official collection of canons and decretals, summarizing and systematizing the work of almost a century; it remained the basic law of the Roman Catholic Church until 1917.

Thus, the canon law of the late Middle Ages, which only today, eight centuries after its creation, is being called into question by some leading Roman Catholics themselves, was the first modern legal system. It prevailed in every country of the West, from England and Spain to Hungary and Poland. It governed virtually all aspects of the lives of the Church's own spiritual army of priests and monks and also a great many aspects of the lives of the laity. The new hierarchy of Church courts had exclusive jurisdiction over laymen in matters of family law, inheritance, and various types of spiritual crimes, and it also had concurrent jurisdiction with secular courts over contracts (whenever the parties made a "pledge of faith"), over ecclesiastical property (and the Church owned one-fourth to one-third of the land of Europe), and over many other matters.[10]

At the same time, it was presupposed by the very existence of the modern canon law, and by the Papal Revolution which gave birth to it, that there were other matters, secular in nature, which were to be governed solely by the secular authorities. Partly in emulation of the canon law, and partly in resistance to it, emperors, kings, great feudal lords, and city and borough authorities created diverse bodies of secular law, diverse professional courts, and diverse types of professional legal literature. Thus the tribal, local, and feudal

---

[9] See Robert L. Benson, *The Bishop-Elect—A Study in Medieval Ecclesiastical Office* (Princeton, NJ, 1968), 12.

[10] See generally Le Bras, "Canon Law," 321-361.

customs which had prevailed throughout Europe until the eleventh and twelfth centuries, were transformed into new secular legal systems governing breaches of the king's peace, property relations, mercantile transactions, and other matters not specifically involving faith or sin. The growth of secular law at this time was greatly stimulated by the rapid growth of commerce in the twelfth century and the concomitant rise of urban centers.

Yet the relationship between the canon law of the Church and the secular law of the kingdoms of Europe could not be one of mere coexistence, or of mere emulation of, or rivalry with, the ecclesiastical law by the secular. There was also a claim of moral superiority by the ecclesiastical authority, coupled with demands for changes in the secular law to conform to moral standards set by the clergy. This was inevitable at a time when the clergy constituted the overwhelming majority of educated persons and hence occupied high positions in the courts of kings and barons. Beyond that, however, the very division of ecclesiastical and secular law presupposed a Church Militant which was determined not only to reform the world but also to protect its own cohesion and its own power. Many of the reforms which it promoted command respect even seven and eight centuries later: the introduction of rational trial procedures to replace magical mechanical modes of proof by ordeals of fire and water, by battles of champions, and by ritual oaths; the insistence upon consent as the foundation of marriage and upon wrongful intent as the basis of crime; the development of equity to protect the poor and helpless against the rich and powerful and to enforce relations to trust and confidence—to give just a few examples. On the other hand, religious sanctity was often attributed to legal standards which were of only temporal value. Universal celibacy of the priesthood, for example, made a legal requirement in the eleventh century, was valuable as a means of insulating the clergy from clan and feudal politics, but it was given the stamp of a divine imperative which made it survive long after it had ceased to be necessary. The law of heresy is an even stronger example of the danger of attaching religious sanctity to legal standards. Here the Church professed its own unwillingness to shed blood but turned the heretic over to the secular arm to be burned at the stake. Likewise, the penalty of excommunication for disobedience to ecclesiastical authority was—and is—a punishment which cannot be justified if the Church is conceived primarily as a legal and political entity rather than as a spiritual community; yet it is a punishment which purports to remove the sinner from the body of Christ.

I have sketched some of the main elements of the Western legal tradition during its formative era in the Catholic Middle Ages. However, substantial changes have taken place in Western law during the four and one-half centuries since the Protestant Reformation. The dualism of church and state has taken many new forms. Ecclesiastical jurisdiction has been greatly restricted, and much of the medieval canon law has been secularized and has passed over—often unnoticed—into the law of the state. Ultimately, Christianity itself has given birth to new secular religions of democracy and socialism, which have in turn threatened to deprive Christianity altogether of its public character, its political and legal dimension; many of the functions of the medieval Church are now performed by the press, political organizations, educational institutions, and the like. Yet, despite these and other changes, the Western legal tradition still bears the marks of its origins. It still stands for the autonomy of law, the autonomy of legal science, the autonomy of legal institutions, the autonomy of the legal profession. It still stands for the coexistence within the tradition of diverse legal systems, each of which challenges the other and each of which is to be judged by reason and morality. The law schools of the West remain one of the last bastions of the scholastic method, by which legal principles of general validity are marked off from those that are variable according to time and place and circumstance. They still teach, at least by implication, that the "body of law," the *corpus juris*, grows organically over generations and centuries, being continually replenished and renewed by legislation and by reinterpretation. The Western legal tradition still stands for the belief that so long as law remains autonomous, so long as it conforms to reason and morality, so long as it develops and grows to meet new challenges, it will continue to be able to resolve individual and social conflicts and to maintain order and justice.

Despite this enormous self-confidence, however, the fact is that the Western legal tradition is *not* able to resolve satisfactorily most of the individual and social conflicts which have confronted it in the twentieth century, and is *not* able to maintain order and justice either within the nations that uphold it or in their relations with each other or in the world as a whole. And that is its crisis.

Foundations of the Western Legal Tradition.—The primary cause of the crisis of the Western legal tradition is, I believe, the disintegration of its religious foundations.

By its religious foundations I do not mean Roman Catholic theology or philosophy of the eleventh and twelfth centuries and thereafter, or the idea of the dualism of secular and spiritual authorities, or the separation of politics and religion. I do not mean the sources of Western law in canon law or the belief that law must be judged by higher standards of faith and morals. These are an integral part of the structure of the Western legal tradition—they are part of what is in crisis—they are not its foundations.

A foundation goes in the opposite direction from the structure which is erected upon it. The *structure* of the Western legal tradition, during its formative era, was its division between secular and spiritual authorities, the one chiefly responsible for order and justice, the other chiefly responsible for faith and morals, and the consequent proliferation of diverse autonomous bodies of law as a means of maintaining the jurisdiction of each and the equilibrium between the two. The foundation of that structure was an entirely different concept and an entirely different experience, namely, the integration of law with religion, of order and justice with faith and morals, in an integrated community which transcended both.

Prior to the revolution of the eleventh and twelfth centuries, law was not an autonomous body of rules and concepts found in books and cultivated by a corps of professional jurists but rather an integral part of the common consciousness and common conscience of the various European peoples. In this earlier period from the sixth to the eleventh centuries every tribe had its own law: the Franks, Alemanns, Visigoths, Ostrogoths, Lombards, Burgundians, and other peoples who were eventually combined in the Frankish Empire, embracing much of what later became Germany, France, and northern Italy; the Angles, Saxons, Jutes, Celts, Britons, and other peoples of what later became England; the Norsemen of Scandinavia and later of Normandy, Sicily, and elsewhere; and many, many others, from Picts and Scots to Hungarians and Slavs.[11] The legal orders of all peoples (whom, for the sake of simplicity, I will call the Germanic people, since most, but not all, were Germanic, although they were certainly not German in the modern sense), though largely independent of each other were nevertheless remarkably similar. On the one hand, the basic legal unit within the tribe was the household, a community of comradeship and trust based partly on kinship and partly on oaths of mutual protection and service. Violation of the peace of the household by an outsider would lead to retaliation in the form of blood-feud or else to interhousehold or interclan negotiations designed to forestall or compose blood-feud. On the other hand, there were also territorial legal units consisting typically of households grouped in villages, villages grouped in larger units often called hundreds and counties, and hundreds and counties grouped in dukedoms or kingdoms. In the local territorial communities, the chief instrument of government and law was the public assembly ("moot" or "thing") of household elders. Together with kinship and local territorial

---

[11] See generally Arthur S. Diamond, *Primitive Law Past and Present* (London, 1971).

communities, there were also various kinds of lordship—in that sense, feudal—bonds, often formed by households "commending" themselves to great men for protection.[12]

At the head of the tribes and of the local and feudal communities there stood royal and ecclesiastical authorities. In the course of time, these became more and more important. Nevertheless, in the period prior to the latter part of the eleventh century, royal and ecclesiastical authorities did not attempt to alter in any fundamental way the essentially tribal and local and feudal character of the legal orders of Europe. This may seem less strange if it is added that the economy of Europe at that time was also almost wholly local, consisting chiefly of agriculture and cattle-keeping, with subsidiary hunting; population was sparse and there were few large towns; commerce played only a small role, and communications in general were extremely rudimentary.

When higher royal and ecclesiastical rulers did assert their authority over law, it was chiefly to guide the custom and the legal consciousness of the people, not to remake it. The bonds of kinship, of lordship units, and of territorial communities *were* the law. If those bonds were violated, the initial response was, as I have already indicated, to seek vengeance, but vengeance was supposed to give way—and usually did—to negotiation for pecuniary sanctions. This was the famous system of fixed tariffs of monetary composition for various types of injuries which was a predominant feature of the Anglo-Saxon, Frankish, and other legal orders of Germanic Europe,[13] as it is a predominant feature of many contemporary systems of primitive law. Adjudication, whether by ordeals of fire or water or by ritual oaths, or by local assemblies or "moots," was often a stage in the interfamily or interclan negotiations. The jurisdiction of moots usually depended upon consent of the parties, and the moot generally could not compel them to abide by its

---

[12] Cf. Henry R. Loyn, *Anglo-Saxon England and the Norman Conquest* (London, 1962), 292-314.

[13] For example, Ethelbert's Laws, promulgated in 600 A.D. and the earliest of the Anglo-Saxon compilations of laws, are remarkable for their extraordinarily detailed schedules of tariffs established for various injuries: so much for the loss of a leg, so much for an eye, so much if the victim is a slave, so much if he is a freeman, so much if he is a priest, and so on. The front teeth were worth six shillings each, the teeth next to them four, and other teeth one; thumbs, thumb nails, forefingers, middle fingers, ring fingers, little fingers, and their respective fingernails were all distinguished and a separate price, called a *bot*, was set for each. Similar distinctions were made between ears whose hearing is destroyed, ears cut off, ears pierced, and ears lacerated; between bones laid bare, bones damaged, bones broken, skulls broken, shoulders disabled, chins broken, collar bones broken, arms broken, thighs broken, and ribs broken; and between bruises outside the clothing, bruises under the clothing, and bruises which do not show black. See Laws of Ethelbert paras. 34-42, 50-55, 58-60, 65-66, in F.L. Attenborough ed., *The Laws of the Earliest English Kings* (New York, 1963).

decision. And so peace, once disrupted, was to be restored ultimately by diplomacy. Beyond the question of right and wrong was the question of reconciliation of the warring factions. Again, these statements can also be made concerning the law of many contemporary primitive societies of Africa, Asia, and South America, and also concerning the law of many ancient civilizations which exist on those continents.

In Germanic law, proof was formal and dramatic. Legal rules, being largely unwritten, were often expressed in poetic images, which helped to stamp them on the memory. Common phrases were: "unbidden and unbought, so I with my eyes saw and with my ears heard," "foulness or fraud," "house and home," "right and righteous," "from hence or thence." Ritual oaths were elaborate,[14] and were to be sworn "without slip or trip." The law was contained in a multitude of proverbs. The earliest Irish law was in the form of poetry.

The dramatic and poetic qualities of Germanic law were associated with its substantive plasticity. It would be laid down that something shall be the rule as far as a cock walks, or flies, or a cat springs, or one can reach with a sickle, or that so much land shall be acquired as can be ridden round in a certain time on a horse, or turned over with the plow.[15] Because life was much less compartmentalized than it later became, much more a matter of total involvement, poetic and symbolic speech, which is closely associated with the whole being and with the unconscious, was more appropriate than prosaic and literal language, especially on solemn occasions involving the law.

Some of the symbols and ceremonies of Germanic law still survive in modern times, such as the handclasp as a confirmation of a contract and various rituals of sitting and standing at the installation of officeholders.[16]

From a Western, that is, post-eleventh century point of view, the Germanic folklaw appears defective because of the absence of law reform movements, sophisticated legal machinery, a strong central lawmaking authority, a strong central judicial authority, a body of law independent of

---

[14] For example, an oath used in suits affirming title to land reads:

So I hold it as he held it, who held it as saleable, and as I will own it—and never resign it—neither plot nor plough land—nor turf nor tuft—nor furrow nor foot length—nor land nor leasow—nor fresh nor marsh—nor rough ground nor room—nor wold nor fold—land nor strand—wood nor water.

Sir Francis Palgrave, *The Rise and Progress of the English Commonwealth* (London, 1832), 135.

[15] See Rudolf Hübner, *A History of Germanic Private Law*, trans. F. Philbrick (Boston, 1918), 10-11.

[16] Ibid. at 11-12.

religious beliefs and emotions, or a systematic legal science. But that is only one side of the coin. The other side is the presence of a sense of the wholeness of life, a sense of the interrelatedness of law with all other aspects of life, a sense that legal institutions and legal processes as well as legal norms and legal decisions are all integrated in the harmony of the universe. Law, like art and myth and religion, and like language itself was, for the peoples of Europe in the early stages of their history, not primarily a matter of making and applying rules in order to determine guilt and fix judgment, not an instrument of the separation of people from each other on the basis of a set of principles, but rather a matter of holding people together, a matter of reconciliation. Law was conceived primarily as a mediating process, a mode of communication, rather than primarily as a process of rulemaking and decisionmaking.

In these respects the early folklaw of Europe had much in common with Eastern legal traditions. In the tradition of the Chinese and of other peoples who have lived under the strong influence of Buddhist and Confucian thought, social control was not to be found primarily in the allocation of rights and duties through a system of general norms but rather in the maintaining of right relationships among family members, among families within lordship units, and among families and lordship units within local communities and under the emperor. Social harmony was more important than "giving to each his due." Indeed, "each" was not conceived to be a being distinct from his society or from the universe but rather an integral part of a system of social relationships subject to the Principle of Heaven. Therefore, in the ancient civilizations of Asia the intuitive, mystical, the poetic side of life was emphasized, and the intellectual, the analytical, the historical—and hence the legal—was subordinated to it.

This was true also of the peoples of Europe in the period with which we have been concerned, before the great explosion of the late eleventh and twelfth centuries. The Germanic folk myths, which dominated their thought prior to the introduction of Christianity, and which had a lasting influence upon them, did not make a sharp division between magic and logic or between fate and the rules of criminal law. Nor did Christianity, an Eastern religion, make a sharp division between faith and reason.

The old myths were about warring gods, spirits in rivers, woods, and mountains, the divine descent of tribal kings, and similar matters; they were based on an overriding belief in honor and in fate. In the fifth sixth, seventh, eighth, ninth, and tenth centuries Christianity gradually spread across Europe, replacing the old myths with the gospel of a universal Creator, father of all men, who once appeared on earth as the man Jesus Christ, worship of whom brings freedom from bondage to all earthly ties, freedom from fate, freedom from death itself. Moreover, Christianity taught that all believers form a community, a Church, which transcends kindred, tribe, and territory. The king continued to be exalted as the supreme religious leader of his people—"Christ's deputy," as he was called in one Anglo-Saxon legal document; nevertheless, Christianity treated even a king as a human being, subject like every other human being to punishment by God for his sins and only able to be saved by God's grace.

These new beliefs had a great appeal to Germanic man. They brought, for the first time, a positive meaning to life and to death, a larger purpose into which to fit the tragedies and mysteries of his existence. Beside these new beliefs the old pagan myths seemed poor and bleak. But by the same token, one might also suppose that the new beliefs would have wholly undermined the social institutions of the old order. On the other hand, one might also wonder how, if Christianity constituted so fundamental a threat to Germanic social institutions, it could have succeeded in making converts among Germanic tribal chiefs and Kings. For it was primarily those chiefs and Kings who determined the religion of their respective peoples.

To understand the implications of Christianity for Germanic law, one must recall that Germanic Christianity was much closer to Eastern Orthodoxy than to modern Christianity, whether Roman Catholic or Protestant. It was hardly concerned with the reform of social institutions. It was above all concerned with the life of the world to come, and with preparation for that life through prayer and through personal humility and obedience. The highest ideals of Christianity in the first thousand years of Church history, both in the East and in the West, were symbolized above all in the lives of holy men and women living in various forms of monastic communities, with their emphasis on fellowship, on charity, and on withdrawal from the temporal world.

This is not to say that Christianity had no effect whatever on Germanic legal institutions. It affected them in the first instance by influencing kings from time to time to write down the folklaw in the form of short collections of rules. This helped to prevent blood-feud and to keep the peace. The Germanic "codes" also show the gradual effect of some Christian concepts, such as that of the fundamental equality of all persons before God. Thus one may observe some amelioration of the position of women, slaves, and children and some protection of the poor and helpless. Yet on the whole the Church did not challenge the basic features of the barbarian law.

Both the strength and the weakness of Christianity in the centuries in which if first came to prevail among the peoples of Europe lay in its willingness to be integrated with the whole social, political, and economic life of those peoples. The Church as an organization did not stand opposite the political order but within it. Religion was united with politics and economics and law, as they were united with each other. The Church taught sanctity and produced saints; this was something new for the Germanic peoples, who previously had glorified only heroes. But the Church did not oppose heroism and heroes; it only held up an alternative ideal. Similarly, the Church did not oppose blood-feud and ordeals; it only said they could not bring salvation, which came from faith and good works. The majority of bishops and priests of the Church became, in fact, wholly involved in the corruption and violence that characterized the age; this was inevitable, because they were generally appointed by leading politicians from among their friends and relatives. Christianity was Germanized at the same time that the Germanic peoples were Christianized.[17] Thus Christianity had the effect, prior to the eleventh and twelfth centuries, of devaluing Germanic legal institutions without replacing them by new ones. It left village and tribal feudal law intact. It accepted the fundamental Germanic values of blood and earth, only attempting—with occasional successes—to subordinate them to Christian values of salvation by faith and works.

It was not primarily the bishops and priests but the monastic movement which, by its example more than its doctrine, taught Christian ideals of sacrifice and service and love of neighbor (and, at the same time, scientific agriculture) to the Germanic peoples. But the monasteries offered no program of law reform to the world outside.

The monasteries did create miniature legal orders within. Each of the monastic communities had its own law, its own "rule" of work and prayer and of administration and discipline. In the sixth century and thereafter, they adopted "penitentials," consisting of collections of rules assigning punishments for various sins. The earliest ones defined the number of strokes or blows to be imposed on a monk for various forms of misconduct. Eventually, more subtle penalties of repentance, good works, compensation, and pilgrimage were added. Thus Christianity, without denouncing the old communal methods of dispute resolution and punishment, offered its own procedures and its own standards of reconciliation and penance, which were more concerned with the cure of souls than the appeasement of vengeance.

Finally, it is important to note that in the tenth and early eleventh centuries, one monastic order, Cluny in southern France, established the first system of administration in which many individual monasteries were united

---

[17] Cf. Heinrich Boehmer, "Das germanische Christentum," *Theologische Studien und Kritiken* 86 (1913): 165.

under a single head, the abbot of Cluny. Within a century after it was founded in 910, Cluny numbered about 1450 monasteries. It was Cluny which paved the way for the Papal Revolution by its program of moral reform of Church life and its attack on the buying and selling of Church offices and the involvement of bishops and priests in local, clan, and feudal politics. And it was Cluny, the first translocal corporation,[18] which served as a model for Pope Gregory VII in his reorganization of the Roman Church as a whole.

These, then, were the religious foundations of the Western legal tradition which was initiated by the Papal Revolution of the late eleventh and twelfth centuries; a Church which for some centuries had been wholly integrated in the social, economic, and political life of the community, except to the extent that monks, whether alone or in monasteries, represented a different world and a religious faith which for centuries had not challenged existing political and legal institutions, but which had served to soften their harsh effects. If we are to look for a modern parallel it is in Eastern Orthodoxy; I think especially of the Russian Orthodox Church which has agreed even to support an atheist state in return for the sole right to keep the churches open so that the Russian people may experience in the worship service the presence of God.

The Crisis of the Western Legal Tradition.—The crisis of the Western legal tradition—its impotence to resolve the crucial conflicts of the twentieth century and to maintain order and justice in a world mortally imperiled by violence and oppression—is primarily due, I am convinced, to the breakdown of the communities on which the Western legal tradition is founded. The establishment, in the late eleventh and twelfth centuries, of the Western Church as a visible, corporate, legal entity, standing opposite the secular authorities, and the articulation of autonomous bodies of ecclesiastical and secular law to maintain the cohesion of the Church and of the State and the equilibrium between the two, made sense—and still makes sense—as a way of protecting spiritual values against corrupting social, economic, and political forces in essentially stable Christian communities. These communities, the *populus Christianus*, constituted the true religious foundations of Western law. Where, however, as in America today, and increasingly throughout the West, social life is characterized by religious apathy and by fundamental divisions of race, of class, of the sexes, and of the generations, where bonds of faith are weak and bonds of kinship and of soil have given way to a vague and abstract nationalism, it is useless to suppose that law can effectuate its

---

18 See Rosenstock-Huessy, *The Driving Power,* 54.

ultimate purposes. Unless it is rooted in community, law becomes merely mechanical and bureaucratic.

The disintegration of the religious foundations of Western law renders wholly barren the dualism of the secular and spiritual aspects of life. Today, law is something which is taught in law schools, practised in law offices, tested and applied in law courts, made in legislatures. Today religion is something which is taught in schools of theology, practiced in churches, tested and applied by the clergy, made by holy synods, or else, as in some Protestant traditions, religion is something which resides in the heart and conscience of the individual believer. Religion is irrelevant in the law schools, and law is alien to the religious mind. Law becomes just a mechanism, religion just an escape. This is the end of the 900-year-old era of Western law; dualism, or rather pluralism, becomes simply fragmentation and disunity.

It would be presumptuous to attempt, in a few words, to project a way out of this impasse.[19] I will only present two general thoughts: first, the solution will not be found in a return to simpler things. There is no going back. Second, the Western legal tradition must adapt itself to the new age that is emerging out of the confrontation of East and West. These are not primarily geographical terms but temporal terms. For Christianity, East is the first thousand years on which the second is founded. The third era must build on the first two.

I close by paying tribute to Pope John, in whose name this chapter is written. He faced squarely the real predicament of the Church in the twentieth century—not the Church as the clergy but the Church as the people, the *populus Christianus*. He said that "the sons of the church . . . should make themselves part of the institutions of civil society, and have an impact on them from within."[20] He opened the doors to the winds of change and to the spirit of renewal. He sought solutions from both the East and the West. He was a man of the next thousand years of the history of mankind.

---

[19] For some suggestions, however, see Harold J. Berman, *The Interaction of Law and Religion* (Nashville, TN, 1974), 107-131.

[20] Encyclical Letter, Pacem in Terris, in *The Sixteen Documents of Vatican II and the Instruction on the Liturgy, with Commentaries by the Council Fathers* (Boston, 1963), 749.

∽ 4 ∾

MEDIEVAL ENGLISH EQUITY*

E quity is probably the most mysterious character in the detective story of English legal history. The Yearbooks compete for that honor; but of the Yearbooks we may at least say that if we only knew more facts about them we should probably be able to understand them. The "facts" of equity are at our disposal, but no one has been able to give a satisfactory explanation of those facts.

Maitland, half-humourously, defines modern equity as that part of the law which would be administered by the Courts of Equity if the Courts of Equity had not been abolished in 1875.[1] Yet in the heyday of the Courts of Equity, in the sixteenth and early seventeenth centuries, the law administered by the Chancellors and the Judges of Star Chamber and Requests and High Commission was—if we are to believe the seventeenth-century champions of the common law—not a system of justice at all, but a cloak for the despotic desires of the Tudors and their councillors. "Tis all one as if they would make the standard of measure the Chancellor's foot," complained Selden.[2] And if we go back further, to the Middle Ages, the era roughly from the Conquest to the Reformation, we find equity administered by no particular set of courts but rather by many different sets of courts; we find it under various names,

---

* Presented in a seminar in English Legal History given by Professor T.F.T. Plucknett, London School of Economics, February 1939.

[1] F.W. Maitland, *Equity: A Course of Lectures* (Cambridge, 1936), 1.

[2] John Selden, *Seldenia, or, The Table Talk of John Selden, Esq.* (London, 1789), 45 (modernized spelling).

unformulated and unsystematic—yet (as I hope to prove) the most powerful factor for new development in the entire medieval legal process.

"Equity in law is the same that the spirit is in religion, what everyone pleases to make it," wrote Selden.[3] In tracing the position and function and nature of equity in medieval english law, I should like to take the first half of this quotation as my text; equity in law is the same as the spirit is in religion—remembering that in medieval Christendom the spirit in religion was no vague or mythical abstraction but a potent and vital force, which entered into the life-fibre of every person and every social institution, and which, so far from being what everyone pleased to make it, was shaped from the eleventh to the sixteenth centuries by one of the most unified and power-ful organizations mankind has ever known, the Church of Rome. Likewise, equity, throughout the four centuries of the era, though undefined and unclassified, injected into the English legal process certain principles and practices which enabled our law not only to throw off its more primitive Anglo-Saxon shackles, but also to adapt itself continually to the changing social needs of the medieval period.

Equity in the Court of Chancery.—Before discussing further this deeper problem of the nature of equity, let us transplant ourselves into the Court of Chancery of the late fourteenth and fifteenth centuries, that we may see medieval equity actually applied.[4]

The Chancellor has before him a bill, or petition. Perhaps it has been addressed to the king, perhaps to himself, perhaps to the Chancellor of the king and to his Council. Perhaps it is in French, perhaps English. As time

---

[3] Ibid.

[4] The following sketch of medieval equity as practised in the fourteenth and fifteenth centuries in the Court of Chancery is drawn chiefly from William P. Baildon, ed., *Select Cases in Chancery (1364-1471)*, Selden Society, vol. 10 (London, 1896); George Spence, *The Equitable Jurisdiction of the Court of Chancery* (Philadelphia, 1846); Christopher C. Langdell, *A Brief Survey of Equity Jurisdiction*, 2d ed. (Cambridge, 1908); James B. Ames, "The Origin of Uses and Trusts," in Association of American Law Schools, ed., *Select Essays in Anglo-American Legal History* (Boston, 1908), 2: 737; Willard T. Barbour, "The History of Contract in Early English Equity," in Paul Vinogradoff, ed., *Oxford Studies in Social and Legal History*, (Oxford, 1914), 4: 9-237.

Much of both the doctrine and the procedure of Chancery is difficult to date, and some of the principles stated here as being practised in the fourteenth and fifteenth cen-turies were undoubtedly not developed in any definite form until the sixteenth century, when equity gradually became systematized. The medieval chancellor might grant a certain remedy in one case and might refuse it in another which to us today seems almost identi-cal. The purpose of the present description is not to codify medieval equity, which would be false to the whole legal outlook of the Middle Ages, but rather to re-create impression-istically its general character.

goes on the bill will be most frequently addressed to the Chancellor and most frequently in English. The bill is quite informal; there is no particular phraseology, no set definition or description of the cause of the suit. Certain facts are detailed, which indicate that the petitioner requires relief against another person but that he cannot get it in the ordinary courts of the king for one of several reasons. He is poor and "lothe to spende on plee;" or he is old or sick, and helpless against the wealth and power of his adversary who will bribe or intimidate the jurors; or the sheriff is corrupt and refuses to bring the defendant to trial; or no one dares to act as his counsel for fear of the defendant's malice. Or else the common law has no remedy for his complaint, it being one of breach of trust or confidence, or of accident, or of fraud, or of duress; or else the remedy at common law is insufficient or too slow.[5] Therefore the petitioner prays a subpoena (or perhaps a writ of *habeas corpus cum causa*, or writ of *certiorari*, or perhaps a subpoena together with one or the other of those writs); and sometimes he asks for a serjeant-at-arms to bring the defendant up and perhaps for an injunction, or for surety of the peace; or maybe he merely prays relief generally asking "such a writ as to you shall seem reasonable in this case." He appeals to the Chancellor most commonly in the name of conscience, often in that of good faith, right, or reason, most rarely in that of equity. He concludes in terms of supplication; the Chancellor is prayed to find a remedy "for the love of God and in way of charity," or "at the reverence of God," or "in honour of God."

If the Chancellor, often in consultation with the Justices of the King's courts as well as with the other members of the Council, considers the case stated in the bill to warrant prosecution, he issues a subpoena to the petitioner's adversary. The subpoena is in Latin, and it may say merely:

> Richard by the grace of God King of England and of France and Lord of Hibernia to John Seymour of London Greeting. Because of certain matters concerning ourselves, we command you to be before us in your proper person in our Chancery on next Tuesday, wherever it will be then, to respond to what will then be objected to you on our behalf and further to do and to receive whatever will then be decided by us. And you will by no means fail to do this under whatever peril

---

[5] See Baildon, ed., *Select Cases in Chancery*, Case 5 (defendants will not be justified by the sheriff against their will, nor will they at any time unless the king betakes himself against them seriously); Case 6 (plaintiffs, who are constables of a Hundred, say they dare not perform their office unless defendants find sureties for the peace); Case 10 (defendant's maintenance pleaded); Case 24 (no one dares to act as plaintiff's counsel for fear of defendant's malice); Case 41 (defendant so great in kinsmen, alliance, and friends); Case 67 (no speedy remedy at common law (case of forcible entry and ouster)).

will befall (or under penalty—subpoena—of 100 livres). And have there this
writ. . . ."[6]

If the defendant is not impressed by this document, sealed with the Great
Seal, and decides to risk not appearing, the Chancellor will issue an attachment against him, and sometimes a second and third attachment. In the early
times, the sheriff is ordered to distrain on his property; later, he is sent to the
Fleet and fined at the discretion of the Court. If he cannot be found, a commission of rebellion issues against him. Ultimately, a commission issues to
put the plaintiff in possession till the defendant should appear or answer.

But let us suppose our defendant appears at the appointed time. The
plaintiff, who has also received a subpoena, also appears. In the presence of
the Chancellor, perhaps together with other members of the Council and/or
with Justices of the Kings' Bench and/or Common Pleas, the plaintiff and
defendant examine each other. The examination is under oath, and sentence
by sentence. The plaintiff makes his complaint. The defendant makes his
answer. The original bill may be amended or supplemented with additional
facts—either before or after the answer. If matters are not settled, the plaintiff
makes his replication, which may be by way of general denial of the defendant's answer, or which may introduce other facts and circumstances to avoid
the effect of the answer to support his own case. Witnesses may be subpoe-
naed by the Chancellor and examined by him freely.[7]

As to rules of pleading—there are none. There are attorneys; in time, in
fact, a Chancery Bar; but their attempts to introduce technical rules of pleading are successfully resisted. As Edward IV's Chancellor, Bishop Stillington,
said in 1470, "In the Chancery, a man shall not be prejudiced by mispleader,
or for default of form, but according to the verity of the matter; we have to
judge according to conscience, and not to what has been alleged. . . . If a man
should allege by his bill that one had done him wrong, and the defendant
should say nothing, yet if it should appear to us that the defendant had done
no wrong to the plaintiff, he should not recover."[8]

Yet (in Spence's words) as a matter of discovery though not of pleading, a
party is bound to answer with precision to those facts which are within his
own knowledge. He may be imprisoned for putting into the replication
"much impertinent and idle matter." For slander, he may be sentenced to

---

[6] See ibid., Case 2.

[7] Witnesses are examined *"ad informandum conscientiam judicis."* Depositions taken
for this purpose are delivered to the judge sealed up. They are not sent to the arbitrators if
the cause is referred, nor to the judges if an issue or action is directed to be tried, unless by
consent.

[8] Quoted by Spence, *Equitable Jurisdiction*, 376-377.

commitment and ignominy. And parties who cause vexatious bills to be filed may be punished and made to pay costs.[9]

The Chancellor, having reached a decision, issues a decree. The decree is directed to one or both of the parties, and it is not tied by forms. "It can direct many things to be mutually done and suffered." It can adapt its remedy to the particular exigencies of the case. It can retain the case until, by means of successive orders, "all the ends of justice in reference to all the parties interested are effectually carried out."[10] And, if necessary, there can be rehearings and appeals.

Such is the procedure of the Court of Chancery in the later Middle Ages. Its substantive law is still harder to define, is even more flexible.

In general, we may say that its law, at least in the fourteenth century, is the same law as that administered in the King's Bench and Common Pleas; that where the common law courts give a sufficient remedy, the Chancellor will not intervene; and that where the Chancellor does intervene it, as Maitland says, is not to administer any body of substantive rules that differ from the ordinary law of the land, but to administer the law in cases which escape the meshes of the ordinary courts.[11]

Yet many cases escape the meshes of the ordinary courts because the wrong requires a remedy unavailable under the ordinary law as established by legal decisions of the king's judiciary; and, on grounds which I shall discuss later, the Chancellor may develop his own remedy. Thus, contrary to the law of the King's Bench and the Common Pleas: an obligee who from loss or accident cannot produce his bond may nevertheless enforce the obligation in Chancery; where the lessor enters on the tenant and thus by rule of law suspends the rent, he may have relief in Chancery; in certain cases, where forfeitures have been clearly incurred according to the rules of law, Chancery may nevertheless give relief against them; one executor and one joint-tenant may in Chancery sue his companion; a man may in Chancery recover property of which he has been defrauded or which he had given to the defendant under duress; a man may in Chancery recover the consideration for a promise which the defendant refuses to perform; a bailor may in Chancery recover a chattel from a defendant in possession of it after the death of the bailee.

In many types of cases which the King's Bench and Common Pleas declared themselves powerless to handle, the Court of Chancery likewise developed rules of its own. Thus, as regards debts which only affect lands by force of a trust created for their payment, Chancery follows the rule that all

---

[9] See ibid. for illustrations of these rules of discovery.

[10] Ibid.

[11] Maitland, *Equity*, 107ff.

debts are equally due in conscience and therefore all, of whatever rank, are to be paid pro rata according to the amount of the debt; and where land is devised for the payment of debts and the Chancery executes the trust (this being a distinct substantive remedy of its own, since the creditor has no remedy against the devisee at law), the same rule of equal distribution between all creditors claiming under the trust is followed. On the other hand, where lands are assigned in trust for the payment of debts, the Chancellor, in administering the trust, directs the judgments to be paid in accordance with their legal preference, since the Chancery remedy is in that case merely a substitute for the common law remedy which the creditor had on judgments.

The Early History of Equity in England.—If this rough picture which I have given of the law and custom of the Court of Chancery (in respect to its equitable jurisdiction) seems fragmentary and unsystematic to the modern legal mind, the fourteenth- and fifteenth-century Chancellors are partly to blame. For medieval equity was a fragmentary and unsystematic thing. As Professor Plucknett puts it, "first one point, then another, developed." There was no body of rules called equity; Chancery was not (in the modern sense) a court of equity. The creation of equity-as-such, and its opposition to the common law-as-such, came only with the breakdown of the medieval era in the sixteenth century and the rise of the Tudor national state.

We can understand this better if we realize that the (what for lack of better word we must call) equity of the Court of Chancery in this period was nothing new to medieval English society, but rather a continuation by a new branch of the King's Council of doctrines and methods which, prior to the rise of that new branch, had not only been administered by the Council, but had also left their mark upon each of the many kinds of law by which medieval England was governed—upon the custom of the manor, upon the custom of the borough and the early law merchant, upon the laws of universities and other special franchises, upon the canon law administered by the ecclesiastical courts, upon the common law of freeholders, upon the law administered by the Justices in Eyre. In the heyday of the medieval legal (and social) organization in England—that is, in the two centuries, roughly, from the reign of Henry II to that of Edward III and beyond, all of these various laws were infused with principles and practices which at a later date would be inherited by the Court of Chancery, and at a still later date would come to be systematized under the title of equity.

In the twelfth and thirteenth centuries there was no need for a special equitable jurisdiction in a Court of Chancery, because not merely the King's Court, but all courts, could do whatever equity required. Yet in doing what equity required, none of them considered that they were administering any extraordinary justice. The fact was simply that rules which today we call equitable were part and parcel of the law and custom of every court in the medieval legal hierarchy.

In order to understand the role of equity in this earlier period from the later twelfth through the early fourteenth centuries, we must remember an important characteristic of this medieval legal hierarchy. Today, generally speaking, any man may appear before any court, the particular court which he does appear before, in any particular case, depending upon the legal nature of the case; whether it is criminal or civil, in appeal or in first instance, involving a major or minor infraction of the law, and so forth. In medieval times, generally speaking, the situation was the opposite; any court could try any kind of a case, the particular court in which a case was tried depending upon the status of the men involved in it. Thus, every court was court of first instance; every court adjudicated whatever wrongs were inflicted upon members of the estate over which it had jurisdiction. Broadly, the manorial court dealt with members of the manor, the borough courts with members of the borough, the common law courts with freeholders, and so forth. Standing guard over these various jurisdictions, however, were two figures representing estates to which every man belonged automatically, and before whose justice every man might be brought; the king, as keeper of the peace between all men of the realm, and the pope, as interpreter of the will of God regarding the conduct of all members of Christendom.

From Henry II to the first half of the fourteenth century, the law of each of these types of courts was in the process of constant formation. The custom of manors and boroughs, the canons of the church, the laws of the king's courts, were flexible and changing. To meet a new wrong there was no hesitation about devising a new remedy; and in devising new remedies, there was no hesitation about administering what later generations called equity.

If we turn to the rolls of a manorial court at the close of the thirteenth century, we shall find that that vigorous and highly flexible institution, "the custom of the manor,"[12] gave special protection to the underling, that it

---

12 See T. F. T. Plucknett, *Concise History of the Common Law* 2d ed. (Rochester, NY, 1936), 227ff., who quotes Azo, the famous late twelfth- and early thirteenth-century legal scholar, to the effect that "a custom can be called *long* if it was introduced within 10 or 20 years, *very long* if it dates from 30 years, and *ancient* if it dates from 40 years." After describing methods by which medieval communities adapted custom to changing social needs, Plucknett states that "the custom of a medieval community may well have been much more intimately a product of the work and thought of those who lived by it, than is a modern statute enacted by a legislature whose contact with the public at large is only occasional."

permitted villeins to sue each other for breach of simple "oral" agreements, that it granted the remedy of specific performance,[13] all this quite informally, and with no consciousness that later historians would consider this equitable jurisdiction extraordinary.[14]

Turning to the vast domains of the canon law[15] we find not merely the essential method and procedure of the later Chancellors; the libel, exception, rejoinders and sur-rejoinders, the examination under oath of the parties to a suit by each other, the personal decree of specific performance, the punishment of contempt of court, etc.[16] We also find the same types of wrongs—

---

[13] See F.W. Maitland and W.P. Baildon, eds., *The Court Baron* (London, 1890), 115-116:

> H.T. was attached to answer J.B. of a plea that he should make him a thousand of sedge whereof he says that he has made 600. Therefore be he in mercy for covenant broken. And [he] is commanded to distrain him to make him the said 400.

> It is found by inquest that P.I. broke covenant with W.M. as to make him a new 'rother', to his damage taxed at 2d. . . . . And it is commanded to distrain the said P. to [make] the 'rother'. . . .

> [Maitland comments,] The agreements enforced at [the Bishop of Ely's court of] Littleport are called 'conventiones'; still we may well doubt whether this word implies that they were agreements which had been put into writing. It is hard to believe that these Littleport villeins, who dared not send their children to school without the lord's leave, were very ready with the pen, or that when they made agreements about their petty affairs, they procured parchment and ink and wax and a clerk. But they certainly do sue upon agreements touching very petty affairs; they sue for 'unliquidated damages' and this clearly marks off the action on a 'conventio' from an action of debt.

[14] See F.W. Maitland, "Introduction," to *Select Pleas in Manorial Courts: Reigns of Henry III and Edward I* (London, 1888): "The Court which had been enforcing the custom of the manor did not become some other court when it turned to punish breaches of the peace or to adjudicate upon actions of debt between the tenants."

[15] I omit a discussion of equity in the borough and fair courts and in the courts of London which has often been hinted at but seems never to have been thoroughly investigated.

[16] This was canon law rather than Roman procedure—or better, it was Roman law procedure molded and reformed by the canonists. One of the chief changes introduced by the canon law into the Roman law was the requirement that each party to a suit must submit to examination under oath by his adversary, his answers being evidence against him as admissions or confessions, but not in his favor. This rule was taken over by the Chancellors. See Langdell, *A Brief Survey of Equity Jurisdiction*, 26. Langdell also points out that since the ecclesiastical courts had no jurisdiction *in rem* but only *in personam*, they were forced in property matters to adjudicate upon the duties of litigants, and to compel performance thereof specifically. Thus they first ordered the party to do or refrain from doing the thing in question; if he refused obedience he was pronounced contumacious and excommunicated; excommunication was then signified to the king, a writ *de excommunicato capiendo* issued, and arrest and imprisonment by the sheriff followed. The system was

breach of fiduciary obligations is the outstanding example—being remedied by the ecclesiastics, as they were later remedied by the ecclesiastical Chancellors.

In regard to the equity of the earlier common law courts it must be noted that the entire writ system (which, incidentally, was used by other courts as well, notably the manor courts and the church courts) was at this period based on the equitable concept of specific relief and the principle that a new wrong may have a new remedy. The writ process of the courts themselves was likewise essentially equitable, the justices not only giving judgments *in rem* but also, in Hazeltine's words, "what we must call 'decrees *in personam*', decrees that under the influence of the subpoena became so marked a feature of the equity of the Chancellors."[17] Going more deeply into the substantive law of the common law courts, Hazeltine and others have shown that they were, at this period, enforcing by writs of detinue and account obligations of a fiduciary character (actually, uses of chattels and money);[18] that they were using doctrines equivalent to the later "equity of redemption" and "decree of foreclosure" in regulating the gage of land;[19] that they administered the remedy of specific performance in enforcing certain obligations of the contractual nature;[20] that the common law writs of prohibition were essentially decrees *in personam* corresponding to the injunctions issued by the later

---

adopted "literally" by the Chancellor, says Langdell, with the exception that the Chancellor had some jurisdiction in rem. Ibid.

[17] Harold D. Hazeltine, "The Early History of English Equity," in Paul Vinogradoff, ed., *Essays in Legal History* (London, 1913), 261-285.

[18] Oliver Wendell Holmes, Jr., "Early English Equity," in Association of American Law Schools, ed., *Select Essays in Anglo-American Legal History*, 2: 705, argues that uses in lands were also enforced at one time by the action of covenant. Ames contradicts this extreme view, but says that uses in chattels and money were enforced by the actions of detinue and account. Ames, "The Origin of Uses and Trusts."

[19] See Hazeltine, "The Early History of English Equity," who shows that from Henry II, the King's Courts enforced the gage of land. If land was gaged for a term, and the debtor failed to pay at the end of the term, he was brought into court and made to answer to a writ ordering him to "acquit" (redeem) the gage.

[20] See Hazeltine, "Early History of Specific Performance of Contract in English Law," in *Juristische Festgabe des auslandes zu Josef Kohlers 60. Geburtstag* (Berlin/Stuttgart, 1909). The common law courts of this earlier period enforced the covenant of the lessor, the covenant to convey, the obligations arising out of final concord, the agreement of lords to acquit their tenants from suit of court, and the obligations of warrantors. Sometimes the court ordered the defendant in general terms to keep his promise (i.e., specifically perform); sometimes to perform his covenant by giving the plaintiff possession of the land or by executing the conveyance. Upon defendant's failure to comply with the judicial order, security might be exacted from the defendant, his property might be distrained, or he might even be threatened with the loss of his land.

equity courts;[21] and that the common law writs *quia timet* anticipated the Chancery bills *quia timet*.[22]

But to emphasize the judicial discretion and equity of the common law judges as something apart from the jurisdiction of the king and his Council would be false to a period in which the courts still followed the king, in which the judges were chosen from the official household of the king, in which the very phrase *per consilium curiae* was synonymous with judicial discretion and, in a broad sense, equity.[23] The common law system, with the Chancellor at its head, was, in fact, integral in the king's legislative machinery. "It was by decisions of the courts and by writs penned in Chancery that

---

[21] Hazeltine, "The Early History of English Equity," writes:

The early common law jurisdiction in personam by means of prohibition was by no means narrow. The orders of the court were issued not only in cases of waste, nuisance, and other torts, but also in cases of contract and property. . . . Parties were not only ordered not to commit waste, not to commit nuisance, not to sell land, not to distrain the plaintiff to do suite of court, not to destroy the wood in which the plaintiff had housebote and hay-bote, not to expose wares for sale elsewhere than in the plaintiff's market, not to sue in the ecclesiastical courts; but parties were ordered to repair walls and building, to erect house, to place property in the same condition in which it has been and to remove existing nuisances. The orders of the court were not only temporary or interlocutory in character but they were final or perpetual;. . . there were also orders never to commit waste, never to expose wares for sale elsewhere than in the plaintiff's market, never to sue in the ecclesiastical courts. . . ."

The methods of enforcement of such orders is revealing, especially in the light of the collapse of enforcement of common law judgments in the fourteenth and fifteenth centuries. The early common law tribunals, Hazeltine says, did on occasion issue orders which closely resemble the writ of subpoena, and did have an effective machinery of punitive and preventive justice which operated both upon the person and the property of those who did not comply with their command. The writs of prohibition themselves contained no hint of penalties attendant upon disobedience, but "it is nevertheless clear from our study of the sources that disobedience resulted in serious consequences." Ibid. The appearance of offending parties could be compelled by gage and pledge and even distraint of all their lands. If a breach of prohibition was proved, on inquest, damages could be awarded to the plaintiffs, heavy amercements could be collected by the king, the defendant's land could be taken from him, he could even be imprisoned for contempt of the king's prohibition. Also, through sureties or threat of loss of lands, the court could protect the plaintiffs against further breach of the prohibition.

[22] The essence of the writ *quia timet* is to prevent a future wrong from occurring.

[23] Frederick Pollock and F.W. Maitland, *The History of English Law before the Time of Edward I* (Cambridge, 1911), 2: 671, n. 4. Cf. *A Translation of Glanville*, trans. John Beames (London, 1812), bk. 2, chap. 12: "Indeed, if the object is to expedite the proceedings, it will more avail to follow the direction of the Court (*curiae consilium*), than to observe the accustomed course of the Law. It is, therefore, committed to the discretion (*providentiae*) and judgment (*arbitrio*) of the King or his Justices, so to temper the proceeding as to render it more beneficial and equitable (*utilius et equius*)."

English law was being constructed," writes Maitland. "A new form of action might be easily created. A few words said by the Chancellor to his clerks— 'Such writs as this are for the future to be issued as of course'—would be as effectual as the most solemn legislation."[24] And, as I have suggested, the legislative writs of the courts themselves, and the constant creation of new law by judicial decision,[25] was not the work of the courts as a distinct and separate institution but was the product of conference with the king and his Council, was *per consilium curiae*.

Returning to equity, it is important to note that the Council, even more than the common law courts, administering a law that closely resembled the law and custom of the later Court of Chancery (which was, as we shall see, an offshoot of the Council). The Council received cases on petition, admitted suitors legally disabled, showed mercy and leniency often to the defeat of *rigor juris*, required a specific performance in restitution of goods and chattels; etc.[26] And in the same connection, we must note that the itinerant justices in Eyre, who also at this period represented closely the person of the king and also dispensed royal prerogative, administered equity; the bills presented to them by the humblest as well as the greatest litigants strike us not only by their formal resemblance to the later petitions to the Chancellor, but also by the fact that they often sought the (equitable) remedies of injunctions and specific performance, and they embodied complaints of infractions of almost every kind of personal right.[27]

The Separation of the King's Courts from Equity.—As the fourteenth century progressed, or retrogressed, and the dissolution of the manor and decay of the manorial courts set in, the common law gradually became less the law of freeholders and more the law of the country as a whole; and the courts which, as branches of the King's Council, had always administered the common law, in separating from the King's Council abandoned equity. At that time, so integral was equity in the common law, that the Council had to

---

[24] Ibid., 170-171.

[25] See T. F. T. Plucknett, *Statutes and their Interpretation in the First Half of the Fourteenth Century* (Cambridge, 1922).

[26] For the extent to which the Council was a court of Equity, see I.S. Leadam and J.F. Baldwin, "Introduction," *Select Cases before the King's Council: 1243-1482*, Selden Society, vol. 35 (Cambridge, MA, 1918), xxxi-xxxiv. Especially in its procedure it was distinguished from ordinary common law. The petitioner's grievance could be quite general, and was not invalidated by formal mistakes; his prayer was often for no specific remedy; and he concluded with the words "for God," "we shall pray for you." Ibid., xxxvi.

[27] See William C. Bolland, ed., *Year Books of Edward II*, Selden Society vol. 18, (London, 1920); *The Eyre of Kent 6 & 7 Edward II*, Selden Society, vol. 3 (London, 1913); id., *Select Bills in Eyre*, Selden Society, vol. 30 (London, 1914).

create a special court in Chancery to help administer the common law—to administer it "in cases which escaped the meshes of the ordinary courts"— escaped, because the ordinary courts had renounced equity.

Gradually, in the fourteenth century, the King's Bench separated from the Council and became independent of the king; the judges came to be chosen not from clerks in orders, not from the officials of the Church, but from the serjeants of the Inns of Court; the laws of the king's ordinary courts became the secret of a closed caste of professional lawyers, men who seem to have been singularly indifferent to what was going on in the world of politics and economics around them, men who by virtue of the growing centralization of the law at Westminster were largely out of contact with the rest of the realm and the rest of Christendom.[28] Many of them were as litigious and as lawless as the age they lived in.[29]

The common law judges and bar turned in upon themselves and adopted a rigid and mechanical procedure; they voluntarily abandoned their discretionary powers. In 1310, Bereford said, "we ought to maintain ancient writs wherever it is possible, rather than new ones," and new writs began to be quashed with increasing regularity. In 1328, the lawyers who dominated the Commons passed the Statute of Northampton, declaring that no royal command shall disturb the course of the common law, and if such command is issued the judges shall ignore it. Whereas previously cases had moved from court to court with great laxity at judicial discretion, now the various courts began to separate and to vie with each other for jurisdiction. Judicial legislation became rare, and interpretations of statutes became narrow and textual. Professor Plucknett has set the date for crystallization of this tendency to narrowness at 1342: it is in this year that Justice Hilary says, "We will not and *cannot* change ancient usages;" that Justice Thorpe lays down the rule, "Statutes are to be strictly interpreted;" and that the Year-Books first begin to

---

[28] Cf. lecture of Professor Plucknett, LL.M. Seminar at London School of Economics, Oct. 12, 1938: The three outstanding characteristics of the law of that period were its insularity, the intense professionalism of the lawyers, and centralization at Westminster. According to Plucknett:

> The law was intensely wrapped up in itself. . . . It had ceased to look abroad; it had ceased to read books; it had ceased to be interested in politics. . . . The judges for the most part held their offices no matter what political party was in office. . . . The lawyers were related to each other . . . became a caste, closed and exclusive . . . a very small profession . . . The fact that it was so small enabled it to recruit itself . . . completely separate from the Universities and from any cosmopolitan influence. . . . Everything that really mattered was done at Westminster. . . ."

[29] See C.H. Williams, "Introduction," *Year Books of Henry VI* (London, 1933).

contrast law and equity. It is significant, Professor Plucknett comments, that this is the moment when we first hear of the equitable jurisdiction of the Chancellor.[30]

Thus the King's Courts became reactionary and exclusive, and lost their judicial discretion. But from what did they react, and from what did they exclude themselves? Judicial discretion is not necessarily equity. Evidently it was a particular kind of discretion that the common law judges now abandoned and the need for which was supplied by the creation of an equitable jurisdiction in Chancery.

For the rules and remedies which I have mentioned as existing in the Court of Chancery of the later Middle Ages and in the various courts of the earlier Middle Ages, though so fluid as to defy formulation or classification, and though integral in practice in the ordinary law of the entire era, were nevertheless not (as some seem still seem to think) "a broad, vague, mystical doing of justice," nor were they something necessarily inherent in any legal system of any era whatsoever; they constituted rather a definite framework of legal justice, representing the legal, social and religious philosophy of a particular era.

Specifically, in separating from equity in the fourteenth century, the King's Courts abandoned the three principles which underlay the whole of medieval equity, and which up to that time had been practised in all the courts of the realm: (1) the principle that the poor and helpless must be protected against the powerful and lawless; (2) the principle that relationships involving trust and confidence must be enforced by law; and (3) the principle that the law, in thus attempting to preserve peace on earth and good will among men, must not be bound strictly by doctrines of land tenure and status but may deal with persons directly and may compel obedience from the parties. Returning to the law and custom of the Court of Chancery of the latter 14th and 15th centuries, we shall see that it was developed specifically on the basis of these three principles which the now equityless King's Courts had abandoned.

Protection of the Poor and Helpless.—The writ-system, by the middle of the fourteenth century, had become too clumsy and unwieldy to serve the purposes of those who were ignorant of the technicalities of the law and too poor to have a lawyer. Not only were writs that provided new remedies quashed by the courts, but the necessity of specifying the exact nature of the alleged wrong, of sticking to the words of the writ once obtained, and of having it

---

[30] Plucknett, *Statutes and their Interpretation,* 121, 169.

accurately phrased—all played into the hands of those who could pay to bribe judges and to pack or intimidate juries and to retain shrewd lawyers. In contrast, the bill which originated action in Chancery required no set definition of the cause of action, and its general informality of phraseology was highly adapted to the complaints of the man-with-the-hoe, the man who was coming more and more in these centuries to be in need of judicial relief. Likewise, the sacrifice of technical rules of pleading to substantial justice, the use of the cross-bill and set-off, the method of examination under oath in the court of Chancery was protecting of the "poor but honest" against the clever but lawless: "Deus est procurator fatuorum," said Chancellor Stillington in 1467.[31] Moreover, the writs issued by the judges in the course of trial were directed to the sheriff, an officer who in this age was likely to be too corrupt, or too weak, to bring into court the wealthy and lawless men, the "bracoeurs of quarrels and maintainors, who are like kings in the country, so that justice can be done to none," in the words of the Commons in 1382.[32] The power of the Chancellor's subpoena, on the other hand, rested not merely in the fact that it was addressed directly to the parties and required them to appear "in proper person," but also in the fact that it was backed by the authority of the king's Great Seal: the defendant was required to appear "because of certain matters *concerning ourselves*," to answer whatever would be objected to him "on our behalf"—and disobedience either to the subpoena or to the decrees of the Chancellor made him a contemner of the king and a rebel.

The failure of the ordinary courts to protect the poor and helpless, the failure of their commands to compel obedience from the wealthy and lawless, was directly bound up with their new exclusiveness and insularity. In an age when there was neither standing army nor police force, the enforcement of law and order was to a large extent dependent upon common religious faith and upon loyalty to the Crown: once the judges and their law were dissociated both from the Church and the king—by virtue of the rise of a distinct non-clerical professional legal caste, with courts separate from the Council— it was perhaps inevitable that both the judges and their law should turn in upon themselves, and that words which could no longer be identified with either the peace of the realm or the will of God should not command the respect of the people. The seals of the common law courts no longer had the power to compel obedience from the parties, and the procedure of the common law courts was no longer adequate to compel the truth from the lawless.

---

[31] Spence, *Equitable Jurisdiction*, 2:408-427. In a case where the defendant argued that the plaintiff had not taken care to follow the prescribed rules as to covenant.

[32] Ibid.

The underling had no recourse but to seek the protection of the Great Seal of the king himself.

Enforcement of Trust and Confidence.—Breaches of trust and confidence had previously had remedies, as I have indicated, in all of the various courts by which earlier medieval England was governed. But the law of these courts had not developed to a great extent in this respect, partly because trust and confidence had not been economically so important as they were later to become, and partly because they had depended for enforcement largely on the honor of the parties and the moral coercion of the Church and its confessors.[33] The same factors at work in the decline of the manorial courts were, however, at work in the tremendous expansion in the popularity of uses and of simple contracts—and were likewise at work in the weakening of the sense of honor among men and of the moral coercion of the Church. Under these circumstances, the common law courts refused to expand their old actions of debt, detinue, and account; refused to simplify and make easier the now cumbersome procedure upon these actions; refused to infringe upon the rights of the franc tenement and the old doctrines of tenure and livery of seisin; above all, refused to receive the custom of the manor which the manorial courts were too disrupted to deal with and under which peasants were exercising their power to incur fiduciary obligations and enter upon contractual relationships. Yet, in a situation in which the greatest part of the land of England was gradually being held in feoffment to uses,[34] and in which (in Barbour's words) "there were hosts of 'accords' and 'bargains' among people of humble life, who from ignorance or lack of means did not observe the technicalities of legal forms"[35]—the need to give to honor and moral coercion a legal backing was greater than ever before.

Here again the Chancellor stepped in to administer the law in cases that escaped the meshes of the ordinary courts. On the one hand, the ordinary courts had restricted themselves to doctrines of land tenure. "A confidence contrary to a man's own feoffment could not be regarded," they said. Moreover, their procedure had become ill-adapted to dealing with conduct and words that had not been consecrated in writing. As Maitland says, "a

---

[33] Ibid., 410-411.

[34] Fenwick, J., 15 Henry VII. 13, said that when the Statute, 2 Henry V., c. 3, stat. 2 (enabling the *cestui que trust* to be a juror) was passed, the greatest part of the land in England was in feoffment to uses. Richard III held estates of a vast number of persons as feoffee to uses. During the Wars of Roses, every one accused of having sided with the guilty party were liable to attainder and hence to confiscation of his estates, this leading to secret conveyances to uses.

[35] See Barbour, "Contract in Equity," 153.

system of law which will never compel, and rarely even allow, the defendant to give evidence—and which sends every question of fact to a jury—is not competent to deal adequately with uses," and, we may add, with contracts. On the other hand, the Chancellor could make a decree ordering conveyances to be executed by the trustee according to the directions of the *cestui que* trust; and he could make a decree for carrying into execution trusts declared by the will of the feoffor. And as regards contracts, the Chancellor not only enforced those written and sealed agreements which were remediable at common law in theory but which were in practice more effectively remediable in Chancery, but also enforced contracts to convey land, promises in marriage settlements, executory contracts for sale of chattels, parol promises of indemnity and guarantee, contracts of agency, and executory parol contracts in general as well as contributions between persons liable for the same debt, contributions between partners, and other relations not expressly contractual but from which an obligation might arise—all of which were without remedy in the ordinary courts.[36]

Coercion of the Person.—Finally, where the common law courts failed most miserably was in their refusal at a time when society was moving rapidly from status to contract, to continue to expand their power to compel obedience directly from the parties to a cause. Thus, if the sheriff could not find the defendant's personal property which was awarded to the plaintiff, the courts could do nothing but give damages. If the defendant refused to perform under a "real" contract, the courts could likewise do nothing but give damages. If irreparable injury were threatened, the courts could only award damages after it was committed. Where there were more than two parties or two sets of parties to a controversy, the courts could not deal with it. Where a division of property among several co-owners was necessary, the courts were helpless. If the trustee refused to perform the trust, or the promisor his unwritten promise, the courts could give no remedy.

Previously, ordinary common law procedure had been quite adequate in reaching persons (as it had been in enforcing its judgments and in remedying breaches of trust and confidence)—because previously "the most convenient way to reach a man was through his land." But now, as Professor Plucknett explains, "the law had to deal with people who could not be reached quickly, if at all, by a procedure directed against land . . . with people not identified with certain acres." In this situation, the ordinary courts chose to continue

---

[36] Ibid., 156.

their bond with the land (and with title by written document) rather than their bond with the person.[37]

Chancery came to the rescue. Not only was its procedure peculiarly adapted to reaching and examining persons directly, but it could compel these persons to produce all the evidence and knowledge in their possession (discovery) which would aid the Chancellor to make a just decision, and it could by its decrees enforce specific performance, issue injunctions, and in general "direct many things to be mutually done and suffered."

The Rise of the Court of Chancery.—By the middle of the fourteenth century, therefore, those who needed protection against the wealthy and lawless, or enforcement of fiduciary and contractual obligations, or remedies that compelled obedience from the person directly, had little other recourse than to petition the king for relief.[38] And so great was the pressure of their demands, that the king found it necessary gradually to delegate jurisdiction over them to a special court.[39]

That that special court should be the Chancellor's court testifies both to the importance of the matter and to its nature. For the Chancellor, throughout the era from the Conquest to the Reformation, was the representative of the two domains which stood guard over the unity of medieval English society; the domain of the realm and the domain of the Church. It was in the Chancellor, in fact, that the two domains met.

Prior to the decline of the manor court and the tightening up of the common law of king's courts, the Chancellor had exercised his influence without a special Court of Chancery, as the most learned and most distinguished member of the Council. He was typically a man versed in both the common law and the canon law. As the "secretary of state for all

---

[37] The sacredness of the written document, itself formerly a means of coercing the person, now became an instrument of extortion; and now the common law regarded the written document with reinforced sanctity. Cf. "Seyntnicolas v. Pygherde," *Year Books of Richard II: 11 Richard II, 1387-1388* (Cambridge, MA, 1914), 12-14 in which the plaintiff leased a manor to the defendant at an annual rent, and took a bond under seal as security for the rent. The lease was later determined in another way, and the bond restored. Later still, the landlord got hold of the bond by force and sued upon it. Chief Justice Belknap refused to accept the proposition that the return of the deed to the tenant deprived it of all its force. "Answer to the deed," he said. Thus the plaintiff was forced to plead duress, undertaking to prove (in accordance with the common law then current regarding duress) that the plaintiff drew his sword and put the defendant in fear of his life, thus forcing him to make the deed.

[38] For a while, in some parts of the country, baronial councils were set up, with procedure based on civil law and equity. The Council of St. Albans is the famous example. The failure of these courts meant that the villeins had to go to the Chancellor.

[39] See George W. Keeton, *An Introduction to Equity* (London, 1938).

departments," including the department of justice, he had the important voice both in the selection of common law judges and in the shaping of the common law itself; and as an important ecclesiastic, often as the Archbishop of Canterbury, he was personally comparatively immune from secular control and was responsible in this conduct to the Church and to the pope.[40] By his power to issue new writs to remedy new grievances, he was the chief legislator of the realm. His importance, both judicial and political, was symbolized by his control of the Great Seal, "the key of the kingdom," without which no document or statute or decree could be enforced, and which is the symbol of sovereignty in England until this day. The Chancellor indeed was the most powerful man in England next to the king—and the king, prior to the fourteenth century, spent most of his time outside of England.

Until the fourteenth century, the Chancellor (in Council) had shared his legislative power with the common law judges, who by virtue of their close connection both with the Council and the Church had been able to exercise a broad discretion. By asserting their right to quash new writs, however, and by their general insularity, the fourteenth century justices in effect resigned from this legislative partnership, gaining, it is true, real control over that section of the law which they still recognized as common law, but abandoning all control over the legislative function of changing the really "common" law to meet the changing needs of society.

It was the pressure of petitions to the king and Council—petitions which had been entrusted for the most part to the Chancellor anyway—which necessitated, in the middle of the fourteenth century, the creation in the Council of a special Court of Chancery. And it is significant that this court had both a common law and an equity jurisdiction, that is, administered a law which could do what both common law and equity required.[41]

Its common law jurisdiction was derived largely from the administrative functions of the Chancellor as the king's "secretary of state for all

---

[40] Up to 1530, 160 ecclesiastics had held the office as against a few laymen. From the third year of Richard II to the end of his reign, with the exception of de la Pole (1383-1386), the Chancellors were ecclesiastics and included two archbishops and five bishops. The significance of the ecclesiastical status of the Chancellors is reserved for discussion below.

[41] That the common law side and the equity side were separate, that each had its own procedure and its own jurisdiction, does not warrant the usual assumption that they were not part of the same law. On both sides, the Chancellor administered law which the ordinary courts were incompetent to handle: on the common law side because of the interest of the king in the matter, on the equity side because of the narrowness of the ordinary courts. It was the ordinary courts which caused the breach between the two sides, and it was the Chancellor who healed the breach by administering both.

departments." Thus, the Chancery held pleas of *scire facias* for repeal of letters patent, pleas of petitions of right, and *monstrans de droit* for obtaining possession or restitution of property from the Crown, pleas of traverses of offices, executions upon statutes, and so forth. Likewise, the Chancellor represented the ordinary jurisdiction of the king in hearing appeals of false judgment when any lord would not do right to those under his jurisdiction and in taking security for keeping the king's Peace. In administering the common law in these capacities, the Chancery established in an ordinary and regular procedure which was in many ways similar to that of the King's Bench and Common Pleas, though it combined ordinary procedure with that of the council, and thus administered the common law as part of the king's prerogative.

As more and more cases escaped the meshes of the ordinary courts, however, petitions to the king and to the Chancellor requiring new remedies—remedies based on the three principles under which I have summarized the equity side of Chancery—increased. In developing these remedies, the Chancellors, with the close cooperation of common law judges and lawyers as well as members of the Council, did not consider that they were administering equity at the expense of the common law, but rather that they were administering the common law in matters "of Grace" and "of Conscience."

There were many complaints on the part of the Commons and the common lawyers against this extension of the common law in the Court of Chancery. The conservatives of the time charged the Chancellors with infringing upon the sacred rights of the franc tenement, with proceeding according to the practice of the Holy Church, and with abusing their process for purposes of extortion. But none complained that the Chancellor did not have a constitutional jurisdiction over the matters which he adjudicated. All agreed that the poor and helpless should be protected, that relations of trust and confidence should be enforced, that persons must be coerced directly— and that the Chancellor had a right to do these things.

Antagonism was futile, since the Chancellor was *not* infringing sacred traditions and radically altering the common law system, but was reevaluating and reshaping the old traditions and thereby preserving the equilibrium of the common law system—an equilibrium which the common lawyers and judges had forsaken by refusing to administer even that equity which had always been a part of common law. It was the common law courts that had threatened the very existence of the common law—by distilling it down almost to pure land law—and had thus made the Chancellor's equitable jurisdiction essential to the preservation of law itself.[42] Antagonism was futile before the march of time, and eventually, in the fifteenth century, the opposition of the lawyers faded before the co-operation between judges and Chancellor; Commons, instead of attacking the Chancellors, now attempted to set bounds to their jurisdiction and to share in controlling it.[43]

The Source of Medieval Equity.—We have gone as far as the experts' "facts" will take us: and the most important problem remains to be considered: the Chancery was a court of conscience, but of *whose* conscience, and why *conscience*? On what authority, in the light of what motives and what ideas, did the various courts prior to the fourteenth century, and the Court of Chancery in the latter fourteenth and the fifteenth centuries, protect the poor and helpless, enforce relations of trust and confidence, and compel obedience from persons directly? Were the authority and the motives and the ideas the same for the earlier courts as they were for the later Chancellors? Who originated equity, and why?

First, some of the underbrush of fictions must be cleared away. I hope it has become clear, from the foregoing analysis, that the usual statement, "equity separated from the common law," is false: actually, the ordinary common law courts separated from equity. Likewise, I trust it has been plainly indicated that the familiar slogan, "equity follows the law," cannot be applied

---

[42] F.W. Maitland and F.C. Montague, *A Sketch of English Legal History* (New York, 1915), 128: "Were we to say that equity saved the common law . . . even in this paradox there would be some truth."

[43] The complaints against innovations into the law by Chancellors may be dated from the middle of the thirteenth century, when Parliament (representing the barons and prelates, for the most part) began to complain against new and unaccustomed writs. This complaint found expression in 1258 in the Provisions of Oxford, in which it was demanded that the chancellors issue no writs save "writs of course" without warrant from the baronial council. This principle was relaxed in the famous clause in the Statute of Westminster II allowing writs to be issued in cases "similar" (*in consimili casu*) to those for which writs had previously been issued.

> With the rise of a separate Court of Chancery in the fourteenth century, the Commons objected frequently and strenuously, at first, to its methods and practices and urged that the jurisdiction it exercised (especially in regard to protection against maintenance) should be left to the common law courts. At the same time, however, the judges of the common law courts were cooperating with the Chancellor and even sitting with him. And the complaints against the Court of Chancery by the Commons are gradually superseded by attempts to control it (cf. 17 Richard II, c.6, in which it was enacted that where persons were compelled to appear before the Council or Chancery on suggestions found to be untrue, the Chancellor should have the power to award damages according to his discretion).

to what is called the Middle Ages: actually, inasmuch as every important development in the law, every new law, came from the equity of the king and Chancellor and Council, it may be said that prior to the fourteenth century the law followed equity, and that in the later Middle Ages, to the extent that the ordinary law did not follow equity it lost its capacity to undergo real change. And finally, I hope the literal truth of Maitland's statement has been proved—that the Chancellors administered the same law in substance as did the ordinary courts, but administered it in cases that escaped the meshes of the ordinary courts—and that it can therefore be understood that equity and common law, were, even in the later fourteenth and fifteenth centuries, part of the same system, which was practised in the earlier period by all courts and in the later period (due to the withdrawal of the ordinary courts from equity) was practised by two complementary sets of courts. To ignore the petitions to the Chancellors and the procedure under oath, in discussing the common law of the fourteenth and fifteenth centuries, is tantamount to ignoring the acts of Parliament in discussing the common law of the nineteenth and twentieth centuries—or the writs in Chancery in discussing the common law of the twelfth and thirteenth centuries.

The proposition that equity was that part of the common law which enabled new wrongs to be met by new remedies, which made for change and innovation, is however, insufficient. For equity was not merely a spirit of justice, not merely a force for new development: it was force plus direction— it was a spirit of a particular kind of justice—a direction and a kind of justice whose legal effects I have attempted to summarize under the three functions of protecting underlings, enforcing good faith, and dealing with persons directly.

Now, in the medieval sense, it is natural justice that these three functions be performed. But it is by no means "natural" that they will be performed, in all ages, by law: nor is it at all likely that any two systems of law which did perform them would do so in the same way. In modern law, for example, persons are dealt with *en masse* in the creation of new law: the legislature passes an act to remedy a grievance of the people as a whole, and if a man is wronged and there is no law on the statute books or no precedent in the courts under which his wrong can be remedied, he cannot generally go to the legislature and get a new act passed specifically to help him. Today, both in Parliament and in court, a man is to a large extend treated as an anonymous individual—as an "average," a norm—which is quite different from being dealt with as a unique person in a unique set of circumstances, which is, after all, the way the medieval litigant was dealt with under the earlier writ system and later in Chancery.

Thus, even under law, there are various ways of protecting underlings and enforcing good faith and of dealing with persons. Prior to the fourteenth century, it was possible in the common law courts to perform these functions effectively, to a certain extent, not by dealing with underlings and agreements and persons directly but by dealing with them through the documents and land with which they were identified. And today, in the twentieth century, it is gradually coming to be realized that the most effective way of dealing justly with many persons is to identify them with certain groups or classes: for example, in industrial disputes to bring before the law not the individual laborer and the individual employer but the representative of the labor union and the representative of the industrial corporation—for in modern industry it is not a question of protecting a poor litigant against his powerful and lawless adversary, or of enforcing a private agreement between two people, or of reaching two persons directly, so much as one of giving certain rights and powers to groups-as-such (contrast the rights of a union on strike with the rights of an individual who threatens to quit his job), and of enforcing *collective* bargaining, and of reaching persons through the organizations to which they belong.

Even assuming, therefore, that every legal system will attempt to protect the helpless, enforce relations of trust, and deal with persons, we must recognize that different legal system attempt to perform these functions in entirely different ways, and that the attempt of the legal system of one age may not be successful in the next. We must therefore search elsewhere than in the realm of mere "natural justice" for the source of Medieval Equity. We must ask, *whose* natural justice?

The clue to the source of equity is in the word conscience. As we know, the Court of Chancery was empowered, by the statute, 22 Edward III, to deal with all matters "of Grace" and "of Conscience," and the Chancellor was most often appealed to in the name of conscience. "What is 'conscience'? According to linguistic testimony it belongs to what we know most surely;" in some languages its meaning is hardly to be distinguished, Freud tells us, from "consciousness." Thus in the case of a guilty conscience, as Freud once said, we become aware of the *inner* condemnation of the act committed. "Confirmation seems superfluous here; whoever has a conscience must feel in himself the justification of the condemnation, and the reproach for the accomplished action."

Now, man's conscience is older than the Middle Ages. But in the Middle Ages, for the first time, the conscience of Christendom was organized: that which Western Man knew most surely he called the law of God and he swore allegiance to the Holy Church which interpreted and protected that law. This was not the taboo conscience of primitive tribes, with its identification of the family or clan with the animal or plant totem; nor was it our modern national consciousness, with its identification of the anonymous individual (or the "natural" man) with the people of the nation. It was rather the conscience of Christendom, and the identification of the inner convictions of every Christian with the teachings of the Church of Rome.

It is for this reason that the procedure of medieval equity was the source of its jurisdiction: the Chancellors dealt with each person as a conscionable Christian, examined him on oath, ordered him in God's name to do right. The protection of underlings and the enforcement of relations of trust and confidence were inextricable from the duty of the person as a member of the Christian Church (as contrasted with the duty of the savage as a member of the tribe, or of the modern individual as a member of the nation).

Through equity, the conscience of Christians was made universal in the social and legal structure of medieval Christendom. And through the Chancellors it made its way into the realm of England, a semi-autonomous province of Christendom. The ultimate source of English equity in Christian conscience was succinctly and practically expressed by Chancellor Cardinal Morton in 1489: "Every law should be in accordance with the law of God; and I know well that an executor who fraudulently misapplies the goods and does not make restitution will be damned in Hell, and to remedy this is in accordance with conscience as I know it."[44]

The ordinary courts were by this time wrapped up in the technicalities of land law and were not interested in the law of God and the conscience of Christians. But the point is that both the members of Council and Chancery and the country as a whole *were*. The Chancellors who administered equity in the fourteenth and fifteenth centuries were the king's personal representatives in matters of conscience, matter for which they were directly responsible to God and to his vicar in spiritual affairs, the pope. It was not the king's conscience which the Chancellors kept in the Middle Ages: that came later, and with it came tremendous changes in English law. It was rather, as one Justice put it, "the general conscience of the Realm," which the Christendom-conscious Chancellors kept in the king's behalf.

I have been speaking of the source of equity in the Middle Ages, not of the needs which it satisfied. The economic historian will point to the demand for protection of uses and contracts arising out of the changing economic scene, especially in the fourteenth and fifteenth centuries. The social psychologist will point to the inner need for religious faith in an agrarian age at the

---

[44] Y.B. 4 Hen. VII, 11. No 8.

mercy of pestilence and famine. The politician will point to the political causes and effects of the increasing centralization of power in the hands of king and Council. The practical lawyer will point to the procedural exigencies of particular cases. But economic and social and political and procedural needs are not always satisfied peacefully by law—as we know too well today. Indeed, in the closing generations of the medieval period, civil disorder was so great that even the Chancellors' equity was often unable to meet these needs, and they were dealt with privately by force of arms. As legal historians, therefore, we are interested primarily in the way in which equity, throughout the Middle Ages, satisfied those needs and we are interested ultimately in where equity came from.

We know that the *words* of equity, at least of the equity of the Council and the Chancery, came from the language of the Church. This applies especially to its procedure; but also applies to its doctrine. "Breach of confidence clearly goes back to the *fidei laesio* which ecclesiastical tribunals had claimed as their province," says Vinogradoff.[45] "A use, according to legal language, was created by *confidence*, preserved by *privity* (i.e., continuation of confidence), and ordered and guided by *conscience*," writes Spence.[46] Underlings were protected "in way of charity" and because they would "pray for you."

We know also that these words were uttered—and equity was administered—by ecclesiastics, men dignified by high office in the Church, men with some knowledge of the canon law. Prior to the fourteenth century, this applies to the equity administered by all courts. Is it merely a coincidence that when the king's courts became secular they gave up equity, and that the court which took over that equity was composed of ecclesiastics?[47]

---

[45] Vinogradoff, ed. *Oxford Studies in Social and Legal History*, 4:14.

[46] Spence, *Equitable Jurisdiction*, p. 447.

[47] Impiety and ignorance (of Canon law, for example) cannot be ascribed to the clerics in the fourteenth- and fifteenth-century Court of Chancery: the Chancellor was invariably distinguished for his statesmanship, and even if he happened to be not well versed in the intricacies of church procedure and practice, there were twelve, and afterwards six, clerks de prima forma and Masters of the Chancery who were assistants in the court to show what is the equity of the Civil Law, and what is Conscience. Moreover, the fact that office in the church was integral in the economic and political framework testifies further to the material influence which was bound up inextricably with spiritual and ideological influence.

Spence places special emphasis upon the prestige and dignity of the clerical office as a necessary prerequisite of the Court of Chancery. "No one but a dignified ecclesiastic would ever have thought of establishing a court, constituted in effect of one man, for the correction of the law, when there was a legislature consisting of king, Lords and Commons who were engaged at the very time in providing for the amendment of the law and securing its due administration." Spence, *Equitable Jurisdiction*, pp. 355.

Thirdly, we know that the authority which the ecclesiastics cited in speaking the words of equity was the religious authority of God. All was done "in the name of God," or "for the sake of God," and the Chancellors constantly appealed to "the law of God."

But the natural conclusion of all this, that the actual law and custom called equity was derived from the Church of Rome, that in Stubbs' words, "the whole subject of Equity is strange to the national growth of the common law"[48]—is definitely out of favor with the modern experts on English legal history, who perhaps inherit a little too much of the insularity of the later medieval common lawyers. The best of them make certain concessions. Maitland writes, "On the whole my notion is that with the idea of a law of nature in their minds [the Chancellors] decided cases without much reference to any written authority, now making use of some analogy drawn from the common law, and now of some great maxim of jurisprudence which they borrowed from the canonists or the civilians." But he adds immediately that in their treatment of uses and trusts they "stick marvellously close to the rules of the common law;" and he says elsewhere that "the Chancellors seem to get most of their dominant ideas from the common law."[49] And Professor Plucknett admits that the Chancellors "acted in the spirit of the canon law, which was impatient of pedantry and inclined to place substance before form," and that "the old canonist idea of good faith is transformed into conscience." But the whole emphasis in Professor Plucknett's treatment of the Chancellor's equity is upon the point that it grew out of the English law and procedure of the earlier common law courts and the Council.[50] Hazeltine expresses the enlightened patriotism with which modern English historians approach the subject (though most often they ignore it) when, after his excellent study of the early history of equity in the common law courts, he states in conclusion that thus "not all the ideas which we associate with English Equity were either borrowed from the Roman system by the Chancellors or original with them."[51]

---

[48] William Stubbs, *History of Canon Law in England*, (Oxford, 1882), 1. Stubbs also points out that while the common law judges may not have been canonists or civilians, the statesmen often were. Stubbs was unable to know (in 1882) what modern research has brought to light: that equity was practised in the common law courts of the pre-fourteenth-century period, but I believe his statement that it is strange to the *national* growth of the common law can still stand.

[49] F.W. Maitland, *Lectures on Equity*, 4-6; Maitland and Montague, *A Sketch of English Legal History*, 125-126.

[50] Plucknett, *Concise History*, 234-259.

[51] Hazeltine, "Early History of English Equity," 285.

Now certainly equity was not original with the Chancellors. But just as certainly, it was not original with the common law courts. It was, as I have indicated, present in the manorial courts, in the borough and fair courts, in the ecclesiastical courts, in the courts of universities, in the courts of the city of London, in the courts of the justices in eyre, in the Council—and in general in all the courts of the realm—before the Court of Chancery existed. This fact supports the argument of Maitland and the modern medievalists that "the number of thoroughly new ideas introduced by the Chancellors of the Middle Ages was by no means large."[52] But with a different set of assumptions, it also argues forcibly for the debt which all the courts *throughout* the medieval period owed to the universal influence of the Church.

The essential procedure and the doctrinal framework of medieval English equity constituted, in fact, the major innovation which the canon law made in the doctrines of the civil law when those doctrines were rediscovered and remolded in the twelfth and thirteenth centuries.[53] It was present in all the courts of Christendom, fluid and unformulated. It represented the "divine and natural justice" of the Church—but represented it not in a vague, mystical way, as those who stop short with a contract between *aequitas* and *rigor juris* are apt to believe; but rather in a concrete, legal way. In England, it represented that divine and natural justice administered chiefly by the king through his Council and his Courts, though also, while they remained in full vigor, by the other courts of the realm not closely associated with the king.

Thus, in developing the law of uses and trusts, the Chancellors could, on the one hand, "stick marvellously close to the rules of the common law," and, on the other hand, could apply those rules as they had always been applied while the common law courts were elastic and equitable "by a series of decisions, firstly, upon the question of what were the duties which a conscientious man in the position of a feoffee to uses would consider that he owed to the *cestui que* use; and secondly, upon the question of what persons who had

---

52 F.W. Maitland, "Introduction," *Year Books of Edward II* (London, 1904) 2: xiii-xiv.

53 In dealing with the source of medieval equity, which is the church and the law of God, it is necessary to remember that the canon law was a revaluation of the earlier civil law of Rome. Equity in Roman Law developed the principle of good faith (bona fides) in contractual obligations; prohibited unjust enrichment at the expense of another; and demanded that judges look at the intention rather than the form of the law. In remolding Roman law into canon law, the founders of medieval equity gave these principles new meaning by making their subject the conscionable Christian, reshaping equitable procedure around a doctrine of good faith transformed into conscience, a doctrine of prohibition of unjust enrichment transformed into protection of underlings, a doctrine of substantial justice transformed into justice substantial to the person and his conscience.

got possession of the land could be considered to be bound in conscience to do to fulfill these duties."[54]

In his *Statutes and their Interpretation*, Professor Plucknett points out a fact that is often lost sight of by specialists who dissect medieval law without trying to put it together again, namely that the essential unity of the medieval legal system of Council, courts, and parliament extends into the fifteenth century, despite the increasing distinctness of these institutions throughout the fourteenth and fifteenth centuries. It seems to me that that unity, which lasted from the Conquest to the Tudors, was dependent for its very life upon the constant infusion of equitable principles into the various laws of the various estates of the realm.[55] The continuity of medieval English equity, from its earlier development in the various courts of the realm to its later history in the Court of Chancery, has been accepted by the best historians;[56] but what must be made clear is that without this continuous stream of developing equity, English law could not have overthrown its Anglo-Saxon shackles— that it was only by virtue of their ability to change their law equitably to protect underlings, to enforce good faith, and to deal with persons directly as equal in the sight of God, that the lords of the manors and the councillors and justices of the king were able to maintain peace and order in a turbulent age, and to retain their jurisdictions, despite continual social and economic change, for four centuries.

The procedure and idea of justice of the Church was extremely flexible, and when infused by English courts into English conditions and English customs it produced a law considerably different in detail—though not in outline and effect—from that of other provinces of Christendom. Yet when the common law began to separate and to become really insular and exclusive, it was the equity of the ecclesiastical Chancellors that brought it once again into line with the medieval legal process of Christendom, substituting the bill and subpoena and decree for the now rigid and ineffective, though formerly equitable, system of writs. Yet even here we must remember that the

---

[54] W. S. Holdsworth, *A History of English Law* (Boston, 1924) 4:430-443.

[55] See Plucknett, *Statutes and their Interpretation in the First Half of the Fourteenth Century*. Cases pass back and forth from court to court, from Common Pleas to Council to Parliament to Chancery—with the greatest of ease. The institutional framework of medieval English law is perfectly described by Fleta's famous sentence: "The king has his court in his council in his parliaments, in the presence of the earls, barons, magnates, and other learned men, where judicial doubts are determined, where new remedies are established as new wrongs arise, and where justice is done to each according to his deserts." Ibid., 20.

[56] See George B. Adams, "The Continuity of English Equity," *Yale Law Journal*, 26 (1917): 550.

Chancellor's power to shape the process of the common law was not a new one, but was merely taking a different and more distinct form; for in earlier times also, the Chancellor, as that official of the King's Council who was most constantly in attendance, most learned in the common and canon law, and judicially and politically most influential, was the man who had (among other methods by issuing new writs to meet new wrongs) constantly extended the scope of the equity of the common law.

"Adjudication, like most other questions of human conduct, depends upon a nice balance between law and equity, rule and exception, tradition and innovation," writes Plucknett.[57] It was the equity in medieval English law that made for innovation and for new development—that enabled a law of persons, living with each other in peace and in good faith despite differences in power and position, continually and gradually to transform the law of land tenure and of status.

In his chapter on the English common law in *Out of Revolution*, Eugen Rosenstock-Huessy makes the point that the medieval English law (like any dynamic law, it must be added) was "not a fact or a collection of rules, but a process"—that "there was no Common Law, but anything could become and be made 'common' law by the intermediation of Chancery;" and that the motive forces which kept the English law *in* process were "the new ideas of righteousness" which "incessantly made their way from the sanctuaries of the Church into the nation."[58] Not so much that the English law deliberately went back to canon law, but more especially that it could go forward only by continually infusing its own basis in English customs with canonical ideas, and chiefly equity. With this in mind, we may restate the underlying facts of the history of Medieval English Equity as follows:

First, that medieval equity was not a system of law, as Tudor equity became; nor was it a vague doing of justice. Rather it was a dynamic framework of law, a continually expanding process, representing a particular way of life; and that it was such throughout the medieval era.

Second, that the basic principles underlying medieval equity were: that the underling must be protected by law, that good faith must be enforced by law, and that the law must deal with persons directly as conscionable Christians.

---

[57] T. F. T. Plucknett, *A Concise History of the Common Law* 5th ed. (Boston, 1956), 681.

[58] Rosenstock-Huessy, *Out of Revolution: The Autobiography of Western Man* (Boston, 1938), p. 270.

---⚬ 5 ⚬---

LAW AND BELIEF IN THREE
REVOLUTIONS*

Periodically in the history of the West there have occurred
revolutionary changes in the predominant system of beliefs held by
the people of a given country or countries. Thus in the early sixteenth century
the rise of Protestantism, especially in its Lutheran form, reflected a major
shift in the belief system of most persons—not only of Protestants—living in
the numerous polities that then made up the German Empire. Some four
generations later, in the mid-seventeenth century, various Calvinist and neo-
Calvinist beliefs became predominant in English social life, espoused not only
by Puritans and other so-called Non-Conformists but also by many who
remained loyal to Anglicanism. And then in the late eighteenth century Deism
became strong, especially in France, and a new outlook came to prevail,
called the Enlightenment, which was essentially individualistic and rationalistic; this outlook found expression in the French Revolution of 1789.

These shifts in religious outlook—from Lutheranism to neo-Calvinism to
Enlightened Deism—were accompanied by parallel shifts in the dominant
political and constitutional outlook. Sixteenth-century German Lutheranism
was associated with a new belief in the supremacy of the Prince, with his
courtiers and civil servants. Seventeenth-century English Puritanism and

* Reprinted from *Valparaiso University Law Review* 18 (1984): 569-629. Delivered as
the Edward A. Seegers Lectures at Valparaiso University Law School November 8, 9, and
10, 1983.

Anglicanism were associated with a new belief in the supremacy of an essentially aristocratic Parliament over the Crown and the Church, and in the independence of the judiciary. Eighteenth-century French Deism and the Enlightenment were associated with a new belief in democracy and the rule of public opinion through a popularly elected legislature.

The interconnections between religious change and political-constitutional change in these three periods of European history have been explored in many books, and in that context certain changes in legal philosophy have also been discussed. Strangely, however, no one, so far as I know, has attempted to relate the changes in the legal system *as a whole* in any of the three periods—that is, the German legal system in the sixteenth century, the English legal system in the seventeenth century, and the French legal system in the late eighteenth and early nineteenth centuries—to the revolutionary changes that took place in the belief system. We have many studies of the relationship of German Protestantism, of English Puritanism, and of the French Enlightenment to political developments, to economic developments, to social developments, to the development of scientific thought—to virtually everything *except* the development of the characteristic legal institutions by which these nations were governed: judicial procedure, criminal law, contracts, property, business associations, family law, and the like.

But even apart from the paucity of such historical studies, our scholarship is woefully weak in discerning contemporary relationships between the legal institutions of a society and that society's underlying system of ideas, ideals, or beliefs. We gladly reach out for an explanation of legal institutions in terms of the economic or political or social "interests" or "policies" that they support. But we are considerably less interested in identifying what Roscoe Pound once called "jural postulates"—the specific philosophical or moral assumptions implicit in specific legal institutions—and in relating those *jural* postulates to *other* postulates upon which our social order rests.

Our predilection for political, economic, and social explanations of legal development, and our corresponding aversion to philosophical and religious explanations, seem to me to reflect a relatively narrow concept of law as a mere device or instrument by which powerful persons or groups may advance their political or economic or social objectives. Even if this narrow concept of law is assumed to be correct so far as it goes, it does not go far enough to be satisfying for it ignores the fact that virtually every law-making regime in the history of mankind has wanted its laws not only to advance its interests but also to reflect its ideas of rightness and of justice. Indeed, if we look to those regimes of recent history in which law was most openly subordinated to the ulterior political-economic-social ends of dictatorial power, namely, those of

Hitler and Stalin, then we see immediately that even the legal systems instituted by these two tyrants strongly reflected their respective philosophies—indeed, their religions, for both Stalin's atheist socialism and Hitler's pagan racism were themselves, in an important sense, religions.

If Communist law reflects a Communist belief system, then surely it is at least plausible to suppose that the legal institutions introduced by the Lutheran princes of German territories in the sixteenth century reflected a Lutheran belief system; that the legal institutions introduced by the Puritan rulers of England in the 1640's and 1650's, and those that were later reaffirmed by their Anglican successors of the 1660's to 1690's, reflected Puritan and Anglican belief systems; and that the legal changes introduced in France after the French Revolution reflected the values, the postulates, the beliefs of the Enlightenment.

It should be emphasized that I am not now talking about "causation." I am not arguing that legal changes are caused by religious or ideological changes. I am talking rather about interconnections, interrelationships, whether or not causal. To take an example: the Puritan emphasis on the moral sanctity of an undertaking may or may not have been a "cause" of the development of the English doctrine of strict liability for breach of contract—a doctrine first clearly laid down in the case of Paradine and Jane, decided by the Court of King's Bench in 1648, at the height of the Puritan Revolution; but the *interconnections* between the religious postulate and the legal postulate need to be understood if either one is to be understood.

Yet one can read the entire scholarly literature on the history of German, England, and France in the sixteenth to nineteenth centuries without finding more than oblique references to such interconnections between legal institutions and fundamental beliefs.

This, then, is the first argument of this chapter, and, indeed the main point. It is a simple one, which I hope that even skeptics of my larger historical perspective would accept: that the new law that emerged in Germany at the time of the Protestant Reformation must be studied in connection with the beliefs to which the Protestant Reformers were committed, including not only their theology in the narrow sense but also their social theories; similarly, that the new law that emerged in England as a result of the upheavals of 1640 to 1689 must be seen in the light of changes in belief that took place during that period, including not only religious belief but also political belief, scientific belief, and other aspects of the belief system; and finally, that the new law that emerged in France—and also in America—in the last years of the eighteenth and the early part of the nineteenth centuries must be understood as part of a shift in the entire system of beliefs that took place in the West at that time.

Why should legal history be viewed in this way? The answer is, once again, elementary: such a view, by helping us to understand the beliefs with which our legal institutions have been associated in the past, will help us also to anticipate the consequences of the decline of those beliefs for the development of law in the future. For at the end of the twentieth century we live once again in the wake of revolutionary upheavals and revolutionary changes both in our legal system and in our general system of beliefs. If we do not understand the close relationship between our legal system and our belief system, we will be unable, in my view, to change either the one or the other to meet the needs that confront us.

I. *The Lutheran Reformation and German Law*

The fifteenth century was something like the twentieth: then, as now, the West lived, in Matthew Arnold's famous phrase, between two worlds, one dead, the other powerless to be born. Then there was widespread clamor for a thoroughgoing reformation both of the church and of the secular order. In the early part of the century the religious revolt of the Hussites was put down, and the conciliar movement within the church was aborted. In the latter decades the campaign by the Northern humanists—Erasmus is the most famous name among them—for more civilized, more humane ecclesiastical policies met with only a weak response from the papal hierarchy, which by that time had sunk into the deepest corruption.

The demand for reformation extended also to the secular realm. As early as 1438, the German Sigismund himself proposed thoroughgoing secular changes, which he expressly called a "Reformation." Little came of it. The depressed peasant masses revolted sporadically without success. There was great poverty and unrest in the German cities as well, and many unsuccessful proposals for urban "reformations." The cities, in turn, put great economic and social pressure on the depressed knightly class, which itself eventually rose up in revolt—again, without success.

Throughout Europe the central political authority was increasing its power, especially vis-à-vis the church and the feudal authorities. The growth of national political consciousness in the fifteenth century was reflected especially in the strengthening of royal power in England, France, Spain, Austria, and the German principalities. Secular authority was also becoming stronger in the cities. Everywhere the church was increasingly on the defensive.[1]

In hindsight we can see that things were building up for an explosion. This was also recognized by many at the time, and many important changes were made in order to forestall such an explosion. None of them, however, prior to Luther, addressed the crucial problem of the times, namely, in Myron Gilmore's words, that "the Gregorian Revolution had finally failed." "The idea that secular government was directed ultimately to the attainment of grace or justice," Gilmore writes, "[was] no longer taken seriously."[2] In other words, the secular world could no longer derive its ultimate meaning from the tasks set for its by the Church of Rome. And there was no other Church!

The Gregorian Revolution of the late eleventh and early twelfth centuries had expressed itself in a revision of the ancient "two swords" theory. As revised by Pope Gregory VII and his successors, the theory postulated that the Church, conceived now as the priesthood, operating under the papal monarchy, had jurisdiction, that is, lawmaking power, over the spiritual life of Christendom. That was the "spiritual sword." It was limited, to be sure, by the "secular sword" wielded by kings, feudal lords, urban authorities, and others. Yet ultimately, the spiritual sword of the Church was to guide the secular authorities into the paths of truth and righteousness. It was the visible Church, under the papacy, that set the rules for leading the good life by which sinful man could be saved. Implicit in this division of jurisdictions was the doctrine that the forgiveness of sins and the salvation of souls rested not only on the faith of the sinner but also on his good deeds, and that the performance of good deeds depended, in turn, partly on his will and reason.

Luther started a revolution by addressing the question of ecclesiastical authority directly and in the most radical terms. He proclaimed the abolition of the ecclesiastical jurisdiction. This was the underlying significance of his 95 theses denouncing papal indulgences in 1517: it was not merely that he was against abuses of papal authority—it was that he denied the validity of the canon law altogether. No priest, he said, is authorized to come between God and the individual human soul that seeks forgiveness for sins. Therefore no priest can promulgate the laws by which Christians should live. The

---

[1] Gerald Strauss, *Manifestations of Discontent in Germany on the Eve of the Reformation* (Bloomington, IN, 1971), 52-63, 130-38, 142-44, 196-207.

[2] Myron P. Gilmore, *The World of Humanism* (New York, 1952), 135. Gilmore adds: "Given that problem, the thinkers of the age occupied themselves with finding a new justification and meaning for the secular world. This is the theme that not only unites Luther, More and Machiavelli, but it is also the theme that gives their writing its 'modern' tone." On the Papal ("Gregorian") Revolution, see Harold J. Berman, *Law and Revolution: The Formation of the Western Legal Tradition* (Cambridge, MA, 1983), chap. 2.

Church, Luther said, has no authority to declare laws at all. It is not a law-making institution. The Church is, rather, the invisible community of all believers in which all are priests, serving each other, and each is a "private person" in his relation to God. Each responds to the Bible as the Word of God.[3]

In testimony to his abolition of ecclesiastical jurisdiction, Luther in 1521 publicly burned the Papal Bull which excommunicated him, together with canon law books supporting the Bull. The Emperor of Germany, Austria, and Switzerland ("the Holy Roman Empire of the German Nation"), supported by the Imperial diet (Reichstag), outlawed Luther; however, his own prince protected him and in 1529 the Lutheran princes and city representatives "protested" the Imperial decrees, and civil war broke out. (It is from this protest that the name "Protestant" is derived.) The princes formed a religious party, the Protestant League, which in 1552, with the help of France, defeated the Emperor. Finally, in 1555, at Augsburg, a religious peace was made, whereby each of the various principalities of the Empire was empowered to establish its own form of religion, either Catholic or Protestant. The religion chosen by the prince was to be the religion of all people in the territory which he ruled—*cuius regio eius religio*, "he who rules shall establish his religion."[4]

Luther replaced the Gregorian "two swords" theory with a new "two kingdoms" theory. The Church, he taught, belongs to the heavenly kingdom of grace and faith; it is governed by the Gospel. The earthly kingdom, the kingdom of "this world," is the kingdom of sin and death; it is governed by Law. It is the secular authority alone which governs the secular society.

Luther withdrew from the church its character as a sword-wielding entity—a visible, corporate, hierarchical, political and legal community. Instead, the church was to be a purely spiritual community, part of the heavenly realm of peace, joy, grace, salvation, and glory. This concept of the church was based on the pivotal doctrine of justification by faith. Luther denied that a person could work his way, so to speak, into the heavenly

---

[3] For discussion of Luther's conceptions of politics and law see F. Edward Cranz, *An Essay on the Development of Luther's Thoughts on Justice, Law, and Society* (Cambridge, MA, 1959); Karl H. Hertz, *Two Kingdoms and One World* (Minneapolis, MN, 1976); August Lang, "The Reformation and Natural Law," in *Calvin and the Reformation* (New York, 1959), 63ff.; William A. Mueller, *Church and State in Luther and Calvin* (Nashville, TN, 1954), 1-59; John Tonkin, *The Church and the Secular Order in Reformation Thought* (New York, 1971), 37-72; Quentin Skinner, *The Foundations of Modern Political Thought* (New York, 1978), 2: 3-20, 81-112. Many of Luther's writings to which this discussion refers are found in John Dillenberger, *Martin Luther: Selections from his Writings* (Garden City, NY, 1961).

[4] The political history of the Reformation in Germany is well told in Hajo Holborn, *A History of Modern Germany, The Reformation* (New York, 1959) and in many other works.

kingdom. Nothing that a person does can "save" him, that is, can make him acceptable to God. Man's fallen nature, his depravity, his essential selfishness, penetrates everything he does—indeed everything he thinks and everything he wants. Therefore salvation is only by grace, which is only bestowed on those who have faith. For this, no mediation by a priesthood is needed, or possible.

But what about the earthly kingdom? Superficially understood, Luther's doctrine seems to take an entirely negative view of it. It is a realm of sin and death, and there is no way out of it by exercise of will or reason. Politics and law are not a path to grace and faith. But are not grace and faith a path to the right politics and the right law?

Here Luther was torn between his belief in man's essential wickedness and his belief that that wickedness itself, and the earthly realm which embodies it, are ordained by God. This dilemma is resolved in part by the doctrine of "the uses of the law." The moral law as well as the law of civil society are ordained, first, in order to make people conscious of their obligations and hence repentant of their sins (the "theological use" of the law), and second, in order to deter recalcitrant people from misconduct by threat of penalties (the "civil use" of the law). Some Lutherans, at least, and most Calvinists, also accepted a third use of the law, called its "didactic" or "pedagogical" use, namely, to guide faithful people in the paths of virtuous living.

Even more important, however, than the doctrine of the uses of the law in explaining Luther's view of the earthly realm was his assumption that its ruler would himself be a Christian and would treat his princely responsibilities as a Christian calling. As the Christian prince, according to Luther, is a private person in his relation with God, "a person for himself alone," so he is a social person, a "person for the sake of others," in his calling as a prince. As such, he should be inspired to serve his people. He should seek to govern in a decent and godly way. He should strive to promote the well-being of his subjects. The Lutheran prince was essentially different from the prince of Niccolò Machiavelli, Luther's contemporary. Machiavelli also believed in the secular state, removed from the divine law, but Machiavelli's prince was to act solely from considerations of power politics, whereas Luther's prince was to strive also to do justice. In this respect, secular politics and law in Protestant principalities continued the older Roman Catholic tradition, though from a different theological and philosophical perspective. The older tradition taught that law is based ultimately on reason and on man's natural inclination toward justice, and that human law, to be valid, must ultimately reflect natural law and divine law. Lutheranism taught, on the contrary, that man's reason and man's will are essentially corrupt, and that human law cannot help but partake of this corruption. Nevertheless, Lutheranism also taught that the Christian lawmaker can and should do his utmost to use his reason and his will to serve God. This was required both by Scripture and by natural law—"the law written in the hearts of men" (Romans 1:18). Further, it was the task of the Christian pastor to preach the Gospel to the prince in order to inspire him to fulfill his calling. Indeed, Luther expanded the concept of "calling," which previously had been applied solely to the clergy, to include the mission of every person to perform his social role in a manner pleasing to God.

Thus the connection between law and religion was preserved by the Lutheran doctrine of the Two Kingdoms, coupled with the concept of the Christian calling. Politics and law were not paths to grace and faith, but grace and faith remained paths to right politics and right law. The Christian was supposed to be law-abiding, and the law of a Christian prince was supposed to achieve both order and justice. Law was supposed to induce people to avoid evil, to cooperate, and to serve the community. The Christian was not to think that by doing good he could earn credits in heaven; nevertheless, he was to use his will and reason—with full consciousness of their defective nature—to do as much good as possible.

And so, ultimately, Luther took a positive view of secular law. More important, the Protestant Reformation which he inaugurated made substantial contributions to the development of law in Germany and elsewhere. In the words of the great German jurist and historian Rudolph Sohm, "Luther's Reformation was a renewal not only of faith but also of the world: both the world of spiritual life and the world of law.[5]

By "the secular authority," Luther meant, above all, the prince; and it was the alliance of Luther with the prince of his own territory, Saxony, and eventually the alliance of Lutherans with other princes, that secured the victory of Protestantism in the territories inhabited by a majority of the people of the German Empire. It was this alliance and this victory which I would call "the German Revolution." Each prince became head of the church in his principality. Not only did his choice of religion determine the established religion of the principality, under the doctrine *cuius regio eius religio*, but the Protestant prince exercised legislative, administrative, and judicial powers over the temporal affairs of the church in his territory. Lutheranism thus strengthened the authority of the prince—not only in Germany but also in other parts of Europe to which it penetrated.

Moreover, Lutheran support for the authority of the prince was not merely a matter of political strategy. It was a matter of theology as well.

---

[5] Rudolph Sohm, *Weltliches und geistliches Recht* (München, 1914), 69.

Luther found in Scripture and in Christian faith the source of royal power. Under the Fourth Commandment, he said, the citizen owes the same duty of obedience to the prince that the child owes to a father, the wife to a husband, or the individual to God. "The powers that be," in St. Paul's words, "are ordained by God" (Romans 13:11).

The Legal Reformation.—I have given the very briefest account of some familiar features of Lutheran religious thought and of their significance for political and legal theory. I would like now to give the very briefest account of some basic changes in German law that took place in Luther's lifetime. My hope is to lay a foundation for some concluding remarks on the interconnections between these two reformations—the reform of religion and the reform of law in Germany.

Germany in 1500 formed an Empire, called the Holy Roman Empire of the German Nation. The German Emperor might rule territories outside of Germany as well, depending to a certain extent on his marital connections. But even the German part of the Empire was a very loose and a very weak structure. Within it there were an incredibly large number of principalities— some 350 all told. These ranged from very large territories (Länder), such as Saxony, Bohemia, Bavaria, Swabia, and others, some of which were sizeable kingdoms, to small counties and town, and from large archbishoprics to small abbeys (some 120 of the principalities were ecclesiastical). In previous centuries the emperor had had very little control over the law by which the constituent principalities were governed. In 1495 Emperor Maximilian finally succeeded in establishing a permanent imperial high court to hear some important cases, and in 1532 Emperor Charles V issued the first important modern imperial legislation, a code of criminal law and procedure. Even then, the principalities had a decisive voice in determining whether to be bound by that code.

Nineteenth and twentieth century German historians have complained bitterly about the fragmentation of Germany; they have envied France and England, which had already achieved a higher degree of national political unity in the fourteenth and fifteenth centuries.[6] Yet the absence of strong political and legal institutions at the imperial level did not necessarily signify disunity. In fact, there had developed in the twelfth to fifteenth centuries in

---

6 Rudolph Hübner, for example, characterized the German law of the Reformation period and before as "much disintegrated and lacking in unity," "particularistic," "disjointed," "parochial," due in part to the multiple sources of law and the lack of an integrated court system and an integrated legal science. Rudolph Hübner, *A History of Germanic Private Law* (London, 1918), 1-40. From a similar perspective one might say the same about American law in the nineteenth century or perhaps even today.

Germany a very strong "common law" on several levels. In the first place, the law applied in the German ecclesiastical courts was the *jus canonicum*, or canon law, common to the whole of Western Europe. For the peoples of Germany, as for all other peoples of Western Christendom, bishops' courts applied the learned law taught in virtually all the European universities, consisting partly of papal and conciliar legislation and papal court decisions (decretals), partly of Gratian's *Decretum* and other great treatises, and partly also of Roman law as reflected in the texts of Justinian that had been redis-covered in Italy in the late eleventh century and had been glossed, commented on, and systematized by many generations of scholars. Both canon law and Roman law were called *jus commune*, "common law."[7]

In addition to canon law, with its Roman law component, Germany was governed, secondly, by a common customary law, including a common customary local law and a common customary feudal law; this was system-atized in the *Sachsenspiegel* of 1220 and in other private German lawbooks which in fact had a quasi-official validity everywhere. Thirdly, many hundreds of German cities had adopted the collections of laws and had followed the court decisions of several leading cities, which, in turn, had many features in common. Finally, the Länder, in developing their own judi-cial and other legal institutions, borrowed extensively from each other.[8] The widespread notion, then, that in comparison with other European countries, pre-Reformation Germany was fragmented in its legal development and backward in legal sophistication needs to be substantially revised.

On the other hand, the legal institutions of pre-Reformation Germany were indeed in great need of reform. The reasons were manifold; let me give two. First, there was an enormous problem of crime, especially on the high-ways. Huge numbers of wanderers—unemployed vagabonds, robbers, gypsies, ex-monks, ex-students, and others—were at large. The traditional local criminal law, based as it was on more stable conditions, was not adequate to deal effectively with widespread and mobile crime of a quasi-pro-fessional character. Second, the ecclesiastical courts, which had had an extremely broad civil and criminal jurisdiction in Germany, even broader, it is usually said, than in England, were losing substantial parts of that jurisdic-tion, especially to city and princely courts, whose procedures and norms were, once again, not well adapted to the increased number and variety of cases.

Here it is necessary to say more about the nature of the German secular courts in the period before the Reformation. For centuries there had existed

---

[7] See Berman, *Law and Revolution*, 199-254.

[8] Ibid., 317-80, 482-511.

in Germany, at the city and territorial level as well as at the imperial level, a tradition and a system of judging by tribunals composed of a number of prominent laymen, called *Schoeffen* ("assessors"), who sat with an official called a *Richter* ("director"). The word Richter, of course, now means "judge," but prior to the Reformation period, the Schoeffen were the *Urteiler*, the "judges"—they gave "judgment." This tradition and this system was fundamental to the development of German secular law in the twelfth to fifteenth centuries. The chief source of that law was custom, and the Schoeffen, being responsible, intelligent, educated (though not university-trained) leaders in the community, knew the custom or else were capable of finding it out. The fact that a substantial part of the customary law came to be expressed in written treatises, such as the *Sachsenspiegel*, or written collections of city laws, did not change its character; it was presupposed in the written texts themselves that the law contained therein remained customary law, to be found and developed by benches of amateur, part-time Schoeffen sitting under the direction of an official Richter.

It was this tradition and this system which came under challenge in the late fifteenth and early sixteenth centuries. Eventually it gave way, first, to a system of tribunals consisting entirely of professional university-trained judges—officials educated in the kind of learned law that hitherto in Germany had been practiced only in the ecclesiastical courts; and second, to a tradition of law whose principal source was not custom but rather legislation—*not*, to be sure, legislation in the contemporary sense, but legislation in the sense of a system of written rules contained in authoritative texts.

This change, which a distinguished German legal historian refers to as the *Verwissenschaftlichung* of German law[9]—literally, the "scientificizing," the rationalizing and systematizing of it as a body of authoritative rules—did not, of course, come all at once. At first, important learned officials were named by the territorial princes to preside at the trials as Richter; eventually, the princes began to choose trained jurists to be Schoeffen; finally, the courts became wholly professional and the Schoeffen more or less disappeared.

Moreover, the "scientific" element in law—perhaps we should call it the "intellectual" element—was given its ultimate expression in the practice, which first became widespread in the sixteenth century, of submitting the most difficult cases to law professors, that is, to university law faculties, for decision.

---

9 Franz Wieacker, *Privatrechtsgeschichte der Neuzeit* (Göttingen, 1967), 131ff.. Another prominent German historian defines the legal reformation of this period as the "gelehrte Bearbeitungen des einheimischen Rechts." Hans Hattenhauer and Arno Buschmann, *Textbuch zur Privatrechtsgeschichte der Neuzeit* (München, 1967), 11.

Courts of territories and of cities as well as the Imperial High Court itself, when faced with a particularly difficult application of the law, were supposed to send the entire file of the case to a law faculty, and the law professors would study and discuss the case and render a reasoned judgment binding upon the court. Called *Aktenversendung*, "the sending of the file," this institution, which lasted in Germany until 1878, was not only highly lucrative for the professors; it also had an enormous influence on the substance as well as on the style of German law.[10] It reflected and embodied an emphasis—new for the German secular courts—on written (instead of oral) procedure, on secrecy (instead of publicity) of proceedings, and on separation of issues of fact (on which findings below were final) from issues of law (on which errors below were subject to appeal). Even more fundamental was the shift from the concept that the court was to find the law, and thereby "set right what was wrong," to the concept that the court was to apply the law, that is, bring the case before it under the appropriate rule "by a process of logical subsumption."[11] The latter intellectual process necessarily involved a new kind of systematization of legal rules.

We may understand better the significance of the "scientificization" of German law in the last years of the fifteenth and the first half of the sixteenth century if we examine its connection with the reform of criminal law and procedure.[12] I have already mentioned that there was an enormous increase in

---

[10] Cf. Eugen Rosenstock-Huessy, *Out of Revolution: The Autobiography of Western Man* (New York, 1938), 402-403. A vivid account of the institution of *Aktenversendungen* is found in John P. Dawson, *The Oracles of the Law* (Ann Arbor, MI, 1968), 198-213, 240-241. A precursor of the sixteenth-century German development is to be found in the practice of courts in various parts of Europe to consult individual learned jurists about difficult cases. This practice became formalized in some Italian cities in the fourteenth century. Cf. G. Kisch, *Consilia: Eine Bibliographie der juristischen Konsiliensammlungen* (Basel, 1970).

[11] Wieacker, *Privatrechtsgeschichte.*

[12] Legal "reformations" preceded or accompanied religious "reformations" in major cities, including Nürnberg (1479), Worms (c. 1499), Frankfurt (1509, 1578), and Freiburg (1520). For a general survey of the city reformations, see Bernd Moeller, *Imperial Cities and the Reformation* (Philadelphia, PA, 1972) and Steven E. Ozment, *The Reformation in the Cities* (New Haven, CT, 1972). For detailed studies of the legal reformations in individual cities, see for Nürnberg, J. W. Ellinger, *Die Juristen der Reichsstadt Nürnberg vom 15. bis 17. Jahrhundert* (Nürnberg, 1954); Andreas Gedeon, *Zur Rezeption des römischen Privatrechts in Nürnberg* (Nürnberg, 1957); Fritz Winter, *Beiträge und Erläuterungen zu Geschichte und Recht der Nürnberger Reformation* (Nürnberg, 1903); Daniel Waldmann, *Entstehung der Nürnberger Reformation von 1479* (Nürnberg, 1908). For Worms, see Carl Koehne, *Die Wormser Stadtrechts Reformation vom Jahre 1499* (Berlin, 1897); Carl Koehne, "Der Ursprung der Stadtverfassung in Worms, Speier, und Mainz," in Otto von Gierke, ed., *Untersuchungen zur deutschen Staat-und Rechtsgeschichte* (1890). For Frankfurt, see H. Coing, *Die Frankfurter Reformation von 1578* (Weimar, 1935); id., *Die Rezeption des*

violent crime in the late fifteenth century. Governmental authorities reacted by harsh measures of law enforcement. This, in turn, produced its own reaction. In 1497-1498 the Imperial Reichstag of Freiburg resolved: "Because complaints have been brought to [the imperial] court against princes, imperial cities, and other authorities, that they have allowed innocent people to be condemned to death and executed unlawfully and without sufficient cause . . . it is therefore necessary to undertake a general reformation and ordering in the Empire of the mode of proceeding in criminal matters."[13]

In light of our situation today, we can appreciate the poignancy of the conflict that raged in Germany at the end of the fifteenth and the beginning of the sixteenth century between adherents of what we would now call the "crime control" and the "due process" "models" of criminal procedure. We can also admire their resolutions of this conflict.

The great name, the great man, in criminal law reform was Johann von Schwarzenberg.[14] He was born twenty years before Luther in a noble family in

---

römischen Rechts in Frankfurt am Main (Frankfurt am Main, 1939, 1962). For Freiburg, see Helmut Knoche, *Ulrich Zasius und das Freiburger Stadtrecht von 1520* (Karisruhe, 1957). A collection of city codes of this period may be found in Wolfgang Kunkel et al., *Quellen zur neueren Privatrechtsgeschichte Deutschlands* (Weimar, 1936).

Apart from city reformations, the *Polizeiordnungen*, promulgated first by the Empire and later by the Länder, became new sources of private law. Although Stobbe had emphasized their significance as early as 1860, later scholars subordinated them to what they called "the Reception of Roman Law" of the late fifteenth and early sixteenth centuries. More recent scholarship has placed that "Reception" much earlier and has revived interest in the Polizeiordnungen. See Otto von Stobbe, *Geschichte der Deutschen Rechtsquellen* (Braunschweig, 1860), 2:200, 220, 229ff.; Otto von Stobbe, *Handbuch des Deutschenprivatrechts* (Berlin, 1864); Winfried Trusen, *Anfänge des gelehrten Rechts in Deutschland* (Wiesbaden, 1962). The best survey of the Polizeiordnungen is Gustaf Klemens Schmelzeisen, *Polizeiordnungen und Privatrechte* (Münster, 1955). Kunkel, et al. eds., *Quellen zur Neueren Privatrechtsgeschichte Deutschlands*, vol. 2, includes many of the original ordinances.

[13] Quoted in John H. Langbein, *Prosecuting Crime in the Renaissance* (Cambridge, MA, 1974), 155.

[14] A short biography and appreciation of Schwarzenberg is given in Erik Wolf, *Grosse Rechtsdenker der deutschen Geistesgeschichte* (Tübingen, 1963), 92-128. The emphasis placed here on Schwarzenberg is not intended to exclude the importance of other great German jurists of the time, notably the famous Ulrich Zasius, an inspired scholar of Roman, canon, and civil law, a friend of Erasmus, an admirer and associate of Luther, and author of the Freiburg legal reformation of 1520. Zasius is sometimes said to be the jurist who best synthesized the Lutheran Reformation and the new humanism of Erasmus in their application to law. See ibid., 55-92; Erik Wolf, *Quellenbuch zur Geschichte der deutschen Rechtswissenschaft* (Frankfurt am Main, 1949), 7-48; R. Stintzing, *Ulrich Zasius: Ein Beitrag zur Geschichte der Rechtswissenschaft im Zeitalter der Reformation* (Leipzig, 1857); Knoche, *Ulrich Zasius*; R. Schmidt, *Zasius und seine Stellung in der Rechtswissenschaft* (Leipzig, 1904); Guido Kisch, *Zasius und Reuchlin* (Konstanz, 1961); id., *Erasmus und die Jurisprudenz seiner Zeit* (Basel, 1960), 317-43. Recently Steven W. Rowan has

the episcopal principality of Bamberg. He eventually became the chief official (*Holfmeister*) of Bamberg, under the bishop, and sat as chief judge of the Bamberg high court. He was a man of great intelligence and dedication, a deeply religious person, very widely read, a folk-poet, with many learned friends, though he himself had not had a university training and did not know Latin. In 1507, when Schwarzenberg was in his early forties, he produced for Bamberg a code of criminal law and procedure that acquired almost instant fame throughout Germany. Other principalities copied it. The Emperor Charles V eventually employed Schwarzenberg to rework his code for adoption by the Empire and in 1532, a few years after Schwarzenberg's death, the imperial code, called the *Constitutio Criminalis Carolina*, or *Carolina* for short, closely modelled on the Bamberg code, was in fact adopted.[15]

Schwarzenberg's code was the first of its kind in history—that is, the first systematic codification of a single branch of law. There had been, to be sure, in the previous three centuries, systematic treatises on particular branches of law, including criminal law and procedure, written by canonist and Romanist legal scholars; and Schwarzenberg drew heavily on concepts and definitions contained in some of those treatises. Yet those treatises, though often treated by European courts as authoritative, were not legislation; they were not the same as comprehensive statutes promulgated by the legislative power of the state. Such comprehensive statutes on particular branches of law began to be promulgated in various German cities in the last decade of the 15th century. Schwarzenberg built on that practice. His genius was not that of a scholar but that of a judge, an administrator, and, ultimately, a legislator. Erik Wolf has called him "the great German legislator of the Reformation period."[16]

The starting-point of Schwarzenberg's Bamberg code of 1507—and hence of the *Carolina* as well—was the existing secular law of Bamberg as reflected in contemporary judicial practice. To this were added basic rules of the common law, as it was called, generally recognized throughout the Empire, which in turn were influenced by the categories of canon law, and to a certain extent Roman law, especially with regard to definitions of types of offenses. A third element was the conceptual framework that had been developed since the end of the thirteenth century by outstanding European canonists and Romanists,

---

emphasized the theological and humanistic contributions of Zasius. See, e.g.., S. Rowan, "Ulrich Zasius and the Baptism of Jewish Children," *Sixteenth Century Journal* 6 (2) (1975): 3, and Ulrich Zasius, "Death Penalty for Anabaptists," *Bibliotheque D'Humanisme et Renaissance* 41 (1979): 527.

[15] With the creation of the *Reichskammergericht* in 1495 came a movement to systematize an imperial criminal law that would be valid throughout the Empire.

[16] Wolf, *Grosse Rechtsdenker*, 96ff., 109ff.

especially the Italians Durantis, Gandinus, Bartolus, Baldus, and others. Finally, the whole was permeated with a spirit of reform, and in this connection Schwarzenberg drew not only on the Bamberg court reform of 1503, of which he himself had been the chief author, but also on the so-called reformations of city law in Nürnberg, in Worms, and elsewhere. His own chief personal contribution, as Wolf has said, was synthesis, based on the two fundamental principles of "justice and the common weal" (*Gerechtigkeit und Gemeinnutz*).[17]

Of critical importance was the combination of systematic legal science with a procedure still characterized by lay participation. The code was to govern the Schoeffen; therefore, it had to be understandable to them; and for that purpose Schwarzenberg wrote it in clear, strong German. Three hundred years later—in 1814—the great German jurist Savigny was to say that no German legislation of the eighteenth century could compare with the *Carolina* in seriousness and strength.

Incidentally, Schwarzenberg scattered little poems—rhymed couplets— through the various sections of his code, in order to dramatize the meaning of the rules and to make it easier to remember them. He also inserted many handsome woodcuts, with similar effect.

The purpose of codifying the criminal law was not to make the Schoeffen into learned jurists. Nor was the purpose to import a foreign law. The purpose was, rather, to reform the German secular law and, in that connection, to give it the benefit of the legal science that had developed first in the church courts and second in the scholarly literature of the university jurists.

Some of the major changes in secular German criminal law embodied in the Bamberg code and later in the *Carolina* are the following:

- Most major crimes were defined in a systematic way. Concepts such as self-defense, complicity, and attempt were defined. Emphasis was placed on intent, causation, and exculpating circumstances.

- Private criminal prosecutions were severely limited. Archaic forms of private remedies, such as wergeld, were finally eliminated. Proof by oath-helping was finally eliminated.

- The power of officials, the *Obrigkeit*, to initiate and carry out criminal prosecution was enhanced, while at the same time limits on their power were set with care. The proceedings were to take the form of an inquest, that is, an official investigation (*Inquisition*), with the judges inquiring and collecting evidence. The Schoeffen were to operate under the supervision of officials.

- The extraordinary procedures against persons charged merely with being socially harmful ("of evil repute") were eliminated. (These procedures,

---

[17] Ibid., 109. Cf. *Carolina*, art. 104.

summary and harsh, together with the vagueness of the charges, had been a main source of complaint against unjust repression in the late fifteenth century.)

- The system of cruel punishments (including, for example, burial alive in the case of some crimes) was alleviated to some extent.

- High standards of proof were set. For capital crimes, in addition to convincing proof of each element of the crime it was required that there be two eye-witnesses or else a confession reiterated voluntarily in court. In such cases, unless there were two eye-witnesses, torture was permitted in order to extract a confession. However, such torture could only be used if there was sufficient evidence to convict without a confession.

- The Schoeffen were instructed repeatedly, in various contexts, that in difficult cases they should "seek counsel" of those who are "learned in the law"—a reference to the institution of the *Aktenversendung*.

Law AND Belief in the German Reformation.—I come, finally, in our consideration of the Lutheran Reformation and German law, to the word "and."

A leading contemporary Roman Catholic theologian told a friend that he had been asked to give a talk on "Freedom and the Church." His friend said, "Of course you know a great deal about freedom, and you are a recognized expert on the church. But I think you will have a lot of difficulty with the 'and'."

By focusing attention on Schwarzenberg's great reform of German criminal law—first enacted ten years before Luther's denunciation of papal indulgences—I seem to have foreclosed any argument that the great changes in German law in the sixteenth century were caused by the Lutheran Reformation. It is true that the *Carolina* was not enacted until fifteen years *after* Luther took his stand, but it was based on Schwarzenberg's earlier work and, moreover, it was promulgated by Emperor Charles V, an archfoe of Lutheranism.

On the other hand, Schwarzenberg did become a Lutheran. Indeed, he became an ardent and prominent Lutheran, corresponded with Luther, and wrote tracts in defense of Lutheranism. While he was working for the Emperor to prepare the *Carolina*, Schwarzenberg used his position to protect Luther and Lutherans from repression.

No doubt it is partly because the reformation of German law began *before* the reformation of the church, and partly because it was supported by many Catholics as well as by many Protestants (and also was opposed by many in both camps), that historian have generally ignored the relationship between the two reformations, the legal and the religious. Yet the fact that Lutheranism did not "cause" the *Carolina*, in some simple *post hoc-propter hoc* sense of causation, does not mean that the two may properly be viewed as independent of each other. The biography of Johann von Schwarzenberg suggests that the word "and" in this context has a more complex meaning.

The complexities multiply when we add other factors to the equation: the New Humanism, the so-called Reception of Roman Law, the increased importance of nationalism, the expansion of commerce, the exploration of new continents, and others. I mention these only to show some of the dimensions of the word "and," and some of the limits of my inquiry into it here. I am focusing simply on some of the connections between the Lutheran Reformation of the church in Germany in the early sixteenth century "and" the movement to reform German law.

There were clear *political* connections. Although the transfer to territorial and city courts of matters previously within the jurisdiction of the ecclesiastical courts had started well before Luther, this secularization—which was an important stimulus of the law reform movement—cannot be separated from Lutheranism. It received a tremendous impetus from the Lutheran attack on the very concept of ecclesiastical jurisdiction. With the abolition of the ecclesiastical courts in the Protestant principalities, the secular courts took jurisdiction over the crimes of heresy, blasphemy, sumptuousness of dress, and other religious and moral offenses. There was a secularization also of the canon law of marriage and divorce, wills, charitable foundations, and other civil matters previously within the ecclesiastical jurisdiction. Secular public schools and libraries were established to replace cathedral schools and libraries, and all universities were placed under civil authority. Poor relief, protection of widows and orphans, medical care, and other forms of public welfare, which previously had been chiefly the responsibility of monastic and other ecclesiastical charitable foundations, were now left to the secular authority and to secular law.

Also jurisdiction over the church itself was transferred from the ecclesiastical to the secular authority. The Protestant prince became the head of the churches in his principality. He was now responsible for the development of a body of secular ecclesiastical law for the government of their temporal affairs.

Moreover, the Protestant princes, lacking a Roman Catholic clergy trained to administer the affairs of state, developed a secular civil service to constitute their advisors, administrators, judges, diplomats, and other officers. The Lutheran Reformation enhanced immeasurably the authority not only of the prince but also of the prince's official retinue, the *Obrigkeit*. In addition, it was a pan-German *Obrigkeit*, for German civil servants could go from one prince to another, just as the university professors could go from the university of one principality to that of another. This extraordinary mobility of the civil service, which contributed to its strong sense of calling, distinguished Germany from England and France in the period of what is usually called absolute monarchy in Europe.[18]

Thus far I have stressed political connections between the religious reformation and the legal reformation. As a political matter, the suppression of ecclesiastical jurisdiction, which Lutherans demanded on theological grounds, inevitably resulted in a further rapid expansion of secular jurisdiction; and this expansion inevitably gave the opportunity to reform the substantive secular law which was to be applied.

There were, in addition, what might be called *intellectual* connections between the legal and the religious reformations. It is interesting, for example, to compare the rhetoric and style of the *Carolina* with the rhetoric and style of Luther's translation of the Bible and his commentaries on it. The *Carolina*—like Schwarzenberg's Bamberg code before it—was written in clear, simple, vivid German, to be understood by the lay judges and lesser legal officials, untrained in law, who participated in German criminal proceedings, just as Luther's Bible and his commentaries were written in clear, simple, vivid German, to be understood by all believers who could read them. One may even compare Schwarzenberg's use of figures and woodcuts with Luther's use of hymns.

The "scientific" character of the new criminal codes, and of the legal reformation generally, also linked them with Lutheranism. Like Lutheranism, the *Carolina* was intended to be comprehensive, systematic, integrated, complete; it proceeded from interlocking basic principles and showed their application to typical concrete situations. The *Carolina* was professors' law, just as Lutheranism was professors' theology, an attempt to embrace and unify the entire Christian belief-system.

The paradox of a systematic legal codification understandable to all literate subjects, like the paradox of a systematic Biblical theology understandable to all literate believers, was resolved by assigning a special role to university professors. Just as especially difficult cases involving application of the *Carolina* were to be sent to university law faculties for resolution, so especially difficult theological questions that troubled princes and pastors were to be resolved by university professors of theology. These practices reflected a profound trust not only in learning but also in the university, which in a sense replaced the papal curia.

---

[18] Rosenstock-Hussey, *Out of Revolution*, 394-95. Rosenstock-Huessy's entire chapter on the German Reformation is filled with important insights.

I have mentioned political and intellectual connections between the legal changes and the religious changes in sixteenth-century Germany. There are even closer *moral* and *philosophical* connections. Both Lutheranism and the *Carolina*—again, I use the *Carolina* as one example of the overall legal reformation that took place—share a revulsion against cruelty and arbitrariness; both place a high value on humaneness and rationality. Yet both accept a certain amount of cruelty as inevitable—neither is willing to proclaim its complete abolition. Luther wrote, after the peasant rebellion of 1524, that "stern, hard civil rule is necessary in the world. . . . The civil sword shall and must be red and bloody."[19] Many other violent statements can be found in his voluminous writings. He was a revolutionary, fighting enemies by the most ruthless means. Yet the faith for which he fought was one through which love was to triumph over hatred, virtue over sin, reason over irrationality. Similarly, Schwarzenberg was a man of piety and idealism, one of whose main purposes was to put an end to the cruelty and arbitrariness that had infected German criminal law and procedure in the fifteenth century. Yet the *Carolina*, though it substantially limited torture, did not abolish it.[20] It eliminated death

[19] "Von Kaufshandlung und Wucher," in *D. Martin Luther Werke*, (Weimar, 1883-1979), 15: 302.

[20] It is something of a mystery why the requirement of a confession was retained even after it had become, in effect, a formality. John Langbein takes the traditional view that with the abolition of the ordeals in 1215 by the Fourth Lateral Council, so-called statutory proofs—that is, by a confession or by two eyewitness—were introduced because of the prevailing distrust of judicial evaluation of so-called subjective proofs (circumstantial evidence, one eye-witness, prior statements of the accused, etc.). Torture was then perceived to be a logical consequence of the requirement of a confession. Thus Langbein concludes that "The Roman-canon system . . . was simply unworkable without torture." J. Langbein, *Torture and the Law of Proof: Europe and England in the Ancien Regime* (Chicago, 1977), 11. This argument neglects the point made elsewhere by Langbein (ibid., 13) that in the realm of lesser offenses the "Roman-canon" system worked quite well without the requirement of statutory proofs. Apparently there was something about capital punishment that made the usual standards of proof inadequate to justify the imposition of the death sentence, though only persons who were guilty by ordinary standards could be required to confess. It may be that in these circumstances unwillingness to give up the requirement of two eye-witnesses or a confession (and hence the option of torture) in capital cases was due partly to the belief that for the good of his own soul a guilty person should be made to confess before he is executed. It may also have been due partly to the fact that a confession, even when extorted, could help the investigating authorities to "solve" the crime—it could help them, for example, to track down accomplices; and that may have seemed especially important in cases of more serious offenses.

As Langbein shows, in the sixteenth and seventeenth centuries new forms of punishment for the most serious crimes—including imprisonment, galley service, workhouses, and banishment—developed alongside the death penalty, and to impose these milder sentences a confession was considered unnecessary and hence torture could be dispensed with. Langbein concludes from this that torture had become obsolete long before it was subjected to the criticism of the philosophers of the Enlightenment and eventually

by burial alive as the penalty for infanticide, but substituted death by drowning. It did not eliminate the crime of sorcery, but it did require proof that the act of sorcery caused harm.[21]

In terms of legal theory, conflicts between Schwarzenberg's two guiding principles, justice and the common weal—in other words, between humaneness and civil order—were to be reconciled by the wisdom of the prince, whose will was the source of all earthly law. Luther did not adopt the modern theory of legal positivism in its strict form. He acknowledged the independent existence of moral law, or natural law, which he identified sometimes as that which is known to the conscience and sometimes as that which is reflected in the spirit of the Mosaic law. He also left some room, though not much, for civil disobedience when the ruler commands his subject to act in evil or ungodly ways. Nevertheless, he attacked the belief that man can truly understand the will of God by his reason or truly reflect it in his law, and he attacked the concept of God as a God of reason and of law. Thus the moral law, or natural law, was associated for him with the earthly rather than the heavenly realm. These theological positions give support to the positivist view that the source of all law is in the will of the ruler. Because Lutheran theory, in contrast to Roman Catholic, did not consider human law to be a *given*, an integral part of the objective reality of God himself, it had to put the question: What are the uses of the law? Thus Luther took an essentially utilitarian view of law—which also is congenial to a modern positivist jurisprudence. Moreover, like the modern positivists, he considered the *civil* use of the law to be to deter misconduct by threat of penalties.

Modern positivist jurisprudence is often attacked for its neglect of justice as a necessary dimension of law. It should be stressed, therefore, that the tendencies toward positivist jurisprudence in Lutheran thought in the sixteenth century were *not* antagonistic, but in fact highly congenial, to the zeal for law reform in the direction of justice. Lutheran thought could accept philosophical propositions that law is the will of the ruler, that it operates by imposing sanctions for violations of rules, and that justice—indeed, reason itself—is corrupted by man's total depravity. Yet German Lutherans of the sixteenth century could not accept the Machiavellian view that makes human

---

abolished. Mirjan Damaska has shown, however, that the death penalty remained applicable in the sixteenth to eighteenth centuries for numerous crimes, including magic, witchcraft, homicide, and treason, and that even in cases where milder punishments were applicable, judges often resorted to torture to be assured of the defendant's guilt and to extract additional information. See Mirjan Damaska, "The Death of Legal Torture," *Yale Law Journal* 87 (1978): 860 (a review of Langbein's book).

[21] H.J. Berman, "Religious Foundations of Law in the West: An Historical Perspective," *Journal of Law and Religion* 3 (1983): 22-24.

selfishness the basic principle of political action for the individual Christian, be he subject or prince. They were unwilling to abandon the earthly kingdom to its own Satanic devices. It was presupposed that the ruler would be a Christian prince.

The religious doctrine which, perhaps more than any other, guided sixteenth century Lutheranism between the Scylla of Machiavellian cynicism and the Charybdis of political passivity was the doctrine of the Christian calling. I have stressed earlier that the Gregorian Revolution had placed the responsibility to reform the secular society primarily on the priesthood: this was part of the two swords theory of the Roman Catholic Church in the late eleventh to sixteenth centuries. Protestantism placed that responsibility on every Christian, and especially on the prince and the *Obrigkeit*. Each was a "private person" in his relation to God; but each had a public responsibility in his calling.

In a civilization reduced almost to despair by the failure, after four centuries, of the Gregorian Revolution, this Lutheran vision gave a new meaning to secular life. It was this vision that gave German society the energy to renew its legal institutions. The fact that reform had been in the air for a hundred years before Luther only enhances the importance of his role as a catalytic agent in bringing it to fruition. But beyond that, it places the Revolution itself in a better perspective. It was not simply Luther's Revolution. It was also Schwarzenberg's. Indeed, it was Germany's Revolution, in which many participated who were not Lutherans. The precise chronological timing of their participation is not important for us. The Revolution should be judged in terms not of *chronos* but of *kairos*: it came in the fullness of time.

II. *The Puritan Revolution and English Law*

The religious upheaval that took place in England in the seventeenth century and the transformation of English law that accompanied it were aspects of a general political, economic, and social revolution similar in scope to the German Reformation of a century before and the French Revolution of a century later. These three successive upheavals—the German, the English, and the French—were Great Revolutions in the classical sense, with civil war, class struggle, and apocalyptic visions of a new era; each was characterized by fundamental changes both in the nation's political and legal systems and in its system of beliefs and values.

The main political and constitutional events of the English Revolution are familiar and may be re-told quickly. For more than a hundred years the Tudors and Stuarts had ruled England as absolute monarchs—the Tudors, on the whole, quite successfully, the Stuarts much less so. The reign of Charles I was particularly unhappy. From 1629 to 1640 he did not once call a parliament into session. The landed gentry and merchants complained bitterly about extraordinary royal taxes used to finance unpopular wars. Religious Non-Conformists were persecuted; in the decade of the 1630's some 20,000 Puritans fled to Massachusetts Bay and a comparable number crossed the channel to the Netherlands; "they flew out of England," it was said, "as out of Babylon." Royal measures were rigorously enforced by the so-called "prerogative courts" of Star Chamber, High Commission, Admiralty, Requests, and others—courts which had been established by the Tudor kings and which were immediately responsive to the royal will. But even the common-law judges of the more ancient courts of King's Bench, Common Pleas, and Exchequer, with jurisdiction chiefly over felonies and rights in land, were at the king's mercy: he could dismiss them at will—indeed, he could have easily put them in the Tower.

In November 1640 the King at last convened a parliament. Under severe provocation, its leaders, mostly Puritans, seized power. A civil war broke out between the supporters of Parliament and the supporters of the Crown. A Puritan "Commonwealth" was established. In 1649 Charles Stuart was tried for treason and executed. But after Oliver Cromwell's death in 1658, Puritan rule quickly collapsed. In 1660 Charles's oldest son returned to England to take the throne as Charles II. This was called "the Restoration," but it was also a phase of the Revolution. Finally, in 1688, when James II—brother of Charles II—began to exercise powers similar to those exercised fifty years earlier by his father, Charles I, Parliament forced him to abdicate and installed a new dynasty on the throne. This was called "the Glorious Revolution;" it ended almost fifty years of acute civil strife, and established a system of government which survived into the twentieth century.

Henceforth it was clear that Parliament, not the king, reigned supreme in England. The English system of political parties took its shape. The Bill of Rights was enacted. Judges were given life tenure. With the abolition of the perogative courts, the common law courts were recognized as subordinate only to Parliament. The content of the common law also changed, both in procedure and in substance.

There was also a new religious settlement. An Act of Toleration gave freedom of association and worship to the Non-Conforming churches (although not to the Catholics). Anglican theology itself changed substantially, partly under the influence of Calvinism.

That is a bare outline of some of the major political-constitutional events of the English Revolution of 1640-1689. I propose now to examine in somewhat more detail, first, the religious changes that took place in that period, and second, the legal changes.

Religious Aspects of the English Revolution—Let me start with the religious side, and especially with Puritanism.

The Puritans—they were first called that by their enemies in the late sixteenth century—were English followers of the French reformer, John Calvin. In the mid-1530's, as a very young man, Calvin had established a Protestant religious community embracing the city of Geneva, Switzerland. He and his followers shared many of the theological doctrines that were being proclaimed by Martin Luther at the time. They denied the authority of the Church of Rome. They believed in the primacy of the Bible. They accepted, though with some modifications, the Lutheran doctrine of the two kingdoms, justification by faith alone, the fallen nature of man, predestination, the priesthood of all believers, and the Christian calling. They put great emphasis on the sovereignty of God and the providential character of human history.

The Calvinist conception of the church, however, differed substantially from the Lutheran. For Luther, the church as a visible institution was to be organized territorially under the secular ruler of the territorial polity, the prince. The prince was believed to be ordained by God to be the ruler of the institutional affairs of the church within his polity—not its faith and doctrine but its legal structure, its political and economic and social activities. The church was not a lawmaking body: church law was merely the law of the secular ruler relating to the secular affairs of the church. Calvin and his followers, on the other hand, viewed the church in its visible, institutional aspect as consisting of politically independent local congregations, each with its own elected minister and elders, each with its own legal authority. The legal authority of the local congregation, or synod of local congregations, was to be balanced against that of the civil polity and might even dominate the civil polity. The Calvinist churches had their own law, by which they regulated not only the worship and the theological doctrine of the civil society but also its morals, including many aspects of its political, economic, and social life. In contrast to Luther, Calvin, who was himself trained as a lawyer, had a well worked out philosophy of secular law.[22] He added, in effect, a new Two Swords doctrine to the Lutheran Two Kingdoms doctrine.

---

[22] Calvin's views on law and government are discussed in Mueller, *Church and State*, 73-103; Tonkin, *The Church*, 93-130; John T. McNeill, "John Calvin on Civil Government," *Journal of Presbyterian History* 47 (1964): 71; Hans Baron, "Calvinist Republicanism and its Historical Roots," *Church History* 8 (1939): 30; Josef Bohatec, *Calvin und das Recht* (Aalen, 1934); id., *Calvins Lehre von Staat und Kirche* (Aalen, 1961).

I will not attempt to recount the dramatic spread of Calvin's teachings through many parts of Europe in the sixteenth and early seventeenth century, other than to say that Calvinism became a transnational movement, but with many variations of doctrine and of policy in different times and places.[23] Calvin's writings were known to educated people throughout Europe. Calvinist doctrines were studied and were taken seriously even by those who opposed them—Roman Catholics, Anglicans, Lutherans, and others.

Most English Calvinists, in the century prior to 1640, did not contest the authority of the English Crown over the church in England, nor did they attempt to draw its followers away from the Anglican Church. Instead, English Calvinists sought chiefly to reform the Church of England from within. They penetrated the Anglican clergy, from which vantage point they attacked traditional Anglican ritualism, resisted the Book of Common Prayer, denied the hierarchical authority of the episcopacy, and preached the right and duty of every believer to read and interpret Scripture for himself. Needless to say, they were, from an early time, a thorn—and eventually a knife—in the side not only of the Anglican Church as such but also of the Crown, whose authority derived in substantial part from its ecclesiastical supremacy. As King James I put it, "No bishops, no king."

Yet despite some repressive measures, neither the monarch nor his bishops seriously tried to rid the English church entirely of its Calvinists. One reason for this was that the Puritans were strongly anti-Roman and were needed by the Crown in the struggle against the papacy and its Spanish and French supporters. (By the same token, the Crown was needed by the Puritans.) Moreover, the Puritans were great patriots, who with dedication entered English public life as justices of the peace, members of Parliament, and in many other capacities. In addition, Puritanism was quite strong among the minor landed gentry and among artisans and merchants—classes that did

---

[23]Herbert D. Foster has used the phrase "international Calvinism" to refer to the Calvinist and Neo-Calvinist teachings that spread throughout Europe in the sixteenth and seventeenth centuries. Herbert D. Foster, *Collected Papers of Herbert D. Foster* (New York, 1929), 147. See also John T. McNeill, *The History and Character of Calvinism* (New York, 1957). A Calvinism largely consistent with Calvin's *Institutes of the Christian Religion* (1st ed., 1536) had entered Britain via the chief Reformers, Knox, Bucer, and Bullinger, the returning Marian exiles, and exiled Dutch and French Huguenot Calvinists. From 1575 to 1610, 96 editions of Calvin's writings were published in England, and of the 85 editions of the Bible printed in Elizabeth's reign sixty were the Geneva Bible in which Calvin's teachings were summarized. See Charles D. Cremeans, *The Reception of Calvinist Thought in England* (Urbana, IL, 1949), 65-66. Yet Calvinism was accommodated to the scholasticism of Beza, the rationalism of Perkins and his followers, Armininiasm, various forms of mysticism, and neo-Platonism. See Peter Toon, *The Emergence of Hypercalvinism in English Non-Conformity* (London, 1967), 18ff..

not have influence at the royal court but that nevertheless had to be reckoned with. Finally, although the excesses of Puritan doctrine and zeal were deplored by the Establishment, a number of Calvinist tenets penetrated high places. In the 1590's, when at last a strong campaign against Puritanism was launched, it was considerably restrained by the fact that Archbishop Whitgift, who led the campaign, considered himself to be at least partly a Calvinist in theology. Eventually, Puritanism survived not only Archbishop Whitgift's campaign, but also the much more severe campaign of Archbishop Laud in the 1630's.

Was there something in the Puritan belief system that helps to explain why the Puritans were able to assume leadership in Parliament in 1640 and 1641, to mobilize the pro-Parliament, anti-royalist forces of the country in 1642, and thereafter to lead an insurrectionary army and to establish a revolutionary government? Was there something in the Puritan belief system that helps to explain why the Puritans were able to transform the English system of government and law?

Several elements of that belief system deserve mention in that connection. The first is the Puritan view of history. The English Puritans—despite all the differences of belief among different branches, different sects, indeed, different congregations—shared the belief that human history is wholly within the providence of God, that it is not primarily a secular story of man's struggle to achieve his own ends but rather primarily a spiritual story of the unfolding of God's own purposes, with man acting always as God's agent. Moreover, patriotic English Puritans in the seventeenth century were led by their belief in divine Providence to view England as God's elect nation, destined to reveal and incarnate God's mission for mankind.[24]

---

[24] For an excellent short account of the providential view of history taken by Puritans, see Donald R. McKim, "The Puritan View of History or Providence Without and Within," 1980 Evangelical Quarterly (1980): 215-31, esp. 227. See also Timothy H. Breen, The Character of the Good Ruler: Puritan Political Ideals in New England, 1630-1730 (New Haven, CT, 1970), 15; William Haller, The Elect Nation (New York, 1963), 244-50. Breen writes:

> [The Puritans] insisted that the Lord had made a compact with the English at some indeterminable time in the past, granting them peace, prosperity and Protestantism in exchange for obedience to scriptural law. The Puritans regarded this agreement as a real and binding contract for which all men could be held responsible. If the nation failed the Lord by allowing evil to flourish, He punished the entire population, saints and sinners alike. The ruler [thus] became a crucial figure for the Puritans, because it was his duty to make Englishmen uphold the terms of their compact [with the Lord] whether they wanted to or not.

Ibid., 15.

Second, the English Puritans were committed to radical reform as a religious activity. They believed that God willed and commanded "the reformation of the world." "The spirit of the whole creation," wrote a leading Puritan, "was about the reformation of the world." "Reform all places, all persons and callings," said another, in a sermon preached before the House of Commons in 1641. "Reform the benches of judgment, the inferior magistrates . . .," he continued. "Reform the universities, reform the cities, reform the counties, reform the inferior schools of learning, reform the Sabbath, reform the ordinances, the worship of God. Every plant which my heavenly father hath not planted shall be rooted up."[25] Although the zeal for "the reformation of the world" subsided somewhat in England after the Restoration, it continued for some decades in Puritan-led colonies of North America, and was revived from time to time thereafter, both in England and America.

Third, the Puritan concept of reformation of the world was closely connected with the emphasis on law as a means of reformation. When the Puritans were in power during the 1640's and 1650's over ten thousand different pamphlets were published urging law reforms of various kinds. This zeal for law reform reflected a deep religious conviction in a God of law, who inspires his followers to translates his will into legal precepts. Calvinism emphasized the didactic, or pedagogical, use of law, that is, its use in guiding faithful persons in the paths of virtuous living. Calvin had written that in addition to making people conscious of their sins and calling them to repentance (Luther's "theological" use of the law), and in addition to deterring recalcitrant persons from misconduct by threat of penalties (Luther's "civil" use of the law) there is a "third and principal use, which pertains more closely to the proper purpose of the law," and which "finds its place among believers in whose hearts the Spirit of God already lives and reigns." The law serves to help such believers to know better the divine will and to arouse them to obedience.[26]

Calvin, to be sure, did not share the older Roman Catholic understanding of law as something given, part of the very nature and being of God. Law for

---

[25] Quoted in Michael Walzer, *The Revolution of the Saints: A Study in the Origin of Radical Politics* (Cambridge, MA, 1965), 12.

[26] John Calvin, *Institutes of the Christian Religion*, ed. John T. McNeill, trans. Ford Lewis Battles (Philadelphia, PA, 1960) bk. 2, ch. 7, para. 12. The enormous outpouring of pamphlets and the general aims of the pamphleteers are discussed in Henry N. Brailsford, *The Levellers and the English Revolution* (Stanford, CA, 1961), 453, 523-40; D. Veall, *The Popular Movement for Law Reform* (Oxford, 1970), 97-224. The Puritans attested to their belief in the didactic use of the law by placing on the walls of their churches and homes long lists of simple rules and by recitation of the Ten Commandments every Sunday morning. See Gerald Robertson Cragg, *Freedom and Authority: A Study of English Thought in the Early Seventeenth Century* (Philadelphia, PA, 1975), 147ff.

Calvinists, as for Lutherans, was part of the earthly kingdom of sin and death rather than of the heavenly kingdom of grace and joy; nor was obedience to law a formula of works necessary to enter that heavenly kingdom. Law was, indeed, ordained by God but it was discerned and given expression by man's defective will and reason. For Calvin, as for Luther, law was something that had *uses*. More than Luther, however, Calvin—and the English Puritans—stressed the positive role both of the moral law (which he identified with natural law) and of the civil law in teaching man to walk in the paths that God has set for him.

A fourth element in the Puritan belief system that contributed to legal reform was its strong social dimension. The ultimate purpose of law, according to Calvin and his followers, was not only to help individual Christians to be upright but also thereby to create an upright Christian community. The congregation of the faithful was to be "a light to all the nations of the world," "a city on a hill."[27] Calvinist Puritanism was essentially a communitarian religion. Each was responsible for all. By the same token, all were responsible for each. Breach of God's commandments by one incurred God's punishment of the whole corporate body—be it the family, the church, or the nation.[28]

A fifth link in the chain that bound Puritan theology to Puritan political and legal philosophy was its stress on hard work, austerity, frugality of time and money, reliability, discipline, vocational ambition, individual commitment to improvement of self, of neighbor, and of society. This "Puritan ethic" was rooted in theological assumptions. The Puritan considered his life to be a part of the divine unfolding of God's plan for the world. To waste time was to do a disservice to God. To be drunk or play cards or keep ill company was to disturb his contemplation of the will of God for his life. Thus the Puritan saw his own life as bound by a multitude of rules. His morality was a legal morality, and he inevitably extended his legal morality to the local community and to the nation.

Finally, and most directly connected with the English Revolution itself, is a basic Calvinist principle of government, namely, the principle that government by representative leaders of the community, "the elders," "the lower magistrates," is superior to government by a single ruler, the prince. Calvin

---

[27] Quotation from a sermon given in 1630 on "The Arabella," by Governor John Winthrop entitled "A Model of Christian Charity," printed in *Winthrop Papers* (Boston, MA, 1931), 2: 295.

[28] Universal punishment is discussed in Gerald R. Cragg, *Puritanism in the Period of the Great Persecution* (Cambridge, MA, 1957), 137, 168; J.S. McGee, *The Godly Man in Stuart England* (1976), 129; Breen, *The Character*, 15.

wrote that the best form of government is either "aristocracy or a system compounded of aristocracy and democracy," such as "the Lord established among the people of Israel." The theological basis of this theory of tempered aristocracy was the doctrine of the sinfulness of man, his fundamental selfishness and lust for power. It is "safer," Calvin wrote, "for a number to exercise government, so that . . . if one asserts himself unfairly, there may be a number of censors and masters to restrain his willfulness."[29]

This theory was the basis also of Calvin's doctrine that when royal government becomes too tyrannical, then the lower magistrates, as leaders and protectors of the community, are commanded by God "to withstand the fierce licentiousness of kings." Thus the zeal for reformation might lead to revolution, which, however, was itself to be limited by aristocratic communitarian principles. Although Calvin himself had muted his advocacy of resistance to tyranny, his followers throughout Europe during the next century proclaimed it a basic religious doctrine.[30]

In 1640 the English Puritans provided the theory and vision needed to fight a civil war, overthrow the monarchy, and establish Parliamentary supremacy. Ultimately, however, Puritanism foundered in England, since its essentially congregational conception of government was wholly inadequate as a system for ruling a whole nation. It led first to factionalism and disintegration and eventually succumbed to Cromwellian dictatorship. Nevertheless, even though the Anglican Church and the Stuart dynasty were restored in 1660, there was no going back to pre-Puritan times. The basic Puritan beliefs that had made the Revolution survived. I have listed six: the belief that God is working in history through his chosen nation, England; the belief in reformation of the world as a religious commitment; the belief that law is a prime instrument of such reformation; the belief in the corporate character of the local community; the belief in the "Puritan ethic;" and the belief in government either by aristocracy or by aristocracy tempered with democracy. These beliefs remained strong in England, although they lost their original Puritan fervor and some of their Puritan theological foundations.

The Transformation of English Law.—I turn now to some of the changes in English law that took place during this period.[31]

---

[29] Calvin, *Institutes*, bk. 4, ch. 2, para. 8., 31.

[30] Ibid., bk. 4, ch. 20, para. 31. The doctrines of civil disobedience advocated by the Huguenots in France were built squarely on this teaching of Calvin.

[31] Among many sources see Veall, *The Popular Movement*; Stuart Prall, *The Agitation for Law Reform During the Puritan Revolution 1640-1660* (The Hague, 1966); Barbara Shapiro, "Law Reform in Seventeenth Century England," *American Journal of Legal History* 19 (1975): 280-312; id., "Codification of the Laws in Seventeenth Century England," *1974*

That English *constitutional* law underwent fundamental changes between 1640 and 1689 is undisputed. Parliamentary supremacy was established. The newer courts that had been created by the Tudor kings were abolished, and the older common-law courts became supreme over all others. Judges were given life tenure. Religious toleration was extended to Protestant denominations. Royal powers were limited by a written Bill of Rights.

More controversial is the scope and nature of the changes in other branches of law, especially criminal and civil law in their procedural and substantive aspects. Legal historians have usually emphasized sixteenth-century more than seventeenth-century developments in these branches of law. Moreover, they have tended to see both sixteenth and seventeenth century developments, and for that matter eighteenth century developments as well, as gradual, incremental changes arising from within the legal system itself rather than as rapid, fundamental changes responding to pressures from outside the law. Plucknett even speaks of "the remarkable continuity and stability of English law during the vicissitudes of the seventeenth century."[32]

I propose a different view, namely, that in the late seventeenth and early eighteenth centuries there were fundamental changes in the English legal system as a whole, including not only its constitutional aspects but also its criminal and civil aspects—indeed, what I would call a modernization of the English common law; and that these changes were generated not only from within the law but also, and more important, from within the entire political, economic, and social upheaval of the time.

In the sixteenth century there had been, indeed, important developments in English law, including the law applicable in the older courts of King's Bench, Common Pleas, and Exchequer. These courts had existed since the twelfth century; they had jurisdiction chiefly over serious crimes ("felonies") (though not over treason) and over civil disputes involving freehold land. Their civil procedure was characterized by an elaborate process of pleadings, designed to reach an issue of fact that could be presented to a petty jury of neighbors for decision "Yes," or "No," based on the previous knowledge of the jurors. In criminal procedure, indictment was by grand jury and conviction or acquittal was, once again, by a petty jury that, prior to any trial, had informed itself of the guilt or innocence of the accused.

Wisconsin Law Review (1974): 428-65; M. Cotterell, "Interregnum Law Reform: The Hale Commission of 1652," *English Historical Review* 83 (1968): 689-704; G.B. Nourse, "Law Reform Under the Law of England," *University of Toronto Quarterly* 10 (1941): 469-81 .

[32] T.F.T. Plucknett, "Bonham's Case and Judicial Review," *Harvard Law Review* 40 (1936): 30.

This archaic procedure was subjected to the same vigorous critique in sixteenth century England as the Schoeffen procedure in sixteenth century Germany. As in Germany, so in England, many called for a rationalization and systematization of the law. In fact the prerogative courts of the Tudor-Stuart kings operated on quite different principles from those of the common-law courts. None of them—including the Court of Star Chamber, the Court of High Commission, the Court of Requests, the High Court of Admiralty, and others—used the common-law system of pleadings in civil cases or of indictment in criminal cases, and none of them used the jury method of decision. Nor did the Chancery, which had older credentials but which in many ways had become like the prerogative courts. All of these non-common-law courts used a system of interrogation of parties and of witnesses by the court, with written depositions under oath; all of them were in the "civilian (as it later came to be called)—actually, it was the canonist procedural—tradition.

Under the pressure of competition from the prerogative courts and from Chancery, the older common law courts gradually began to reform their procedure and to expand their jurisdiction. This was a very slow process, chiefly because the common law courts owed their very survival to the fact that by their antiquity they lent a legitimacy to Tudor justice that it might otherwise not have had. By declaring royal supremacy over the church in England, Henry VIII had cut English law adrift from its moorings in the Church of Rome and had anchored it instead to the supreme political authority of the state. The shock of this break with the past was somewhat softened by the perpetuation of the older royal courts, with their older, more popular, less learned procedures. Consequently, those older courts were reluctant to change those procedures; when they did change them they usually sought justification in the past. Hence there slowly emerged in the sixteenth century an increasing emphasis on precedent as a justification for both continuity and change.

In the sixteenth and especially in the first decades of the seventeenth century, the common law judges began to invoke precedent in order to control the rival courts and to limit their jurisdiction; this eventually brought them—and especially the Chief Justice of the King's Bench, Sir Edward Coke—into direct conflict with the king himself. Coke's historicism eventually became an important part of the ideology of the English Revolution. The radical Puritan John Lilburne used to go into the House of Commons in the 1640's with the Bible in one hand and Coke's Institutes in the other.

The abolition of the prerogative courts by the Puritan-led Parliament in 1641 signified an enormous change in English law. On the one hand, it meant the elimination of both the substantive and the procedural law of those courts and, on the other hand, it stimulated radical changes in the substance and procedure of the common law that was now made applicable to cases previously decided in those courts.

Thus the common law courts acquired exclusive jurisdiction over criminal cases, with right of trial by jury for all serious offenses. This meant the end of the inquisitorial system as it had been practiced in the Court of Star Chamber, the Court of High Commission, and in criminal cases in Admiralty, Chancery, and other courts. The notorious ex officio oath, under which a mere suspect could be required to swear to answer truthfully any questions that might be put to him by the investigator, and against which the common law courts had sometimes inveighed without much effect, now disappeared from English jurisprudence. Preliminary investigation of crimes was henceforth controlled partly by the writ of habeas corpus, which was considerably expanded and finally, in 1679, made the subject of a comprehensive statute; and partly by bail, which was also modernized by statute. Excessive fines were condemned, as were cruel and unusual punishments. The privilege against self-incrimination appeared for the first time. Torture was eliminated from English criminal procedure.

Also the nature of the jury trial changed. Previously, the jury had been an active investigative body, which was supposed to find out the guilt or innocence of the accused in advance and then merely to report its verdict when summoned by the court; now it became a passive body, which, knowing nothing of the crime in advance, was supposed to listen to evidence presented at trial. A system of more rational proofs, which in England had previously existed only in the ecclesiastical courts, the Chancellor's court, and the prerogative courts, was now introduced in a new form into jury trials in the common law courts. There appeared first the right and then the duty of witnesses to testify in the common law courts. The common law courts took over the contempt power of the ecclesiastical courts, Chancery, and the prerogative courts. The distinction between fact and law was sharpened, and the jury was given considerable independence in determining questions of fact at the same time that it was subjected to new forms of judicial supervision in matters of law.

These developments also affected civil procedure at common law, since jury trial was used there as well. In civil cases written pleadings were introduced, and witnesses were subjected to examination and cross-examination by counsel for the parties. (In criminal cases, counsel for the accused was not allowed until 1695, and then only in cases of treason; it was not until 1836 that counsel for the accused was allowed in cases of felonies.) Also the language of court reports, which previously had been Law-French, was shifted to English.

In addition, civil law was affected by the transformation of the forms of action. By an abundant use of fictions, the action of ejectment was transformed into an action to try title to land, the action of trover was transformed into an action to try title to chattels, the action of special assumpsit was transformed into an action for breach of contract, and the action of general assumpsit was transformed into an action for unjust enrichment. Thus the old forms were retained, but their functions were modernized.

Of critical importance in these developments was the fact that after 1640 the courts of common law inherited the vast jurisdiction of the prerogative courts. Prior thereto, the common law courts were concerned, in criminal law, principally with felonies and, in civil law, principally with rights in land. Now they had to be concerned with the entire range of criminal and civil causes; even those matters that continued to fall within the remaining jurisdiction of Chancery, Admiralty, and the ecclesiastical courts were now for the first time subjected to the regulation of the common law courts, which had the final say in the matter of jurisdiction.

One may speak, indeed, in this context, of a certain nationalization of English law. Mercantile law, for example, which had been applied in the sixteenth and early seventeenth centuries in the courts of Admiralty and Chancery, with their flourishing commercial jurisdiction, embodied many rules of canon law and Roman law that were accepted by merchants throughout Europe. These now passed over into the common law, at first in the form of commercial custom declared by juries of merchants and eventually by integration into the substantive common law itself.

Also the common law courts inherited some of the laws of morality that had been developed previously in the ecclesiastical and other courts. Thus in the famous case of the King against Sir Charles Sidley, decided in 1664, Sir Charles was indicted for "having shown his nude body in a balcony in Covent Garden to a great multitude of people, and had said and done certain things to the great scandal of Christianity." The Court of King's Bench took jurisdiction, stating that "since at this time there is no longer a Star Chamber . . . this Court is the *custos morum* ["guardian of morals"] of all the subjects of the King, and it is now high time to punish such profane actions done against all modesty. . . ." The Court stated further that since the defendant was "a gentleman of a very old family (of the county of Kent) and his estate was encumbered (not intending his ruin but in order to reform him)"—he was to be fined 2000 marks and imprisoned for a week and placed on good behavior for three years.[33]

Two generations later, the common law courts also succeeded to the jurisdiction of the ecclesiastical courts over the crime of obscenity.

In addition to such important changes in jurisdiction and procedure, with their tendency toward unification of English law under the supremacy of the courts of King's Bench and Common Pleas, a new technique of precedent was gradually introduced. I have mentioned the ideological need for a doctrine of precedent that would enable the common law to adduce the authority of the past for adaptation of its rules to new circumstances. In the latter seventeenth century and thereafter, as it became increasingly important to rationalize and systematize the common law, the earlier historicism was supplemented by a sophisticated technique of precedent. Previous decisions were subjected to a close analysis, with a distinction made between dictum and holding. This meant much greater predictability of results. Holdings in cases came to have a function somewhat similar to that of codified rules. A science of reasoning by analogy of cases came to be developed.

There was also a rationalization of common law rules concerning property and contract. I have referred to the transformation of older forms of action to serve the functions of trying title to land (ejectment) and chattels (trover). The device of the "strict settlement" was invented to permit landed gentry to make effective arrangements, despite the rule against perpetuities, to keep land in the same family for many generations.

Also this was the period when it was established that a bargained exchange was binding and actionable on breach, regardless of the absence of fault. In the famous case of Paradine and Jane, decided in 1648, at the height of the Puritan Revolution, a lessor sued a lessee for nonpayment of rent. The tenant defended on the ground that due to the occupation of the leased premises by Prince Rupert's army, it was impossible for him to enjoy the benefit of his contract and he therefore should be excused from liability. He cited canon law, civil (i.e. Roman) law, military law, moral law, the law of reason, the law of nature, and the law of nations. The court held that by the common law of England a lessee for years is liable for the rent, even though the land be impossible to occupy.[34] This was an early—perhaps the earliest—authoritative formulation of the principle of strict liability for breach of contract. The court said that where a duty or charge is created by law, the party will be excused if he is not at fault, "but when the party by his own

---

[33] LeRoy v. Sir Charles Sidley, 1 Sid. 168, *English Reports* 82 (1664): 1036 .

[34] Paradine and Jane, Style 47, 82 *English Reports* 519 (1647); also reported in Aleyn 26, 82 *English Reports* 897.

contract creates a duty or charge upon himself he is bound to make it good, if he may, notwithstanding any accident or inevitable necessity, because he might have provided against it by his contract."

Law AND Belief in the English Revolution.—We come back once again to the word "and": law "and" belief, law "and" revolution. I have indicated certain revolutionary changes that took place in the English belief system after 1640; I have also indicated certain revolutionary changes that took place in the English legal system in roughly the same period. But what is the connection between the two sets of changes?

Some external connections are obvious. Puritanism was undoubtedly the spark which ignited the Civil War, which in turn led eventually, after many upheavals, to the victory of Parliament over the Crown and of the common law courts over its rivals. The Puritans in seventeenth century England—like the Lutherans in sixteenth century Germany, the Jacobins in eighteenth century France, and the Bolsheviks in twentieth century Russia—provided not only the zeal but also the theory and the vision that were needed to change radically the political, the constitutional, and ultimately the prevailing legal system. This "but for" causal connection between Puritanism and English constitutional law is not without importance, and it does not deserve to be ignored, as it often has been in the conventional historiography. All our modern Western legal systems, including the English, have their origins in violent revolutions, which in turn have their origins in radical ideologies.

We are looking, however, for more intimate connections between belief systems and legal systems. Do seventeenth century English religious beliefs help to explain why England opted for Parliamentary supremacy as against royal supremacy, for the common law as against rival systems, for jury trial as against trial by professional judges, for the adversary system of proof as against the inquisitorial system, for the doctrine of precedent as against systematization by codes, for strict liability for breach of contract as against contractual liability based on fault? In other words, is English law rooted in the Puritan Revolution merely in a chronological sense or is it rooted in it in the sense that it derives nourishment from it?

I have already suggested some positive connections of this kind. Calvinist theology itself favored aristocratic government over monarchical and advocated the God-given right and duty of lower magistrates to resist tyrants. These and other Calvinist teachings were invoked to support limitations placed on the English monarchy by the Long Parliament in 1640-1642 and during the Civil War that followed, the subjection of the monarchy to Parliament in the period after its restoration in 1660, and, finally, in 1688, the forced abdication of the monarch and his replacement by a new dynasty subject to the severe restrictions placed on it by the Bill of Rights of 1689. The sixteenth century Lutheran and Anglican conception of the prince as the bearer of the religious mission to be the supreme governor of the earthly kingdom gave way to the Calvinist conception that the supreme duty of government is borne by the "magistracy," which ultimately meant, in England, the landed gentry, especially as they were represented in Parliament. Locke's theories of social contract and of government by consent of the governed, expounded in his *Two Treatises of Government*, published in 1689-90 as a justification of the Parliamentary system as established by the Glorious Revolution, were based essentially on liberal Calvinist doctrine. Underlying Locke's theory was the Calvinist emphasis on man's inherent selfishness. It was this that required the reciprocal limitations on power—on the power of subjects as well as on the power of rulers—that are implicit in the concept of a contract.[35]

The Calvinist doctrine of original sin also supported the idea of a written constitution, which in effect embodied the social contract and made it, by virtue of the writing, more difficult to break. In 1649, a written constitution called the "Agreement of the People," had been proposed but not adopted, and in 1653 a written constitution, called the "Instrument of Government," had been adopted—the first national written constitution in history. It was, however, wholly ineffective against Cromwell's dictatorship. Such experiments were not repeated after the Restoration. Nevertheless, they bore fruit in the Bill of Rights of 1689 and in the acceptance of that document, together with Magna Carta, the Petition of Right of 1628, and other written texts, as constituent parts of England's "unwritten" constitution. It is true that the theory of an "unwritten"—one might better call it a "half-written"—constitution left the way open to the acceptance of a parallel theory of absolute Parliamentary power. Parliament, some said, could, if it wished, enact a law turning all men into women. Fortunately, the matter remained hypothetical. In theory, the omnicompetence of Parliament was qualified by its duty to preserve the liberties of the subject and to respect the requirements of natural

---

[35] "Locke's political views were little more than a distillation of concepts that had long been current coin in Calvinist political theory." Winthrop S. Hudson, *Religion in America: An Historical Account of the Development of American Political Religious Life*, 3rd ed. (New York, 1981), 94. See also id., "John Locke: Heir of Puritan Political Theorists," in George L. Hunt, ed., *Calvinism and the Political Order* (Philadelphia, PA, 1965), 108-29, where many of Locke's ideas are traced to the devout Presbyterian Samuel Rutherford, author of *Lex, Rex* (1644). For an account of Locke's Puritan upbringing and the liberal character of his Calvinist background, see Foster, *Private Papers*, 153-78; Lang, "The Reformation and Natural Law," 86ff.

justice. In practice, Parliament rarely invoked a competence to wield unlimited power. (When it did so with respect to the American colonies, they made their own Revolution.)

In tracing such basic constitutional principles to Calvinism, one must bear in mind not only Calvinist doctrine but also Calvinist practice. Aristocracy—or aristocracy tempered with democracy—had not only been advocated by Calvin as the best form of government; it had also been introduced into the ecclesiastical polity. Calvinist churches were governed by elected ministers and lay elders. Similarly, the Calvinist doctrine of social contract was introduced into practice in Geneva, where all citizens were summoned in groups to accept the "covenant" between God and the church, to take an oath to obey the Ten Commandments, and to swear loyalty to the city.[36]

Their experience, and not only their theory, was also of crucial importance in the development by the Puritans of constitutional principles of civil rights—particularly their experience in openly disobeying, on grounds of Christian conscience, the oppressive laws of the Tudor-Stuart monarchy. Many Puritans had refused to take the ex officio oath as required by the Court of High Commission under Archbishop Laud: such an oath, they said, which would require them to swear, in advance of any charges made, to answer truthfully any question that might be asked, violated their sacred obligation, based on the Bible, not to swear oaths; and furthermore, it violated the English common law. Puritans also resorted to the writ of habeas corpus to challenge the jurisdiction of courts established by the king on the basis of his own prerogative—the Court of Star Chamber, the Court of High Commission, and others; and when they came to power they abolished such "prerogative" courts. They asserted a right to refuse to testify against themselves in criminal proceedings, and a right not to be prosecuted for an act that had not previously been declared to be criminal. They objected to excessive bail, excessive fines, cruel and unusual punishments, the presumption of guilt, the subjection of the jury to the will of the judge, royal interference in adjudication, and torture. They objected to these on principle: first, that they were against the will of God; second, that they violated "the ancient constitution," the

---

[36] Cf. McNeill, *History and Character*, 135-42. In Puritan New England as well, Roscoe Pound comments, "covenants and compacts were the basis of all community life, political and religious." Roscoe Pound, "Puritanism and the Common Law," *American Law Review* 15 (1911): 810, 819.

common law of former times—that is, before the Tudor-Stuart monarchy had assumed supremacy over the church.[37]

Men like John Hampden, John Lilburne, Walter Udall, William Penn, and thousands of other Puritans (I use the name in its broadest sense) gave England—and ultimately America—civil rights by being willing, on grounds of Christian conscience, to go to prison for them. Later, a Puritan-led Parliament enacted legislation guaranteeing many of the rights on which Puritans had previously insisted in vain. Still later, Parliaments not led by Puritans reaffirmed and added to such legislation.

It may be somewhat less easy to discern religious influences in the seventeenth century tendency to rationalize the common-law rules of property and contract. Here major roles were played by political and economic considerations as well as by the new scientific outlook of the seventeenth century. There was a drive toward security of property rights and of contractual transactions; there was a drive toward rationality, in the sense of calculability or predictability.

Puritanism also played a role. Efforts to rationalize the English common law, as well as to secure property and contract rights, were connected with the Puritan emphasis on order and discipline: "God being the God of order and not of confusion hath Commanded in his word and put man into a Capasitie in some measure to observe and bee guided by good and wholsome lawes...."[38] "Discipline," Calvin had said, "serves as the sinews [of the church] through which the members of the body hold together, each in its own place."[39] Developments in the law of contract and property were also connected with the Calvinist emphasis on voluntary action, the act of will, in the service of God, together with God's faithfulness in response. Calvinists taught that there were two covenants, one between God and the community, including the ruler and the people as parties, the other between the ruler and the people. These covenants were seen in terms of the same values of rationality, predictability, and security that were emphasized in the law of property and contract.

Finally, there were important connections between Puritan casuistry and Puritan historicism, on the one hand, and the seventeenth century English lawyer's emphasis on analogy of cases and on historical precedent.

---

[37] Cf. J. G. A. Pocock, *The Ancient Consititution and the Feudal Law: A Study of English Historical Thought in the Seventeenth Century* (Cambridge, MA, 1957).

[38] "The Address to the General Laws of New Plymouth" (1658), in David Pulsifer, ed., *Records of the Colony of New Plymouth Laws, 1623-82* (1861), 11: 72 .

[39] Calvin, *Institutes,* bk. 4, ch. 12, para 1.

To stress these links between seventeenth century English legal developments and Puritanism is not to ignore their links also with Anglicanism, including not only those features of Anglicanism which it shared with Puritanism but also those features which contrasted with Puritanism.[40] For example, the historicism of the seventeenth century English common lawyers, exemplified above all in the writings of Sir Edward Coke and in his judgments when on the bench, is much more akin to the historicism of Bishop Hooker and of the Church of England than to that of Calvin and his English followers. The English Puritans followed Calvin in looking first to Biblical history and Biblical examples. They added, however, a vision of England as an "elect nation" destined to fulfill God's plan of history. Anglican historicism—developed only partly in response to Puritanism—taught the fiction of a continuously developing Anglican church, always fundamentally the same, always English, never really Roman, "comprehensive" enough to embrace widely differing intellectual approaches, founded not on doctrinal consistency but on historical continuity. This, of course, was the kind of historicism adopted ultimately by the English common law.

Also the language and style of seventeenth century English common law was more similar to that of the Book of Common Prayer than to that of Calvin's Institutes or the English Puritan tracts. Indeed, Calvinist doctrine was congenial to codification of law, and it was no accident that in the Puritan period of the English Revolution there were great pressures toward codification of the English common law. Ultimately, however, English law adopted a quite different mode of systematization, namely, systematization by forms of action and by precedent—one that was controlled primarily by the judiciary rather than by the university professors. English Puritans were eventually able to find a good deal in their religious upbringing to support a judge-made systematization of the law, even though they might have found even more to support codification. The Anglican outlook, however, would have found codification quite uncongenial.

The interconnection between the transformation of the English system of law and the transformation of the English system of beliefs found vivid expression in the life and work of Matthew Hale, who, like the sixteenth century German von Schwarzenberg, represented in his own person both the legal genius and the religious genius of his time.

Holdsworth has called Hale a "consummate master of English law," "easily the greatest English lawyer of his day," "the first of our great modern

---

[40] For comparison and contrast of Anglican and Puritan theology and ideology, see Herschel Baker, *The Wars of Truth* (Gloucester, MA, 1969), chap. 5; John F. New, *Puritan and Anglican* (Stanford, CA, 1964).

common lawyers."[41] Born in 1609, he had already distinguished himself at the bar when the Puritans seized power in 1641. In 1652 he headed an important law reform committee appointed by Parliament, known as the Hale Commission, which proposed fundamental changes in English law. From 1653 to 1657 he was judge of the Court of Common Pleas. In 1660, with the return of Charles II, Hale became Chief Baron of the Exchequer and in 1671 Chief Justice of the King's Bench, which he remained until just before his death in 1676. His reputation as a lawyer rested not only on his great ability in these practical roles but also, and even more, on his scholarship. He was a master of constitutional and legal history and the author of the first history of English law ever written.[42] His writings of English criminal and civil law represent the first systematic studies in those fields.[43] Moreover, he was a serious student of the Roman law and also wrote tracts in the fields of mathematics, natural science, philosophy, and theology.[44]

Hale's career as a lawyer and legal scholar cannot be divorced from his deep religious convictions. Raised a Puritan, he retained a passion for piety, order, discipline, and moral responsibility. Yet he was also loyal to the Church of England. He wrote a number of meditational and devotional tracts which reflected his adherence to both Calvinism and Anglicanism. In the

---

[41] William S. Holdsworth, *History of English Law* (London, 1927), 6: 581. The account of Hale's life and work given in the text is drawn chiefly from ibid., 6: 574-95 and from E. Heward, *Matthew Hale* (London, 1972). See also David E.C. Yale, *Hale as a Legal Historian* (London, 1976).

[42] Hale's *History of the Common Law* was first published in 1713. None of Hale's voluminous legal writings were published in his lifetime, though many of them circulated widely in manuscript.

[43] Hale's *History of the Crown*, first published in 1736, was not a history but a textbook on criminal law and procedure dealing with capital crimes. Heward writes: "This book is a tour de force. It is systematic and detailed. . . . Hale succeeded in reducing the mass of material to a coherent account of the criminal law relating to capital offenses. . . ." Heward, *Matthew Hale*, 133-134.

Hale's *Analysis of the Law* divides the law into two main divisions, namely, civil law and criminal law, but itself deals only with civil matters, which it divides into civil rights or interests, wrongs or injuries related to those wrongs. Civil rights are subdivided in the Romanist style into rights of persons and rights of things.

[44] Hale admired Roman law and, in the words of his contemporary biographer, Burnet, "lamented much that it was so little studied in England." Quoted in Heward, *Matthew Hale*, 26. Hale's systematization of English law was greatly influenced by Romanist legal science as it had developed in the West since the late eleventh century. However, Hale did not write any tracts of Roman law. His systematization of English law was also greatly influenced by his knowledge of the exact and natural sciences, on which he did write several long tracts. He was well acquainted with Boyle and Newton and with some of the founders of the Royal Society of London. Three of his discourses on religion were published after his death by his friend the Puritan minister, Richard Baxter. They are summarized in Heward, *Matthew Hale*, 127-128.

period of Puritan ascendancy, he remained a royalist and advised Strafford, Bramston, Laud, and other persons accused by the Long Parliament, and when Charles I was tried for treason by a special court, the so-called High Court of Justice, Hale advised him to plead to the jurisdiction. Nevertheless, he was able conscientiously to serve under Oliver Cromwell (though he refused to be reappointed to the Court of Common Pleas in 1658 by Oliver's son and successor Richard), and after the restoration of the Monarchy, which Hale had helped to facilitate, he befriended and defended Protestant Non-Conformists with the same openness and integrity with which he had formerly befriended and defended Anglican royalists.

Hale was driven by a deep Christian faith to live and to work without deceit, without greed for money or power, without injustice; he represented in his person the new "public spirit" which the English Revolution put forward as a principal basis of legitimacy.[45] At the bar, Hale refused to take cases that he considered to be unjust; also he would often forego fees in order himself to arbitrate disputes that came to him. As a judge, he would subordinate strict law to equity or else use his mastery of the techniques and subtleties of strict law to achieve a result dictated by conscience. He refused the gifts that were customarily offered by persons seeking favors or else, if it was necessary to accept them, he would require that they be in the form of money, which he then gave to the poor. His extraordinary generosity was

---

[45] As "public opinion" became a principal source of the legitimacy of governmental authority in France from the time of the French Revolution, so "public spirit" was a principal source of the legitimacy of governmental authority in England from the time of the English Revolution of the seventeenth century. Public spirit included not only civic zeal but also loyalty to tradition as well as other "aristocratic" virtues. It was defined by de Tocqueville in the early nineteenth century as including "the affections of a man with his birthplace . . . united with a taste for ancient customs and a reverence for traditions of the past, . . . patriotism sometimes simulated by religous enthusiasm." Alexis de Tocqueville, *Democracy in America*, ed. Phillips Bradley (New York, 1945), 274. The phrase itself goes back to 1654, when Whitlock wrote: "Persons with Publike Spirits, are of a goodnesse Angelicall." Quoted in *Oxford English Dictionary* (Oxford, 1933), under heading "Public spirit." Lecky characterizes the late seventeenth and eighteenth centuries in England as an age of public spirit; although public spirit diminished substantially in the middle of the eighteenth century, he writes, it nevertheless remained stronger than in other countries of Europe. William E.H. Lecky, *England in the Eighteenth Century* (London, 1892), 1: 188-98, 489-90, 505-12. In the early 1700s the coffee houses in London were called "the School of Publick Spirit, where every Man . . . learns the most hearty contempt of his own Personal Sordid Interest . . . and devotes himself to . . . his Country. . . ." *Daily Gazeteer, London*, (July 4, 1737). A pamphleteer in London in 1714 sharply criticized the Whigs for neglecting public spirit and being "ready to gratifie their Ambition and Revenge by all desperate Methods; wholly alienated from Truth, Law, Religion, Mercy, Conscience, or Honour." Pamphlet entitled *The Publick Sprit of the Whigs* (London, 1714) (available in Widener Library, Harvard University).

made apparent by the relatively small estate that he left when he died. "His dread of ostentation and vanity led him to go so shabbily clothed that even [his close friend the Puritan minister Richard] Baxter remonstrated with him."[46] In Holdsworth's words, "Hale was a man of a really saintly character, who, by his genuine goodness, attracted the affection [not only of those who knew him well but also] of all those with whom he came into merely passing contact."[47]

In combining impeccable moral and personal qualities with superb professional skills and intellectual powers, Hale, like Schwarzenberg before him, inevitably made a strong impact on his contemporaries. Even more important, in both cases, was the nature of the impact. Hale, like Schwarzenberg, helped to bring about fundamental changes in the pre-existing legal system that were responsive to fundamental changes that were taking place at the same time in the belief system of the society. Hale's deepest beliefs, which were characteristic of the beliefs of his time, not only influenced his own personal and professional life but also found expression in the substantive contributions which he made to the development of English law.

Many examples can be given of specific legal contributions that reflected Hale's religious outlook. As a judge, he set an example of scrupulous fairness to prisoners in criminal cases. He once persuaded a jury, with some difficulty, to acquit a man who had stolen a loaf of bread because he was starving. He shared the overriding Puritan concern with poor relief; his "Discourse Touching Provision for the Poor," written in 1659, contained a detailed plan for providing work for the poor, anticipating reforms that were only carried out a century-and-a-half later. On the other hand, he also shared the Puritan horror of witchcraft and in 1664 he imposed the death penalty, as provided by statute, on two women found by the jury to be guilty of bewitching certain children.[48]

More important than these and other specific contributions which Hale made as a judge and as an advocate of law reform was his more general contribution to the very conception of law. Hale, above all in his writings, introduced a systematization of English law based primarily on the concept of its historical development. This historical jurisprudence had been nourished initially in his university days at Oxford, where he had come under the influence of the great Puritan legal historian John Selden. Living in the prerevolutionary period of struggle between the common law courts and the prerogative courts, Selden had emphasized the medieval tradition of limitations upon

---

[46] Holdsworth, *History*, 6: 578.

[47] Ibid., 579. Holdsworth compares Hale's character to that of Sir Thomas More.

[48] See Heward, *Matthew Hale*, 71-86, and Holdsworth, *History*, 6: 578-79.

the royal prerogative. Living in the postrevolutionary period, Hale emphasized not only the medieval roots of the English legal tradition but also its
capacity to evolve and to adapt itself to new needs. Laws must change with
the times, he wrote, or they will lose their usefulness.[49]

Hale also went far beyond Selden in deriving from the evolution of the
English legal tradition a systematization of rules, principles, concepts, and
standards. Here he was helped both by his deep knowledge of Roman law and
by his studies of natural science.

Hale's biographer, Burnet, reports that some persons once said to Hale
that they "looked on the common law as a study that could not be brought
into a scheme, nor formed into a rational science, by reason of the indigest-
edness of it, and the multiplicity of cases in it." Hale's reply was decisive. He
"was not of their mind," he said; and he drew on a large sheet of paper "a
scheme of the whole order and parts of it . . . to the great satisfaction of those
to whom he sent it."[50]

Hale proved by his own example that English common law was not a
wilderness of single instances, but an evolving system which he, at least,
could grasp as an integrated whole.

That Hale's historical systematization of English law was rooted in his
religious convictions, both Puritan and Anglican, may be demonstrated by
contrasting it with other methods of systematization of law. Hale did not
attempt to show that English law is to be understood and tested primarily by
reference to divine law and natural law, as Roman Catholic jurisprudence
maintained. Nor did he attempt to show that English law is to be understood
and tested by justice and the common weal, as taught in Schwarzenberg's
Lutheran jurisprudence. Hale asserted, of course, the validity of divine law
and natural law, which he equated with Christian revelation and the Christian
religion, respectively; and he asserted the claims of justice and utility. But he
also asserted the independent validity of English law as such, which evolved
in the first instance through experience, through custom and usage, and
which was suited to the character of the English people.

Hale's historical jurisprudence may be contrasted not only with Roman
Catholic and Lutheran legal thought but also with the rationalistic and

---

[49] Hale wrote: "The matter changeth the custom; the contracts the commerce; the
dispositions educations tempers of men and societies change in a long tract of time; and so
must their lawes in some measure be changed, or they will not be usefull for their state and
condition." Quoted in Holdsworth, *History*, 6: 593. Hale's *Considerations Touching the
Amendment and Alteration of Laws* is a systematic analysis of policies and techniques of law
reform. It is digested in Heward, *Matthew Hale*, 156-166.

[50] Quoted in Holdsworth, *History*, 6: 584.

individualistic legal thought that was characteristic of the eighteenth century Enlightenment and of the period following the French Revolution.

The links between Hale's jurisprudence and his religious beliefs are to be found above all in his emphasis on the God-given historicity of the English people and of their legal institutions. Hale denounced the doctrine of sovereignty proclaimed by his contemporary, Thomas Hobbes; Hobbes's "speculations" concerning the unlimited power of the sovereign to repeal and alter laws or to take the property of his subjects as he pleases, Hale stated, are contradicted in England by the existence of laws and customs that bind the sovereign. "The laws and customs of the kingdom are facts which exist," he wrote in answer to Hobbes.[51] That is, they are historical facts, providential facts, and therefore superior to any sovereignty, any government. By the same token they formed, for Hale, a *system* of facts whose interrelationships with each other could be studied scientifically.

The belief that God has providentially revealed himself in the ongoing history of the English common law is the Puritan and Anglican legacy of the seventeenth century English Revolution to Western jurisprudence.

III. *The Enlightenment, the French Revolution, and the Napoleonic Codes*

France in 1789 was the largest country of Europe, with some twenty-five million inhabitants—three times more than in England. It was divided administratively into thirty-five provinces, thirty-eight military districts, one-hundred-and-forty-two bishoprics, and innumerable local frontiers where tolls and customs duties were imposed on travelers. These units were governed generally by local patrician oligarchies, whether of the higher clergy or of the nobility or both. In addition to the clergy and nobility, which were characterized as the First and Second Estates, respectively, there was a flourishing Third Estate consisting of officials, lawyers, teachers, merchants, artisans, well-to-do farmers, and others.

France was an autocracy. The king was considered to have absolute authority; that is, he was the supreme legislator, judge, and executor of the laws, and was himself "absolved" from obedience to them. All officials, central and local, exercised their authority in his name and as his agents.

There were two symbolic limitations on royal power. The appellate courts, called Parlements, of which there were thirteen, consisted of judges who were noble either by birth or by office, whose families had purchased their judicial office and were therefore irremovable by the king; the

---

[51] Quoted in Heward, *Matthew Hale*, 140. The text of Hale's "Reflections on Hobbes' Dialogue of the Law" may be found in the appendix to Holdsworth, *History*, 5: 500.

Parlements claimed the right to advise the king on the limits of his power—they were custodians of the medieval tradition of constitutionalism, although in fact they had no effective means of checking royal abuses. The second symbolic limitation on the king's power was the historical institution of the Estates General, the assembly of representatives of the three estates, which had power to veto royal taxes and to advise the king. This was an even less effective protection against royal abuses, since it could only meet at the call of the king and the king had not called it into existence since 1614.

Royal government, including royal military activity, was carried on at the king's private expense, except that he could levy taxes within limits set by tradition. The church was not taxed at all, though it owned a substantial part of the land of France. The abundant privileges of the aristocracy also included exemptions from various taxes. King Louis XVI, who had come to the throne in 1774, financed French assistance to the American Revolution largely by extravagant borrowing. By 1787 the servicing of the royal debt had driven the crown to the verge of bankruptcy. The aristocracy would not give up its privileges. Meanwhile there were hunger riots and peasant revolts. The Parlements had already been moved on several occasions to advise the king that he was exceeding the limits of his powers. In 1788, Necker, recalled as Minister of Finance by popular demand, persuaded the king to allow him to call for elections and to convene the Estates General in order to raise money.

The Estates General met at Versailles in May 1789—for the first time in 175 years! There was a sharp conflict between the deputies of the Third Estate and those of the other two estates. In June the Third Estate took the title of National Assembly and assumed full sovereign powers. The king took the side of the other two estates. On July 14 a crowd stormed the royal prison, the Bastille; this act was immediately recognized as a revolution—indeed as "the" Revolution. It symbolized for all Europe the fall of absolute monarchy. The king accepted representatives of the Third Estate as rulers of the city of Paris. The ecclesiastical hierarchy and the nobility now stepped forward to renounce their privileges—solemnly and in detail ("the renunciations"). Throughout France, the old administrative and judicial authorities dissolved.

In August 1789 the National Assembly adopted a Declaration of the Rights of Man and Citizen, which proclaimed civil rights and civil liberties. Its first article expressed a basic ideal of the Revolution: "Men are born and remain free and equal in rights. Social distinctions can only be based on general utility." Article 3 stated: "The source of all sovereignty resides essentially in the nation. . ." A wholesale reorganization of the country's administrative structure was introduced. The entire legal system was reformed.

In the decade after 1789 France was in a constant state of turmoil. The various factions which had helped to bring on the Revolution fought viciously among themselves. Written constitutions came and went—ten different ones between 1789 and 1815. Meanwhile there was the constant threat that the royalists would regain power, backed by the Roman Catholic hierarchy and by various foreign powers. The list of leaders executed or murdered under successive Revolutionary regimes included King Louis XVI, Marie-Antoinette, Marat, Danton, Robespierre—in all, there were over 14,000 victims of the Terror.

Various Revolutionary governments launched a series of wars—most of them disastrous—against Austria, Prussia, Belgium, the Rhineland, Savoy, Nice, England, Holland, Italy, Switzerland, Malta, Egypt. A young military commander from Corsica, Napoleon Bonaparte, became a hero in some of these campaigns. The people of France were ready for a dictatorship, and in 1799 Napoleon seized power. He presented himself as the fulfillment of the spirit of 1798. One might call him the Stalin of the French Revolution.

Wherever Napoleon's armies went in Europe they carried with them something of the French Revolution and especially its slogans of liberation from aristocratic privileges. Even after the final defeat of Napoleon in 1815 and the restoration of the Bourbon dynasty, it was impossible to turn the clock back to the *ancien régime*. The permanent achievements of the French Revolution were finally established in 1830 when the Chamber of Deputies invited Louis Phillipe, Duke of Orleans, to assume the throne as a constitutional monarch.

Thus the French Revolution may be dated not, as it often is, from 1789 to 1799 but from 1789 to 1830, just as the English Revolution may be dated from 1640 to 1689, and the German Revolution from 1517 to 1555.

The Belief System Embodied in the French Revolution; Deism.—The belief system embodied in the French Revolution—that is, the structure of ideas and attitudes reflected in the policies of the new regime—had its origin in the eighteenth century European movement called "the Enlightenment." Among the most famous French participants in this movement were (1) Montesquieu, for many years the presiding judge of the High Court of Bordeaux, whose book *The Spirit of the Laws*, written in 1748, remains a classic of modern social theory; (2) Voltaire, satirist, historian, man of letters and leading *philosophe*, who wrote his first play *Oedipus*, in 1718 and died in full vigor in 1778 at the age of 84; (3) Diderot, a man of universal knowledge, who put together the ideas of the Enlightenment in a huge set of volumes called the *Encyclopedia*; (4) Jean-Jacques Rousseau, whose *Confessions* made him the man of the age and whose *Social Contract*, published in 1762, was a principal source of inspiration for the revolutionary dictator Robespierre among countless others. A great many others could also be listed among the intellectual leaders of the mid-eighteenth century whose ideology became the ideology of the Revolution.[52]

Before describing the tenets of the Enlightenment, I should note that this was the first European belief system that was developed outside of any organized church by people who were for the most part not Christians in the conventional sense, and were, indeed, in many cases avowed anti-Christians. The new belief system was neither Calvinist nor Lutheran nor Roman Catholic—nor any combination of these. It built, to be sure, partly on the writings of seventeenth century English philosophers and scientists such as John Locke and Isaac Newton, who themselves were devout Christians; but it ignored their theology and built only on their secular writings, without regard to the fact that those writings were considered by their authors to be devoted solely to the "earthly kingdom," in which God was present but hidden.

The word "secular" takes on a new meaning when it is applied to the world-view of the eighteenth century *philosophes*. Prior to the sixteenth century political power in Roman Catholic Christendom was divided between the ecclesiastical and the secular "swords." In the sixteenth and seventeenth centuries the idea had become widespread that *all* political authority, including that wielded by the ecclesiastical hierarchy, is secular, "earthly," in contrast to the "heavenly realm" of Gospel and grace—whether conceived in Lutheran or in Calvinist terms. For the intellectual leaders of the eighteenth century Enlightenment, however, there was neither a "spiritual sword" nor a "heavenly realm." The earthly realm—the world of time—had indeed been created a long time ago by a "supreme artisan," or a Supreme Being, and had then been given its direction, its design, its purposes. But the God of Voltaire and Rousseau did not intervene in the nature that he had once created.

These religious tenets, called Deism, were an essential part of the belief system of the Enlightenment. Deism was founded, to be sure, on reason; it was a system of rational propositions based on observation of nature, including human nature. The source of reason was the intellectual capacity of every individual person; Deism had no church. Nevertheless, God was an essential

---

[52] For an account of the influence of the Enlightenment on the French Revolution, see Norman Hampson, *The Enlightenment* (Harmondsworth, 1968), esp. 251-83; D. Mornet, *Les origines intellectuelles de la revolution francaise* (Paris, 1954), esp. 469-477; Henri M. Peyre, "The Influence of Eighteenth Century Ideas on the French Revolution," *Journal of the History of Ideas* 10 (1949): 63; William F. Church, *The Influence of the Enlightenment on the French Revolution: Creative, Disastrous, or Inconclusive?* (Boston, 1964).

part of the Deist belief system. Reason, it was said, teaches every person who is willing to exercise it that the universe was created by God, and that according to God's design man should use his reason to do good and to avoid evil. Although they attacked traditional Christianity, most *philosophes* vigorously denied that they were atheists or pantheists. Voltaire, for example, criticized Spinoza for failing to recognize that there is a divine Providence which has made eyes to see, minds to reason. "How is it that [Spinoza] did not glance at these mechanisms," Voltaire asks, "these agents, each of which has its purpose, and investigate whether they do not prove the existence of a supreme artisan?"[53] "The whole philosophy of Newton," Voltaire wrote, "leads of necessity to the knowledge of a Supreme Being who created everything, arranged all things of his own free will."[54]

Thus the *philosophes*—in general—believed that there is a cosmic order, that it was created originally by the deity, and that it was designed to operate harmoniously for the benefit of mankind. They believed in what Jefferson, in the Declaration of Independence, called "the laws of Nature and of Nature's God." It was, in fact, their belief in the laws of Nature's God that led the *philosophes* to proclaim universal human happiness as the highest goal, and universal liberty, equality, and fraternity as the highest means of achieving that goal. Deism was a Christian heresy. As Carl Becker has put it, "[The *philosophes*] had put off the fear of God, but maintained a respectful attitude toward the Deity. They ridiculed the idea that the universe had been created in six days, but still believed it to be a beautifully articulated machine designed by the Supreme Being according to a rational plan as an abiding place for mankind. . . . They renounced the authority of church and Bible, but exhibited a naive faith in the authority of nature and reason. They scorned metaphysics, but were proud to be called philosophers."[55]

The political, economic, and social implications of the religion of Deism are apparent. Its individualism and its rationalism led inevitably to an emphasis on reform of existing conditions for the benefit of the majority of individuals living in a given society. It was utilitarian in both the popular and technical sense of that term; indeed, it was the young Beccaria who, in 1765, with Voltaire's endorsement, in proposing substantial reforms of criminal law, first coined the slogan of utilitarianism later adopted by Jeremy Bentham, "the greatest happiness of the greatest number."

---

[53] Cited in Hampson, *The Enlightenment*, 81.

[54] Ibid., 78.

[55] Carl L. Becker, *The Heavenly City of the Eighteenth Century Philosophers* (New Haven, CT, 1932), 30-31.

The *philosophes* of the French Enlightenment taught that the privileges of the aristocracy were not only unjust but also illogical—in other words, that the reasons hitherto given to justify them were false. This was an essential precondition of the Revolution.

The *philosophes* also provided major elements of the political program later adopted by leaders of the Revolution. Montesquieu's *Spirit of the Laws* had expounded the theory of separation of powers; he attributed this theory to the English system of government, but in fact he altered the English theory substantially by placing the functions of legislating, executing, and judging in three wholly separate compartments, with legislation supreme over the other two. This paved the way for the development of a theory of the judicial function as the objective, consistent, and logical application of statutory law to specific cases. Montesquieu had also taught that laws have the purpose of promoting individual liberty and economic equality; this, too, became part of the program of the Revolution.[56]

Rousseau may also be credited with providing major elements in the later political program of the Revolution. He taught that law should rectify inequalities that arise from natural differences among people. "For the very reason that the force of things always tends to destroy equality," he wrote, "the force of legislation must always tend to maintain it."[57] Rousseau, like other intellectual leaders of the Enlightenment, attacked specific aristocratic privileges. In his *Discourse on Inequality* he proposed that inheritances ought to be reduced by taxes, and that those who owned no land receive some.

In general, however, the intellectual leaders of the eighteenth century did not prophesy a Revolution such as that which broke out in 1789. They did not propose the overthrow of the monarchy. "In all France there were not ten of us who were republicans before 1789," wrote the Revolutionary lawyer Camille Desmoulins.[58]

The *philosophes* had not preached a revolution. They were reformers, not revolutionaries. They presented a critique of the existing regime, together with proposals for changing it, not for abolishing it. Their critique, and the philosophy that underlay it, became part of the belief system of those who later overthrew the regime and established a new one. Above all, the individualism of the Enlightenment and its rationalism—these two basic elements

---

[56] Charles Louis de Secondat Montesquieu, *Notes sur l'Angleterre* (Paris, 1729), 195. Cf. Montesquieu, *L'Esprit des lois, ou du rapport que les lois doivent avoir avec la constitution de chaque gouvernement, les moeurs, le climat, la religion, le commerce, etc.* (Paris, 1748), bk. 6.

[57] Jean J. Rousseau, *Contrat Social* (Amsterdam, 1762), bk. 2, chap. xi.

[58] Quoted in Peyre, "The Influence," 73. Peyre adds, "Furthermore, he [Desmoulins] was not one of those ten."

from whose combinations were derived its utilitarianism and its emphasis on liberty and equality—became fundamental principles of the Revolution. But the Revolution also added other elements that were only implicit, at most, in the Enlightenment philosophy. One such element was the belief in public opinion as the ultimate political authority. Another was nationalism.

The phrase "public opinion"—*l'opinion publique*—emerged in the 1780's in one of the leading salons of Paris, Necker's circle. This was after more than thirty years of intense agitation among the intellectuals of France, especially in the large cities. Ideas had fermented through salons, clubs, circles, and societies of all kinds; through pamphlets, tracts, periodicals, books; through the theater (Beaumarchais' *Marriage of Figaro*, for example, was an attack upon aristocratic privilege whose repercussions were enormous); through secondary education; through conversation.[59] Then in 1788 the public as a whole was invited—by Necker—to make suggestions of remedies for the great financial crisis of the government; the floodgates were opened, and the *cahiers de doléances* poured in—grievances of all kinds, proposals of all kinds. Now the circulation of ideas was extended beyond the intellectuals to professional people generally, tradesmen, artisans, indeed the entire middle class. Finally, King Louis XVI himself used the magic phrase: "[Let us] raise the results of public opinion," he said, "to the rank of laws, after they have submitted to ripe and profound examination."[60]

---

[59] Ibid., at 75-76; Hampson, *The Enlightenment*, 132-41.

[60] Louis made this statement in 1788 as an invitation to the public to contribute to the initial stages of drafting a criminal code. "All our subjects," Louis declared, "will be allowed to take part in the execution of the project [of the Criminal Code] with which we are occupied. . . ." Quoted in Paul Viollet, "French Law in the Age of the Revolution," in Adolphus W. Ward et al., eds., *The Cambridge Modern History* (Cambridge, 1902), 8: 744-45. See also E.J. Lowell, *The Eve of the French Revolution* (Boston, MA, 1892), 324. Lowell states: "In the decay of religious ideas, the Frenchmen of the Eighteenth century had set up a comparison independent of revelation. They had found it in public opinion. The sociable population of Paris was ready to accept the common voice as arbiter. . . . 'A halberd leads a kingdom', cried a courtier to Quesnay the economist. 'And who leads the halberd?' retorted the latter. 'Public opinion'."

On Rousseau's use of the phrase "public opinion" see Paul A. Palmer, "The Concept of Public Opinion in Political Theory," in *Essays in History and Political Theory in Honor of Charles Howard McIlwain* (Cambridge, MA, 1936), 235-237. Rousseau writes: "Just as the declaration of the general will is made by the law, the declaration of public judgment is made by the censorial tribunal. Public opinion is the sort of law of which the censor is the minister." Cited in ibid., 237. Palmer notes (ibid., 233) that the phrase "*opinio publica*" is found without the political connotation of public opinion in the writings of Marcus Tullius Cicero, *Ad Atticum*, bk. 6, i. 18 and in the writings of John of Salisbury, "The Statesman's Book of John of Salisbury," ed. John Dickenson (New York, 1927), 39, 130. Earlier uses of the term "opinion" in Pascal, Voltaire, Hobbes, and Locke carried a quite different connotation (as did Rousseau's "general will"). See also Wilhelm Bauer, "Public Opinion," in

Eventually the Revolution institutionalized the concept that government should be so organized as to require the maximum responsiveness to public opinion. The theoretical basis for such a political principle may be found in the Enlightenment view that society is an association of rational individuals; for if that is so, their shared opinions are the best indication of their needs. It was revolutionary experience, however, that brought this theory to fruition.

The element of nationalism was also more a product of the Revolution itself than of the Enlightenment as such. Most of the intellectual leaders of the Enlightenment had thought of themselves as Europeans. Rousseau, to be sure, had glorified the nation-state. He had attributed to the nation total sovereignty, and to the state the responsibility of inculcating in its citizens the redemptive virtues of simplicity and honesty and care for the common good. Similarly, the Abbé de Sieyes, in his famous revolutionary tract *The Third Estate—What It Is*, wrote that the nation exists before all and is the origin of all; "its will is always legal, it is the law itself." These doctrines are, indeed, as Jacob Talmon stressed, sources of twentieth century totalitarian democracy.[61] From an eighteenth century viewpoint, however, the glorification of the nation-state was only an indirect reflection of Enlightenment thought; more fundamentally, it was a product of the intense nationalism that was beginning to overcome Europe as belief in traditional Christianity began to decline.[62] But whatever the underlying causes may have been, it was the Revolution itself that put nationalism in the forefront of its belief system and of its domestic and foreign policies. Domestically, the Revolutionary government sought to unify France politically, administratively, and legally, as well as culturally. In foreign relations, the Revolutionary government mobilized a mass army to make war upon France's neighbors in order to secure what she now conceived to be her "natural boundaries."

Encyclopedia of the Social Sciences (New York, 1934); Bernard Fay, *Naissance d'un Monstre—l'Opinion Publique* (Paris, 1965); Hans Spier, "The Rise of Public Opinion," in Harold D. Lasswell et al., eds., *Propaganda and Communication in World History* (Honolulu, 1979), 147-167.

On the emergence of the modern meaning of "public opinion" in Necker's Circle, and the elaboration by him of a theory of government responsive to public opinion, see Ferdinand Tönnies, *Kritik der öffentlichen Meinung* (Berlin, 1922), chap. 8.

[61] J. L. Talmon, *Origins of Totalitarian Democracy* (London, 1952).

[62] On the effect of the French Revolution on the rise of nationalism and the new idea of the nation-state, see Alfred Cobban, *In Search of Humanity: The Role of Enlightenment in Modern History* (New York, 1960), 199ff. ("Making Nationalism a Religion in Revolutionary France"). The links between nationalism and public opinion are stressed by Cobban, as well as by Cornwell B. Rogers, *The Spirit Of Revolution in 1789* (Princeton, NJ, 1949), 20ff., 54ff., 206ff. Rogers refers to revolutionary songs and rituals to show the religious character of the belief in nationalism and in public opinion.

The Transformation of French Law.—As in the case of the German and English Revolutions, the most apparent and most comprehensive legal changes connected with the French Revolution were in the field of constitutional law. I have already referred to many of these changes. A written constitution was adopted for the first time in French history. A republican form of government was instituted, with supreme power given to a legislative assembly elected by popular vote and responsive to public opinion. The church was subjected to state control insofar as that was necessary to protect religious toleration. The judiciary was confined to the application of statutory law. Most hereditary distinctions and social privileges of the aristocracy were abolished. Remnants of feudal law were abolished. In principle, equal civil rights were established for all.

In addition to constitutional law, other aspects of the French legal system underwent transformation. Of special importance was the unification of French law. Diversity of local customs, and especially the striking differences in legal traditions between the south and the north of France, were subordinated not only to a common written constitution and a unified system of legislation and adjudication but also to codification of criminal, civil, and commercial law on a national scale.

In civil law, the famous *Code civil* of 1804, in whose drafting Napoleon himself played a part, and which was intended to express the spirit of the Revolution, gave especially strong protection to rights of private property and contract. With the abolition of the remaining feudal dues and restrictions, ownership was defined broadly as the right to possess, use, and dispose of one's property as one wills, except as prohibited by law. A general contract law was formulated—rules applicable to all kinds of agreement; and the intention of the parties was made central to contractual obligation. Rescission of contract for gross unfairness ("lesion"), duress, or fraud, as well as for minority, was now permitted by law without the former requirement of royal consent. In tort law ("delict"), the principle was established that, as a general rule, liability should be based on fault: the doer of harm should not be civilly liable to the victim unless he intended to cause the harm or else caused it negligently. In family law, the state was accorded general jurisdiction over marriage and divorce. Marriage was viewed as any other civil contract, and divorce was obtainable by mutual consent, for cause, or for proven incompatibility. The father's disciplinary power over his wife and his children was restricted. Wives were accorded greater property rights and greater civil rights generally.[63]

---

[63] See James F, Traer, "From Reform to Revolution: The Critical Century in the Development of the French Legal System," *Journal of Modern History* 49 (1977): 73-88;

Striking law reforms were also introduced in the field of criminal law and procedure. Voltaire had not exaggerated when he wrote that French criminal law and procedure of his time seemed to be "planned to ruin citizens."[64] Although the Criminal Ordinance of 1670 had identified types of crimes and the punishments applicable to them, in fact public prosecutors and judges were free to indict and convict for acts not legally defined as crimes at all; moreover, there was no control over their actions, since proceedings were not public and no reports of the reasons for decisions were given. Von Bar summarized the pre-Revolutionary situation as follows:

> Punishments [were] unequal; they [varied] according to the status of rank of the offenders rather than the nature of the crime. Punishments [were] also cruel and barbarous in their method—the base of the system [was] the death penalty, and a prodigal use of bodily mutilations. Furthermore, punishments [were] variable in discretion; crimes [were] loosely defined, and the individual [had] no security against excess of severity in the state's repression of crime. Finally, ignorance, prejudice, and emotional violence [bred] imaginary crimes; and the scope of penal law [extended] beyond the regulation of social relations and trespasses even upon the domain of conscience.[65]

The arbitrariness and cruelty of the substantive criminal law was more than matched by that of the system of criminal procedure. I have already mentioned the secrecy of it. In addition, suspects could be held indefinitely in prison, incommunicado, while under investigation—this under the notorious *lettres de cachet*. For capital offenses, of which there were a very large number (including not only treason and murder but also sacrilege, heresy, pandering, incest and others), torture could be applied to secure a confession. The judges, who had purchased their offices, were paid by the parties; additional fees were extorted by delays, and bribery was a common practice.

The penal policy of the Revolution was expressed forcefully in the Declaration of the Rights of Man and Citizen of August 1789. Among its provisions were the following:

- The law may inflict only such penalties as are strictly and clearly necessary.
- Retroactive laws are proscribed.

James F. Traer, *Marriage and the Family in Eighteenth Century France* (Ithaca, NY, 1980). For a general survey of French Revolutionary private law legislation preceding the *Code civil*, see Phillippe Sagnac, *La legislation civile de la revolution francaise* (Paris, 1989). See also Viollet, "French Law," 710-53.

[64] Quoted in Leon Radzinowicz, *Ideology and Crime* (New York, 1966), 1.

[65] Karl Ludwig von Bar, *A History of Continental Criminal Law* (Boston, 1916), 315.

- Like offenses are to receive like punishments, regardless of the rank and station of the offender.

- The death penalty or infamous punishment cannot carry a vicarious infamy to the family of the condemned person.

- General confiscation of the property of a condemned person is abolished.

- A criminal action against a party dies when the party dies.

- There shall be no crime, no punishment, without a [previously enacted] law.

- There shall be a presumption of innocence.

In 1791 the fledgling Republic issued a comprehensive Penal Code. Characteristically, it was meticulous in its efforts to define crimes and to fix the severity of the punishments in proportion to the gravity of the crime. It aimed to curtail judicial discretion severely and to provide a predictable, graduated penalty structure. The 1791 Penal Code was revised in 1795. Ultimately it was replaced in 1810. The 1810 Code has served as the basic penal legislation in France—of course, with numerous amendments—until the present.

The 1810 Penal Code—like the 1804 Civil Code—bears the stamp of Napoleon's own ideas. Napoleon was in close touch with the five draftsmen of his Penal Code and with the Council of State which was responsible for accepting or rejecting it.

Napoleon's guiding principle, and that of his draftsmen, was general deterrence of crime, which he believed that the law could foster by intimidation, that is, by threat of penalty. Retribution was rejected, whether in the classical sense of exaction of a price for violation of the law (which I would call general retribution) or in the sense of vengeance (which I would call special retribution). The emphasis on deterrence was characteristic of the utilitarian philosophy which prevailed in the Enlightenment and was embodied in the Revolution. Criminal acts were to be punished because they were socially harmful—*not* because they violated the divine order or the cosmic order, *not* because they were morally wrong, *not* because they were against the traditions of the people. The punishment was to be primarily a deterrent to others. The goal of rehabilitation of the offender is, of course, consistent with utilitarianism and was reflected in the 1791 Code. In the 1810 Code, however, Napoleon opted for general deterrence, and against rehabilitation, as a guiding principle. "Prisons," said Napoleon, "are to punish prisoners, not to reform them."[66] This was also consistent with utilitarianism, and with Beccaria's view that it is not a proper function of the law to enforce moral virtues.

---

[66] Quoted in H.A.L. Fisher, "The Codes," in Ward et al., eds., *The Cambridge History*, 9: 175. Cf. von Bar, *A History*, 335, n. 7.

In addition, Napoleon supported the reintroduction of branding for forgery, which the 1791 Code had eliminated. Confiscation of property was also reintroduced. Life imprisonment was ruled out, but not penal servitude for life. Only limited judicial discretion to move between minimum and maximum penalties was favored. There were other shifts in emphasis between 1791 and 1810, but the basic philosophy was the same: for Napoleon and his draftsmen, as for the draftsmen of 1791, as for Beccaria and the *philosophes* in the generation after 1750, the criminal law was to be, above all, a rational instrument of the state, intended by its nature to deter potential criminals by threat of penalties. Of Luther's first two uses of the law—the political and the theological—only the first was kept; the third use, the educational (to guide the faithful to virtue), stressed by Calvinism, was also discarded ("Prisons are to punish prisoners, not to reform them").

I have touched on a few basic changes in French law that followed in the wake of the French Revolution. Among many other such changes I shall mention only one: the change in legal science itself, and especially in the style and method of legal analysis and of legislation.

Prior to the Revolution, legal science in France was highly developed in the Roman Catholic Church, where it was applied to canon law and to the texts of Roman law that formed one of the sources of canon law and Roman law. French secular law—royal law, customary law, the law of the cities and provinces—had become a university subject in 1697, but prior to the Revolution it remained a stepchild in the curriculum. This was due in part to the extraordinary diversity and complexity of French customary and local law, and in part to the largely unsystematized character of French royal law. Decisions of royal courts were seldom published; indeed, they were, for the most part, secret; and French royal statutes and regulations, though increasingly numerous in the eighteenth century, were for the most part not collected or harmonized. Portalis, a principal author of the 1804 *Code civil*, described the predicament of the codifiers as they considered the pre-existing laws. "What a spectacle opened before our eyes!" he wrote. "Facing us was a confused and shapeless mass of foreign and French laws, of general and particular customs, of abrogated and unabrogated ordinances, of contradictory regulations and conflicting decision; one encountered nothing but a mysterious labyrinth."[67]

Under these circumstances the draftsmen of the civil code seized upon the few available treatises. Of these, the most important was that of Pothier

---

[67] *Fenet Recueil complet des travaux preparatoires du Code civil* (Paris, 1836), xcii, cited in Arthur von Mehren, *The Civil Law System* (Boston, 1957), 12. See also Dawson, *Oracles*, 314-349.

(1699-1772), former judge at Orléans, professor of French law at the University of Orléans after 1750, and prolific writer on civil law and family law. In criminal law as well, the codifiers drew heavily upon leading scholarly writing. Thus in France in the late eighteenth and early nineteenth centuries, as in Germany three centuries earlier, a professorial style of systematization was introduced both into legal analysis and into legislation (though not into French judicial opinions, which, under the influence of the doctrine of absolute legislative supremacy, became more laconic than ever).

French professorial style differed, however, from its German counterpart. Far more than the Germans, the French jurists prized simplicity and clarity and strove to avoid both casuistry and the excessive qualification of general doctrines. These characteristics of the new French legal science linked it with post-Revolutionary French thought and with French letters generally. Stendhal's famous remark is revealing in this regard—that he kept the *Code civil* at his bedside for evening reading, *pour prendre le ton.*

Law AND Belief in the French Revolution.—That both the French legal system and the French belief system underwent substantial transformation in the last decade of the eighteenth century and the first decades of the nineteenth century can hardly be doubted. Moreover, important connections between the two transformations are easily discernible. In this respect the French Revolution differed markedly from its predecessors, the English and the German. As we have seen, it is not obvious—although it is true—that the nature and substance of German law reform in the sixteenth century are traceable in part to Lutheran beliefs and concepts. Similarly, it is not obvious—although it is true—that basic changes in English law in the late seventeenth and early eighteenth centuries are traceable in part to Puritan beliefs and concepts. In the case of these earlier revolutions, the connections between political and legal changes, on the one hand, and changes in the belief system, on the other, are more hidden, partly because the changes in the belief system were expressed primarily in new theologies rather than in new secular philosophies. The secular philosophies of Lutheranism and Calvinism were for the most part implicit rather than explicit. In the French Revolution, on the other hand, the secular philosophies were largely explicit; indeed, it was the theology of the Revolution that was largely explicit. Eventually, the law reforms that took place in France in the decades after 1789 were a conscious reflection of secular philosophies associated with the Revolution—its outlook of rationalism, individualism, and utilitarianism and its emphasis on equality of opportunity, natural rights, freedom of expression, and freedom of will. In many instances the law reforms introduced after the

Revolution were those that had previously been demanded by the opinion leaders of the Enlightenment; for example, in the 1750s, 1760s and 1770s Voltaire, Beccaria, and hundreds of others who called themselves *philosophes* demanded the reform of French criminal law and procedure, and in the period after 1789 their demands were largely fulfilled by new legislation. Thus it has been said that the criminal law reform in the post-1789 period is "one of the clearest 'success stories' of the *philosophes*."[68]

In speaking of the secular outlook of the Enlightenment and of the embodiment of that outlook in the law reforms that followed the French Revolution, one cannot ignore the fact that that secular outlook was itself derived from certain religious beliefs. I have spoken earlier of the belief in Deism. That was, of course, an explicit theology. It postulated a God of creation, who appointed a purpose for everything in the universe. Man was given certain qualities—above all, reason—to enable him to secure his own advancement. By using his reason Man is able—so the *philosophes* taught—to case out error, to discern truth, and to reform the world.

From Deism it followed—and here we move from *explicit* to *implicit* theology—that Man is essentially good, not evil. He is born free and equal. He is born with the capacity to pursue—and to achieve—both knowledge and happiness. His future is governed by a natural law of progress. Thus arose what has been called "a new cosmology," namely, "the belief that all human beings can attain here on this earth a share of perfection hitherto in the West thought to be possible only for Christians in a state of grace and for them only after death."[69]

Not only Protestant Christianity in its Lutheran and Calvinist forms but also Roman Catholic and Anglican Christianity were challenged by this new implicit theology. Faith in the natural goodness of man, in the purity and power of reason, in the promise of science, and in the inevitability of progress—challenged the old belief in Scripture and tradition, in the sinfulness of man, in the providential character of human history, and in the power of grace and revelation.

Standing between the secular outlook (rationalism, individualism, utilitarianism, natural rights, equality of opportunity, freedom of expression, freedom of will) on the one hand, and the implicit theology (Deist creationism, the perfectibility of man, the natural law of progress) on the other hand

---

[68] Antoinette Wills, *Crime and Punishment in Revolutionary France* (Westport, CT, 1981), xii. Cf. von Bar, *A History*, 315ff.

[69] Crane Brinton, *Ideas and Men: The Story of Western Thought* (New York, 1950), 369. The novelty of this conception was expressed by St. Just: "Le bonheur est une idee nueve en Europe." Ibid.

were the twin dogmas of the nation-state and of public opinion. Law was to be the law of the nation-state as determined by public opinion. Its ultimate justification was to bring about progress and perfect happiness, and thus to fulfill the purpose of creation, but it was to do so, in the first instance, by responding to the national interest democratically expressed.[70]

Yet it would be wrong to say that the philosophy and theology of the eighteenth century Enlightenment and of the French Revolution marked a total break with the philosophy and theology of the English and German Revolutions or of Western Christendom in the Roman Catholic era of the eleventh to fifteenth centuries. The answers were different, but the basic questions and the terms of reference were the same.

Similarly, it would be wrong to suppose that the changes in French law that took place in the late eighteenth and early nineteenth centuries lacked continuity with prerevolutionary law. Like the reformed German law of the sixteenth century and the reformed English law of the seventeenth and eighteenth centuries, so the reformed French law of the nineteenth century had its roots in an older European legal tradition that dated from the late eleventh and twelfth centuries. Each of the Great Revolutions of modern Western history represented both a break with the tradition and a renewal of it.

---

[70] The origin of the ideas of natural progress and of human perfectibility in eighteenth century Deism, and their relationship to public opinion and democracy, is discussed in J.B. Bury, *The Idea of Progress* (New York, 1932), 112ff., 118, 141ff., 162-67, 204-205. See also Charles Vereker, *Eighteenth Century Optimism: A Study of the Interrelations of Moral and Social Theory in English and French Thought Between 1689 and 1789* (Liverpool, 1967), 39–106, 232-286; Hampson, *The Enlightenment*, 79-84, 97-119; Paul Hazard, *European Thought in the Eighteenth Century* (London, 1954), 14-25, 309-324.

$$\sim\!\!\circ\!\! 6 \,\circ\!\!\sim$$

THE TRANSFORMATION OF WESTERN LEGAL PHILOSOPHY IN LUTHERAN GERMANY[*]

I t should not be surprising to find that the Lutheran Reformation had an enormous influence on the development of legal philosophy in sixteenth-century Europe, especially in Germany. How could it be otherwise? Could such a fundamental transformation of both the religious beliefs and the political institutions of one of the major European nations have taken place without substantial changes in legal thought? Yet virtually nothing has been written, either by historians or by philosophers, to show a relationship between religious and political thought, on the one hand, and legal thought, on the other, in Lutheran Germany. Most accounts simply jump from (twelfth- to fifteenth-century) Roman Catholic natural-law theory to (seventeenth- and eighteenth-century) Enlightenment social contract theory, treating the sixteenth-century, at most, as a transition period. Those writers who do discuss sixteenth-century developments in legal philosophy usually regard the Lutheran contribution as a mere abridgement of medieval Roman Catholic thought.[1] Others even argue that there was no such thing as a

---

[*] Excerpted from *Southern California Law Review* 62 (1989): 1575-1660 (coauthored with John Witte, Jr.). Omitted here are most of the footnotes, including many quotations of original Latin and German sources, together with translations, as well as copious references to secondary literature.

[1] This thesis has been argued most forcefully by the German historian and theologian Ernst Troeltsch (1865-1923). See, e.g., Ernst Troeltsch, *Protestantism and Progress: a Historical Study of the Relation of Protestantism to the Modern World*, trans. W. Montgomery,

Lutheran legal philosophy, since Luther and his followers had made law and religion mutually irrelevant.[2]

The Lutheran reformers did, however, have a distinctive legal philosophy rooted in their basic theological and political beliefs, and this legal philosophy had a great influence not only in Germany but also in other European countries and eventually America as well. The reformers did not, to be sure, break totally with the legal thought that had come to predominate in the Roman Catholic tradition since the late eleventh century. They retained much of the terminology and many of the concepts that had been first articulated by the scholastic jurists.[3] They also accepted certain basic postulates of Roman Catholic legal theory: that human law is rooted in the nature of the universe; that it takes its character in some degree from natural law as revealed in creation, in Scripture, and in human reason and conscience; and that, on the other hand, human selfishness and pride may give rise to unjust laws that are contrary to natural law and are, therefore, to be condemned. Yet the Lutheran reformers, starting from radically new theological and political premises, cast these traditional concepts and postulates in a new ensemble, with new meanings, new emphases, and new applications. Their legal philosophy thus differed markedly not only from that of the earlier Roman Catholic tradition

---

repr. ed. (Boston, 1958), 101; Ernst Troeltsch, *The Social Teaching of the Christian Churches*, trans. Olive Wyon (New York, 1931), 2: 528; Ernst Troeltsch, *Aufsätze zur Geistesgeschichte und Religionsgeschichte*, ed. Hans Baron (Tübingen, 1925), 4: 161, 180; see also John T. McNeill, "Natural Law in the Teaching of the Reformers," *The Journal of Religion* 26 (1946): 168.; Jürgen Habermas, *Theory and Practice*, trans. John Viertel (Boston, 1973), 62; Max Weber, *Gesammelte Aufsätze zur Religionssoziologie* (Tübingen, 1920), 1: 69; E. Erhardt, *La notion du droit naturel chez Luther* (Paris, 1901).

[2] This thesis has been advanced primarily by Troeltsch and Emil Brunner. See Emil Brunner, *The Christian Doctrine of the Church, Faith and the Consummation*, trans. David Cairns (Philadelphia, PA, 1962), 306ff.; Emil Brunner, *The Divine Imperative: A Study in Christian Ethics*, trans. Olive Wyon, 5th impr. (London, 1953); Emil Brunner, *Justice and the Social Order*, trans. Mary Hottinger (London, 1945), 21; Troeltsch, *Protestantism and Progress*. For a criticism of the dualistic assumptions made primarily by Brunner, see Harold J. Berman, *The Interaction of Law and Religion* (Nashville, TN, 1974), 77-105; H. Richard Niebuhr, "Love and Law in Protestantism and Catholicism," *The Journal of Religious Thought* 9 (1952): 95.

[3] We use the term "scholastic" to refer to those writers who, after the Papal Revolution, adopted a dialectical method of analysis and synthesis to organize and systematize law, theology, and philosophy. The founder of the dialectic method was Peter Abelard (1079-1142). The method was utilized by Gratian (c.1095-1150) to systematize the canon law, by Peter Lombard (1100-1160) to systematize theological doctrines, and by Thomas Aquinas (1225-1274) to systematize the various branches of philosophy. See Harold J. Berman, *Law and Revolution: the Formation of the Western Legal Tradition* (Cambridge, MA, 1983), 131-132 and sources cited therein.

but also from the legal philosophies that came to prevail in Europe in the seventeenth and early eighteenth centuries.

Lutheran legal philosophy is an important historical and philosophical source of the two major competing schools of contemporary Western legal philosophy, namely, legal positivism and natural-law theory. In terms of positivism, Lutheran legal philosophy defines law as the will of the state expressed in a body of rules and enforced by coercive sanctions. It sharply separates law and morals. In terms of natural law, Lutheran legal philosophy postulates the existence within every person of a conscience, or sense of justice, which enables him or her to apply to concrete circumstances general rules that, precisely because of their generality, are necessarily unjust. Thus, Lutheran jurisprudence seeks to cure the inevitable injustice of rules by the resort to equity in their application. A positivist theory of legal rules is combined with a natural-law theory of the legal application of rules.

The tension between rule and application of rule, strict law and equity, is reflected, in Lutheran legal philosophy, in the equal duty of civil obedience to lawful authority and civil disobedience to laws that offend conscience. Lutherans affirm that such laws are laws and, therefore, morally binding; at the same time, they affirm that morality may require that such laws be disobeyed. The only sure way of escape from this dilemma is, once again, by resort to conscience.

The reliance upon conscience is aided by the correspondence between the dictates of conscience and the revealed truth of the Ten Commandments. Lutheran theologians teach that God has implanted in the conscience of every person moral insights that correspond to the Biblical injunctions to worship God, to respect authority, not to steal, not to kill, to be honest, to deal fairly with others, to respect the rights of others, and the like. Lutheran jurists called this the moral law or natural law. It differed, however, from the natural law of the Roman Catholic Church, which was founded on reason and on the synthesis of reason and revelation rather than on the conscience of the individual.

The Legal Philosophy of Martin Luther.—Throughout his career, Luther maintained an active interest in questions of law and legal philosophy. After he matriculated at the University of Erfurt in 1501, his father presented him with a book of Roman law and urged him to pursue legal studies. Accordingly, Luther took preparatory courses in philosophy, theology, and canon law, and after receiving the master's degree in 1505 he enrolled in the doctorate program in civil law. Some two months later—apparently having been nearly killed by a bolt of lightning—Luther left the university and entered the Augustinian monastery at Erfurt. While cloistered, however, he continued his study of canon law and ecclesiastical politics, and in 1510 he journeyed to the papal curia in Rome to represent the Erfurt chapter in a legal dispute within the Augustinian order.

In 1511 he forsook the monastic order to join the theology faculty of the newly founded University of Wittenberg. He received his doctorate in theology in 1512 and began his famous lectures on the Psalms and on the Epistle to the Romans, which first set forth the rudiments of his radical new theology.

During the course of his revolt against Rome from 1517-1522, Luther drew not only on his new theological insights but also on his extensive knowledge of the canon law. In his Ninety-Five Theses of 1517 and in his subsequent debates and polemics, he cited a litany of abuses and injustices not only in the confessional practices of the church but also in its canon laws. He also exposed what he considered to be the "fallacious legal foundation" of papal authority and the "myriad" inconsistencies between "the divine precepts and practices" of Scripture and the "human laws and traditions" of the Roman Catholic Church.[4]

In the course of the next two decades, Luther prepared a number of learned commentaries and sermons on the Old Testament Torah and devoted a large portion of his famous catechisms to exegesis of the Ten Commandments. He embellished even his densest exegetical writings on other Biblical passages with citations to and quotations from Roman law and earlier canon law texts. He gave public lectures and published learned tracts on various legal and moral questions of marriage, crime, usury, property, commerce, sumptuousness, and social welfare. He enthusiastically endorsed the efforts of legal humanists to reconstruct the ancient texts of Roman law and to reform legal education in the German universities. He corresponded regularly with jurists and politicians throughout Europe and counted among his closest friends two of the most outstanding German jurists of his day, Hieronymous Schuerpf (1481-1554) and Johann Apel (1486-1536), both of whom were his colleagues at the University of Wittenberg.

Although Luther did not write systematically about either legal or political philosophy, he drew many legal and political implications directly from his theology. He drew the implications that it is the duty of Christians to carry out God's work in the earthly kingdom and that they are to accept the Ten Commandments as a divine law to be applied not only directly in their

---

[4] See the collection of quotations from Luther in Jaroslav J. Pelikan, *Spirit Versus Structure: Luther and the Institutions of the Church* (New York, 1968), 20-24.

personal lives but also indirectly through laws of civil authorities derived from it in their practical lives.

Luther believed not only that the power of civil rulers is ordained by God but also that the laws through which they exercise their power are ordained by God.[5] The civil ruler, he argued, holds his authority from God. He serves as God's vice-regent in the earthly kingdom. His will is to appropriate and apply God's will. His law is to respect and reflect God's law. The civil ruler is thus not free to rule arbitrarily. He is under a duty to rule according to divinely inspired principles of justice. Luther found those principles of justice expressed most perfectly in the Ten Commandments, which he believed to be a summary of the natural law and, thus, accessible to pagans as well as to Christians. He found justice also expressed, though less perfectly, in Roman law, which was in his view an embodiment of human reason—a reason implanted by God but corrupted by human sinfulness.[6]

"The polity and the economy," Luther wrote, "are subject to reason. Reason has first place. There [one finds] civil laws, civil justice."[7] Such reason is to be found not only in Christian texts. "The heathen on their side have their heathen books," he wrote, "[and] we Christians on our side [have] our books of Holy Scripture. Theirs teach virtue, rights, wisdom for the temporal good, honor, peace on earth. Ours teach faith and good works for eternal life, the kingdom of heaven . . . . The poets and historians, like Homer, Virgil, Demosthenes, Cicero, Livy, as well as the ancient jurists [are] prophets, apostles, and theologians or preachers for worldly government."[8]

Contrary to what some commentators have argued, Luther's more favorable view of reason in matters of law and politics is not inconsistent with his less favorable view of reason in matters of doctrine and belief. Luther predicated this distinction on the two-kingdoms theory, which separates the

---

[5] *D. Martin Luthers Werke* (Weimar, 1883-1979), 11:247; 30:556; 31:191. In various places in his writings, Luther did distinguish between a variety of types of laws: divine law, Mosaic law (with its moral, judicial, and ceremonial types), natural law, civil (or statutory) law, and customary law—though neither his taxonomy nor his terminology is consistent. For Luther, however, all these types of law are merely manifestations of one law, God's law, which he has allowed to appear in a variety of guises.

[6] Although Luther often deprecated Roman law and Roman society (see, e.g., ibid., 51: 241), he occasionally also gave it unstinted praise (see, e.g., ibid., 30: 557; 51: 24). Nevertheless, Luther continued to criticize specific provisions of Roman law, such as those relating to slavery, marriage and family, and property, and in such contexts he often denounced Roman law in general. See, e.g., ibid., 12: 243; 14: 591, 714; 16: 537. For a more general treatment, see Gerald Strauss, *Law, Resistance and the State: The Opposition to Roman Law in Reformation Germany* (Princeton, NJ: 1986), 201.

[7] *D. Martin Luthers Werke*, 40: 305; see also ibid., 51: 211; ibid., 17: 102.

[8] Ibid. 51: 242-43; see also ibid., 11: 202; 32: 394; 45: 669.

spiritual knowledge and activity of the heavenly kingdom, based on faith, from the temporal knowledge and activity of the earthly kingdom, based on reason. This ontological distinction allowed Luther, on the one hand, to dismiss reason as "the devil's whore" and "Aristotle's evil brew" (when it intrudes on the heavenly kingdom) and, on the other hand, to treat it as "a divine blessing" and "an indispensable guide to life and learning" (when it remains within the earthly kingdom).[9]

Luther's understanding of law differed, however, from that of his Roman Catholic predecessors in both its philosophical and theological foundations.

Philosophically, Luther espoused a radically different ontological view of the relationship between human reason and conscience and a radically different epistemological view of their respective roles in the apprehension and application of natural law. The prevailing scholastic doctrine had made conscience a handmaiden of reason. It had distinguished between a rational faculty of apprehension, which was called *synderesis* (reason), and a practical faculty of application, which was called *conscientia* (conscience). A rational person, it was said, uses his *synderesis* to apprehend and elucidate the principles and precepts of natural law; he uses his *conscientia* to apply those principles and precepts to concrete practical circumstances. Thus, for example, through the exercise of *synderesis* a person apprehends and understands the principle of love of neighbor; through the exercise of *conscientia* he connects this principle with the practice of aiding the poor and helpless or of keeping his promises. For the scholastics, reason was considered a superior cognitive or intellectual faculty, conscience an inferior practical or applicative skill. Luther, by contrast, subordinated reason to conscience. Conscience, he taught, is not merely the skill of applying rational principles of natural law and knowledge. Conscience is the "bearer of man's relationship with God," the "religious root of man"[10] that shapes and governs all the activities of his life including both his rational apprehension and his application of the natural law. "Where a man's conscience remains fallen," Luther wrote, ". . . his reason will also inevitably be darkened, distorted and deficient." Where his conscience is redeemed, "his rational apprehension will also be enhanced."[11]

Theologically, Luther's conception of law differed from that of the scholastics in that he considered not only civil law but also natural law and

9 See generally Bernhard Lohse, *Ratio und Fides. Eine Untersuchung über die Ratio in der Theologie Luthers* (Göttingen, 1958), 70; B.A. Gerrish, *Grace and Reason* (Oxford, 1962), 10, 57, 84.

10 See Emanuel Hirsch, *Lutherstudien* (Gütersloh, 1954), 1: 127-28 and sources cited therein.

11 Quoted by Friedrich J. Stahl, *Die Kirchenverfassung nach Lehre und Recht der Protestanten*, 2d ed. (Erlangen, 1862), 37.

divine law to be ordained by God only for the earthly and not for the heavenly realm. Luther did not consider law to be an integral part of the objective reality of God himself, nor did he consider that law was ordained by God as a way of leading people to union with him. In Luther's theology, all law, including the Ten Commandments, was ordained by God solely for sinful man, fallen man. Obedience to it did not rescue man from his sinfulness, nor did it make him acceptable to God.

The Uses of the Law.—Once it is granted that salvation does not depend on "the works of the law," the question arises: Why does God ordain the law? What are, from God's point of view, its "uses"? This is an essentially different question from that asked by earlier Roman Catholic theologians, who made obedience to the moral law together with faith essential to a person's justification and salvation. For the scholastic theologian, to speak of "the uses" of the law would be like speaking of "the uses" of faith—or, indeed, the uses of God.

Luther set forth in rough terms two "uses of the law" (*usus legis*) and endorsed a third. One such use is to restrain people from misconduct by threat of penalties. He called this the "civil" or "political" use of the law. God, Luther argued, wants even sinners to observe the moral law—to honor their parents, to avoid killing and stealing, to respect marriage vows, to testify truthfully, and the like—so that "some measure of earthly order, concourse and concord may be preserved."[12] Fallen man, not naturally inclined to observe these commandments, may nevertheless be induced to do so by fear of punishment—divine punishment as well as human punishment. This "first use" of the law applies both to the Ten Commandments and to the civil laws derived therefrom.[13]

Luther's civil use of the law helped to lay the foundation for modern theories of legal positivism. "Stern hard civil rule is necessary in the world," he wrote, "lest the world be destroyed, peace vanish, and commerce and common interest be destroyed."[14] He emphasized that to maintain order it is important that there be precise legal rules, not only to deter lawbreakers but also to restrain officials, including judges, from their natural inclination to wield their powers arbitrarily. Especially in wicked times, he wrote, written

---

[12] *D. Martin Luthers Werke*, 10: 454; see also ibid., 11: 251.

[13] Luther generally spoke of the "civil use" as the "first use of the law," and the "theological use" as the "second use of the law" (see, e.g., ibid., 10: 454; 40: 486). But "for Luther the primary emphasis is on the theological use of the law . . . particularly later in his career." Frank S. Alexander, "Validity and Function of Law: The Reformation Doctrine of Usus Legis," *Mercer Law Reivew* 31 (1980): 509, 515.

[14] *D. Martin Luthers Werke*, 15: 302.

laws are needed because of the excessive generality of natural law.[15] Thus, Lutheran jurisprudence was an important source of the nineteenth-century legal positivist's definition of law as the will of the state expressed in rules and enforced by coercive sanctions.

In contrast to nineteenth-century legal positivism, however, Lutheran jurisprudence postulated that the state, its will, its rules, and its sanctions are ordained by God, and that they have, in addition to their civil use, a second and even more important "theological" or "spiritual" use. The natural law as well as the civil laws derived therefrom serve to make people conscious of their duty to give themselves completely to God and their neighbors while at the same time making them aware of their utter inability to fulfill that duty without divine help. Through the law man is thus driven to seek God.[16] Here Luther relied on St. Paul's explanation of the significance of the Ten Commandments for Christians: to make them conscious of their inherent sinfulness and to bring them to repentance.[17]

Luther also acknowledged a third use of the law, its "pedagogical" use, namely, to educate the faithful—those who are already penitent and do not need to be coerced to obey—in what God wants of them and, thus, to guide them to virtue. Luther himself never expressly expounded this third use, although he endorsed without qualification those confessions and treatises in which it was set forth.[18] It was his colleague and close friend Philip

---

[15] Ibid., 4: 3911, 4733ff.

[16] See, e.g., *D. Martin Luthers Werke*, 40: 481-486.

[17] Romans 7:7-25; Galatians 3:19-22. See generally *D. Martin Luthers Werke*, 16: 363-393.

[18] See, e.g., *Apology of the Augsburg Confession*, Art. 4, in *Triglot Concordia, The Symbolical Books of the Evangelical Lutheran Church* (St. Louis, MO, 1921), 127, 161, 163 (Melanchthon speaks of the virtues that the law teaches). In the 1535 edition of his *Loci communes*, Melanchthon argues that "the third office of the law . . . is to teach us the good works that are pleasing to God." See G. Bretschneider et al. eds., *Corpus Reformatorum* (Brunsvigae, 1834-1860): 21: 406. Luther approved of both these writings by Melanchthon.

In several places in his writings, Luther also suggested the idea of, although not the precise phrase, the pedagogical use of the law. In his 1522 commentary on Galatians, for example, Luther spoke generally of "a three-fold use of the law" and endorsed strongly Paul's comment that "the law was our teacher until Christ came," Galatians 3:24, but then went on to elaborate only two uses of the law. *D. Martin Luthers Werke*, 10: 449ff. See G. Ebeling, *Word and Faith*, trans. J. Leitsch (Philadelphia, PA, 1963), 64. In his famous *Table Talk*, Luther distinguished obliquely between a written law, an oral law, and a spiritual law and then wrote, "the spiritual law cannot operate without the holy spirit, which touches the heart and moves it, so that a man not only ceases to persecute, but . . . desires to be better." *The Table Talk or Familiar Discourse of Martin Luther*, trans. William Hazlitt (London, 1848), 135-136, Cf. similar sentiments in *D. Martin Luthers Werke*, 38: 310. In his *Large Catechism of 1529*, which he described as a set of instructions for the daily lives

Melanchthon who systematically developed the doctrine of the threefold use of the law in both theological and jurisprudential terms.

The Legal Philosophy of Philip Melanchthon.—It has been said that whereas Luther taught the justice of God, Melanchthon taught the justice of society, and that his teaching on social justice "deserves to be viewed alongside the teachings of an Aristotle, a Thomas Aquinas, a Leibniz, and alongside the teachings of the German school of jurisprudence of the nineteenth century."[19] Wilhelm Dilthey calls him "the ethicist of the Reformation" and the "greatest didactic genius of the [sixteenth] century, [who] liberated the philosophical sciences from the casuistry of scholastic thought . . . . A new breath of life went out from him."[20] Indeed, in his own time Melanchthon was called "the teacher of Germany" (*praeceptor Germaniae*).[21]

What needs also to be said, however, is that Melanchthon's teachings on social justice and on ethics were combined with a new theory of natural and positive law which came to replace Thomistic and other Roman Catholic theories in those parts of Europe where Lutheranism triumphed.

Born in 1497 and orphaned by the age of ten, Melanchthon was a child prodigy. He received his bachelor's degree at the University of Heidelberg in 1511 and his master's degree at the University of Tübingen in 1514. From 1514 to 1518 he worked as an editor at a publishing house and prepared both his own translations of Greek verse and an important book of classical grammar, *Rudiments of the Greek Language.*

In 1518, at the age of 21, Melanchthon was called to the University of Wittenberg to serve as its first professor of Greek. In his brilliant inaugural address entitled "The Improvement of Education," he urged his colleagues to abandon the "arid, barbaric fulminations of the scholastics" and to return to

---

of Christian believers, Luther devoted more than fifty pages to exegesis of the Decalogue, concluding that outside of the Ten Commandments, no work can be good or pleasing to God, however great or precious it may appear in the eyes of the world. Reprinted in *Triglot Concordia*, 670-671. He includes a similar exegesis in *D. Martin Luthers Werke*, 6: 196 and 39: 359, 418, 486, respectively. It is clear from these and other passages that for Luther law could serve not only as a harness against sin and an inducement to faith but also as a teacher of Christian virtue.

[19] H. Fild, "Justitia bei Melanchthon" (Th.D., Diss. Erlangen, 1953), 150.

[20] Wilhelm Dilthey, *Gesammelte Schriften (Weltanschauung und Analyse des Menschen seit Renaissance und Reformation)*, (Leipzig, 1921), 21: 193; Albert Haenel, "Melanchthon der Jurist," *Zeitschrift für Rechtsgeschichte* 8 (1869): 249; Otto Krause, *Naturrechtler des sechzehnten Jahrhunderts: Ihre Bedeutung für die Entwicklung eines natürlichen Privatrechts* (Berlin, 1821), 106.

[21] Cf. Karl Hartfelder, *Philip Melanchthon als Präceptor Germaniae* (Berlin, 1889).

the study of classical and Christian sources.[22] Melanchthon's iconoclastic manifesto won the accolade of Luther, who was in the audience. Luther defended his young colleague against detractors and ultimately became one of his staunchest friends and supporters.

Under Luther's inspiration, Melanchthon joined the cause of the German Protestant Reformation. In his first year at Wittenberg, he studied theology while he taught Greek and rhetoric, and early in 1519 he received the bachelor's degree in theology. He soon became a gifted professor of theology—as many as 600 students attended his lectures. He also became an eloquent exponent of Lutheran theology. In 1519 and 1520 he wrote several learned defenses of Luther against his Roman Catholic opponents and a number of short popular theological pamphlets. In 1521 he published his famous *Loci communes rerum theologicarum*, the first systematic treatise on Protestant theology.

During the 1520s and 1530s, Melanchthon played a leading role in the debates between the Lutheran reformers and their Roman Catholic and radical Protestant opponents. He drafted the chief declaration of Lutheran theology, the Augsburg Confession (1530) and its Apology (1531), and participated in the drafting of the Schmalkald Articles (1537), another important Lutheran creed. He prepared a number of Lutheran catechisms and instruction books and published more than a dozen commentaries on Biblical books and ancient Christian creeds as well as several revised and expanded editions of his *Loci communes*.

Although Melanchthon's theological writings were more systematic, irenic, and logical in form than Luther's, they differed little in substance. At no time did Luther and Melanchthon ever oppose each other on any substantial point of theology or, indeed, of moral, political, or legal philosophy.[23]

Melanchthon wrote much on legal philosophy, chiefly in the context of moral and political philosophy. He taught university courses in Roman law and wrote widely on the theological and philosophical foundations of legal institutions. He also participated in the drafting of a number of urban and territorial statutes and was frequently consulted on cases that raised intricate legal, political, and moral questions.

---

[22] Philip Melanchthon, *De corrigendis adolescentiae studiis* (1518), in Robert Stupperich et al. eds., *Melanchthons Werke in Auswahl* (Gütersloh, 1951), 3: 29-42.

[23] Luther's correspondence is filled with glowing accolades of Melanchthon and of his writings. Luther was particularly impressed with Melanchthon's chief theological work *Loci communes*. See, e.g., *Table Talk*, 21; *D. Martin Luthers Werke*, 18: 601; 1: 514. For a general treatment of the relationship between Luther and Melanchthon, see Vilmos Vatja, ed., *Luther and Melanchthon in the History and Theology of the Reformation. Referate des 2 internationalen Lutherforschungskongress* (Philadelphia, PA, 1961).

Melanchthon's writings, taken as a whole, set forth a systematic Lutheran legal philosophy. To be sure, Melanchthon drew freely on the entire tradition of Western legal philosophy, particularly on Graeco-Roman sources, but he restated and revised that tradition in a new way, reconciling it with and subordinating it to the cardinal Lutheran doctrines of the two kingdoms, total depravity, justification by faith alone, *sola Scriptura*, the Christian calling, and the priesthood of all believers.

We shall summarize Melanchthon's legal philosophy under three headings: (1) the relationship of natural law to divine law (the Ten Commandments), (2) the uses of natural law in civil society, and (3) the relationship of natural law to positive law.

(1) The Relationship of Natural Law to Divine Law (The Ten Commandments).—Melanchthon departed in only some minor respects from the traditional Roman Catholic conception that there are certain moral principles inscribed on the hearts of all people by which they should be governed in their relations with each other and that these are accessible to human reason.[24] Like his Roman Catholic predecessors and contemporaries, he called these moral principles the law of nature (*lex naturae*), or natural law (*ius naturale*). He postulated, as did they, that reason was given to man by God partly in order to discern and apply this natural law.

Melanchthon offered, however, a radically new theory of the ontology of natural law, that is, its origin in the essential nature of man.[25] Building on the

---

[24] Philipp Melanchthon, *Annotations in Evangelium Matthaei of 1519-1520*, in Stupperich et al. eds., *Melanchthons Werke*, 4: 164; *Corpus Reformatorum*, 21: 116. In this early period, Melanchthon identified at least nine principles or precepts of natural law: (1) to worship and honor God and his law; (2) to protect life; (3) to testify truthfully; (4) to marry and bear children; (5) to care for one's relatives; (6) to harm no one; (7) to obey all those in authority; (8) to distribute and exchange property on fair terms; (9) to oppose injustice. See notes in ibid., 21: 25-27. In his *Loci communes* of 1521, Melanchthon summarized these principles thus: "(1) Worship God. (2) Since we are born into a common social life, harm no one but help everyone with kindnesses. (3) If it is impossible that absolutely no one be harmed, act in such a way that the fewest be harmed, letting those suffer who disturb public order and for this purpose let magistracies and punishments for the guilty be set up. (4) Property shall be divided for the sake of public peace. For the rest, some shall supply the needs of others through contracts." Ibid., 21: 119-20. For a provocative discussion of Melanchthon's development of the principles of natural-law and the relation of these principles to broader Lutheran theological doctrines, see Wilhelm Maurer, *Der junge Melanchthon* (Göttingen, 1967), 2: 288-95.

[25] For an introduction to Melanchthon's theory of human nature, see Heinrich Bornkamm, "Melanchthons Menschenbild," in *Philipp Melanchthon: Forschungsbeiträge zur vierhundertsten Wiederkehr seines Todestages*, ed. Walter Ellinger (Berlin, 1961), 76. The significance of Melanchthon's theory of human nature has been lost even on some of those who are most sympathetic to Melanchthon's contribution. See, e.g., Dilthey, *Gesammelte*

two-kingdoms theory, he taught that God has implanted in all persons, certain "elements of knowledge" (*notitiae*), which are a light from above, a "natural light," without which we could not find our way in the earthly kingdom.[26] These *notitiae* include not only certain logical concepts, such as that the whole is bigger than any one of its parts, and that a thing either exists or does not, but also certain moral concepts, such as that God is good, that offenses which harm society are to be punished, and that promises should be kept.[27]

These inborn moral concepts, Melanchthon argued, are "facts of [human] nature," which form the premises, not the objects, of rational inquiry.[28] They are thus beyond the power of human reason either to prove or to disprove. This was a marked departure from the Roman Catholic scholastic tradition, which taught that human reason can prove moral propositions that are consistent with divine revelation. Melanchthon also rejected the related scholastic doctrine that the universal acceptance of a given principle of justice is proof of its rationality; thus, he did not include the law of nations (*ius gentium*) automatically within the category of natural law.[29]

Human reason, according to Melanchthon, is capable neither of proving the existence of certain fundamental inborn moral concepts nor of

---

Schriften, 2: 193 (who traces Melanchthon's teachings to Aristotle, Plato, the Church Fathers, and the scholastic theologians and philosophers of the twelfth to fifteenth centuries); McNeill, "Natural Law," 168 (there is "no real discontinuity" between Melanchthon's theory of natural law and that of the scholastics). See also Franz Wieacker, *Privatrechtsgeschichte der Neuzeit*, 2d ed. (Göttingen, 1967), 165 (Melanchthon is a "restorer of scholastic jurisprudence"); ibid., 264 (Melanchthon represents "the later return of Lutheran theology to a natural-law theory rooted in Thomistic Aristotelianism").

[26] *Corpus Reformatorum*, 13: 150, 647; 21: 71.

[27] See ibid., 16: 228; 21: 117; Stupperich et al. eds, *Melanchthons Werke*, 3: 20. Melanchthon describes his general doctrine of the inborn elements of knowledge in greater detail in Philip Melanchthon, *Compendaria Dialectices Ratio* (1520), in *Corpus Reformatorum*, 20: 748; Philip Melanchthon, *De loci communibus ratio* (1526), in *Corpus Reformatorum*, 20: 695 and Philip Melanchthon, *Dialectices* (Wittenberg, 1534). A systematic exposition of Melanchthon's epistemology appeared in his *Erotema Dialectices* (1547), in *Corpus Reformatorum*, 13: 642. For a careful analysis of Melanchthon's theory of the *notitiae nobiscum nascentes* in his earlier and later works, see Dilthey, *Gesammelte Schriften*, 2: 162. Dilthey describes Melanchthon as: "The middle link (*Mittelglieder*) who . . . tied the natural knowledge of God and the world as revealed in the renewed classics with faithful piety as revealed in the renewed Christendom. In this universal spirit a balance was struck between Humanism and Reformation." Ibid., 162; see also comments of Manschreck in the introduction of *Loci communes* (1555), xxviii; Ernst Troeltsch, *Vernunft und Offenbarung bei Johann Gerhard und Melanchthon* (Göttingen, 1891), 46ff.

[28] Melanchthon, quoted by Herman Dooyeweerd, *Encyclopedie der Rechtswetenschap* (Amsterdam, 1946), 58.

[29] *Corpus Reformatorum*, 16: 70-72.

apprehending and applying them without distortion.[30] The scholastics had also recognized that human reason can be distorted by self-interest, but they had argued that it need not be. For Melanchthon, however, as for Luther, human reason not only can be but also is inevitably corrupted by man's innate inclination to greed and power.[31]

Melanchthon's strong emphasis on the limitations of human reason rendered his doctrine of natural law paradoxical. On the one hand, he argued that "the law of nature is the law of God concerning those virtues which the reason understands."[32] On the other hand, he argued that "in this enfeebled state of nature," human reason is "darkened" and thus "the law of nature is distorted . . . and invariably misunderstood."[33] His resolution of this paradox was to subordinate the natural law that is both discernible to and distorted by human reason to the Biblical law that is revealed to faith.[34] The Biblical law (which Melanchthon also called the divine law)[35] reiterates and illuminates the natural law. This Biblical law is summarized in the Ten Commandments,[36] whose two "tables" Melanchthon divided into the first

---

30 Ibid., 13: 547-555; 21: 116-117, 399-400. In his *Loci communes* of 1535 and in his Latin edition of the *Loci communes* of 1555, Melanchthon added one minor qualification to this view. He first distinguished between (1) theoretical principles (*principia theoretica*), which he defined as the principles and axioms of geometry, arithmetic, physics, dialectics, and other (what we now call) exact sciences; and (2) practical principles (*principia practica*), which he defined as the principles and norms of ethics, politics, law, and theology. He then argued that man's rational knowledge of theoretical principles is far less distorted by sin than is his rational knowledge of practical principles. Theoretical principles, therefore, command greater assent than do practical principles. All men can agree, he argues, that two and two equal four or that an object thrown into the air will eventually come down. Not all men can agree, however, that God must be worshipped, that adultery is evil, that property must be respected, or that honorable contracts must be kept. *Corpus Reformatorum*, 21: 398-400, 711-713. See the further discussion in Dilthey, *Gesammelte Schriften*, 2: 173-174.

31 Philip Melanchthon, *Annotations in Evangelium Matthaei*, in Stupperich et al. eds, *Melanchthons Werke*, 4: 146ff.; [Philip Melanchthon,] *Apology of the Augsburg Confession*, Art. 3 ("Of Love and the Fulfilling of the Law"), in *Triglot Concordia*, 157-159; *Corpus Reformatorum*, 21: 399-402.

32 *Corpus Reformatorum*, 16: 23.

33 Ibid., 16: 24; 21: 400-401.

34 See ibid., 21: 392; 22: 256-257; 16: 70. See also Maurer, *Der junge Melanchthon*, 2: 288-290; Bauer, "Der Naturrechtsvorstellungen," 67-71.

35 Melanchthon generally used the terms Biblical laws (*leges Bibliae*) and divine laws (*leges divinae*) interchangeably throughout his writings. See, e.g., the definition of divine law (*lex dei*) in *Corpus Reformatorum*, 21: 1077. In his *Loci communes* (1555), however, Melanchthon referred to this Biblical law variously as the "law of morality," "law of virtue," "judgment of God," "Ten Commandments," and "the eternal immutable wisdom and rule of justice in God himself." *Corpus Reformatorum*, 22: 201-202.

36 Like Luther, and like the earlier scholastics, Melanchthon distinguished three

three commandments and the remaining seven.[37] The first three commandments—to acknowledge one God and make no graven image, to utter no blasphemy, and to keep the sabbath holy—correspond to man's need for union with God. The remaining seven commandments—to honor authority, to preserve life, to protect the family, to respect property, to maintain truth, and to avoid envy and greed—correspond to man's need for community.

Thus, following Luther's lead, Melanchthon transformed traditional Western moral and legal philosophy by making not reason but the Bible, and more particularly the Ten Commandments, the basic source and summary of natural law. Earlier Roman Catholic writers—particularly in the fifteenth century—had, to be sure, also discussed and interpreted the Ten Commandments at some length. They had also argued that the Ten Commandments "clearly set forth the obligations of the natural law."[38] Most Roman Catholic writers, however, had relied on the Ten Commandments to develop a moral law for the inner spiritual life rather than a natural law for the outer civil life. Accordingly, most of the discussion of the Ten Commandments in the Roman Catholic tradition occurred in confessional books and in treatments of the internal form and the sacrament of penance, and not in books on law.[39] For

---

types of Biblical laws: the ceremonial, judicial, and moral laws. Only the moral law (which was summarized in the Decalogue, as well as in the Golden Rule, the Beatitudes, and various injunctions in Paul's letters) remained in effect after Christ. The ceremonial laws (dealing with sacrifices, rites, feasts, and similar matters) and judicial laws (dealing with forms of Old Testament monarchical government, law, and similar matters) were no longer binding. See *Corpus Reformatorum*, 21: 294-296, 387-392; *Loci Communes* (1521), in Pauck ed., *Melanchthon and Bucer*, 53-57. For further discussion of the importance of the Decalogue, see *Corpus Reformatorum*, 12: 23.

[37] For a comparison of the Lutheran tradition for numbering and arranging the Ten Commandments with other Christian and Judaic traditions see Bo Riecke, *Die zehn Worte in Geschichte und Gegenwart* (Tübingen, 1973); Ludwig Lemme, *Die Religionsgeschichtliche Bedeutung der Dekalogus* (Breslau, 1880); L. Baumgaertel, "Die zehn Gebote in der christlichen Verkündigung," in *Festschrift O. Procksch* (Tübingen, 1934), 29. In the Bible, of course, the Ten Commandments are not numbered at all. See Exodus 20:1-17, Deuteronomy 5:6-21.

[38] Thomas Aquinas, *Summa Theologica* I-II, Q. 98, Art. 5.

[39] See, e.g., A. de Clavasio, *Summa angelica de casibus conscientiae*, section on "Penitentia;" passages from Huguccio, Laurentius, and Raymond of Peñafort, quoted by Rudolf Weigand, *Die Naturrechtslehre der Legisten und Dekretisten* (München, 1967), 220, 438. For a good example of later sixteenth-century Roman Catholic writing on the Decalogue, see *The Catechism of the Council of Trent*, trans. Jeremiah Donovan (Baltimore, MD, 1829), 406-416. For further discussion, see Steven E. Ozment, *The Reformation in the Cities: The Appeal of Protestantism to Sixteenth-Century Germany and Switzerland* (New Haven, CT, 1975), 17:

In the late 14th and the 15th centuries, the Ten Commandments replaced the

Melanchthon, by contrast, the Ten Commandments were both the ultimate source and summary of the natural law and hence a model for the positive law enacted by the earthly rulers.

This represented a new way of reconciling faith and reason. In contrast to traditional Roman Catholic thought, Melanchthon denied the capacity of human reason to discern divine and natural law unless it is aided by faith.[40] At the same time, he conflated divine and natural law, identifying both with the Ten Commandments. By so doing, he restructured the traditional learning about natural law in such a way as to bring it entirely within the Bible, and he reinterpreted the Bible in such a way as to embrace the traditional learning about natural law.

Basic to Melanchthon's theory of the Ten Commandments was the theory of the two kingdoms. In Melanchthon's conception, the first three commandments relate to a person's direct relationship with God, that is, the heavenly kingdom; the last seven relate to a person's multiple relationships within the human community, that is, the earthly kingdom. Only if people will accept by faith the first table of the Decalogue will they be able, by reason, to establish an ethic, and hence a law, based on the second table.

(2) *The Uses of Natural Law in Civil Society.*—Like Luther, Melanchthon believed that in "the drama" of faith and grace, that is, in the heavenly kingdom, law "plays no useful role."[41] "So one may ask," he wrote, "for what, then, is the law useful?"[42] In this context, by "law" he meant both the natural law embodied in the Ten Commandments and positive law reflecting it. His answer, like Luther's, was that both natural law and positive law have important uses within the earthly kingdom—for Christians and non-Christians alike.

Melanchthon elaborated systematically the "civil" and "theological" uses of the law that Luther had adumbrated. The first use is to coerce people by fear of punishment to avoid evil and do good. Although such "external morality . . . does not merit forgiveness of sin," Melanchthon wrote, "it is

---

Seven Deadly Sins as the main guideline for oral catechesis and confession. This was an important shift which enlarged the areas of religious self-scrutiny of and by the laity. At no other time were the Ten Commandments so zealously promoted and carefully expounded.

See also Reicke, *Die zehn Worte in Geschichte und Gegenwart*, 9 ("[d]uring the Middle Ages, the chief role played by the Decalogue was in the church's confessional practice"); M. B. Crowe, *The Changing Profile of the Natural Law* (The Hague, 1977), 158-165.

[40] See, e.g., *Apology of the Augsburg Confession*, Art. 3, in *Triglot Concordia*, 157.

[41] *Corpus Reformatorum*, 22: 153.

[42] Ibid., 21: 716.

pleasing to God,"[43] since it allows persons of all faiths to live peaceably together within the earthly kingdom that God has created,[44] it enables persons who are Christians to fulfill the vocations to which God has called them, and it allows "God continually to gather to himself a church among men."[45]

The second use of the law, for Melanchthon, as for Luther, is to make people conscious of their inability by their own will and reason, without coercion, to avoid evil and do good.[46] Such consciousness, Melanchthon argued, is a precondition to both their search for God's help and their faith in God's grace.[47]

Melanchthon added a third "pedagogical" or "educational" use of the law not articulated by Luther, namely, to educate the faithful themselves, the righteous, "those saints who now are believers, who have been born again through God's word and the Holy Spirit." They also, Melanchthon said, need the law so they may "know and have a testimony of the works that please God."[48] Melanchthon's third use of the law built on Luther's teaching that the Christian believer, though saved, is not yet perfect. He is at once saint and sinner, citizen of both the heavenly kingdom and the earthly kingdom. Thus even the greatest saints, Melanchthon stated, need the instruction of the natural law, "for they carry with them . . . weakness and sin,"[49] and they "are still partly ignorant of God's will and desire for their lives."[50]

Melanchthon's emphasis on the pedagogical use of the law brought the heavenly kingdom into a close relationship, though not a complete interdependence, with the earthly kingdom. The natural law, which God has implanted in every human heart and has confirmed in the Ten Commandments, guides all persons, whether Christians or non-Christians, in ways that are pleasing to God. It imbues in them a respect for authority, a concern for society, a love for justice and fairness, and a desire for right living. Melanchthon called this a form of "civic" or "political righteousness," which, though "it must be sharply distinguished from religion or evangelical righteousness," is, nonetheless, a "useful benefit" that the law provides.[51]

---

[43] *Corpus Reformatorum*, 22: 250.

[44] Ibid., 22: 151.

[45] Ibid., 22: 249.

[46] Ibid., 21: 69-70; 22: 250-251.

[47] Melanchthon makes clear that not only the divine law (i.e., the Ten Commandments) but also the civil law serves both to make men aware of their depravity and to impel them to grace. See, e.g., ibid., 22: 152.

[48] Ibid., 21: 255.

[49] *Loci Communes* (1555), 127.

[50] Ibid., 132.

[51] *Corpus Reformatorum*, 1: 706-08.

(3) The Relationship of Natural Law to Positive Law.—Melanchthon's concept of the educational role of natural law in guiding saints and sinners alike in their understanding of "political righteousness" is an important link between his theory of the uses of natural law in civil society and his theory of the relationship of natural law to positive law. His theory of that relationship, put briefly, was that even as God sets guidelines for civil society through natural law, so civil society, especially through the state, has the task of transforming the general principles of natural law into detailed rules of positive law. That is what natural law "educates" the state to do. At the same time, the state—and here Melanchthon used the word "state" in its modern sense—is to exercise through its law an educational function with respect to its subjects parallel to the educational function which God exercises through natural law with respect to the state.

For Melanchthon, as for Luther, political rulers were called to be God's "mediators" and "ministers," and their subjects were called to render to them the same obedience that they rendered to God.[52] Melanchthon went beyond Luther, however, in articulating the divinely imposed task of political authorities to promulgate "rational positive laws" for the governance of both the church and the state in the earthly kingdom.[53] To be rational, Melanchthon stated, positive laws have to be based on both (1) the general principles of natural law; and (2) practical considerations of social utility and the common good. Unless both criteria are met, a positive law is neither legitimate nor obligatory.

In elaborating the first criterion, Melanchthon started from the position that it is the office of political rulers to be the "custodians of the first table and the second table of the [Decalogue]."[54] As such, they are responsible for defining and enforcing by positive laws both the right relationship between man and God, as reflected in the three commandments of the first table, and the right relationships among persons, as reflected in the seven commandments of the second table.

As guardians of the first table, political rulers are not only to proscribe and punish all idolatry, blasphemy, and violations of the Sabbath—offenses that the first table prohibits on its face—but they are also to "establish pure doctrine" and right liturgy, "to prohibit all wrong doctrine," "to punish the obstinate," and to root out the heathen and the heterodox.[55] Thus,

---

[52] See *Corpus Reformatorum*, 11: 69-70; 21: 1011.

[53] Ibid., 22: 611-612; 16: 230.

[54] Ibid., 22: 87, 286, 615.

[55] Ibid., 22: 615-618; 16: 85-105 (section entitled: "An principes debeant mutare impios cultus, cessantibus aut prohibentibus episcopis, aut superioribus dominis"). This

Melanchthon laid a theoretical basis for the welter of new religious establishment laws that were promulgated in Lutheran cities and territories, many of which contained comprehensive compendia of orthodox confessions and doctrines, songs and prayers, and liturgies and rites. The principle of *cuius regio eius religio*, which was set forth in the Religious Peace of Augsburg (1555) and again in the religion clauses of the Peace of Westphalia (1648), rested ultimately on Melanchthon's theory of positive law as defining and enforcing the first table of the Decalogue.[56]

As guardians of the second table of the Decalogue, political rulers are responsible for governing "the multiple relationships by which God has bound men together."[57] Thus, on the basis of the Fourth Commandment ("Honor thy parents"), officials are obligated to prohibit and punish disobedience, disrespect, or disdain of authorities such as parents, political rulers, teachers, employers, and others; on the basis of the Fifth Commandment ("Thou shalt not kill")—unlawful killing, violence, assault, battery, wrath, hatred, mercilessness, and other offenses against one's neighbor; on the basis of the Sixth Commandment ("Thou shalt not commit adultery")—unchastity, incontinence, prostitution, pornography, obscenity, and other sexual offenses; on the basis of the Seventh Commandment ("thou shalt not steal")—theft, burglary, embezzlement, and similar offenses against another's property, as well as waste or noxious use or sumptuous use of one's own property; on the basis of the Eighth Commandment ("Thou shalt not bear false witness")—all forms of dishonesty, fraud, defamation, and other violations; and, finally, on the basis of the Ninth and Tenth Commandments ("Thou shalt not covet")—all attempts to perform these or other offensive acts against others.[58]

---

doctrine of religious establishment by civil law was a departure from the original Lutheran message. Luther in 1523, for example, wrote:

> Worldly government has laws that extend no further than to life, property, and other external things on earth. For God cannot and will not allow anyone but himself alone to rule over the soul. Thus when the earthly power presumes to prescribe laws to souls, it encroaches upon God and his government and only seduces and corrupts souls.

D. Martin Luthers Werke, 11: 262.

[56] The basic principle of the Religious Peace of Augsburg, though not the precise formula of *cuius regio eius religio*, was written into Article 7, Sections 1-2 of the Peace of Westphalia (1648), a document which served as the basic constitutional law of German cities and territories until the dissolution of the Holy Roman Empire in 1806. For a translation and discussion of the latter document, see Sidney Z. Ehler and John B. Morrall eds., *Church and State* (Westminster, MD, 1954), 189-193.

[57] *Corpus Reformatorum*, 22: 610.

[58] See ibid. for citations to various passages in which Melanchthon interprets the Ten Commandments. The fullest example appears in *Loci Communes* (1555), 97-122.

Many of these aspects of social intercourse had traditionally been governed by the Roman Catholic Church both through the confessional laws of the internal forum and through the canon laws of the external forum. Melanchthon's legal philosophy provided a rationale for political officials to bring these subjects within the province of the state. Accordingly, new urban, territorial, and imperial ordinances began to appear throughout mid-sixteenth-century Germany, replete with detailed regulations of social conduct.

In elaborating his second criterion of the rationality of positive laws, namely, their correspondence to practical considerations of social utility and the common good, Melanchthon drew from the Ten Commandments as a whole, in the context of Scripture as a whole, a general duty of the state "to maintain external discipline, judgment, and peace in accordance with the divine commandments and the rational laws of the land."[59] Neither the divine commandments, however, nor the rational laws of the land based on them contained a systematic statement of the nature of the legal order required for the maintenance of "discipline, judgment, and peace." In laying foundations for such a systematic statement, Melanchthon developed general theories of both criminal law and civil law.

In criminal law, Melanchthon urged political rulers to develop comprehensive laws that define and prohibit "all manners of offense against the person or the property of another" and to enforce these laws "swiftly and severely." He listed "four most important reasons" for punishment of crime: (1) "God is a wise and righteous being, who out of his great and proper goodness created rational creatures to be like him. Therefore, if they strive against him the order of justice [requires that] he destroy them. The first reason for punishment, therefore, is the order of justice in God." (2) "The need of other peaceful persons. If murderers, adulterers, robbers, and thieves were not removed, nobody would be safe." (3) "[To set an] example. When some are punished, others are reminded to take account of God's wrath and to fear his punishment and thus to reduce the causes of punishment." (4) "The importance of divine judgment and eternal punishment, in which all remain who in this life are not converted to God. As God in these temporal punishments shows that he distinguishes between virtue and vice, and that he is a righteous judge, we are reminded more of this example that also after this life all sinners who are not converted to God will be punished."[60] Thus, for Melanchthon, criminal punishment served as a form of divine retribution, special deterrence, general deterrence, and education.

---

[59] *Corpus Reformatorum*, 22: 615.

[60] Ibid., 224.

In civil law, as opposed to criminal law, Melanchthon postulated the duty of the ruler to facilitate and regulate the formation and functioning of various types of voluntary social relationships. He focused on three in particular: contractual relationships, family relationships, and relationships involving the visible church. Each of these relationships also had traditionally been subject, at least in part, to the jurisdiction of the Roman Catholic Church. The canon law had governed all contracts involving oaths or pledges of faith as well as most aspects of marriage and family life and of church polity and property. Under the inspiration and instruction of Melanchthon and other reformers, these social institutions were also brought within the jurisdiction of the state and subjected to an elaborate system of civil law.

"God has ordained contracts of various kinds," Melanchthon wrote, to facilitate the sale, lease, or exchange of property, the procurement of labor and employment, and the lending of money and extension of credit.[61] Such contracts serve not only the utilitarian ends of exchanging goods and services but also the social ends of promoting equality and checking greed.[62] Accordingly, God has called his political officials to promulgate general contract laws that prescribe "fair, equal, and equitable" agreements, that invalidate contracts based on fraud, duress, mistake, or coercion, and that proscribe contracts that are unconscionable, immoral, or offensive to the public good. Melanchthon was content, for the most part, to state these general principles of contract law in categorical form, although he occasionally applied them to specific cases. He condemned with particular vehemence loan contracts that obligated debtors to pay usurious rates of interest or entitled creditors to secure the loan with property whose value far exceeded the amount of the loan, unilateral labor and employment contracts that conditioned a master's obligation to pay on full performance from the servant, and contracts of purchase and sale that were based on inequality of exchange.[63]

Officials, Melanchthon argued, are also to promulgate rules to govern family relations. Civil laws are to prescribe monogamous heterosexual marriages between two fit parties and to proscribe homosexual, polygamous, bigamous, and other "unnatural" relations. They are to ensure that each marriage is formed by voluntary consent of both parties and to undo relationships based on fraud, mistake, coercion, or duress. They are to promote the created marital functions of propagation and childrearing and to prohibit all forms of

---

[61] Ibid., 22: 241-242.

[62] For Melanchthon's discussion of contracts, see ibid., 22: 128-152, 251-269, 494-508 ("Dissertatio de contractibus"); ibid., 22: 240; Stupperich et al. eds., *Melanchthons Werke*, Part 2, 2: 802-803.

[63] See *Corpus Reformatorum*, 16: 128-152, 251-269, 494-508.

contraception, abortion, and infanticide. They are to protect the authority of the *paterfamilias* over his wife and children but to punish severely all forms of adultery, desertion, incest, and wife or child abuse.[64]

The church, too, in Melanchthon's view, is to be regulated by laws promulgated by the political ruler, not only with respect to doctrine and liturgy, according to the first table of the Decalogue, but also with respect to polity and property. "The prince is God's chief bishop (*summus episcopus*) in the church," Melanchthon wrote.[65] He is to define the episcopal hierarchy within the church—from local congregations to urban ecclesiastical circuits or the territorial council or synod. He is to decide the responsibilities and procedures of congregational consistories, of circuit councils, and of the territorial synod. He is to appoint ecclesiastical officials, to pay them, to supervise them, and, if necessary, to admonish and discipline them. He is to ensure that the local universities and schools produce the pastors, teachers, and administrators needed to operate the church. He is to furnish the land, the supplies, and the services necessary to erect and maintain each church building. He is to oversee the acquisition, use, and alienation of church property.[66]

Thus, Melanchthon, in the style of modern legal positivism, described political rulers as the makers of positive law. Yet he also insisted that the validity of positive law is limited by the natural law revealed in Scripture and written in the hearts of men. It is natural law that both gives the ruler authority to make positive laws and governs the exercise of that authority. Only positive laws that are consistent with natural law are authoritative and legitimate. Moreover, since the ultimate source of positive law is natural law, the ruler is bound by the positive laws that he and his predecessors have made.

Melanchthon described the duties and rights not only of political officials but also of those subject to their authority and law. Early in his career,

---

[64] For Melanchthon's views of marriage and the family, see ibid., 16: 509; 21: 1051; 22: 600; 23: 667; Stupperich et al. eds., *Melanchthons Werke*, Part 2, 2: 801-802. For a more detailed treatment of the Lutheran theory and law of marriage in the sixteenth century, see John Witte, Jr., "The Transformation of Marriage Law in the Lutheran Reformation," in *The Weightier Matter of the Law: Essays on Law and Religion—A Tribute to Harold J. Berman*, eds. John Witte, Jr. and Frank S. Alexander (Atlanta, GA, 1988), 57.

[65] Quoted by Emil Sehling, *Kirchenrecht* (Bonn, 1908), 36-37. For similar sentiments by Melanchthon in his *Instruction to Visitors* (1528), see Emil Sehling, *Die evangelischen Kirchenordnung des sechszehnten Jahrhundert* (Leipzig: 1904), 1: 149-152, 163-165.

[66] See *Corpus Reformatorum*, 16: 241, 469, 570; ibid., 22: 227, 617; Sehling, *Die evangelischen Kirchenordnung des sechszehnten Jahrhundert*, 1: 149; *Corpus Reformatorum*, 22: 617-618. Melanchthon's bold new description of the responsibility of the political authority in ecclesiastical affairs helped to inspire the promulgation of a rich new body of Lutheran ecclesiastical law (*evangelisches Kirchenrecht*) in cities and territories throughout sixteenth-century Germany.

Melanchthon, like Luther, taught that all subjects have the duty to obey and no right to resist political authority and positive law—even where such authority and law has become arbitrary and abusive. If the "magistrate commands anything with tyrannical caprice," he wrote in 1521, "we must bear with this magistrate because of love, where nothing can be changed without a public uprising or sedition."[67] Melanchthon based this theory of absolute obedience on the political texts of St. Paul: that "the powers that be are ordained by God," that unswerving obedience to them is "mandated by conscience," and that to defy them is to defy God and to incur his wrath.[68]

As the power of German princes continued to grow, however, Melanchthon became deeply concerned to safeguard subjects from abuse and to restrain princes from tyranny. At least by 1555, he joined those who recognized a right of resistance against tyrants based on natural law. "Conscious disobedience of the secular *Obrigkeit* and against true and proper laws," he still maintained, "is deadly sin, that is, sin which God punishes with eternal damnation if one in conscious defiance finally persists in it."[69] However, if the positive law promulgated by the political official contradicts natural law, particularly the Ten Commandments, it is not binding in conscience. The principle that positive law cannot bind in conscience if it contradicts the fixed standards of natural law is, of course, consistent with Roman Catholic jurisprudence. The principle, however, had radically different implications in a unitary Protestant state in which there were no longer concurrent ecclesiastical and civil jurisdictions to challenge each other's legislation on the ground of violation of natural law. It was now left to the people—acting individually or collectively through territorial and imperial diets—to resist officials who had strayed beyond the authority of their office and to disobey laws that had defied the precepts of natural law.

In addition, Melanchthon emphasized throughout his career the importance of published written law as a restraint on arbitrary power. He argued that all the great legal civilizations of the past, including the Israelite, Cretan, Greek, and Roman, had met this requirement. Written and published laws are more secure, more predictable, and more permanent. They protect citizens against groundless violations of their person and property by officials. They also protect authorities against unjustified rebellions and groundless charges of arbitrariness or capriciousness. Written positive laws provide "an iron wall

---

[67] *Corpus Reformatorum*, 21: 223-224. Melanchthon, however, did counsel those subject to tyrannical authority and law to escape if they could do so without tumult and uprising. Ibid.

[68] Romans 13:1-7.

[69] *Corpus Reformatorum*, 22: 613.

against the ruthlessness of the crowd" (*die Rucksichtslosigkeit der Menge*) and a common bond between ruler and people for the defense of order and peace.[70]

Melanchthon also considered Roman law to be a restraint on arbitrary authority. The Roman law, he argued, was positive law imposed by the ruler; in that connection he stressed both its written character and its detailed character. Yet he also considered it to be "written reason" (*ratio scripta*) that implemented natural law. He countered the argument that the Roman laws were of pagan, not Christian, origin by stating that they "are pleasing to God, although they were promulgated by a heathen ruler," and that they "stem not from human cleverness [but] rather they are beams of divine wisdom," a "visible appearance of the Holy Spirit" to the heathen.[71] Thus, the Roman law bound the *Obrigkeit*. It was their law, positive law imposed by them, yet since it stemmed from their predecessors (the Roman emperors) and since it was in the form of glosses and commentaries on ancient texts (the *jus commune*), it was to a certain extent beyond their reach. It had a certain objectivity and exercised a certain restraint over them.[72]

Melanchthon's effusive praise of Roman law was not based on ignorance of its content. He studied it intensively and knew its development from the texts of Justinian through the glosses of Irnerius, the commentaries of Bartolus, and the revisions of his contemporaries.[73] Colleagues and friends with whom he discussed Roman law included some of the foremost legal scholars of the age.[74] Yet his interest in Roman law was not primarily that of a legal scholar. It was rather that of an ethicist and political theorist who found in Roman law a source of political order that protects against "seizure of power by the crowd," on the one hand, and a restraint on abuse of authority that "guards us against tyranny," on the other.[75] Thus, Melanchthon set forth the

---

[70] Quoted by Guido Kisch, *Melanchthons Rechts- und Soziallehre* (Berlin, 1967), 177. See further discussion in *Corpus Reformatorum*, 11: 73, 552.

[71] Ibid., 11: 921-922.

[72] Ibid., 11: 218ff., 357ff., 630ff., 922ff.

[73] See particularly Philip Melanchthon, *De Irnerio et Bartolo iurisconsultis oratio recitata A D. Sebaldo Munsero* (c.1537), in *Corpus Reformatorum*, 11: 350.

[74] For an account of Melanchthon's connections with numerous leading German jurists, as a teacher, colleague, and/or correspondent, see Guido Kisch, "Melanchthon und die Juristen seiner Zeit," in *Melanges Philippe Meylan* (Paris, 1963), 2: 135. See further Roderich von Stintzing, *Das Sprichwort "Juristen böse Christen"* (Leipzig, 1875); Roderich von Stintzing, *Geschichte der deutschen Rechtswissenschaft* (Berlin, 1880), 241-338.

[75] Quoted by Kisch, *Melanchthons Rechts- und Soziallehre*, 113.

idea, made popular in the nineteenth century by the famous German jurist Rudolf von Jhering, that "Roman law . . . is in a certain sense a philosophy."[76]

The Legal Philosophy of Johann Oldendorp.—Philip Melanchthon helped to shape the content and character of German legal philosophy until well into the seventeenth century. A whole generation of Germany's leading jurists in the sixteenth century—Johann Oldendorp (c.1480-1567), Konrad Lagus (c.1499-1546), Basilius Monner (c.1501-1566), Melchior Kling (1504-1571), Johannes Schneidewin (1519-1568), and many others—came under his direct influence as students, colleagues, and correspondents. Generations of students thereafter studied his legal, political, and moral writings, many of which were still being published in the late seventeenth century and being used as textbooks in the universities. His basic jurisprudential insights dominated German legal scholarship until the early Enlightenment.

Melanchthon's legal philosophy, however, was neither the only nor the most comprehensive Lutheran legal philosophy developed in the sixteenth century. Although sixteenth-century Lutheran jurists and moralists accepted Melanchthon's basic insights, they often criticized the formulation and focus of these insights and systematized and supplemented them in their own way. Perhaps the most significant such critical systematization of Lutheran legal philosophy was that of Johann Oldendorp.

Oldendorp was "one of the strongest legal figures of his epoch,"[77] "surpassing all others," in Roderich von Stintzing's words, "in the power of his personality . . . and in his significance as a writer and as a teacher."[78] Born in Hamburg in the 1480s,[79] he studied law from 1504 to 1508 at the

---

[76] *Corpus Reformatorum*, 11: 358.

[77] Peter Macke, *Das Rechts- und Staatsdenken des Johannes Oldendorp, Inaugural-Dissertation zur Erlangung der Doktorwürde einer Hohen Rechtswissenschaftlichen Fakultät der Universität zu Köln* (n.d.; date of oral examination 25 May 1966), 165. Most of the biographical information presented below is derived from Hans Dietze, *Johann Oldendorp als Rechtsphilosoph und Protestant* (Königsberg, 1933), 448-484; Krause, *Naturrechtler der sechszehnten Jahrhunderts*, 115-125; Macke, *Das Rechts- und Staatsdenken*; Erik Wolf, *Grosse Rechtsdenker der deutschen Geistesgeschichte*, 3. Aufl. (Frankfurt am Main, 1951), 129-132; S. Pettke, "Zur Rolle Johann Oldendorps bei der offiziellen Durchfuhrung der Reformation in Rostock," *Zeitschrift der Savigny-Stiftung* (Kan. Ab.) 101 (1984): 339.

[78] Stintzing, *Geschichte*, 311. Stintzing also calls Oldendorp "the most significant of the German jurists of the middle of the sixteenth century." Ibid. Ernst Troeltsch describes him as the "most influential jurist" (*massgebendster Jurist*) of the age of the Reformation. Ernst Troeltsch, *Die Soziallehren der christlichen Kirchen und Gruppen*, 545, n.253.

[79] The year of Oldendorp's birth remains a point of controversy. The date 1480 is accepted by Stintzing, *Rechtswissenschaft*, 311, as well as by many later historians. More recently, however, Wieacker has given Oldendorp's birthdate as 1486, Wieacker, *Privatrechtsgeschichte*, 283, and Macke has adopted the date 1488, Macke, *Das Rechts- und*

University of Rostock and from 1508 to 1515 at the University of Bologna, then a leading center of humanist thought. In 1516 he became a professor of Roman law and civil procedure at the University of Greifswald. In these early years, Oldendorp was steeped in the new humanism. He became a close student of the classics—Plato, Aristotle, and Cicero—and of Roman law. He was in close contact with the leading German exponents of legal humanism—Claudius Cantiuncula (d. 1560) and Christophus Hegendorf (1500-1540).

In the early 1520s, Oldendorp resolved to dedicate his life to the cause of the Lutheran Reformation. Accordingly, in 1526 he left Greifswald to become a leading city official (*Stadtsyndikus*) of Rostock and leader of the city's Reformation party. Eventually he was influential in inducing the Rostock City Council to adhere to the Reformation, and he himself played an important part in supervising church activities there and in establishing a public school for the education of the young. Roman Catholic opposition, however, led him in 1534 to leave Rostock in order to accept the post of *Stadtsyndikus* in Lubeck, one of Germany's chief commercial centers. There, too, he worked to bring Protestantism to the city, but there, too, Roman Catholic opposition eventually forced him out. In 1536 he accepted a teaching position in Frankfurt an der Oder, where he had also taught for a short time, from 1520-21. In 1539 he was invited to Cologne both to teach at the university and to serve the city government. The Roman Catholic Archbishop of Cologne, Cardinal Hermann von Wied (1477-1552), was himself drawn to Protestantism and befriended Oldendorp. Oldendorp came in personal contact there with Melanchthon and the Strassburg reformer Martin Bucer (1491-1551). Once again, however, facing opposition, Oldendorp left Cologne in 1541. Following a brief term as professor at the University of Marburg, he returned to Cologne at the urging of Cardinal Hermann, but in 1543 he was finally expelled from the city by the Roman Catholic authorities. He returned to Marburg, where Protestantism was firmly established, and taught in the law faculty there for twenty-four years until his death in 1567.

Oldendorp accepted the call to Marburg on condition that he be freed from the usual requirement of lecturing on the texts of the *Corpus Juris Civilis* in the order and manner imposed by the post-glossators—the famous *mos italicus* that had dominated European legal education and legal scholarship for some two centuries. He would come, he insisted, only if he could "teach the laws with special attention to their just consequences and in their relationship to God's word, which, above all, must be pursued and taught."[80]

Staatsdenken. Even later dates have been argued by other historians. In light of Oldendorp's career, 1486 or 1488 seems more plausible.

[80] Oldendorp, quoted by Stintzing, *Rechtswissenschaft*, 323.

Eventually Oldendorp was authorized by the founder of the university, Landherr Philip the Magnanimous, to introduce a basic reform of legal education at Marburg, whereby the entire body of law was considered philosophically and historically in its relationship to the Word of God.

Oldendorp's copious legal writings[81] present a complex legal philosophy in which classical Greek, Roman, scholastic, humanist, and other elements are recombined in an original way and are subordinated to Biblical faith and the Christian conscience. Thus, one may say that Oldendorp, like Melanchthon, was both a humanist and a Lutheran.

Oldendorp started with a deceptively simple definition of law (*Recht, ius*) as the totality of legal norms. Legal norms, in turn, he defined as general rules issued by certain authorities that command, prohibit, permit, or punish conduct. Thus, Law with a capital "L" (*Recht, ius*) is identified with law with a small "l" (*Gesetz, lex*), in the style of modern legal positivism.[82]

Laws issued by civil authorities (*leges rei publicae*), that is, positive laws, are subordinate, in Oldendorp's theory, to the laws that are implanted by God in the human heart and that are discerned by conscience. These Oldendorp called variously the "law inside people" (*lex in hominibus*), the law of nature (*lex naturae*), and natural law (*lex naturalis, ius naturae*). He considered these

---

[81] Oldendorp wrote at least 56 separate tracts, of which three are in old German and the rest in Latin. The German writings are among the earliest. The fullest bibliography of Oldendorp's writings is given in Dietze, *Johann Oldendorp als Rechtsphilosoph und Protestant*, 18-21. Macke's bibliography, *Das Rechts- und Staatsdenken*, viii-xi, while not as exhaustive as Dietze's, includes six works not found in Dietze.

Two of the German works have been translated into modern German and published in Erik Wolf, *Quellenbuch zur Geschichte der deutschen Rechtswissenschaft* (Frankfurt am Main, 1949). These are Johannes Oldendorp, *Was billig und recht ist* (Rostock, 1529), in Wolf, *Quellenbuch*, 29 [hereinafter Oldendorp, *Billig und Recht*], and Johannes Oldendorp, *Ratmannspiegel* (Rostock, 1530), in Wolf, *Quellenbuch*, 69 [hereinafter Oldendorp, *Ratmannspiegel*]. The latter work is also published separately as *Ein Ratmannenspiegel von Joh. Oldendorp, Doctor und Stadtsyndicus zu Rostock* (Darmstadt, 1971). Two of Oldendorp's Latin works, Johannes Oldendorp, *Isagoge iuris naturalis gentium et civilis* (Köln, 1539) [hereinafter Oldendorp, *Isagoge*] and Johannes Oldendorp, *Divinae tabulae X praeceptorum* (Köln, 1539) [hereinafter Oldendorp, *Divinae Tabulae*], are reproduced in edited form in Carl von Kaltenborn, *Die Vorläufer des Hugo Grotius* (Halle, 1848), Appendix A, 1-25. (Kaltenborn mistakenly identifies the *Divinae Tabulae* as Title V of the *Isagoge*, though the two works were written separately. The two works, however, were bound together, along with Oldendorp's *Epitome successionis ab intestato & alia quaedam pro tyronibus juris* in a 1539 Antwerp publication, available in the Treasure Room, Langdell Library, Harvard Law School.)

[82] See Oldendorp, *Isagoge*, 7. But see Oldendorp, *Billig und Recht*, 57, where Oldendorp also puts customary law on an equal level with enacted law: "Law, or laws, is [sic] twofold: written and unwritten." Under written law, he included the civil law (Roman law) and positive law, and under unwritten law he included custom, the law of nations, and natural law.

to be directly binding upon the civil authorities.[83] Laws promulgated by God in the Bible (*leges Bibliae*) are themselves to be discerned, in Oldendorp's view, by the conscience of each believer.

Thus, in Oldendorp's theory, as in the traditional Roman Catholic scholastic jurisprudence first enunciated systematically by the great twelfth-century canonist Gratian, there are three states, or levels, of law, which form a hierarchy: divine law, natural law, and human law. In contrast to the scholastic theorists, however, Oldendorp restricted the divine law (*lex divina*) to the laws set forth in the Bible, which in effect meant chiefly the Ten Commandments. In doing so, he followed both Luther and Melanchthon, who declared that of the many rules laid down in the Old Testament only the Ten Commandments are binding on Christians. Also, like Luther and Melanchthon and unlike the scholastics, Oldendorp did not speak of an eternal law (*lex aeterna*) transcending the Bible.

Oldendorp also departed from Roman Catholic teaching in deriving the law inside people, or natural law, not from human reason as such, that is, the reason that originates in the mind, but, once again, from the Bible. Natural law, Oldendorp wrote, is derived from those parts of the Bible, especially the Ten Commandments and portions of the New Testament, that establish general moral principles of love and truthfulness—especially love of one's fellowmen as a community, love of one's individual neighbors, the golden rule, and the duty to be truthful in one's relations with others.[84] This is a God-given, Biblical natural law, and through his God-given conscience each person has the capacity to discern it and to observe it. Conscience was, for Oldendorp, indeed a form of reason—not, however, ordinary human reason or civil reason (*ratio civilis*), but a divine reason implanted in man, which Oldendorp called natural reason (*ratio naturalis*). For nature, in Oldendorp's concept, is the creative power of God; indeed, "nature is God the creator of all things."[85] The natural law implanted by God in man's conscience "does not depend on the power of the person but stands free, unchangeable. God has written it into your reason. Therefore you must apply your unbiased mind and read diligently."[86] "Conscience," he wrote, "is an infallible guide."[87]

---

[83] Echoing Melanchthon, Oldendorp defined natural law as "the natural elements of knowledge that God has implanted in us by which we distinguish equity from iniquity" Oldendorp, *Isagoge*, 6. And again: "The source of natural norms . . . lies in the heart and conscience of man, on which God has inscribed them." Ibid., 15.

[84] See Oldendorp, *Isagoge*, 15; Oldendorp, *Divinae Tabulae*, 17. See also Oldendorp, *Billig und Recht*, 58-65.

[85] Quoted in Macke, *Das Rechts- und Staatsdenken*, 30-31. See also Oldendorp, *Isagoge*, 6.

[86] Oldendorp, *Billig und Recht*, 57. We have substituted the term "natural law" for the

Civil reason, which does depend on the power of the person, operates primarily in the sphere of the positive law of the civil polity. That law, however, also is derived ultimately from Holy Scripture. Like Luther and Melanchthon, Oldendorp traced all laws for ordering the earthly kingdom to the Fourth Commandment ("Honor thy father and thy mother"—the prince being the parent). More clearly than Melanchthon, he traced all criminal laws to the Fifth Commandment ("Thou shalt not kill"), the law of private property to the Seventh Commandment ("Thou shalt not steal"), and the law of procedure to the Eighth Commandment ("Thou shalt not bear false witness"). He also (unlike Melanchthon) traced family law to the Tenth Commandment ("Thou shalt not covet . . . thy neighbor's wife") and the law of taxation to the general commandment, "Thou shalt love thy neighbor as thyself."[88]

Oldendorp placed special emphasis on the Seventh Commandment ("Thou shalt not steal"), in which he saw "the common locus for the whole civil law, namely, that which pertains to things," including both property law and contract law.[89] He argues that in the earthly kingdom, given the depravity of human nature, it is ordained by God that property is primarily individual and private and only secondarily and in special circumstances to be held in common.[90]

Thus Oldendorp viewed the positive laws by which Germany was governed in his time (*leges rei publicae*) as ordained by God. Yet he also subjected those laws to the tests of both natural law (the law inside people, *lex in hominibus*) and divine law (the laws of the Bible, *leges Biblicae*), and he said that in the exceptional instances in which they were found wanting it is the duty of the Christian conscience to disavow and disobey them. "A civil law that departs *in toto* from natural law is not binding," he stated.[91] He did in fact find a number of such precepts. He condemned as directly contrary to divine law human laws permitting the sale of church benefices, divorce, and usury, and as contrary to natural law human laws permitting bad faith possession of property, disinheritance of family members, delay of justice, interest of a judge in the outcome of proceedings before him, privileges granted by a ruler against natural law, conduct of war on the basis of a mere advance

---

term "equity" (*Billigkeit*) in the original quotation; Oldendorp uses the two synonymously, as is explained in Hans H. Dietze, *Naturrecht in der Gegenwart* (Bonn, 1936).

[87] Quoted by Dietze, *Johann Oldendorp als Rechtsphilosoph und Protestant*, 81.

[88] Oldendorp, *Divinae Tabulae*, 15-25.

[89] Ibid., 21.

[90] Ibid., 20-22.

[91] Oldendorp, *Isagoge*, 13. Later in the same passage, Oldendorp adduces Melanchthon in support of his position.

declaration, strict forms of servitude such as slavery, and some others.[92] More generally, he argued that natural law requires an owner to use his property for social ends and not, for example, to exclude others from use of it in instances where such use does him no harm.[93] He also argued that natural law imposes substantial duties on the state.[94]

Thus, the positivist character of Oldendorp's definition of law ("law is the totality of legal norms") was corrected, to a certain extent, by his innovation of divine legal norms revealed in the Bible, and revealed through the Bible in the individual conscience.

Oldendorp's Theory of Equity.—There remained, for Oldendorp, another equally crucial question that neither Luther nor Melanchthon had adequately addressed, namely, by what criteria are legal norms, whether Biblical, natural, or civil, to be applied in individual cases? The very generality of a legal norm or rule, Oldendorp wrote, presupposes that it is applicable in a wide variety of different situations, each with its own unique circumstances; yet the rule itself contains no indication of how the multiplicity of differences are to be taken into account. Two centuries after Oldendorp, Immanuel Kant expressed this point succinctly in his dictum that "there is no rule for applying a rule."[95]

Melanchthon had addressed the problem in the manner of the scholastic jurists. Rulers were required, he wrote, to "tailor" the general principles of natural law "to fit the circumstances."[96] General principles, he said, anticipat-

---

[92] Ibid., 12-13. See also the collection of quotations from other works of Oldendorp in Macke, *Das Rechts- und Staatsdenken*, 49-50; Oldendorp, *Isagoge*, 13.

[93] Oldendorp, *Billig und Recht*, 60-62. Oldendorp urged citizens "to enhance the common good as the highest ideal. For by serving the common good, you not only help one person but many." Ibid.

[94] See Macke, *Das Rechts- und Staatsdenken*; Oldendorp, *Ratmannspiegel*; id., *Lexicon*.

[95] See Immanuel Kant, *Critique of Pure Reason* A/32-B/71-A/34-B/74, and discussion in Kenneth J. Kress, "Legal Indeterminacy," *California Law Review* 77 (1989): 283, 332-333. This is similar to the position Lon L. Fuller took in his debate with H.L.A. Hart in Lon Fuller, "Positivism and Fidelity to Law—A Reply to Professor Hart," *Harvard Law Review* 71 (1958): 630, 661-669. Hart's position was that each rule has "a core of settled meaning" and that it is only in the "penumbral" cases that it becomes unclear how to apply the rule. H.L.A. Hart, "Positivism and the Separation of Law and Morals," *Harvard Law Review* 71 (1958): 593, 606-608. Fuller contended that rules are not to be applied by cataloguing those situations to which their words clearly refer and those to which they refer less clearly. He proposed instead that in every case they should be applied according to their purposes. Translated into Oldendorp's terms, this means that rules are always to be applied "equitably."

[96] *Corpus Reformatorum*, 16: 72-81. See also Melanchthon's definition of *epikeia* in ibid., 21: 1090.

ing a 20th-century American jurist, do not decide concrete cases.[97] If a "generally just law works injustice in a particular case," it is the responsibility of a judge to apply the law "equitably and benevolently," if he can, so as to remove the injustice.[98] Nevertheless, a "generally just law" must be maintained even if in a particular case it results in injustice, since "pious persons may not be left in uncertainty" about the requirements of the law.[99]

Oldendorp filled the gap between rule and application with a new concept of equity (*Billigkeit, aequitas*). Equity, in his view, is that which requires careful examination of the concrete circumstances of the particular case, and which enables the judge properly to apply the general rule, the abstract norm, to those circumstances.[100] Here Oldendorp built on, and went beyond, Aristotle's conception (largely repeated by Melanchthon) that equity corrects the defect in a rule whose excessive generality would work an injustice if the rule were applied in a particular case that literally falls within it but that it was not actually meant to include.[101] The Aristotelian contrast is between equity and strict law, not between equity and all law: equity is for the exceptional case. The scholastic jurists had built on this Aristotelian concept of equity and had filled it with new content: equity, they said, protects the poor and helpless, enforces relations of trust and confidence, and otherwise departs from particular laws that work hardship in particular types of cases. For Oldendorp, however, all law is strict law because all law is general and

---

[97] Ibid. Cf. *Lochner v. New York*, 198 U.S. 45, 76 (1905) (Holmes, J., dissenting) ("General propositions do not decide concrete cases.").

[98] *Corpus Reformatorum*, 16: 66-72, 245-247; Stupperich, *Melanchthons Werke*, Part 1, 2: 159; *Loci Communes* (1555), 332-33; *Corpus Reformatorum*, 11: 218-223.

[99] *Corpus Reformatorum*, 22: 612.

[100] See, e.g., Oldendorp, *Disputation*, 13, where Oldendorp writes: "Equity is the judgment of the soul, sought from true reason, concerning the circumstances of things which pertain to moral character, since [these circumstances] indicate what ought or ought not to be done."

Joseph Story cited this very language in his *Commentaries on Equity Jurisprudence*. After discussing the various rules of equitable interpretation of laws which arise "according to their nature and operation, whether they are remedial, or are penal laws; whether they are restrictive of general right, or in advancement of public justice or policy; whether they are of universal application, or of a private and circumscribed intent." Story cited Grotius and others, adding: "There are yet other senses in which equity is used, which might be brought before the reader. The various senses are elaborately collected by Oldendorpius in his work De Jure et Aequitate Disputatio; and he finally offers, what he deems a very exact definition of equity, in its general sense, Aequitas est judicium animi, etc.," quoting Oldendorp's definition in full. See Joseph Story, *Commentaries on Equity Jurisprudence, as Administered in England and America*, 12th ed. (Boston, 1877), 7, n.2.

[101] See Aristotle, *Ethics*, ed. J. Thomson (New York, 1953), 5: 10; see also Aristotle, *The Art of Rhetoric*, trans. J. Freese, (1926) 1: 13-19.

abstract;[102] therefore, every application of the law needs to be governed by equity. Thus, law and equity, *Recht und Billigkeit, ius et aequitas,* stand opposite each other and complete each other, becoming a single thing.[103]

Oldendorp concluded that equity has a threefold function: (1) to suspend legal norms that conflict with conscience, (2) to improve legal norms (for example, by favoring widows, orphans, the aged, and the sick), and (3) to interpret legal norms in every case to which such norms are to be applied.[104] The first and second of these functions reflect traditional views of equity and identify it, as Oldendorp identified it, with natural law. The third, to which Oldendorp subordinated the other two, reflects his own distinctive jurisprudence, in which natural law is merged with human law as it is merged with divine law.[105]

Equity is, in fact, for Oldendorp, the law of conscience. It is natural (God-given) law (*lex in hominibus*). It is not the product of human will or of the kind of reason that depends on human will, which Oldendorp called civil reason.[106] Equity, or natural law, is instilled by God in the conscience of the

---

[102] See Oldendorp, *Disputatio,* 72.

[103] Oldendorp writes: "Natural law and equity are one thing." ("Naturlich Recht und Billigkeit ist ein Ding.") Quoted by Dietze, *Naturrecht in der Gegenwart,* 71. Cf. Wolf, *Grosse Rechtsdenker,* 161. Guido Kisch hails Oldendorp as the first great humanist jurist to transform traditional Aristotelian concepts of equity. Guido Kisch, *Erasmus und die Jurisprudenz seiner Zeit: Studien zum humanistischen Rechtsdenken* (Basel, 1960), 228. Kisch's exposition of Oldendorp's theory of equity does not make clear, however, the nature of that transformation. Dietze writes that, with Oldendorp, "thesis and antithesis stand over against each other unreconciled: the thesis [that] equity and law are two types of value, the antithesis [that] both are one and the same." Dietze, *Johann Oldendorp als Rechtsphilosoph und Protestant,* 88-89. It would be more accurate to say that Oldendorp in fact reconciles these contradictory propositions by stating that law and equity are two conflicting parts of a single whole.

[104] See Macke, *Das Rechts- und Staatsdenken,* 63-66.

[105] Here, too, Oldendorp's concept of natural law is sharply distinguished from that of Aquinas, who speaks of natural law as a middle stage between divine and human law. See Aquinas, *Summa Theologica* I-II, qq. 93-95.

[106] Macke, *Das Rechts- und Staatsdenken,* 151 rightly charges both Erik Wolf and Franz Wieacker with oversimplifying Oldendorp's conception of natural law (or equity). The same charge can be leveled against von Kaltenborn, *Die Vorläufer des Hugo Grotius,* 233-36, on whom both Wolf and Wieacker partly rely. Wolf says that natural law for Oldendorp consists of unchangeable principles derived from natural reason, which are above human law; this characterization is derived principally from Oldendorp's *Billig und Recht,* and does not take adequately into account Oldendorp's other writings. See Wolf, *Grosse Rechtsdenker der deutschen Geistesgeschichte,* 161. Wieacker, relying principally on Oldendorp's *Isagoge,* characterizes his conception of natural law as a source of legal norms, equivalent to the Decalogue. See Wieacker, *Privatrechtsgeschichte,* 283-84. Kaltenborn, also relying on the *Isagoge,* describes Oldendorp's natural law as a divine source of legal principles from which the positive law is derived and by which it is tested. In this view, the Decalogue merely aids the human reason to understand and apply the natural law. Such a

individual person, that is, in that faculty that enables us to distinguish good from evil, just from unjust, and to give judgment.[107]

Oldendorp thus drew on an earlier scholastic conception of conscience, insofar as he defined it as an aspect of practical reason through which general moral principles are applied to concrete circumstances. Thomas Aquinas had developed the conception of conscience as an act of applying knowledge of good and evil to a particular case. Aquinas, however, had not translated this moral concept—as Oldendorp did—into a legal concept. Moreover, Oldendorp, in contrast to Aquinas, followed the Lutheran conception of conscience as pertaining to the whole person, including one's faith, and not simply one's intellectual and moral qualities. Thus, for Oldendorp, as for Luther, the conscience of sinful man can be redeemed by faith, through God's grace.

One must ask: How is the individual person, faced with the difficult question of applying legal norms to concrete cases, to retrieve equity from his or her conscience? How is one to determine what it is that conscience tells him and to know whether it is his conscience speaking or merely his civil reason or his will? Oldendorp's answer may not satisfy the non-Lutheran reader. A "conscience-decision" (*Gewissensentscheidung*), he wrote, is a personal spiritual judgment, a judgment of the soul (*iudicium animi*). In the first instance, it is based, as is any legal decision (*Rechtsentscheidung*), on civil reason, that is, on human, legally trained reason, by which the relevant legal authorities are carefully studied, analyzed, and systematized. It is, however, also based on natural reason, that is, on God-given reason, which is instilled into the souls of those who subject themselves to the laws of Holy Scripture. "A judgment cannot be made in conscience," Oldendorp wrote, "without some formula of law which indicates in the heart of man that that which he does is just or unjust. Therefore, law [i.e., the law of Holy Scripture] is in the person."[108] The answer, in short, is that in order to discern what is equitable, the individual jurist, having exercised his or her civil reason to the maximum degree, must study the Bible, pray to God, and search his or her conscience.

---

misunderstanding of Oldendorp stems, in part, from Kaltenborn's unwarranted reduction of Oldendorp's *Divinae Tabulae* to a mere title of the *Isagoge*. Macke, relying on the totality of Oldendorp's writings, argues convincingly that his complete conception of natural law can be derived only from his concept of nature as God himself, creator of all things (*deus creator omnium*). Natural law, therefore, includes both God-given legal norms (the Decalogue), from which civil legal norms are derived, and principles derived from God-given reason, but it also includes much more, namely, the capacity of conscience, implanted in man by God, equitably to apply norms and principles to concrete circumstances.

[107] See Oldendorp, *Isagoge*, 6-11; Oldendorp, *Billig und Recht*, 58-67.

[108] Oldendorp, *Disputatio*, quoted by Dietze, *Johann Oldendorp als Rechtsphilosoph und Protestant*, 129.

Thus Oldendorp built on Luther's belief in the Christian conscience as the ultimate source of moral decisions. Luther had justified his own breach of his monastic vows and his own defiance of Emperor Charles V at Worms as acts "for God and in my conscience."[109] He denounced laws that conflict with conscience. Oldendorp developed the Lutheran emphasis on conscience into a constituent element of a systematic legal philosophy. He treated conscience, as Luther treated faith, as a "passive" virtue instilled in the heart of God's grace, rather than as an "active" virtue that is the result of human will and reason.

Theory of Politics and the State.—Emphasis on the supremacy of the natural law of conscience over the positive laws of the civil polity did not, however, lead Oldendorp to a broad doctrine of civil disobedience. On the contrary, Oldendorp, like Luther and Melanchthon, emphasized that the civil polity—which he variously called the secular regime (*weltliches Regiment*), the political regime (*politien Regiment*), the republic (*res publica*), the civil order (*ordo civilis*), the magistrates (*magistrati*), and the corporation of citizens (*universitas civium*)—is ordained by God and commands the unconditional obedience of its subjects.[110] Yet Oldendorp was willing—in contrast to Luther and Melanchthon—to give an extensive list of exceptional instances in which the citizen's conscience may require him to disobey the civil authorities. Moreover, Oldendorp went beyond both Luther and Melanchthon in providing a systematic conception of the responsibility of the civil authorities to adhere to the laws of the Bible, to the law inside people, and to the civil laws including, in addition to its own civil laws, the laws of nations.[111] "It is an old question," he wrote, "whether the magistrates are superior to the law or whether the law binds the magistrates." His answer was: "the magistrates are ministers [i.e., servants] of the laws."[112] "It is false and simplistic," he

---

[109] See the account of Luther's speech in *D. Martin Luthers Werke*, 7: 838.

[110] Cf. Dietze, *Johann Oldendorp als Rechtsphilosoph und Protestant*, 94. In his famous *Lexicon juris*, which was widely used in the sixteenth and seventeenth centuries, Oldendorp defines the state (*civitas*) as "a corporation of citizens brought together so that it may prosper by the law of associations." Oldendorp, *Lexicon Juris* (Marburg, 1546), 78.

[111] A summary of his discussion of the *ius gentium* appears in Oldendorp, *Isagoge*, 11-13. See also Köhler, *Luther und die Juristen*, 130, who states that Oldendorp was "the first among the [Lutheran] jurists" to treat in a systematic manner the origin, nature, and function of the *ius gentium*."

[112] Oldendorp, *Lexicon*, 272. Cf. Oldendorp, *Divinae Tabulae*, 19; Oldendorp, *Ratmannspiegel*, 73-77.

wrote, "to assert that the prince has power to go against the law. For it is proper to such majesty . . . to serve the laws."[113]

In addition to placing limitations on state power, Oldendorp developed a consistent theory of the tasks of the civil polity, one that not only built on but also went beyond that of Luther and Melanchthon.[114] As servant of the law of nature and of the law of the Bible, he wrote, the civil polity has the legislative task of enacting laws that conform to God's will. In doing so, the civil authorities should compare the laws of other states, present and past. Administratively, it is the task of the civil polity to support the true faith by seeing to it (among other things) that there are enough preachers, that they are well qualified, that they are well enough paid, and so on, so that they may combat unbelief—not by force but only by God's word; to punish acts of greed, idleness, sumptuousness of dress, and other immoral conduct; and to institute and support good schools and universities because only thereby can capable, conscientious people be trained who will enable the civil polity to achieve its God-given objectives.

It is also the task of each civil polity to maintain peace with other civil polities. The people of all republics, he said, form a *corpus Christianum* and should live, as nature (God) requires, "next to each other, not against each other."[115] War is justified only for defense against an unjust attack. Even when attacked, Oldendorp wrote, a civil polity should seek to settle the conflict peaceably, and even when that is impossible it should leave three days before defending itself in order to give the imminent attackers a chance to change their minds. Moreover, defense should be limited to that which is necessary, because its only purpose is to restore peace.[116]

Oldendorp emphasized the legal personality of the civil polity. Like a single person, it has (in addition to tasks) rights and duties. It is bound not only internationally by the principle *pacta sunt servanda* and by the customary laws of war but also domestically by its own citizens. He carried his idea of state responsibility to the point of requiring the civil polity, as a legal person, to compensate for harm done by its illegal acts, citing the great fourteenth-century jurist Bartolus in support of his view that a court (he did not say which court) should have jurisdiction to impose both criminal and civil

---

113 Quoted by Macke, *Das Rechts- und Staatsdenken*, 79-80.

114 The following list of description of such limitations is found in Oldendorp, *Ratmannspiegel*, 81-97.

115 Oldendorp, *Lexicon*, 407.

116 *Ratmannspiegel*, 92-94.

liability on a republic that has failed to perform its legal duties or has otherwise failed in legislating, judging, or administering.[117]

Oldendorp's theory of limitations on state power was derived from the Lutheran concept that earthly authority does not partake either of divine justice or of absolute reason or of human self fulfillment, but is a product of the fall of man from grace and of a lost paradise. As the great German jurist Erik Wolf has written, Oldendorp rejected the doctrine of Roman Catholic theology and of the canon lawyers that "tried to turn divine law into positive law." Oldendorp articulated in Wolf's words, "the first German natural-law doctrine," combining scholastic concepts and Roman law principles with the Lutheran ethic of conscience. This doctrine, Wolf states, was distinguished from the later Enlightenment concept of a rational law of nature by its emphasis on common needs, on the natural orders of the various social classes ("estates"), and on Holy Scripture.[118]

Peter Macke states that Oldendorp was closer to Erasmus than to Luther in his concern to Christianize public life through law.[119] Oldendorp's concern, however, was based directly on Lutheran principles. "The purpose of law," Oldendorp wrote, "is that we may peacefully pass through this shadowy life and be led to Christ and to eternal life."[120] He emphasized "the third use" of the law—its pedagogical, or educational, function; Oldendorp called law *paedagogus noster ad Christum*—our teacher in the path to Christ.[121] This involved a certain confidence in human reason; while emphasizing the depravity of man, Oldendorp wrote that despite the Fall, sparks (*igniculi*) of human reason had been retained.[122] To be sure, he built a huge fire out of those sparks by uniting them with conscience and by uniting conscience, as Luther and Melanchthon did not do, with Holy Scripture.

Summary and Conclusions.—Conventional accounts of the history of Western legal philosophy have obscured the contribution of the Lutheran Reformation of the sixteenth century—in substantial part because of their narrow view of the sixteenth century, of Lutheranism, and of legal philosophy in general.

Many writers have treated the sixteenth century as a mere transition period in the history of legal philosophy between the scholastic Middle Ages

---

[117] Ibid., 80-82.

[118] Wolf, *Grosse Rechtsdenker*, 140-41.

[119] Macke, *Das Rechts- und Staatsdenken*, 110.

[120] Oldendorp, *Lexicon*, 249.

[121] Ibid.

[122] See, e.g., Oldendorp, *Isagoge*, 9-10.

and the seventeenth-century inauguration of modern times. "The jurists of the 16th century," it is argued, "were doorkeepers to the modern age of legal philosophy," who "were largely incapable of entering ideas of their own."[123] At best, they served as middle links between Gratian, Aquinas, and Ockham, on the one hand, and Grotius, Hobbes, and Locke, on the other. Indeed, when sixteenth-century legal thought has been taken more seriously, it has usually been connected not with the Reformation but with "the Renaissance," an indefinite time period whose beginnings are often traced to the late thirteenth and fourteenth centuries and whose ending is variously located in the sixteenth or even early 17th century. The novelty and significance of the reformers' teachings have thus been lost on most contemporary interpreters. Lutheran legal philosophy has remained largely in the shadows of legal humanism and Machiavellian politics.

Many writers have also analyzed Lutheran thought in general from too narrow a perspective. They have confined their analysis to the writings of Martin Luther alone and have found therein only the rudiments of a legal philosophy haphazardly arranged. They have failed to consider the systematic exposition of Lutheran teachings in the many confessions, catechisms, and creeds of sixteenth-century Germany; in the voluminous writings of Melanchthon, Bucer, Brenz, and other important Lutheran theologians and ethicists; and in the treatises of Oldendorp, Lagus, Kling, and other important Lutheran jurists.

These writers have further confined their attention to Luther's reform of dogma and liturgy and thus come to regard Lutheranism as merely a spiritual, even mystical, movement. "Luther's Church," writes a leading Reformation historian, "was confined exclusively to the Word and to the spiritual comfort of the individual. . . . Luther [was] wary of attaching any significance to details of a secular order."[124] The fact that Luther and his colleagues consigned law to a secular realm under civil authority has misled many scholars to suppose that they had made law and religion mutually irrelevant, and, further, that their new beliefs and doctrines were applicable only to religion. Starting from this assumption, it is easy to conclude that the few contributions that Lutheran writers did make to legal philosophy remained unoriginal, eclectic, and superficial, comprised of little more than patristic and Roman Catholic commonplaces. In fact, just the opposite is true. Lutheran conceptions of the relationship of the earthly to the heavenly realms and of law to

---

123 Ernst Cassirer, quoted by Dooyeweerd, *Encyclopedie der Rechtswetenschap*, 1: 93.

124 Hajo Holborn, *A History of Modern Germany: The Reformation* (Princeton, NJ, 1964), 188, 190.

faith was the source not only of a new theology but also of a new jurisprudence and a new political science as well.

Finally, many writers have stopped with the question of whether Lutheran legal philosophy belongs to the natural-law school or to the positivist school of jurisprudence. They have sought answers in those terms to analytical questions that are currently in vogue—concerning the nature of rules, the sources and sanctions of law, the definition of a legal system, the nature of legal obligation, and the like. These categories and questions of contemporary jurisprudence leave large portions of Lutheran legal philosophy untouched.

The basic structure of Western legal philosophy was first established during and after the revolutionary upheaval of the late eleventh and early twelfth centuries. Then, for the first time, great scholars of the newly revived and resystematized Roman law and the new system of canon law undertook to formulate a coherent set of principles concerning the nature and purposes of law, the sources of law, the various kinds of law, and the relationship of law to justice and order. They drew, to be sure, on the works of Plato, Aristotle, and the Greek and Roman Stoics as well as on the writings of the Church Fathers and later moralists and theologians. Nevertheless, none of their predecessors had treated legal philosophy as a separate comprehensive body of knowledge, distinct from, though related to, both moral philosophy and theology.

Not only the basic structure but also some of the basic postulates of Western legal philosophy were first articulated in the twelfth and thirteenth centuries. The early scholastic jurists taught that human law, including both customary and statutory law, derives its legitimacy from natural law, which is in turn a reflection of divine law. Natural law was thought to be immediately accessible to human reason. Divine law was revealed to human reason in sacred texts and in the traditions of the Church. At the same time, the scholastic jurists recognized that human selfishness, pride, and the drive for power are sources of unjust laws, which are contrary both to natural law and to divine law. Thus, human law, though a response to divine will, was seen to be also a product of a defective human will, which could be and needed to be corrected by human reason. Human reason, it was said, coincided with natural law and divine law in postulating that crimes should be punished, that contracts should be enforced, that relationships of trust and confidence should be protected, that accused persons should be heard in their defense, and, in sum, that legal rules and procedures should conform to standards of justice.

Stated broadly, these and other postulates of Western legal philosophy, first articulated by Roman Catholic jurists and theologians, survived in the writings of the Lutheran reformers. Lutheran legal philosophy must, therefore, be understood, in the first instance, in terms of its continuity with Roman Catholic teachings. The Lutheran assault upon scholastic legal philosophy was from within a tradition that the scholastics had first established.

Nevertheless, the Lutheran reformers introduced revolutionary changes in that tradition. In analyzing those changes we have drawn on the writings of the two persons who may be said to have founded Lutheran legal philosophy—Luther himself and his cohort Philip Melanchthon—and the one person, Johann Oldendorp, who developed that philosophy most fully. All three were trained in theology, philosophy, and law, though Luther was more the theologian, Melanchthon was more the philosopher, and Oldendorp was more the jurist. Despite differences among them, they all shared the same basic theological, philosophical, and legal outlook. In this summary we shall stress what they had in common.

By their theology, and especially by their twin doctrines of justification by faith alone and the priesthood of all believers, the Lutheran reformers undermined the canon law and the sacramental system, and, therewith, the entire jurisdiction of the Roman Catholic Church. This gave to civil rulers the sole prerogative of legislation, administration, and adjudication within their respective territories. By the same token, however, laws enacted by civil rulers now lacked the sanctity that they had formerly had by virtue of ecclesiastical endorsement under the two-swords theory, with its division of powers between the universal church organized under the papacy and the plurality of secular kingdoms, feudal lordships, and urban polities.

Moreover, the reformers attacked the Roman Catholic belief that reason, standing alone, is compatible with faith and is capable of proving independently what is revealed by faith. It was this belief in the synthesis of reason and revelation that underlay the Roman Catholic doctrine of natural law.[125] Lutherans, on the other hand, taught that not only human will but also human reason itself is corrupted by innate pride, greed, and other forms of egoism. They did not doubt that there were transcendent moral principles by which human conduct and human laws were to be judged, but they did not believe that such principles could be derived ultimately from reason as such.

---

[125] "The central problem of late medieval intellectual and religious history was the mentality that had given birth to the synthesis of reason and revelation, the presumptuous, seductive vision of high medieval theology." Steven E. Ozment, *The Age of Reform 1250-1550: An Intellectual and Religious History of Late Medieval and Reformation Europe* (New Haven, CT, 1980), 21.

Lacking the endorsement of an independent ecclesiastical hierarchy, and lacking a foundation in objective and disinterested human reason, what was to justify civil laws other than mere expediency? Why should anyone obey the law unless compelled to do so? What made them laws and not mere commands?

The theological answer to these fundamental jurisprudential questions was rooted in the Lutheran two-kingdoms theory, with its postulate that God is present, though hidden, in the earthly kingdom. Despite their corruption, Christians living in the earthly kingdom are called to carry out God's work there. They are called to maintain order and to do justice, however defective such order and justice will inevitably be. Order and justice are not paths to salvation, but they are forms in which God's presence in the earthly kingdom is concealed. They are ordained by him partly to make human life livable and partly to point the way—though they themselves are not the way—to faith.

Although these theological beliefs do not in themselves constitute a legal philosophy, they nevertheless negate the conventional view that Lutheran theology is concerned solely with the spiritual life of the individual and is indifferent to politics and law. In addition, they provide a theological basis for distinguishing between the duties that the individual person owes to God and the duties that he owes to his neighbors.

Both sets of duties, according to Lutheran theology, are set forth in the Bible, especially in the Ten Commandments. Not only for Lutheran theology but for legal philosophy as well, the Ten Commandments replaced ecclesiastical tradition and the canon law as the transcendent source of divine, natural, and human law. With respect to that part of law that regulates civil relationships, the last seven Commandments were interpreted as an authoritative statement of fundamental principles of public and private law, including respect for political authority, for human life, for property rights, for family relationships, for procedural justice, and for the rights of others.

Lutheran legal philosophy was not content, however, to rest the ultimate test of the validity of law on the Bible alone, although early in his career Luther was tempted to do so. The Bible speaks to the faithful, but not all people subject to civil authority are believers. God ordains civil authority and civil law for pagans as well as Christians. Indeed, it is because of the fallen state of humankind that law in any form is needed—primarily to show sinful man what is required of him and how helpless he is to fulfill those requirements. Therefore, outside the Bible, and independently of it, God has implanted in the conscience of every man certain moral insights, which, in fact, correspond to the principles revealed to faith in the Ten Commandments. Melanchthon classified these universal moral insights, among the "elements of knowledge," which themselves shape reason and hence cannot be proved by reason. Nevertheless, if reason is guided by faith, it can understand and accept, even though it cannot prove, that which is revealed directly to conscience. Thus, reason can be rescued, so to speak, by faith. In Oldendorp's terms, conscience is a higher form of reason—not ordinary reason but divine reason.

As the Lutheran theory of conscience brought faith into contact with reason, so the Lutheran theory of civic, or political, righteousness brought the heavenly kingdom into contact with the earthly kingdom. Here the "third use" of the law, emphasized by both Melanchthon and Oldendorp, played a major role. Natural law—the moral legal principles known to conscience and confirmed in the Decalogue—serves as a guide to faithful people, especially those in high places, in the ways of justice, fairness, altruism, and peace.

The concept of the educational role of law was carried over in Lutheran legal philosophy from natural law to positive law. As it is an important function of natural law to educate the civil authorities, Melanchthon and Oldendorp wrote, so it is an important function of the positive law of the civil authorities to nurture the moral attitudes and sentiments of those who are subject to such laws. Here Melanchthon and Oldendorp spelled out in detail the ways in which various branches of positive law, including criminal law, civil law, ecclesiastical law, and constitutional law, contribute not only to social order and social welfare but also to the moral improvement of society.

Of special significance for the development of Western legal philosophy was Oldendorp's insight that the generality and objectivity inherent in legal rules is both their great virtue and their great vice. Equally important was his further insight that the vice of generality and objectivity in legal rules can be cured and the virtue preserved through their conscientious application in specific circumstances. Melanchthon the philosopher sought to reconcile legal norms with reason and conscience in the general sense of those terms. Oldendorp the jurist explored at length and in depth particular applications of rules and principles, and showed the paradoxes that arise when general rules and principles are invoked in concrete cases. Oldendorp concluded that conscientious application of rules was required not only in exceptional cases but in all cases, and not only from the point of view of fairness in the particular case but also from the point of view of the ultimate consistency of the rules themselves. He found that ultimate consistency in the purposes that the rules were intended to serve in their specific applications. Thus, Oldendorp made conscience the master key to the unity and integrity of the legal system in action. This was perhaps the most important specific contribution made by Lutheran legal thought to Western jurisprudence. Oldendorp's theory of

equity as a higher reason that is brought into play in the conscientious application of rules is reflected in many modern Western legal concepts and
institutions. Perhaps the most striking of these is the Anglo-American concept
of "jury equity."

The Lutheran emphasis on the role of individual conscience as a source of
justice must be balanced against its equal emphasis on the role of civil
authority in defining and enforcing justice and, more generally, in guarding
religious worship, morality, and social welfare ("the common weal"). Luther
himself considered that his conception of the dignity and mission of the
state—the *Obrigkeit*—was one of his most important contributions to the
religious and political thought of his time.[126] Indeed, the Lutheran Reformation created the modern secular state by allocating to the holders of state
offices ultimate responsibility for the exercise of functions that had previously
been in the jurisdiction of holders of ecclesiastical offices. Thus, state officials
in Lutheran territories assumed jurisdiction over the clergy, church property,
education, poor relief, medical care, moral and religious crimes, marriage and
family relations, wills, and many other matters which in Roman Catholic
territories were regulated by ecclesiastical officials operating under canon law.
The very concept of secular state sovereignty was closely associated with the
expanded role of the secular *Obrigkeit*, a German cognate of the Latin word
superanitas, which literally means (as *Obrigkeit* literally means) "overness" or
"highness" ("superness"), and that was translated into French as *souveraineté*
and into English as sovereignty.

The elimination of the checks upon secular authority traditionally exercised by the Roman Catholic hierarchy substantially increased the danger that
the prince would assert absolute power, that is, a power above the law.
Moreover, Lutheran theology emphasized that the prince ruled by divine right
and that his subjects were bound to honor and obey him as the father of his
country. It is this aspect of Lutheranism that has led some to see in it a basis
for totalitarian dictatorship.[127] Nevertheless, Lutheran legal philosophy, like

---

126 See *D. Martin Luthers Werke*, 32: 390; 38: 102.

127 In *From Luther to Hitler: the History of Fascist Political Philosophy* (Boston/New
York, 1941), William M. McGovern argues that Luther was the founder of the German
national identity, which found its ultimate expression in Nazi totalitarianism and
antisemitism. Similarly, William Ebenstein in *Great Political Thinkers: Plato to the Present*,
4th ed. (New York, 1969), 305, writes that "Luther added to his strong respect for the state
an equally passionate feeling of German nationalism and even racialism; thus he became—
the only Protestant leader to have such progeny—one of the spiritual ancestors of Prussian
nationalism and German Nazism."

The view that the totalitarian state has roots in Lutheran thought of the sixteenth
century is sharply criticized by Thomas Brady, who points out that Luther's doctrine of the
two kingdoms, far from deifying the state, relegated it to the kingdom of this world, which

Roman Catholic legal philosophy, contained important counterbalances to tyranny. First, like Roman Catholic legal philosophy, it emphasized the principle that the ruler is bound by his own laws because their ultimate source is in natural law. The concept of the prince as a father to his people itself implied a responsibility on his part inconsistent with tyranny. Second, Lutheran legal philosophy emphasized the importance of written published laws, whose function was, in part, to restrain wicked rulers. Third, it declared the authority of Roman law as the written embodiment of reason; although each territorial prince was thought to have succeeded to Roman imperial authority, nevertheless, Roman law was also seen as a transnational *jus commune*, whose interpretation was entrusted to learned jurists who glossed and commented on and synthesized the ancient texts. Finally, the Lutheran jurists found both in Scripture and in conscience a general right of resistance to tyrannical rule. Conscience was the seat of both civil obedience and civil disobedience. When positive law contradicts natural law, the conscientious Lutheran Christian is torn between one's duty to obey the divinely ordained

---

is also the kingdom of the devil, and further, that Luther placed the state alongside the family and the church as three autonomous but interacting modes of social relationships. Brady attributes the source of the "Luther-to-Hitler legend" to certain German Lutheran theologians of the 1920s and early 1930s who supported Hitler and to Nazi propaganda. See Thomas Brady, in James D. Tracy, ed., *Luther and the State: The Reformer's Teaching in its Social Setting* (New York, 1986), 31, 33, 35-37, 43-44.

To be sure, a large majority of German Lutheran leaders supported Hitler after 1933, while only a very small minority, including Dietrich Bonhoeffer and Martin Niemoeller, stood up boldly against him. Yet this in itself proves only that Luther's sixteenth-century doctrine of "inner-worldliness" (as Bonhoeffer put it) was susceptible of being exploited in the twentieth century to justify nonresistance to evil and the fusion of church and state. In Norway, for example, Lutheran Bishop Berggrav invoked Luther's call for passive resistance to secular tyranny and active resistance to papal heresy as a basis for open opposition to the Nazi occupation of that country.

The view that Luther preached antisemitism is based on his violent denunciations of the Jews, which, however, must be understood, as Heiko Oberman has shown, in the context of his own time, which knew neither religious tolerance, on the one hand, nor antisemitism, on the other. Thus Luther could vehemently advocate the most severe repression of the Jews—and also of Turks, papists, and Anabaptists—because of their religious beliefs while at the same time praising Jews as the "blood-friends, cousins, and brothers of the Lord." It was the supposed sinfulness of adherents to Judaism, that is, to the Jewish faith, not any supposed biological or other inferiority of Jews as an ethnic group, that was offensive to Christians in an age when it was universally accepted that religion is essentially a communal, and not merely a personal, matter and that it is necessary that a given community should have a single common religious belief system. In fact, Luther rejected the earlier Roman Catholic doctrine of the collective guilt of the Jewish people for their part in the crucifixion of Christ and based his strong anti-Judaic doctrine on their present refusal to accept Christ as their savior. See generally Heiko A. Oberman, *The Roots of Anti-Semitism in the Age of Renaissance and Reformation*, trans. J. Porter (Philadelphia, PA, 1983).

"powers that be" and one's duty to obey one's own divinely ordained sense of justice.

A contemporary American legal philosopher may be frustrated by the inability of Lutheran legal philosophy to resolve the tension between law and morals by rational means. Yet it is important to recognize that Lutheran legal philosophy is a primary source, in the philosophical as well as the historical sense, of both contemporary legal positivism and contemporary natural-law theory. Viewed as a positivist theory, Lutheran legal philosophy defines the law of civil society as the will of the lawmaker expressed in a system of rules, backed by coercive sanctions, whose primary function is to preserve social order. Melanchthon wrote that "politics"—which he also called "the state" and sometimes "the *Obrigkeit*"—is simply the method of "creating legitimate order within the community" and of creating laws "to govern property, contracts, succession, and other matters."[128] This was the first statement of the German concept of the *Rechtsstaat*, "the law-state."[129] To be fully effective, legal rules, Melanchthon and Oldendorp stressed, must be promulgated, predictable, generally applicable, and binding on both political authorities and their subjects. The claim of a legal system, or of a given law or legal decision, to be an expression of reason and justice cannot be verified, according to Lutheran legal philosophy, from within the legal system itself but only on the basis of moral standards derived from outside the legal system. Thus, Lutheran legal philosophy accepted the basic premise of contemporary legal positivism, namely, that law and morals are to be sharply distinguished from each other and that the law that is should not be confused with the law that ought to be. To identify law with morality is to foster uncertainty and instability in the law and hence disorder; it is also to make the civil law the source rather than the object of moral criticism and thus to foster injustice.

Lutheran legal philosophy rejects the definition of law propounded by Thomas Aquinas: that law is an ordinance of reason for the common good made by one entrusted with the care of the community.[130] Such a definition, according to Lutheran thought, gives an unwarranted sanctity to both law and

---

[128] *Corpus Reformatorum*, 16: 436.

[129] On the development of the German Rechtsstaat theories in the later nineteenth and twentieth centuries, see Otto von Gierke, *Johannes Althusius und die Entwicklung der naturrechtlichen Staatstheorien* ("Die Idee des Rechtsstaats"), ed. J. Gierke, 5th ed. (Breslau, 1958), 264; F. Daemstaedter, *Die Grenzen der Wirksamkeit des Rechtstaats* (Berlin, 1930); Herman Dooyeweerd, *De Crisis der humanistischen Staatsleer in het Licht eener calvinistische Kosmologie en Kennistheorie* (Amsterdam, 1931), 40. On the contributions of Lutheranism to the modern idea of the state, see Gunther Holstein, *Luther und die deutsche Staatsidee* (Tübingen, 1926).

[130] Aquinas, *Summa Theologica*, I-II, q. 90, article 4.

reason. It rests on an overoptimistic conception of human nature and, consequently, on an overoptimistic conception of the role of the state as an instrument of justice. A lawfully promulgated decree of a sovereign is law, in Lutheran legal philosophy, even though it is arbitrary in its purpose and effect.

Viewed, on the other hand, as a natural-law theory, Lutheran legal philosophy postulates that every person has within himself or herself certain moral sentiments relating to legal justice, including a respect for civil authority, for human life, for property, for family responsibilities, for fair procedures, and, in general, for the rights of oneself and of others. These moral sentiments, insights, or inclinations reside partly in reason and will but primarily in conscience. The conscience of every person is thus a source of a natural law, that is, of a principle of thought and action that is inherent in human nature. Lutheran natural law theory, in contrast to Roman Catholic, is essentially a moral theory, not a legal one. It rests primarily on an innate sense of justice, to which reason is subordinate. Reason, from a Lutheran standpoint, is too weak, too biased by egoism, to sustain such a sense of justice. Thus, there are bound to be rational disagreements among people concerning the meanings of the various principles of the law and concerning their application to concrete cases. In the event of rational disagreement, each person must turn to his or her own conscience in making such application.

To the extent that the Lutheran theory of natural law is essentially a moral rather than a legal theory, it is reconcilable with contemporary legal positivism. It goes beyond the parameters of legal positivism, however, in invoking conscience for the application of legal rules to specific circumstances. In the legal process of judging or administering, injustices that would flow from a purely rational application of broad rules to concrete cases can only be corrected by sensitivity to the particular circumstances of the case, including the character of the parties, their motivation, the consequences of alternative decisions, and other specific factors. Similarly, in the legal process of legislating, legislators should be concerned not only with policy in the general sense but also with the specific circumstances that give rise to the need for the law in question and the specific consequences entailed in its application. Thus Lutheran legal philosophy is congenial to—and, in fact, in sixteenth-century Germany led to—a massive classification and systematization of the rules of law coupled with a flexibility in their application based on conscience and called equity. Stated in this condensed and abstract form, Lutheran legal philosophy has something to offer to contemporary jurisprudential thought. Above all, it suggests a mode of reconciling differences between what may be called the "higher law" school of legal thought, which would treat such values as equality and privacy as transcendent rights that are beyond the jurisdiction of the political community to infringe, and, on the other hand, what may be called the "political realities" school, which would deny the character of law to principles that have not been formally accepted as such by the duly constituted lawmaking authorities. Lutheran legal philosophy claims that the conflict between these two schools cannot be resolved by the exercise of reason. It claims further that it can be resolved, in practice, by the exercise of conscience. It offers no guide, however, to the exercise of conscience except a theological one. Those who cannot accept a theological guide are thus left with a hard but nevertheless interesting and even valuable lesson.

7

THE RELIGIOUS SOURCES
OF GENERAL CONTRACT LAW:
AN HISTORICAL PERSPECTIVE[*]

I n his dramatic, if not mystical, account of the birth, growth, senescence, and death of American contract law, and of its ultimate dissolution into the law of tort, Grant Gilmore certainly did not intend to join forces with those who would later seize on his story as evidence that both contract and tort, and, indeed, law all together, are merely artificial devices to support an hierarchical and hegemonic political structure and to facilitate economic exploitation of the weak by the strong.[1] Yet Gilmore's exposé of the logical circularities and fallacies of contract doctrine (especially as it is taught in first-year courses in American law schools) does add fuel to the already raging fires of skepticism—skepticism not only about the coherence of individual branches of the legal tree (contracts, torts, property, etc.) but also about the validity of doctrinal legal analysis and ultimately of law itself.

---

[*] Reprinted from *The Journal of Law and Religion* 4 (1986): 103-124. Presented at a colloquium held in 1985 at Loyola Law School in Los Angeles devoted to the place that religion should occupy in the first year law school curriculum.

[1] Grant Gilmore, *The Death of Contract* (Columbus, OH, 1974). Cf. Clare Dalton, "An Essay in the Deconstruction of Contract Doctrine," *Yale Law Journal* 94 (1985): 997, 1012, 1040-1043, 1067-1071, 1084-1087; Betty Mensch, "Freedom of Contract as Ideology," *Stanford Law Review* 33 (1981): 753; Peter Gabel and Jay M. Feinmann, "Contract Law as Ideology," in David Kairys, ed., *The Politics of Law: A Progressive Critique* (New York, 1982), 172, 177.

Arthur Corbin—Gilmore's mentor and the hero of his book—did not share that skepticism, although he strongly opposed the rigidities of the then prevailing contract doctrine, especially as represented in the teachings of his friend and rival, Samuel Williston. Unlike Williston, Corbin was prepared to give a contractual remedy for losses caused by reliance on a promise, and thus to bring contract and tort into a common focus. He was also more willing than Williston to expand concepts of fairness at the expense of strict liability for breach. Nevertheless, Corbin did not doubt, and surely did not seek to undermine, the coherence of contract law.

Although Gilmore went farther than Corbin in his critique of traditional doctrine, he, too, was concerned to restructure contract law, not to destroy it. Above all, Gilmore retained a commercial lawyer's respect for *contracts*—in the plural; his attack was rather on the notion of *contract*—in the singular—as an abstract entity, a thing-in-itself, reflecting in its very essence the coherent body of concepts, principles, and rules that had come to surround it: offer and acceptance, consideration, formal requirements, defenses of fraud and duress and mistake, excuse based on impossibility or frustration, and the rest. This entire body of learning was now thought to be based on a questionable theory of the priority of intent, or will, which in turn was based on a questionable theory of the priority of party autonomy. It was the logical symmetry of the doctrines and their basis in the will-theory and the autonomy-theory of contract law that came under attack in Gilmore's *Death of Contract*, as it had come under attack for the preceding fifty years—in the first instance by those scholars who called themselves "legal realists," but also by other legal scholars, like Corbin, who opposed the Legal Realist Movement, and, most important, by courts and legislatures which, by their decisions and statutes, were breaking down the old categories in response to fundamental changes in the economy itself.

Looking back at what has happened to contract law *in action* during the twentieth century, and especially to accepted contract practices, one is struck by the fact that the priorities of contractual intent and party autonomy, which still form the basis of contract law *in theory*, no longer correspond to reality in most situations. Contracts of adhesion, regulated contracts, contracts entered into under economic compulsion, and other types of prefabricated contractual arrangements, are now typical rather than exceptional. Doctrines of frustration and of substantial performance have been greatly expanded. The defense of unconscionability has become a reality in consumer sales and is a potential obstacle to contractual autonomy in other types of transactions as well. Duties of cooperation and of mitigation of losses have begun to change the nature of many types of contractual relationships. Promissory estoppel has spawned nonpromissory estoppel, notably in the form of implied warranties which, though contractual in theory, nevertheless "run with the chattel," as someone has said, "half way around the world."

The breakdown of traditional contract law in practice has given some support to those legal theorists who contend that all law must be judged not in terms of doctrinal consistency but in terms of social consequences. Some of these theorists go so far as to contend that the very effort to apply rules on the basis of their consistency with other legal rules, or their conformity to underlying legal principles, serves only to obfuscate the political and economic functions that every such purported application inevitably performs.

To understand the significance of the attack that has been launched against general contract law in the past two generations, however, one must go back much farther in time than Gilmore went. One must also go much farther in space. Gilmore imagined that Christopher Columbus Langdell and Oliver Wendell Holmes, Jr. invented the modern system of contract doctrine which Williston later refined. In fact, Langdell in 1870 carried over into American legal thought ideas that had been propounded in France, Germany, England, and elsewhere for a hundred years. The Enlightenment of the late 18th century stimulated the desire to rationalize and systematize the law in new ways. In England, Jeremy Bentham called for the "codification"—a word of his own creation—of the various branches of law. In the wake of the French Revolution, France adopted separate codes for civil law, civil procedure, criminal law, criminal procedure, and commercial law. Although England and the United States, like Germany, resisted codification of substantive civil law, nevertheless the idea was taken up everywhere in the West that the entire body of civil law, and, within it, its component parts, should be rationalized and systematized anew, whether in a code (as in France) or in scholarly treatises (as in Germany) or in court decisions collected by law teachers (as in England and the United States). Indeed, in the United States, a generation before Langdell, William Story wrote *A Treatise on the Law of Contracts Not Under Seal* (1844) and Theophilus Parsons wrote *The Law of Contracts* (1853).

And so Langdell and others did for American contract law what Powell (1790), Chitty (1826), Addison (1847), and Leake (1867) had done for English contract law, and, in effect, what the French commentators on the *Code civil* and the German Pandectists had done for contract law in their respective countries. They attempted to reduce it to a set of concepts, principles, and rules which would be applicable to all contracts.

It is, however, a great mistake to suppose that this was the first time that any such attempt had been made, and an even greater mistake to suppose that the nineteenth-century systematizers of contract law simply invented the concepts, principles, and rules upon which they founded their new system. The "general law of contract" was, in fact, invented much earlier, and the nineteenth-century jurists drew upon the older learning, and the older tradition, in establishing their new version of it.[2]

Yet the nineteenth-century jurists differed from their predecessors in several crucial respects. Perhaps the most important of these was their concern to cut the general law of contract loose from its moorings in a religious—more specifically, a Christian—belief system. They sought to replace those moorings with their own Enlightenment belief system, based on rationalism and individualism. It was that Enlightenment faith which found expression, in nineteenth-century contract law, in the overriding principles of freedom of will and party autonomy. Those principles were applied, however, to an already existing system of contract law, many of whose basic features were preserved.

The Origins of Modern Contract Law in the Canon Law of the Roman Catholic Church.—Modern contract law originated in Europe in the late eleventh and early twelfth centuries. It was that epoch that gave birth to the modern Western belief in the autonomy of law, its professional character, its integrity both as a system of institutions and as a body of learning, and its capacity for organic growth over generations and centuries. It was then that consciously integrated systems of law came to be formed, first in the church and then in the various secular polities—kingdoms, cities, feudal domains, mercantile communities. It was then that various branches of law, within those systems, were first given structure: criminal law, family law, corporation law, mercantile law, and others.[3]

Starting in the last two decades of the eleventh century, the glossators of Roman law began to construct out of Justinian's massive texts, newly discovered after more than five hundred years of virtual oblivion, a coherent *corpus juris* that had only been adumbrated in the original writings. (Justinian had not called his texts a *corpus juris*.) Equally important, the canon lawyers began to create, partly with the help of the new Romanist legal science, a consciously integrated legal system to be applied in the newly created

---

[2] See James R. Gordley, "Review of Grant Gilmore, *The Death of Contract*," *Harvard Law Review* 89 (1975): 452, 453-454. Gordley stresses the Romanist contract law of the twelfth century and thereafter. The canon law of contract that emerged in those centuries was in some ways even more integrated and systematized.

[3] This is the main theme of Harold J. Berman, *Law and Revolution: The Formation of the Western Legal Tradition* (Cambridge, MA, 1983).

hierarchy of ecclesiastical administrative and judicial agencies, culminating in the papal curia. Eleventh- and twelfth-century Roman law (I shall henceforth call it "Romanist law," to distinguish it from the earlier Roman law whose vocabulary and rules it selectively adopted and transformed) was not as such the positive law of any jurisdiction; it was law taught as *ratio scripta* in the emerging universities of Europe and it was drawn upon selectively by every jurisdiction, ecclesiastical and secular, as a subsidiary law, to fill gaps, to interpret, and sometimes to correct the positive law. Canon law, on the other hand, after 1075, was the positive law of the church, replenished by papal decrees and decretals and by the legislation of church councils; it was directly applicable throughout Western Christendom to most aspects of the lives of the clergy and to many aspects of the lives of the laity.[4]

To say that modern contract law was gradually formed in the late eleventh and the twelfth centuries is not to say that there were not, before then, contracts, in the sense of legally binding agreements. There was, however, among the peoples that inhabited Western Europe in the year 1000, no general principle that a promise or an exchange of promises may in itself give rise to legal liability. Legal liability attached to promises only if they were embodied in formal religious oaths, which were almost always secured by some kind of pledge. The obligation that was enforced was not the mutual contractual obligation of the parties but the oath, that is, the obligation to God (or, before Christianity, to the gods); the legal liability that was imposed was the forfeiture of the pledge. Originally the pledge might consist of the surrender of the oath-taker's own person, symbolized in the formal transfer of his faith (*fides facta*) through the ritual of shaking hands. Alternatively, other persons could be pledged as hostages, and eventually property could also be pledged as security.[5] A sharp distinction was made between the oath-taker's obligation (*Schuld*) and his liability (*Haftung*). The breach of obligation triggered liability but was not itself a basis of liability. In itself it had no legal consequences, though it had spiritual consequences and could be punished as a sin in the penitential processes of the local monastic order or parish

---

[4] Pope Gregory VII's revolutionary document of 1075, *Dictates of the Pope* (*Dictatus papae*), declared for the first time the independence of the Roman church from secular rulers and the supremacy of the papal curia over all ecclesiastical courts. See Berman, *Law and Revolution*, 94-99. Though the Dictates were never made a formal part of the canon law, they formed the basis of many of its main principles.

[5] See Raoul Berger, "From Hostage to Contract," *Illinois Law Review* 35 (1940): 154 and literature cited therein; Johannes Bärmann, "Pacta sunt servanda: Consideration sur l'histoire du contrat consensual," *Revue internationale de droit comparé* 13 (1961): 18.

priesthood.[6] The legal consequences were wholly interwoven with the pledge and consisted simply of its forfeiture. If forfeiture was resisted, resort was had either to conciliation or to blood-feud.

Germanic law (including Frankish, Anglo-Saxon, Burgundian, Lombard, and many other varieties of clan law) also recognized a duty of restitution arising from a half-completed exchange: a party who had transferred property to another was entitled to receive from the other the purchase price or other equivalent. This also was *not* a contractual remedy in the modern sense of the word "contractual."

The older Roman law of contracts, reflected in Justinian's compilation, was, to be sure, much more sophisticated than the Germanic law. Names were provided for various ways of forming contracts and for various types of contracts that fell within those forms. Thus certain named ("nominate") contracts were formed by following a prescribed verbal formula, others by formal entry in certain account books, a third category by delivery of the object covered by the contract, and a fourth by informally expressed consent. The fourth category included sale, lease, partnership, and mandate (a form of agency). Unnamed ("innominate") contracts included a gift for a gift, a gift for an act, an act for a gift, and an act for an act. Innominate contracts were actionable only after one party had performed his promise. In addition to an elaborate classification of categories and types of contracts, the Justinian texts included hundreds of scattered rules—opinions of jurists, holdings in decided cases, decrees of emperors, and so forth—concerning their operation.

Nowhere, however, did the texts of Justinian contain a systematic explanation of the reasons for the rules of contract law or for the classification of types of contracts. Nowhere was there stated a theory or even a general concept of contractual liability as such. Law in the Justinian texts, including those parts of it which we think of today as "contract" law, was not only unsystematized but casuistic in the extreme; its rules were sometimes classified, but the taxonomy was not explained in theoretical terms.[7]

The glossators of the late eleventh and the twelfth centuries, in indexing the Roman texts, collected the various statements of the older Roman jurists on contracts and, in glossing them, elaborated general concepts and principles that they found to be implicit in them. The canonists went even farther,

---

[6] See John T. McNeill and Helena M. Gamer, *Medieval Handbooks of Penance: A Translation of the Principal Libri Poenitentiales and Selections From Related Documents* (New York, 1938). See Berman, *Law and Revolution*, 68-84.

[7] See John P. Dawson, *The Oracles of the Law* (Ann Arbor, MI, 1968), 114ff.; Fritz Schulz, *The History of Roman Legal Science* (Oxford, 1946); Berman, *Law and Revolution*, 127ff.

offering a general theory of contractual liability and applying that theory to actual disputes litigated in the ecclesiastical courts.

The canonists developed for the first time the general principle that an agreement as such—a *nudum pactum*—may give rise to a civil action. Drawing partly on the texts of Justinian but also on the Bible, on natural law, on the penitentials, on canons of church councils and of bishops and popes, and on Germanic law, the canonists drew a conclusion which none of those sources, taken individually, had ever before drawn: that consensual obligations as such are, as a general principle, binding not only morally but also legally, even though they were entered into without any formalities. By legally binding, the canonists meant that the promisee had a right against the promisor, enforceable in an ecclesiastical court, to the performance of the promise or else to compensation for losses. This general principle was in sharp contrast to the then prevailing Germanic law, under which a contractual obligation (*Schuld*) was in itself unenforceable, and a pledge accompanying such an obligation (*Haftung*) was only enforceable if its transfer had been carried out with the proper formalities. The new principle of the canon law erased the Germanic distinction between obligation and liability. It was also in sharp contrast to the rules of the earlier Roman law set forth in the Justinian texts, under which formalities were essential to the validity of most types of contracts, partial performance was essential to the validity of innominate contracts, and special requirements existed for the limited class of contracts that could be concluded informally.

The general principle of contractual liability arising from agreements, developed by the canonists, rested, in the first instance, on the theory that to break a promise is a sin. A sin, however, in and of itself, gave rise not to legal liability but to penitential discipline; it was to be confessed and repented in the internal forum of the church. Legal liability, imposed in the external forum, that is, in the bishop's court, was based not only on the sin of the obligor but also on the protection of the rights of the obligee. This required a new development in moral theology, which was closely connected with new developments in political, economic, and social life.

The twelfth century witnessed an enormous expansion of commerce, including economic transactions between ecclesiastical corporations. In addition, the ecclesiastical courts sought and obtained a large measure of jurisdiction over economic contracts between laymen, where the parties included in their agreement a pledge of faith; the faith that was pledged, it was now said, created an obligation not only to God but also to the church. To justify enforcement of contracts in the external forum of the church it was necessary to add to the theory that to break a promise is a sin the theory that the claim of the party who has suffered from such breach is morally justified. The canonists developed the two theories together. They concluded that a morally binding promise should also be legally binding if it is part of an agreement (a *pactum*, or consensual obligation) that is itself morally justified. The object or purpose (*causa*) of the contract had to be reasonable and equitable.

Based on the theory that contracts should be legally binding if they serve a reasonable and equitable cause, the twelfth-century canonists, with the help of their contemporary Romanists, developed a whole series of principles which, taken together, justify the characterization of "general contract law." Some of these principles were the following:[8]

- that agreements should be legally enforceable even though they were entered into without formalities (*pacta sunt servanda*), provided that their purpose (*causa*) was reasonable and equitable;
- that agreements entered into through the fraud of one or both parties should not be legally enforceable;
- that agreements entered into through duress should not be legally enforceable;
- that agreements should not be legally enforceable if one or both parties were mistaken concerning a circumstance material to its formation;
- that silence may be interpreted as giving rise to inferences concerning the intention of the parties in forming a contract;
- that the rights of third-party beneficiaries of a contract should be protected;
- that a contract may be subject to reformation in order to achieve justice in a particular case;
- that good faith is required in the formation of a contract, in its interpretation, and in its execution;
- that in matters of doubt rules of contract law are to be applied in favor of the debtor (*in dubiis pro debitore*);
- that contracts that are unconscionable should not be enforced.

These principles of the canon law of contract embodied what may be called a *moral* theory of contract law.

The last point, relating to unconscionability, deserves further elaboration. Equity, for the twelfth-century canonists and Romanists alike, required, in contracts, a balancing of gains and losses on both sides. This principle took form in the doctrine of the just price. Both the Romanists and the canonists started with the premise that normally the just price is the common estimate, that is, the market price; a sharp deviation from the market price was prima facie contrary to reason and equity. Usury, which was defined as a charge for

---

8 See Bärmann, "Pacta sunt servanda," 18-25; Berman, *Law and Revolution*, 245-250.

the loan of money in excess of the normal rate of interest, was also condemned by both Romanists and canonists as a breach of market norms.[9]

The canonists, however, in contrast to the Romanists, were more concerned with another aspect of a sale in excess of the just price, or a charge for money in excess of normal interest, namely, the immoral motive that often underlay such practices. Profit-making in itself—contrary to what has been said by many modern writers—was not condemned by the canon law of the twelfth century. To buy cheap and sell dear was considered to be proper in many types of situations—as where one's property had increased in value or a craftsman had improved an object by his art or a merchant resold goods at a profit in order to maintain himself and his dependents. What was condemned by the canon law was "shameful" profit (*turpe lucrum*, "filthy lucre"), and that was identified with avaricious business practices. Thus for the canonists, rules of unfair competition, directed against breach of market norms, were linked also with rules of unconscionability, directed against oppressive transactions.

It should not come as a surprise to us, living in an age when an economic interpretation of history is often taken for granted, that the newly developing contract law of the Roman Catholic Church provided an important source of support for the rapid expansion of capitalist commercial and financial activities in Western Europe in the late eleventh, twelfth, and thirteenth centuries. Perhaps more interesting, however, is the other side of the coin: that within the church, which embraced almost the entire population of Western Europe, there was articulated at that time a public morality, based on a shared belief in a transcendent good, which informed the actual development of the new law of contract.

In subsequent centuries, many of the basic principles of the canon law of contract were adopted by secular law and eventually came to be justified on the basis of the will-theory and party autonomy. It is important to know, however, that originally they were based on a theory of sin and a theory of equity. Our contract law did not start from the proposition that every individual has a moral right to dispose of his property by means of making promises, and that in the interest of justice a promise should be legally enforced unless it offends reason or public policy.[10] Our contract law started, on the contrary, from the theory that a promise created an obligation to God,

---

[9] Berman, *Law and Revolution*, 247-49; James R. Gordley, "Equality in Exchange," *California Law Review* 69 (1981): 1587, 1638. See John T. Noonan, Jr., *The Scholastic Analysis of Usury* (Cambridge, MA, 1957), 105ff.

[10] That our modern contract law *is* based on these propositions is a major thesis of Charles Fried, *Contract as Promise: A Theory of Contractual Obligation* (Cambridge, MA, 1981).

and that for the salvation of souls God instituted the ecclesiastical and secular courts with the task, in part, of enforcing contractual obligations to the extent that such obligations are just.

The Puritan Concept of Contract as Covenant and of Strict Liability for Breach.—If we jump from Roman Catholic Christendom in the late eleventh, twelfth, and thirteenth centuries to Anglican and Puritan England in the seventeenth and eighteenth centuries, we confront a startling paradox. On the one hand, the political, economic, and social situation has changed drastically. On the other hand, the terms of the debates concerning law and government have remained remarkably stable; that is, the same issues continue to be addressed, although the emphasis is different and the answers are different.

Brian Tierney has recently shown the remarkable continuity of Western constitutional theory from the twelfth to the seventeenth centuries—from Gratian and John of Salisbury to Althusius and Locke. Tierney writes that "[t]he juridical culture of the twelfth century—the works of the Roman and canon lawyers, especially those of the canonists where religious and secular ideas most obviously intersected—formed a kind of seedbed from which grew the whole tangled forest of early modern constitutional thought."[11] Tierney's study is a challenge to legal historians to show that continuity existed in the realm not only of constitutional theory but also of criminal and civil law, including the law of contracts.

Prior to the sixteenth century, the law in England governing what we would today call contractual liability had been divided among various jurisdictions, each with its own procedures and its own legal rules. The English ecclesiastical courts, which had a wide jurisdiction over contract disputes involving not only clerics but also laymen, applied the canon law of the Roman Church. In the numerous cities and towns of England, as well as at fairs, mercantile courts applied a customary commercial law, sometimes called the law merchant, whose general features were more or less uniform throughout Europe. English county courts as well as feudal and manorial courts enforced various types of agreements, applying chiefly local and feudal or manorial custom. The royal courts of Common Pleas and King's Bench resolved contract disputes chiefly through the common law actions of debt, detinue, account, deceit, covenant, and trespass on the case. In the fourteenth and fifteenth centuries the chancellor also acquired a wide jurisdiction over contracts in cases which fell outside the common law (such as many types of

---

[11] Brian Tierney, *Religion, Law and the Growth of Constitutional Thought, 1150-1650* (Cambridge, 1982), 1.

parol promises, uses, actions by third-party beneficiaries) or which the common law courts were unable to decide fairly (for example, because of pressures exerted by powerful persons or because of inadequacy of common law remedies). The chancellor's "court of conscience" (as it was often called in those centuries) drew upon canon law, mercantile law, common law, and its own ingenuity and sense of fairness.

All the diverse types of law applicable to contracts were strongly influenced by the religious beliefs that prevailed during those centuries in England as in the other countries of Western Christendom. In the canon law, as we have seen, contractual liability was based ultimately on the sin of the defaulting promisor and the right of the promisee to require performance or compensation insofar as the agreement served a reasonable and equitable purpose. The law merchant stressed the element of trust among merchants and, in the event of dispute, their need for a speedy, informal procedure and for decisions based on mercantile reasonableness. The chief common law actions relating to agreements were founded on the concept of moral wrong as expounded in Roman Catholic theology: debt, detinue, and account presupposed the wrongfulness of retaining money or property that was due the other party to a half-completed exchange; deceit presupposed an intentional wrong; covenant presupposed the wrongfulness of violating a solemn oath; assumpsit—more accurately, trespass on the case upon an assumpsit—developed in the fifteenth century to permit recovery for the wrongful act ("trespass" is, of course, Law French for the Latin *transgressio*, "sin") of negligently performing an undertaking (misfeasance). In Chancery, the influence of moral theology was even more apparent, if only because the Chancellor, in those centuries, was almost invariably an archbishop or bishop, quite familiar with the basic features of the canon law, and his decisions were often grounded expressly in Christian teaching. Indeed, his jurisdiction may be said to have rested on three principles that were attributed to Christian faith: the protection of the poor and helpless, the enforcement of relations of trust and confidence, and the granting of remedies that "act on the person" (injunctions, specific performance, and the like).

In the sixteenth and early seventeenth centuries, the English law applicable to contracts underwent significant development. After the Act of Supremacy (1534), the ecclesiastical courts, now subordinate to the Crown, lost a substantial part of their jurisdiction over matters of property and commerce. The Tudor monarchs created an array of new "prerogative" courts, including the Court of Star Chamber, the High Court of Admiralty, the Court of Requests, and others, and also transformed the chancellor's court into the High Court of Chancery; with the rapid growth of both domestic and overseas trade, these courts exercised an enormously expanded commercial jurisdiction, applying to commercial cases the traditional law merchant as well as many rules and concepts derived from canon law and from Romanist legal science. Partly, no doubt, in order to meet the new competition, and in the spirit of the times, the common law courts also began to reform the action of assumpsit, making it available in certain types of cases of nonfeasance, and simplifying procedures in order to make the action a less unwieldy instrument for settling commercial disputes. In *Slade's Case* (1602), assumpsit was made available in cases of half-performed contracts and half-performed sales of goods, which previously had been subject to the archaic remedies of debt and detinue. By that time the common law courts had also elaborated a doctrine of consideration, similar to that of chancery and of the canon law, by which the validity and enforceability of an undertaking—whether in the case of the half-completed exchange or in the case of a simple promise—was tested in terms of the circumstances which caused or motivated it.[12]

Despite the significant changes in the law of contracts which took place in the sixteenth and early seventeenth centuries, in all the legal systems that prevailed in England, including the common law, the underlying presuppositions of contractual liability remained what they had been in the earlier period. Breach of promise was actionable, in the first instance, because—or if—it was a wrong, a tort, and in the second instance, because—or if—the promisee had a right to require its enforcement in view of its reasonable and equitable purpose. With some qualifications, the common lawyers accepted these premises no less than the canon lawyers. Prior to the latter part of the seventeenth century, assumpsit was essentially an action for breach of (unilateral) promise, not breach of (bilateral) contract in the modern sense, and the required consideration was conceived in terms of the moral justification and purpose of the promise. The action of covenant, on the other hand, was not seen to be a contractual remedy; duress was a defense but fraud in the inducement was not, although relief might be obtained from the Chancellor. The fact that the common law courts used distinctive procedures in enforcing promises, applied distinctive technical rules (often required by the different procedures), and gave only limited contract remedies, reflected the division between the ecclesiastical and the secular spheres and the subdivision of the secular sphere into plural jurisdictions. These divisions and subdivisions were themselves associated with the specific religious worldview that had emerged in the eleventh and twelfth centuries.

---

[12] See A.W.B. Simpson, *A History of the Law of Contract: The Rise of the Action of Assumpsit* (Oxford, 1975), 297-302 (on Slade's Case) and 316-488 (on consideration).

The Puritan Revolution of 1640 to 1660 established the supremacy of the common law over its rivals. In 1641 the Long Parliament, dominated by Puritans, abolished the prerogative courts. Eventually a separate admiralty jurisdiction survived, but it was greatly restricted in its scope and was subordinated to the common law. Chancery also survived but it, too, suffered a reduction of jurisdiction and was no longer able to assert its superiority over Common Pleas or King's Bench. Under the Puritans the common law courts heard cases of breaches of promise to marry, actions for legacies, and other ecclesiastical causes, on the ground that the ecclesiastical courts were not sitting. After 1660 some of that jurisdiction was retained, and the ecclesiastical courts, like the others, were ultimately bound by the common law as interpreted by Common Pleas and King's Bench.

With respect to commercial matters, the vast increase in the amount and variety of cases that came before the common law courts required an expansion and revision of their remedies and doctrines. Especially after 1660, when some of the most important reforms of the Puritan period were confirmed under a restored, chastened, and limited monarchy, the common law courts gradually adopted a great many of the remedies and rules that had been elaborated in the previous hundred years by the prerogative courts and by Chancery.

Other changes, however, in the common law of contracts, as it developed in the later seventeenth and eighteenth centuries,[13] cannot be attributed to

---

[13] A.W.B. Simpson's definitive study *A History of the Law of Contract* is concerned with "the rise" of assumpsit, which, he concludes, had risen by the early 1600s. He therefore deals only cursorily with developments after the 1620s and 1630s. P.S. Atiyah, on the other hand, in his volume *The Rise and Fall of Freedom of Contract* (Oxford/New York, 1979), is concerned with "the rise" of freedom of contract after 1770, and deals only cursorily with developments prior to that date. Similarly, Morton Horwitz, in *The Transformation of American Law, 1780 to 1860* (Cambridge, MA, 1977), makes broad characterizations of English and American law as it existed before 1780 without, however, presenting substantial evidence for them.

Partisans of the approach taken by Simpson, which is the traditional approach of English legal historians, are able to show that the transformation of "medieval" to "modern" contract *doctrine* took place long before the late eighteenth century. See A.W.B. Simpson, "The Horwitz Thesis and the History of Contract," *University of Chicago Law Review* 46 (1979): 533. On the other hand, partisans of the approach taken by Atiyah and Horwitz, which emphasizes the origins of contemporary contract *ideology*, though they often ignore or misinterpret earlier doctrinal developments, are able to show that there was an important ideological shift in the 19th century. Both sides would be greatly aided by a systematic exploration of the *terra incognita* of English legal development in the century and a half after the outbreak of the Puritan Revolution. Some steps toward filling this hiatus have been taken by S.J. Stoljar, *A History of Contract at Common Law* (Canberra, 1975); and Clinton W. Francis, "The Structure of Judicial Administration and the

the adoption or adaptation of doctrines previously elaborated in rival jurisdictions. There was, in fact, a shift in some of the basic presuppositions of
contract law that had developed over the previous five centuries. This shift
may be summarized in three interrelated propositions.

First, the underlying theory of liability shifted from breach of promise to
breach of a bargain. The emphasis was no longer placed primarily on the sin,
or wrong, of the defaulting promisor but rather on the binding character of an
agreement as such and the disappointment of the expectations of the
promisee. This change raised more acutely than before the question whether
the promises of the two sides were to be treated as independent or interdependent. The tendency of the courts in the century from 1660 to 1760 was to
treat them increasingly as interdependent.[14]

Second, the emphasis on bargain was manifested in a new conception of
consideration. The older conception of consideration as purpose or motive or
justification for a promise (analogous to the canonists' conception of *causa*)
gave way to a conception of consideration as the price paid by the promisee
for the promise of the promisor. This change raised more acutely than before
the question of the adequacy or inadequacy of the consideration. The
tendency of the courts in the century after the Puritan Revolution was
increasingly to enforce agreements regardless of the inadequacy of the consideration.[15]

Third, the basis of liability shifted from fault to absolute obligation. The
promisee was entitled to compensation for nonperformance with the terms of
the bargain itself; excuses for nonperformance were to be confined, generally
speaking, to those provided for within those terms.

The shift from a *moral* theory to what may be called a *bargain* theory of
contract is well illustrated in the famous case of *Paradine v. Jane*, decided in

---

Development of Contract Law in Seventeenth-Century England," *Columbia Law Review* 83
(1983): 35. See below notes 14, 15, 18, 19.

[14] See Stoljar, *History of Contract*, Chapter 12; Francis, "Development of Contract
Law," 122-125; William S. Holdsworth, *A History of English Law* (Boston, 1924), 4: 64, 72,
75.

[15] See Simpson, *Law of Contract*, 446. Simpson shows that inadequacy of consideration had not been recognized as a defense at common law in medieval times, but that that
was partly due to the fact that until some time after the sixteenth century "the conception
of consideration was not that of a price for a promise, but a reason for a promise." In other
words, prior to the late seventeenth century the *reason* for the promise had to be
"adequate," even though the *price* paid might have been relatively low or even nominal.
This distinction is often ignored by those who would trace an unbroken continuity in the
doctrine of consideration from the sixteenth to the eighteenth centuries.

1647, at the height of the Puritan Revolution.[16] A lessor sued a tenant for nonpayment of rent. The tenant defended on the ground that, due to the occupation of the leased premises by Prince Rupert's army, it was impossible for him to enjoy the benefit of his contract and therefore he should be excused from liability. He cited in his defense canon law, civil (i.e., Roman) law, military law, moral law, the law of reason, the law of nature, and the law of nations. Disregarding these authorities, the court held that by the common law of England a lessee for years is liable for the rent, even though the land be impossible to occupy. Although as an action of debt for rent the case could have been decided solely on the basis of the law of leasehold tenure, the court enunciated a broad principle of strict contractual liability. It said that where a duty is created by law, the party will be excused if he is not at fault, "but when the party by his own contract creates a duty or charge upon himself he is bound to make it good, if he may, notwithstanding accident or inevitable necessity, because he might have provided against it by his contract."[17]

One may find earlier cases that suggest a doctrine of strict contractual liability.[18] Indeed, one may show that all the doctrinal ingredients of the modern action for breach of contract were present, in embryo, in the action of assumpsit as it developed in the late 1500s and early 1600s.[19] In the history of legal doctrine, it is usually not difficult to find in some earlier decision or text a source for every new development. Yet it is fair to say that before *Paradine and Jane* no English court had ever laid down the *theory* of absolute obligation for breach of a bargained exchange, namely, that obligation in contract is distinguished from obligation in tort by the fact that the parties to a contract set their own limits to their liability; and moreover, that after *Paradine v. Jane* that theory was never effectively challenged.

On the other hand, some historians of English law have said that it "was not until the eighteenth century that a serious search for a general theory of

---

[16] Style 47, 82 Eng. Rep. 519 (1647); Aleyn 26, 82 Eng. Rep. 897 (1648). Most discussions of the case use only the report in Aleyn. The report in Style needs also to be read in order to grasp its full significance.

[17] Aleyn 26, 82 Eng. Rep. 897 (1648).

[18] See Simpson, *Law of Contract*, 31-33. Simpson shows that the sixteenth-century writer Brooke had distinguished the effect of a private contract, where liability was self-imposed, from the effect of the general law, and had stated that a man by private contract could make himself strictly liable, and that at least one case had adopted that point of view. He states that "in the leading case of *Paradine v. Jane* (1648) Brooke's theory eventually triumphed."

[19] This is the burden of Simpson's book, *A History of the Law of Contract*. Yet Simpson is careful to distinguish between the cases and writings that anticipate the establishment of a doctrine and those in which the doctrine eventually "triumphs."

contract was undertaken,"[20] and it was not until the nineteenth century that there emerged a bargain theory of contract, based on agreement of the wills of autonomous parties.[21] These statements depend for their validity on a special meaning of the phrase "general theory of contract." It can hardly be maintained that prior to the 18th century contractual liability was not considered to be based on a coherent set of principles, including the principle of the binding force of a bargained agreement expressing the intent of the parties.

The moral theory of contractual liability, which linked legal liability closely with the sin or wrongfulness of a breach of promise, on the one hand, and the equitable purpose of the promise or exchange of promises, on the other, was attacked in the seventeenth century in England by Puritans, including both lawyers and theologians. The attack was part of a revulsion against the discretionary justice of the chancellor. In the words of the great seventeenth-century Puritan legal scholar and practitioner John Selden: "Equity in law is the same as the spirit is in religion, what everyone pleases to make it;" and again: "Equity is a roguish thing . . . ; equity is according to the conscience of him that is chancellor. . . . It is all one as if they should make the standard for the measure a chancellor's foot."[22] The distrust of equity was linked with a strict view of contractual liability. Of contracts Selden wrote:

> We must look to the contract; if that be rightly made, we must stand to it; if we once grant [that] we may recede from contracts upon any inconveniency that may afterwards happen, we shall have no bargain kept. . . . [H]ow to make our contracts is left to ourselves; and as we agree upon the conveyance of this house, or this land, so it must be. If you offer me a hundred pounds for my glove, I tell you what my glove is—a plain glove—pretend no virtue in it—the glove is my own—I profess not to sell gloves, and we agree for an hundred pounds—I do not know why I may not with a safe conscience take it.[23]

It was not the lawyers, however, but the theologians, who articulated the underlying premises of the new bargain theory of contractual liability. Three basic tenets of 17th-century Puritan theology may be identified as bearing directly on that theory. The *first* was the belief in a sovereign God of order, who requires of his people obedience and self-discipline, on pain of eternal damnation. The *second* was the belief in the total depravity of man and total dependence for salvation on God's grace. The *third* was the belief in a

---

[20] T. F. T. Plucknett, *A Concise History of the Common Law*, 5th ed. (Boston, 1956), 652.

[21] See generally Atiyah, *Freedom of Contract*, and Horwitz, *Transformation*.

[22] John Selden, *Seldeniana; or, The Table Talk of John Selden, Esq.* (London, 1789), 45-46. Selden's *Table Talk* was first compiled in 1654 and first published in 1689.

[23] Ibid., 37-38.

contractual ("covenantal") relationship between God and man whereby God has bound himself to redeem his people in return for their voluntary undertaking to submit to his will.

(1) "God being the God of order and not of confusion hath Comaunded in his word and put man into a Capasitie in some measure to obserue and bee guided by good and wholsome lawes;" said a Massachusetts Puritan in 1658.[24] As John Witte has put it,

> "The austere ethical demands of the Puritan, frugality of time and money, severe church discipline, vocational ambition, and reformist zeal were all tied to theological assumptions. Because the Puritan was a part of the divine unfolding of the providential plan of the world, he viewed his work as holy and he sought to perform as God's agent impeccably."

By the same token, "rules and laws were essential not only to arouse people to obedience to God and to guide them in the paths of virtue but also to bring English society to good order and discipline and to reform it."[25]

The Puritans drew a connection between the belief in a God of order, who governs by strict rules and who requires his subjects also to govern themselves by "good and wholsome lawes," on the one hand, and the belief in strict contractual liability, on the other. "[W]e must keep covenant with each other, when we have contracted one with another," wrote the Puritan leader Ireton in 1647. "Abandon this principle and the result will be chaos."[26] The context of Ireton's statement was a debate among Puritan leaders concerning the duty of submitting to an unjust law enacted by Parliament, in the light of the "contract" between Parliament and the people as ruler and ruled. However, the analogy was often drawn in that debate between social contract and private contract. As Selden wrote,

> "To know what obedience is due to the prince, you must look into the contract between him and his people; as if you would know what rent is due from the tenant to the landlord, you must look into the lease. When the contract is broken, and there is no third person to judge, then the decision is by arms."[27]

---

[24] "General Laws of New Plymouth (September 29, 1658)," reprinted in David Pulsifer, ed., *Records of the Colony of New Plymouth Laws, 1623-82* (Boston, 1861), 11: 72.

[25] John Witte, Jr., "Notes on English Puritanism and Law" (unpublished). See also John Witte, Jr., "Blest Be the Ties that Bind: Covenant and Community in Puritan Thought," *Emory Law Journal* 36 (1987): 579.

[26] Quoted in John W. Gough, *The Social Contract: A Critical Study of its Development* (Oxford, 1936), 90.

[27] Ibid., 92. (Note that Selden's analogy was with the law of leases, in which the doctrine of absolute obligation was firmly established.) The obligation of both social

(2) The belief in the total depravity of man, his inborn lust for power, the corruption not only of his will but also of his reason—reinforced the Puritan's emphasis on strict adherence to rules, including rules agreed upon by parties to a contract. As evidenced in Selden's caustic remarks, quoted above, about the untrustworthiness of the chancellor's conscience, the Puritan view of human nature (including the human nature of judges) did not encourage a resort to general ideas of equity or fault for the resolution of conflict. The Puritan preferred to rely upon something that seemed to him to be more objective, more certain, namely, the will of the parties as manifested in the words of the contract—just as he preferred in matters of personal morality to rely on the words of Scripture rather than on the ratiocinations of moral philosophers.

(3) Perhaps the most direct link between the doctrine of absolute contractual obligation and the Puritan belief system is to be found in the Puritan concept of the covenants—a word meaning, at that time, simply "agreements"—which God has entered into with men. As Witte has written:

> Traditionally, theologians, both Protestant and Catholic, had discussed the Biblical covenants: the Old Testament covenant of works whereby man, through his obedience to God's law, is promised his salvation; and the New Testament covenant of grace whereby man, through his faith in the incarnation, resurrection, and atonement, is promised eternal salvation. The covenant doctrine in this earlier period, however, had remained a footnote to the more important doctrines of God, man, and salvation. In the late sixteenth and seventeenth centuries, English Puritan theologians radically expanded the doctrine with two major innovations.[28]
>
> First, they transformed the covenant of grace as a merciful gift of God into a bargained contract, voluntarily negotiated and agreed upon, and absolutely binding on both sides. This new "federal theology," as it is called (from the Latin word *foedus*, "covenant") is evident in the rhetoric of John Preston, a leading Puritan theologian in the seventeenth century: "You may sue [God] of his bond

---

contract and private contract was traced to the Bible by the Puritan covenant theologian Samuel Rutherford, who wrote that the king and his people should not fight with each other just as "two merchants should keep faith one to another, both because God hath said he shall dwell in God's mountain who sweareth and covenanteth, and standeth to his oath and covenant, though to his loss and hurt (Psalm 15) and also because they made their covenant and contract thus and thus." Samuel Rutherford, *Lex, Rex, or The Law and the Prince* (London, 1644), 201. John Locke drew heavily on Rutherford for his doctrine of social contract.

[28] On the development of covenant theology in seventeenth-century English Puritanism, see Perry Miller, "The Marrow of Puritan Divinity," *Transactions of the Colonial Society of Massachusetts* (Indianapolis, IN, 1937), 247-300; Michael Walzer, *The Revolution of the Saints: A Study in the Origins of Radical Politics* (New York, 1968), 167ff., 222ff.

written and sealed, and He cannot deny it." "Take no denyall, though the Lord may defer long, yet He will doe it, he cannot chuse; for it is part of his Covenant."[29] What Calvin and his earlier followers had often described as God's covenant faithfulness to man became in Puritan theology God's absolute contractual obligation to man; what they had described as God's gracious gift of faith to his predestined became man's voluntary negotiation and agreement of the terms of his covenant with God.

Second, Puritan theologians added parties to the covenant. They characterized many relationships between God and various Biblical figures as covenant relations, whose terms were negotiated and agreed upon voluntarily and were thus absolutely binding. God's relations with the prophets were interpreted as bargains. The relation between the Father and the Son was viewed as a three-fold covenant of redemption, reconciliation, and suretyship. Also the covenant of grace between God and "man" was now understood as a covenant not only with the elected individual Christian but also with the "elect nation" of England, which was called to reform its laws and legal institutions according to God's word. Moreover, within the Biblical covenants the Puritans advocated political and institutional covenants of all kinds: covenants to form families, communities, associations, churches, cities, and even commonwealths, each of which was deemed absolutely binding.[30] This broad theological doctrine provided the cardinal ethical principle of Puritanism that each man was free to choose his act but was bound to the choice he made, regardless of the consequences. This principle was readily applied to contractual obligations as well. Every contract, wrote a leading Puritan minister, "is a voluntary obligation between persons about things wherein they enjoy a freedom of will and have a power to choose or to refuse."[31] But having chosen, they are bound to perform.[32]

Conclusion.—The canonists and Romanists of the late eleventh and twelfth centuries and thereafter based the enforceability of contracts on two principles: first, that to break a promise is a sin, an offense against God, or, more fundamentally, an act of alienation of oneself from God; and second, that the victim of the breach ought to have a legal remedy if the purpose of the promise, or exchange of promises, was reasonable and equitable. These

---

[29] Quoted in Christopher Hill, *Puritanism and Revolution: Studies in Interpretation of the English Revolution of the 17th Century* (London, 1958), 246. Cf. David Zaret, *The Heavenly Contract: Ideology and Organization in Pre-Revolutionary Puritanism* (Chicago, 1985), 161. Zaret draws from sermons and tracts many examples of the tendency of Puritan preachers, in the period before 1640, to analogize the covenant between God and man to commercial contracts in which each party has the right to demand of the other that he "perform his bargain."

[30] Cf. John D. Eusden, *Puritans, Lawyers, and Politics in Early Seventeenth Century England* (Hamden, CT, 1968), 28ff.; Gough, *Social Contract*, 82-99.

[31] Quoted in Walzer, *Revolution of the Saints*, 24.

[32] Witte, "Notes"; Witte, "Blest be the Ties That Bind," 595.

principles served as part of the foundation for the systematization of contract law, that is, the construction of an integrated set of concepts and rules of contract law. Many of these concepts continue to be taught today in courses in law schools throughout the world—concepts and rules concerning fraud and duress and mistake, unconscionability, duty to mitigate losses, and many other aspects of contract law that link it directly with moral responsibility. It would contribute enormously, I believe, to our understanding of modern contract law if teachers and writers were to trace its formation to the canon law of the church as it developed in a pre-capitalist, pre-individualist, pre-rationalist, pre-nationalist era. There is more "mythology" in the law of contract than Grant Gilmore chose to discuss, and more "rationalization" than its current critics on the left seem to realize. Modern contract law, as it was first developed in the West, reflects what Alasdair MacIntyre has rightly called the fundamental tension in a belief system that is concerned with the transformation of man-as-he-is into man-as-he-could-be-if-he-realized-his-telos.[33]

It should be noted that its two underlying principles brought the canon law of contract into close touch with other branches of the law of civil obligations, including tort and restitution. To break a promise is prima facie a wrong, a tort. On the other hand, it may be unjust, though no wrong has been committed, to acquire or retain property or benefits at another's expense. Under what I have called here the moral theory of contract, a remedy (such as debt or detinue) may be applicable both to breaches of contract and to cases of unjust enrichment. It is of some interest in this connection that in English law the concept of unjust enrichment was also concealed in the action of general assumpsit, which is still usually classified as "quasi-contract."

The bargain theory of contract was, in its inception, also a moral theory, but in a different sense of the word "moral." It started from the premise that God is a God of order, who enters into contracts with his people by which both he and they are absolutely bound. Its second premise was that the people of God, in entering into contracts with each other, whether social contracts or private, are also absolutely bound by the contract terms, and that nonperformance is excused only to the extent that those terms permit. However, the Puritan stress on bargain and on calculability ("order") should not obscure the fact that the bargain presupposed a strong relationship between the contracting parties, within the community. These were not yet the autonomous, self-sufficient individuals of the eighteenth-century

---

[33] Alasdair MacIntyre, *After Virtue: A Study in Moral Theory*, 2d ed. (Notre Dame, IN, 1984), 52ff.

Enlightenment. England under Puritan rule and in the century that followed was intensely communitarian.

As in the case of the canon law, the underlying principles of the English law of contracts, as it developed in the late seventeenth and early eighteenth centuries, brought that law into close contact with other branches of English law. In particular, English contract law was not separated from commercial law. There was therefore no independent integrated body of rules governing all kinds of contracts; in that special sense, there was no "general theory of contract." Only in the late eighteenth and early nineteenth centuries were efforts made to synthesize "contract" as an independent branch of law. Instead, English contract law in the late seventeenth and eighteenth centuries remained a law of different *types* of contracts. The parties who entered into a contract of bailment, or of lease, or an insurance contract, or a conditional sale, or a transportation contract, or the sale of land, or a contract of personal services, were bound by the rules applicable to the particular type of contract, except to the extent that they varied them by express terms. What was involved in the first instance was the will of the parties to enter into a type of relationship.

In the late eighteenth and nineteenth centuries, these older theories of contract law were secularized, in the sense that their religious foundations were replaced by a conception based not on faith in a transcendent reason and a transcendent will, from which human reason and will are derived and to which they are responsible, but rather on the inherent freedom of each individual to exercise his own autonomous reason and will, subject only to considerations of social utility. This secular theory drew heavily on contract doctrines and rules that had originally been developed on the basis of the earlier religious theories, but it subjected those doctrines and rules to a new rationalization and a new systematization. It broke many of the links not only between contract law and moral theology but also between contract law and the communitarian postulates which had informed both the Catholic (including Anglican as well as Roman Catholic) and the Protestant (including both Lutheran and Calvinist) legal traditions. The new secular theory also tended to isolate contract law from other branches of civil law, such as the law of torts and of unjust enrichment, whose moral and communitarian aspects were less easy to suppress.

With the decline of individualism and rationalism in the twentieth century, it was inevitable that the prevailing nineteenth-century theory of contract law would come under attack. Both its attackers and its defenders need to be aware, however, of its historical background, and especially of the religious sources from which it was derived and against which it reacted. In the absence of such an awareness, the issues become distorted. We are given a choice between the prevailing theory of general contract law—without its historical roots—and no theory at all. We may learn from history, however, that there is a third possibility: to build a new and different theory on the foundation of the older ones.

—— ℒ 8 ℒ ——

THE INTERACTION OF LAW AND RELIGION IN AMERICAN CONSTITUTIONAL HISTORY*

When the word "law" is juxtaposed with the word "religion," an American lawyer today is apt to think immediately of the First Amendment to the United States Constitution, with its double protection against any governmental interference in "the free exercise" of religion, on the one hand, and against any governmental "establishment" of religion, on the other. From the standpoint of contemporary American constitutional law, religion has become the personal and private affair of individual citizens or groups of citizens. Indeed, in recent decades our courts, in interpreting the "free exercise" clause, have gone very far toward immunizing individual and group activities from governmental control, whether federal or state, whenever they are considered by the persons engaging in them to be of a religious character; and at the same time, under the "establishment" clause, the courts have struck down most forms even of indirect governmental support of religion, whether federal or state.

A theologian, on the other hand, is apt to respond quite differently to the topic "law and religion." He is apt to think first not of the Constitution but of the Ten Commandments, with their implicit assertions that all human law is

* Reprinted from *Capital University Law Review* 8 (1979): 345-356. Delivered as the opening talk at a Conference on Legal and Ethical Aspects of Religious Liberty sponsored by The Institute of Social Ethics of the University of Southern California and the University of Southern California Law Center.

founded on divine law, and that the ultimate purpose of human law is to help create conditions in which love of God and love of neighbor may flourish. From the standpoint of theistic faith, the interrelationship of law and religion is a two-way street, in which not only do legal structures and processes serve to protect religion from governmental intervention but also religious structures and processes serve to motivate and give direction to the society as a whole, including its legal system.

It is a profound mistake, I submit, though one that is very frequently made, to consider the relation of law to religion solely from a legal point of view, that is, solely in terms of the *legal* foundations of *religious* freedom. It is also necessary to consider that relation in terms of the *religious* foundations of *legal* freedom. Otherwise, we shall not do justice to the religious sentiments of the American people, an overwhelming majority of whom state that they believe in God and a lesser majority of whom, though still a majority, state that they adhere to some organized religious community, either Christian, Jewish, or Muslim. Most such believers would say—and many agnostics and even many atheists would also agree—that the very existence of constitutional law in the United States, and therefore of freedom of belief or disbelief, rests ultimately on the religious faith of the American people.

This was undoubtedly the view of the men who framed the Constitution, including the first amendment. Thomas Jefferson, who was perhaps the most freethinking of the Founding Fathers, said in 1801, in his first message as President, "that the liberties of a nation [cannot] be thought secure when we remove their only firm basis, a conviction in the minds of the people that their liberties are the gift of God."[1] Jefferson was an ardent advocate of freedom of every kind of opinion, but he also believed that, despite all diversity, there was a common core of religious belief that was essential to preserve peace and order in society.[2] For Jefferson, the disestablishment of religion was a great "experiment," as he called it,[3] intended to test whether that common core of shared religious belief—which not only he but all the Founding Fathers agreed was necessary to the very existence and well-being of society—could flourish without governmental sanctions.[4]

In other words, the authors of the Constitution, including those who were personally skeptical of the truth of traditional theistic religion, did not

---

[1] Isaac A. Cornelison, *The Relation of Religion to Civil Government in the United States of America* (New York, 1895), 93.

[2] See Saul K. Padover, *The Complete Jefferson* (New York, 1943), 676; Cf. Sidney E. Mead, *The Lively Experiment* (New York, 1963), 40.

[3] Mead, *Lively Experiment*, 59.

[4] Ibid., 63.

doubt that the vitality of the legal system itself depended on the vitality of religious faith, and more particularly, of the Protestant Christian faith that predominated in the new American Republic.

Moreover, while many, like Jefferson, opposed governmental control or support of religion, the majority were in favor of such control and support, but at the state level, rather than the federal level. The first amendment was well understood to be applicable to the federal government alone: "*Congress,*" it said, "shall make no law respecting an establishment of religion, or prohibiting the free exercise thereof." But nothing was said to restrict the states in this regard. The establishment of religion was not listed among the measures which the states are prohibited from taking under article I, section 10. As Justice Story said: "Thus, the whole power over the subject of religion is left exclusively to the state governments, to be acted upon according to their own sense of justice, and the state constitutions."[5]

In the early part of the nineteenth century, most states did enact laws that had the effect of establishing Christianity—or, more often, Protestant Christianity—as the religion of the state. Thus one may find state constitutional and statutory provisions declaring it to be "the duty of all men to worship the Supreme Being, the great Creator and Preserver of the Universe,"[6] regulating membership in Christian denominations, imposing fines for failure to attend worship services on the Lord's day, requiring elected officials to swear that they "believe the Christian religion, and have a firm persuasion of its truth,"[7] and establishing public education for the purpose of promoting "religion, morality, and knowledge."[8]

In New York in 1811, the highest state court upheld an indictment for blasphemous utterances against Christ. Speaking for the court, Chief Justice Kent stated that "we are a christian people, and the morality of the country is deeply ingrafted upon christianity. . . ."[9] The New York State Convention of 1821 endorsed the decision in that case, declaring that the court was right in holding that the Christian religion is the law of the land and is to be preferred

---

[5] Joseph Story, *Commentaries on the Constitution of the United States* (Cambridge, MA, 1833), 3: 731.

[6] Connecticut Constitution of 1818, art. VII, 1. See also Cornelison, *Relation of Religion to Civil Government*, 96.

[7] Massachusetts Constitution of 1780, ch. VI, art. I. See also Cornelison, *Relation of Religion to Civil Government*, 105.

[8] "Religion, morality, and knowledge, being necessary to good government and the happiness of mankind, schools and the means of education shall forever be encouraged." Cornelison, *Relation of Religion to Civil Government*, 111 (citing The Northwest Ordinance of 1787, art. III.)

[9] People v. Ruggles, 8 Johns. 290, 295 (1811).

over all other religions.[10] These statements were confirmed in an 1861 New York case in which the court said: "Religious tolerance is entirely consistent with a recognized religion. Christianity may be conceded to be the established religion, to the qualified extent mentioned, while perfect civil and political equality, with freedom of conscience and religious preference, is secured to individuals of every other creed and profession."[11]

Similarly, in Pennsylvania in 1822 a man was convicted of blasphemy for saying that "the Holy Scriptures were a mere fable" and that "they contained a great many lies."[12] The Supreme Court of Pennsylvania, in affirming the conviction, stated: "Christianity, general Christianity, is and always has been a part of the common law of Pennsylvania, . . . not Christianity founded on any particular religious tenets; not Christianity with an established church, and tithes and spiritual courts; but Christianity with liberty of conscience to all men."[13]

On the same grounds, laws restricting commercial activities on Sundays were upheld by courts of many states. In one such case the Supreme Court of Missouri stated:

> Those who question the constitutionality of our Sunday laws seem to imagine that the constitution is to be regarded as an instrument framed for a state composed of strangers collected from all quarters of the globe, each with a religion of his own, bound by no previous social ties, nor sympathizing in any common reminiscences of the past; . . . [S]uch is not the mode by which our organic law is to be interpreted. We must regard the people for whom it was ordained. It appears to have been made by Christian men. The constitution, on its face, shows that the Christian religion was the religion of its framers.[14]

Similar judicial statements may be found in other states in similar cases, involving blasphemy, violations of Sunday laws, and other religious offenses.

In addition, states did not hesitate to require the teaching of the Christian religion in state colleges and universities as well as in prisons, reformatories, orphanages, homes for soldiers, and asylums. Also states required the reading of the Bible and singing of hymns and saying of prayers in elementary and secondary schools.

In 1890 the Supreme Court of Illinois considered the case of a student at the University of Illinois who had been expelled because of his refusal to

---

10 Cornelison, *Relation of Religion to Civil Government*, 129.

11 Lindenmuller v. People, 33 Barb. 548, 562 (1861).

12 Updegraph v. The Commonwealth, 11 Serg. & Rawl. 393, 394 (1822).

13 Ibid., 399.

14 State v. Ambs, 20 Mo. 214, 216-217 (1854).

attend daily chapel exercises. He contended that the chapel requirement violated a provision of the Illinois Constitution stating that "[n]o person shall be required to attend or support any ministry or place of worship against his consent."[15] The Court held that so long as the rules of chapel attendance were reasonable, permitting excuse on grounds of religious or other conscientious objections, the University had a right to impose the requirement, and the student could not escape it on the mere ground that he considered it unlawful. There is nothing in the Illinois Constitution, the court said, that prevents state colleges and other institutions of learning from adopting "all reasonable regulations for the inculcation of moral and religious principles in those attending them."[16]

With regard to religious exercises and religious education in elementary and secondary schools, the courts of many states went so far as to uphold regulations requiring attendance, on pain of expulsion, regardless of religious objections. The Supreme Court of Maine stated:

> The right of one sect to interdict or expurgate would place all schools in subordination to the sect interdicting or expurgating. . . . If the claim is that the sect of which the child is a member has a right of interdiction [in fact she was a Roman Catholic who objected to the reading of the Protestant version of the Bible as part of a general course of instruction], and that any book is to be banished because under the ban of her church, then the preference is practically given to such church, and the very mischief complained of, is inflicted on others.[17]

I have rehearsed these ancient cases *not* for their current legal significance—in fact, they have all long since been overruled—but rather for what they tell us about the religious roots of our constitutional guarantees of religious freedom. In 1835, Alexis de Tocqueville wrote: "[T]here is no country in the world where the Christian religion retains a greater influence over the souls of men than in America. . . ."[18] In 1888, James Bryce wrote that "the influence of Christianity seems to be, if we look not merely to the numbers but also the intelligence of the persons influenced, greater and more widespread in the United States than in any part of western Continental Europe, and probably as great as in England."[19]

I myself can testify that even fifty years ago, if you had asked whether the United States is a "Christian" country, the overwhelming majority of

---

15 Illinois Constitution of 1870, art. 2, 3.

16 North v. Board of Trustees, 137 Ill. 296, 305; 27 N.E. 54, 56 (1891).

17 Donahoe v. Richards, 38 Me. 376, 407 (1854).

18 Alexis de Tocqueville, *Democracy in America* (New York, 1945), 1: 303.

19 James Bryce, *The American Commonwealth* (New York, 1915), 2: 778.

Americans would have said yes. That was certainly what I was taught as a young boy at the Noah Webster School in Hartford, Connecticut. And when at the Wednesday morning assemblies, together with readings from the Old and New Testaments, the hymn was "Onward Christian Soldiers," the few of us kids who were Jewish would sing at the top of our lungs, "Onward *Jewish* Soldiers." We knew even better than the rest that America professed itself to be a Christian country.

In those times, if you had asked Americans where our system of law came from, on what it was ultimately based, the overwhelming majority would have said, "the Ten Commandments," or "the Bible," or perhaps "the law of God." John Adams' conception that our law is rooted in a common religious and moral tradition[20] was shared not only by the Protestant descendants of the English settlers on this continent, and by their black slaves, but also by tens of millions of immigrants from western and southern and eastern Europe, most of whom were Roman Catholics and Jews. Indeed, throughout the entire nineteenth and into the early twentieth century, America studied its law chiefly from Blackstone, who wrote that

> [the] law of nature . . . dictated by God himself . . . is binding . . . in all countries and at all times; no human laws are of any validity if contrary to this; and such of them as are valid derive all their force, and all their authority, mediately or immediately, from this original.[21]

In the past two generations the public philosophy of America has shifted radically from a religious to a secular theory of law, from a moral to a political or instrumental theory, and from a communitarian to an individualistic theory. Law is now generally considered—at least in public discourse—to be simply a pragmatic device for accomplishing specific political, economic, and social objectives. Its tasks are thought to be finite, material, impersonal—to

---

[20] Cf. Sanford Levinson, "The Specious Morality of the Law," *Harper's* 254 (1977): 35, 36. Levinson writes:

For Adams and most other pre-nineteenth-century adherents of the rule of law, law . . . was linked with moral norms. . . . [L]aw was defined by the medievalists as the product either of natural reason given by God or of immemorial custom itself incarnating natural justice, or as the commands of political leaders ordained by God and therefore given the right to rule.

Adams' notion of the rule of law was based on this older conception of law as rooted in a common religious and moral order.

Ibid., 36.

[21] J. Stewart, ed., *Blackstone's Commentaries*, 23d ed. (1854), 1: 36. (footnotes omitted).

get things done, to make people act in certain ways. Rarely, if ever, does one hear it said that law is a reflection of an objective justice or of the ultimate meaning or purpose of life. Usually it is thought to reflect, at best, the community's sense of what is expedient, and more commonly, the more or less arbitrary will of the lawmaker.

This view of law, founded on utilitarianism, goes back to the Enlightenment of the late eighteenth century and to the French and American Revolutions which were the product of the Enlightenment; and it had strong support, especially among intellectuals, in nineteenth-century America. It is important to remember, however, that prior to World War I, and even up to the Great Depression, Americans *as a people* continued to believe that the Constitution and the legal system were rooted in a Covenant made with God by which this country was to be guided in its mission to be a "light to all the nations."

It is only in the last two generations that the Enlightenment concept of law as something wholly instrumental, wholly invented, as contrasted with the pre-Enlightenment concept of law as something ordained, something partly invented but also partly given, has penetrated not only the ideology of the intellectuals but also the social consciousness of virtually all classes of the population. Likewise, it is only in the last two generations that the Enlightenment concept of religion as something wholly private and wholly psychological, as contrasted with the pre-Enlightenment concept of religion as something public, something partly psychological but also partly social and historical, indeed, partly legal, has come to dominate our discourse.

The radical separation of law and religion in twentieth century American thought—I am speaking now not of constitutional law but of jurisprudence, of legal philosophy—creates a serious danger that law will not be respected. If law is to be measured only by standards of expedience, or workability, and not by standards of truth or rightness, then it will be difficult to enforce it against those who think that it does not serve their interests. It is usually said by those who espouse an instrumental theory of law that enforcement in the last analysis is always obtained by threat of coercive sanctions. This is, however, an unsatisfactory argument. Far more important than coercion in securing obedience to rules are such factors as trust, fairness, credibility, and affiliation.[22] It is precisely when law is trusted and therefore does not require coercive sanctions that it is efficient; one who rules by law is not compelled to be present everywhere with his police force. Today this point has been proved in a negative way by the fact that in our cities that branch of law in which the

---

[22] Harold J. Berman, *The Interaction of Law and Religion* (Nashville, TN, 1974), 28. See also sources cited in ibid., 146-147, n.7.

sanctions are most severe—namely, criminal law—has been powerless to create fear where it has failed to create respect by other means. Today everyone knows that no amount of force which the police are capable of exerting can stop urban crime. In the last analysis, what deters crime is the tradition of being law-abiding, and this in turn depends upon a deeply or passionately held conviction that law is not only an instrument of secular policy but also part of the ultimate purpose and meaning of life.

Similarly, the radical separation of law and religion in contemporary American thought creates a serious danger for religion—namely, the danger that it will be viewed as a wholly private, personal, psychological matter, without any social or historical or legal dimensions. Jefferson's experiment may be in the process of failing, for though religion is flourishing in America, it is increasingly a "privatized" religion, with little in it that can overcome the forces of strife and disorder in society.[23]

In stressing the dangers of too radical a separation of law and religion, we must avoid, of course, the opposite dangers of making too close an interconnection between them. Law is surely more directly concerned with social action and social utility, and religion more with personal aspirations and a sense of the holy. Each is therefore in some tension with the other; each challenges the other. Religion, by standing outside the law, helps to prevent legal institutions from being worshipped. Conversely, law, by its secularity, leaves religion free to develop in its own way. The separation of law and religion thus provides a foundation for the separation of Church and State, protecting us against caesaropapism, on the one hand, and theocracy on the other.

Yet the radical separation of legal and religious institutions does not require the radical separation of legal and religious values. It does not require the total secularization of law and the total spiritualization of religion. These two aspects of life have now been separated to the point of disaster. On the one hand, we have cults like the People's Temple—many others could also be mentioned—which are given immunity from social control on the sole ground that they are religious. On the other hand, our public schools are inhibited from transmitting our common religious heritage on the sole ground that they are secular.

The practical danger of any organic theory of society is that it may be used irresponsibly to sanctify and petrify the particular existing laws and the particular existing orthodoxies of a given social order. This danger is particularly acute when law and religion do not carry within themselves built-in

---

[23] Cf. Mead, *Lively Experiment*, 69-71, citing John P. Williams, *What Americans Believe and How They Worship*, rev. ed. (New York, 1962).

principles of change. The danger is much less acute in a society such as our own, where our religious traditions, as well as our legal traditions, are founded on the concept of change. Indeed, in the Western tradition it is a fundamental purpose of religion to challenge law to change continually in order to be more humane, and a fundamental purpose of law to challenge religion to change continually in order to be more socially responsible. An organic theory of society does not protect the status quo when the theory itself conceives the society in terms of a dynamic process of development.

In America the dynamic character both of law and of religion—the capacity of each to change, to develop, and even to die and be regenerated—makes it possible for them to serve each other without overstepping the constitutional boundaries that separate them. Despite the broad interpretations that have been given to the "free exercise" clause, I believe that our courts would uphold governmental action against religious groups that use duress or fraud to induce support. Also, despite the broad interpretations that have been given to the "establishment" clause, it is clear that the legislature may take some measures to protect the free exercise of religion without necessarily effecting an establishment. For example, it may permit religious organizations to be exempt from taxation; it may permit contributions to religious causes to be deducted from taxable income; it may permit chaplains to be employed by the armed forces; it may exempt from military service persons who object to such service on religious grounds; it may give some kinds of indirect support to parochial schools; it may provide programs of released time or shared time in public schools to enable pupils to have religious instruction elsewhere; it may not provide for religious instruction or the saying of prayers as part of public school exercises, but it may provide for instruction about religion—courses in religious history, religious philosophy, religious literature, and the like. The view that law needs religion for its inspiration does not imply that responsibility for the encouragement of religions should be shifted from the people—where it belongs—to the government or to the legal system. It only implies that the government, by law, should cooperate to the extent of its constitutional powers in providing an environment in which religion may flourish.[24]

I have argued that our Constitution, while requiring a high degree of separation of religious institutions from political and legal institutions, also presupposes a high degree of interaction between religious values and political and legal values. It presupposes that an important purpose of the guarantee of religious freedom is to help create conditions in which religious faith

---

[24] This and the preceding four paragraphs are drawn in large part from Berman, *Interaction*, 138-140.

can be purified and strengthened; it presupposes further that such purified and strengthened religious faith will help to give motivation and direction to the political and legal system. These presuppositions, or postulates, are part of a jurisprudence that conceives of law all together as a manifestation of something beyond itself, a witness to something greater, a guide to some historical destiny.

In recent decades these postulates have been substantially eroded. Increasingly, law has come to be seen not as a pointer or witness to the collective fulfillment of a higher aspiration and destiny but as an end in itself, the very purpose of our national existence, the ultimate bond of our unity as a people. We have come to believe in the Constitution for its own sake—to believe in the "free exercise" clause and the "establishment" clause for their own sake. We find legal neutrality in matters of religion to be *convenient*, and we know of no other principle that would be *acceptable* in a "pluralistic," that is, a first amendment, society. No other justification is thought to be needed.

This is, I believe, itself a form of secular religion, or idolatry. It involves the worship of a constitutional principle for its own sake, coupled with a high degree of skepticism concerning any justification for such worship other than immediate self-interest, whether individual or collective.

Such skepticism concerning the ultimate meaning and purpose of the constitutional protection of religious freedom threatens to undermine that very freedom. On the one hand, the cult of self, which is becoming our dominant faith, threatens to make us indeed a nation "composed of strangers . . . each with a religion of his own, bound by no . . . social ties, nor sympathizing in any common reminiscences of the past,"[25] or in any common vision of the future. The cult of self has already begun to have the effect both of gradually removing from public education and public discourse all references to traditional religion and of gradually substituting its own jargon and ritual and its own morality and belief system. Thus there is a danger that this new secular religion will, indeed, place all other religions in subordination to itself, inflicting on others the very mischief of which it complains.[26]

On the other hand, the cult of society—which in dynamic terms is the eventual consequence of the cult of self, though logically they are in conflict—lurks in the background as an alternative option. It, too, would introduce a state-supported secular religion—the religion of total social involvement, of absolute patriotism—in violation of the spirit of the first amendment.

---

[25] State v. Ambs, 20 Mo. 214, 216 (1854).

[26] See Donahoe v. Richards, 38 Me. 376 (1854).

It will be said that it is a misuse of the word "religion" to apply it to personal and social philosophies such as those that I have identified as the "cult of self" and the "cult of society." It is this very argument, however, that is used to support both state "establishment" of such philosophies and state interference with their "free exercise." Here the example of the Soviet Union is instructive. The Soviet Constitution provides for the separation of church and state and for freedom of religion. Since virtually all education in the Soviet Union is state education and virtually all publication is by state publishing enterprises, the teaching of religion and the circulation of religious literature are severely limited. Moreover, since religion is considered to be the private affair of each citizen, the free exercise of religion is construed to consist merely of freedom of worship. On the other hand, the public teaching of so-called scientific atheism is required in all schools and is promoted in the press and elsewhere. Thus atheism, by claiming to be not a religion, but a science or a philosophy, is in fact "established," and traditional religions such as Christianity, Judaism, and Islam are withdrawn from public discourse.[27]

It seems to me that this example shows quite well that it is not, in and of itself, the constitutional guarantee of freedom of religion from governmental control or support that is our final protection against religious oppression, but rather it is that guarantee coupled with its original purpose: namely, to help create a society in which political and legal values, on the one hand, and religious values, on the other hand, freely interact, so that law will not degenerate into legalism but will serve its fundamental goals of justice, mercy, and good faith, and religion will not degenerate into a private religiosity or pietism but will maintain its social responsibility.

---

[27] See David E. Powell, *Antireligious Propaganda in the Soviet Union* (Cambridge, MA, 1975); R. Marshall, Jr., ed. *Aspects of Religion in the Soviet Union 1917-1967* (Chicago, 1971); A. V. Belov, ed., *O Religii i Tserkvi* (Moscow, 1977).

∽❧ 9 ❧∽

RELIGIOUS FREEDOM AND THE CHALLENGE
OF THE MODERN STATE*

I f we are to undertake, in the words of the Williamsburg Charter, "a fresh consideration of religious liberty in our time and of the place of the religion clauses of the First Amendment in our national life," we must ask, first, what religion meant in America when the Bill of Rights was framed, and what its relationship was to government; and second, how both religion and government have changed in the course of time, and especially in the last two generations. It is only on this broad background of historical development that the "free exercise" and the "establishment" clauses of the First Amendment can be interpreted and applied in a way that is true both to the text of the Constitution and to the future of the nation.

It should be noted at the outset that although the First Amendment is usually said to provide for the separation of church and state, in fact it does not contain the word "church" but speaks instead of "religion;" and it does

---

* Reprinted from *Emory Law Journal* 39 (1990): 149-164 as part of a symposium held in April 1988 at Emory Law School on Religious Dimensions of American Constitutionalism; also presented in April 1988 at a national symposium organized by the Williamsburg Charter Foundation, a body established to celebrate the Bicentennial of the United States Constitution and to reaffirm the religious liberty clauses of the First Amendment. The chapter was also published in James Davison Hunter and Os Guinness, eds., *Articles of Faith, Articles of Peace: The Religious Liberty Clauses and the American Public Philosophy* (Washington, DC, 1990). The Williamsburg Charter, to which reference is made in the chapter, was drafted by representatives of America's leading faiths. It is reproduced at pages 127-145 of the above book.

not contain the word "state" but speaks instead of "Congress." Moreover, in the extensive public discussions that were carried on in the late eighteenth and early nineteenth centuries concerning the religion clauses of both the federal and the state constitutions, reference was rarely made to relations between "church" and "state;" debate centered, rather, on the extent to which "religion" and "government" should be free from each other's control. This, indeed, was Madison's own terminology.[1] Despite Jefferson's famous remark that the First Amendment erected "a wall of separation between church and state," it is important to recognize that in America at that time there was no "state" in the sense in which that word is used in classical Western political theory; nor was there then (nor is there now) a "church," either in the sense of a single universal ecclesiastical entity such as the Roman Catholic Church, which maintained an autonomy vis-à-vis the various secular polities of Europe in the eleventh to sixteenth centuries, or in the sense of the established churches that existed in the various kingdoms of Europe after the Protestant Reformation.

As John Noonan has eloquently stated:

'Church and State' . . . is a profoundly misleading rubric. The title triply misleads. It suggests that there is a single church. But in America there are myriad ways in which religious belief is organized. It suggests that there is a single state. But in America there is the federal government, fifty state governments, myriad municipalities, and a division of power among executive, legislative, administrative, and judicial entities, each of whom embodies state power. Worst of all, 'Church and State' suggests that there are two distinct bodies set apart from each other in contrast if not in conflict. But everywhere neither churches nor states exist except as they are incorporated in actual individuals. These individuals are believers and unbelievers, citizens and officials. In one aspect of their activities, if they are religious, they usually form churches. In another aspect they form governments. Religious and governmental bodies not only coexist but overlap. The same persons, much of the time, are both believers and wielders of power.[2]

The Framers of the American federal and state constitutions were keenly aware of the historical experience that is implicit in the phrase "church and state." They chose at the federal level, and eventually in all the states as well, a new and different solution, namely, the right of all persons, both

---

[1] Cf. Madison Brant, "On the Separation of Church and State," *William and Mary Quarterly,* 3d ser., 8 (1951): 3. Despite Brant's title, none of his numerous citations of Madison include the phrase "church and state." For example, he quotes Madison's Essay on Monopolies, written some time after 1817, stating that "the separation between religion and government" is "strongly guarded . . . in the Constitution of the United States." Ibid., at 21.

[2] John T. Noonan, *The Believer and the Powers That Are* (New York, 1987), 16.

individually and in groups, to exercise their religion free of restraint by government, and also the duty of government to exercise its powers and functions without identification with religion. But the fact that religion and government were to be free of each other's control was not understood to exclude their reciprocal influence on each other. Officeholders, as Noonan indicates, were not expected to shed their religious commitments at the door of the office.

In considering what was meant by religion and what was meant by government when the federal and state constitutions were adopted, and what is meant by religion and government today, one should have in mind not only the various kinds of beliefs that may properly be called religious, and not only the various kinds of speech and worship associated with those beliefs, but also their manifestation in social action. Today religion is often defined solely in terms of personal faith and collective worship. Such a definition neglects the repercussions of such faith and worship in social life. In the Puritan theology that prevailed in America throughout the eighteenth century,[3] often in association with both Anglican and "free church" traditions, religion was understood not only in terms of a covenant of grace but also in terms of a covenant of works.[4] A person's relationship to God was understood to involve his active participation in the life of the community. More than that, religion was understood to be not only a matter of personal faith and personal morality but also a matter of collective responsibility and collective identity.

In seeking the meaning of the religion clauses of the First Amendment, I propose, therefore, in the first part of this essay, to focus attention on the role which religion played in the social life of America in the eighteenth and nineteenth centuries. To do so is to be faithful to Madison's conception that religion comprises not only "the duty which we owe to our Creator" but also "the manner of discharging" that duty.[5] For Madison, as for Americans generally in the 1780s and 1790s, and indeed for generations thereafter, free exercise of religion included freedom of religious groups to take an active part in regulating family responsibilities, education, health care, poor relief, and various other aspects of social life which were considered to have a significant moral dimension.

---

[3] "At the time of the Revolution, at least 75 percent of American citizens had grown up in families espousing some form of Puritanism." A. James Reichley, *Religion in American Public Life* (Washington DC, 1985), 53.

[4] See John Witte, Jr., "Blest Be the Ties that Bind: Covenant and Community in Puritan Thought," *Emory Law Journal* 36 (1987): 579, 580-581.

[5] James Madison, "Memorial and Remonstrance Against Religious Assessments," in Gaillard Hunt, ed., *The Writings of James Madison* (New York, 1901), 2: 183-184.

Conversely, the concept of government which prevailed when the federal constitution and the first state constitutions were adopted, and which continued to prevail for generations thereafter, was that government's role in the regulation of family responsibilities, education, health care, poor relief, and other similar matters of social welfare, as distinct from political and economic concerns, is not a direct but an indirect one, namely, to help maintain conditions in which the carrying on of such activities by religious associations, or associations inspired by religious motivation, can flourish.

Yet the prevailing social roles and functions of religion and government in the United States today are quite different. The contrast between the earlier situation and the present situation is obvious enough. In the 1780s religion played a primary role in social life, as I have defined that phrase, and government played a relatively minor, though necessary, supportive role. In the 1980s religion plays a relatively minor, though necessary, supportive role and government plays a primary role. On the other hand, the role played by government in the social life of America in the 1780s (and for almost a century and a half thereafter) was openly and strongly influenced and directed by religion, whereas in the 1980s that is much less true and in many respects not true at all, while the role played by religion in the social life of America in the 1980s is openly and strongly influenced and directed by government.

To put this last point in strong terms, and perhaps with some exaggeration: Whereas two centuries ago, in matters of social life which have a significant moral dimension, government was the handmaid of religion, today religion, in its social responsibilities, as contrasted with personal faith and collective worship, is the handmaid of government.

Lest this be misunderstood as a plea for a return to some golden age, it should be emphasized that what is described here is the irrevocable transition of twentieth-century America from a nation which had previously identified itself as Protestant Christian to a nation of plural religions, including not only many varieties of Protestants, Catholics, Jews, and Muslims but also diverse other groups whose belief systems, though non-theistic, have much of the character and many of the functions of religion. Most of these theistic and non-theistic belief systems have come to be defined largely in terms of personal life rather than in terms *both* of personal life *and* of social, or public, or civic responsibilities.

Thus the first two parts of this essay will address two paradoxical situations in which America now finds itself by virtue of (a) having a constitutional text which, when it was adopted, presupposed the active role of religion, on the one hand, and the relative passivity of government, on the other, in various realms of social life; and (b) living now in a time when, on the one hand, religion is becoming increasingly privatized, and, on the other hand, its public or civic or social functions are being increasingly swallowed up by—what now by reason of that very fact may properly be called—the secular state.

The third and concluding part of this essay will consider the significance of this shift in the social roles of religion and government for our understanding of how the religion clauses of the First Amendment should be interpreted and applied.

Religion and Government.—In sketching the social role of religion in America in the late eighteenth and early nineteenth centuries, it will be useful to specify its role in a number of areas of social life.

First, take family life. In the late eighteenth century and, indeed, for some generations thereafter, the family in America was widely thought to be not only a civil but also a religious unit. Births, marriages, deaths, and other family events were often recorded in family Bibles. Family prayers were not uncommon. Attendance at church was generally by families, with seating in family pews. Marriage was subject to ritual and law derived from church traditions. As late as 1917, the United States Supreme Court spoke of marriage as a "holy estate."[6] A leading treatise on family law published in 1899 stated that marriage is a "state of existence ordained by the Creator," "a consummation of the Divine command 'to multiply and replenish the earth'," and "the only stable substructure of our social, civil, and religious institutions."[7] Bigamy, polygamy, incest, and homosexuality were punishable offenses. Betrothals were required to be formal and marriages were required to be contracted with parental consent and before witnesses. Divorce laws in the various states were derived from English ecclesiastical law, which was itself derived partly from the canon law of the Roman Catholic Church and partly from Protestant religious norms. Couples who sought divorce had to publish their intentions and to prove in court adequate cause or fault.[8]

Following English precedent, American statutes and court decisions in the late eighteenth and early nineteenth centuries gave the husband and

---

6 Caminetti v. United States, 242 U.S. 470 (1917) (quoting Murphy v. Ramsey, 114 U.S. 15, 45 (1885)).

7 John Witte, Jr., "The Reformation of Marriage Law in Martin Luther's Germany: Its Significance Then and Now," *Journal of Law and Religion* 4 (1986): 293, 347, (quoting William C. Rodgers, *A Treatise on the Law of Domestic Relations* (Chicago, 1899), 2).

8 Witte, "Reformation of Marriage Law," 347. See also sources cited in ibid., at 347, n.130. In the following pages of his article, Witte goes on to show the transformation of these marriage laws and concepts in the twentieth century.

father the dominant role in family life. He had the primary right to control his wife and children and the household. Indeed, the wife could not sue or be sued except with her husband. In case of separation or divorce, the father was given preference in the custody of children. These legal rules favoring male domination were identified to a large extent with religious tradition, including traditional interpretations of the Bible.

In the realm of education the pattern was similar. In 1787 and for many decades thereafter, education in the home was widespread. Outside the home it was largely in the hands of the churches and of private teachers, a considerable percentage of whom were clergymen. Education at all levels had a strong religious purpose and character. There was little public education, although three of the thirteen original states provided for it in their constitutions. In the majority of states, most education was provided by the dominant churches, such as the Congregationalist church in Massachusetts and other parts of New England and the Episcopal and Presbyterian churches in Virginia.

Not until the 1820s and 1830s did government gradually assume responsibility for the education of the youth. Even then, however, this responsibility was conceived to be fundamentally religious in character. That is apparent from the speeches and writings of the great apostle of the public school, Horace Mann, who continually emphasized that only through public education could a Christian social consciousness and a Christian morality be inculcated in the population as a whole.[9]

Horace Mann did not invent these views. As early as 1787, the Northwest Ordinance promulgated by the Continental Congress, stated that "[r]eligion, morality, and knowledge being necessary to good government and the

---

[9] The Massachusetts Board of Education was established in 1837 largely as a result of Mann's inspiration. As secretary of the Board, Mann gave a lecture at a convention held in each county in the state to explain the aims, costs, and benefits of education. Lecture 5, given in 1841, contains the following language:

> As educators, . . . our great duty is . . . to awaken the faculty of thought in all the children of the Commonwealth; . . . to cultivate in them a sacred regard to truth; . . . to train them up to the love of God and the love of man; to make the perfect example of Jesus Christ lovely in their eyes; and to give to all so much religious instruction as is compatible with the rights of others and with the genius of our government—leaving to parents and guardians the direction, during their school-going days, of all special and peculiar instruction respecting politics and theology; and at last, when the children arrive at years of maturity, to commend them to that inviolable prerogative of private judgment and of self-direction, which, in a Protestant and a Republican country, is the acknowledged birth-right of every human being.

Reprinted in Horace Mann, *Lectures On Education* (New York, 1969), 263.

happiness of mankind, schools and the means of education shall forever be encouraged."[10]

As the number of religious sects and the prevalence of public schooling increased in the first half of the nineteenth century, state support of specific, doctrinal education dwindled. But at the same time, schools did not lose their more general Christian aspect. Prayer and a reading from the Protestant Bible, usually at the beginning of the day, set a religious tone to instruction. Though some states passed laws requiring Bible reading, most states did not bother to legislate established custom. "Even Thomas Jefferson, though questioning the value of religious education for children, insisted only that in the public schools of Virginia, 'no religious reading, instruction or exercise, shall be prescribed or practiced, inconsistent with the tenets of any religious sect or denomination'."[11]

Not only public elementary and secondary schools but also state colleges and universities were intended to promote Christian education. The University of North Carolina, which opened in 1795, had as its president during most of the first third of the nineteenth century a Presbyterian minister, who, with strong support from the state legislature, "insisted on regular attendance by students at religious worship and on orthodox religious instruction."[12] Of the 246 colleges and universities founded in America before 1860, the great majority were denominational foundations; most of the others were founded by union of several churches; only seventeen were state institutions, and even these considered themselves Christian and required students to attend religious services.[13]

Much of the same can be said of social welfare. Poor relief was also primarily a responsibility of religious groups in many parts of the United States during the late eighteenth and early nineteenth centuries. In Virginia, for example, the parishes regularly provided money and food to parishioners who were in need. Also the vestry of the parish would levy tithes on the parishioners to reimburse those members of the parish who supported aged paupers, orphan children, and indigent parents, as well as to maintain a workhouse and poor farm.[14]

In the northern states the townships took responsibility for poor relief, but this was under the strong influence of Puritan conceptions and with

---

[10] Northwest Ordinance of 1787, art. III, 1 Stat. 50, 51-53 (1789).

[11] See Reichley, *Religion in American Public Life*, 136-137.

[12] Anson P. Stokes, *Church and State in the United States* (New York, 1950), 629-630.

[13] Ibid., 636-637.

[14] See George C. Mason, ed., *The Colonial Vestry Book of Lynnhaven Parish, Princess Anne County, Virginia, 1723-1786* (Newport News, VA, 1949), 7: 113-114.

active participation of the churches. In general, those who were willing to work but had fallen on hard times were to be helped, but those who were "idle or vicious" were to be punished.[15]

Philadelphia was a pioneer in establishing a secular system of public poor relief, administered by city officials who assessed and collected a poor tax. Nevertheless, the need for private charity remained a pressing one, and the various religious denominations maintained parallel systems of relief for their own adherents. The public and the private systems worked together. Thus in combating successive epidemics of yellow fever in the late 1700s and early 1800s, Philadelphia physicians, ministers, and merchants cooperated in administering both public and private funds. Moreover, public and private relief of disease and of poverty was combined with "reclamation" and "uplift" of the "idle or vicious" poor onto the path of industry and morality.[16]

In comparison with the role of religion, the role of government in social life in 1787 and thereafter was very limited. Although it was indeed a responsibility of government to regulate family life through laws on marriage and divorce, parental powers, and the like, government regulation of these matters consisted chiefly in the implementation of religious norms and concepts. Using the language of "church and state," one may say that family law, which had once been in the province of canon law and ecclesiastical courts, was, in the American Republic, a part of secular law administered by secular courts. But if we use the language of "religion and government," we must say something rather different, namely, that family law, while administered by government, remained essentially religious in character and, more specifically, Protestant Christian.

Similarly, much of the criminal law, which was enacted and enforced by agencies of government, embodied religious concepts. Not only did the legislative, executive, and judicial branches of government prohibit, prosecute, and punish such religious crimes as blasphemy, Sabbath-breaking, sexual deviation, gambling, and duelling, but also the entire concept of crime and punishment was rooted in religious doctrines of sin and penance.

While religion played a guiding role and government an implementing role in both family law and criminal law, in education the role of government was even more restricted. Government-sponsored education was in its infancy. When it did begin to flourish a generation later, the guiding role of

---

[15] See Louis B. Wright, *The Cultural Life of the American Colonies 1607-1763* (New York, 1957), 23-27.

[16] See generally John K. Alexander, *Render Them Submissive: Responses to Poverty in Philadelphia, 1760-1800* (Amherst, MA, 1980).

religion was paramount and the role of government was, once again, an auxiliary one.

With regard to poor relief, health care, and other forms of social welfare, the role of government at all levels, local as well as state and federal, was minimal. These matters were left almost entirely to voluntary associations, and especially to religiously motivated associations.

It would be a mistake to attribute the limited role of government in social welfare to a laissez-faire theory of the state. It is not true that the founders of the American Republic conceived the role of government to be that of a "night watchman," with the duty solely to police the operation of a free-market, individualistic society. Especially in the economic sphere, government at all levels was thought to have an important positive role to play. But in *social* life, in the sense in which I have employed that term, including, to be sure, the economic function of poor relief, the role of government was minimal—compared with what it has become in the twentieth century—and the role of religion was maximal.

Specifically, government was thought to have an auxiliary role, an implementing role, while religion was thought to have a directing role, a motivating role. This relationship was dramatically symbolized by the sermons preached at openings of legislative sessions at the state level as well as at other state occasions. Sometimes lasting two hours or more, such sermons emphasized the Christian covenant of works between God and man as well as the mission of public servants to maintain civic virtue.[17]

That government had the function of implementing goals set by religion is evident in the large amount of governmental support given to religion, and especially to religious education, even at the federal level. For example, the Northwest Ordinance, in addition to its general endorsement of such support, specifically provided for government establishment of religious schools.[18] The Ohio Company was given a huge grant of land with the specification that a substantial acreage be used "for the support of religion."[19] The federal government provided a Roman Catholic school for the Indians of the

---

[17] Cf. Harry S. Stout, *The New England Soul: Preaching and Religious Culture in Colonial New England* (New York, 1986). This book focuses solely on the colonial period. However, the practice of preaching "occasional" sermons at public events continued into the nineteenth century.

[18] Act of Aug. 7, 1789, ch. 8, 1 Stat. 50.

[19] Act of Apr. 21, 1792, ch. 25, 1 Stat. 257; Act of Feb. 20, 1833, ch. 42, 4 Stat. 618. See Noonan, *The Believer*, 138. Cf. Northwest Ordinance of 1787, art. III, 1 Stat. 50, 51-53 (1789).

Northwest Territory[20] and subsequently sent missionaries to Indians.[21] Congress gave a land grant in 1832 to a Baptist university and in 1833 to Georgetown College (in what is now Washington, D.C.), which was a Jesuit college for educating Roman Catholic boys. At the state level, widespread governmental aid to religious activities continued into the twentieth century.[22]

Religion and Government Today.—In the twentieth century, we see a complete reversal of the respective roles of religion and government in American social life. Defined in terms of their social functions, these two have radically changed their meaning.

It is unnecessary to introduce data to prove that government today is largely responsible for education at the primary and secondary level and plays a major role at the level of higher education as well. Public education today is almost wholly secularized—not only in the sense that it is operated by government but in the sense that government, and not religion, sets its goals.

Similarly, health care is no longer primarily a religious or even a charitable concern. It is primarily a political, a governmental, concern. Although it is benefitted by charitable contributions to medical services, its standards and goals are set to a considerable extent by government. Where religion enters the hospital, chiefly in the form of chaplains' services, it does so in an auxiliary and private capacity.

Relief of poverty is also, above all, a governmental concern. Religion makes an important contribution, but it is, once again, essentially an auxiliary contribution. Church shelters for the homeless are an excellent example: the relationship of the churches to the people whom they shelter is largely impersonal. These homeless are not, as they would have been in 1787, the

---

[20] The bill enabling this action was signed by President Jefferson. Jefferson's letter to the Senate, presenting the treaty with the Kaskaskia Indians for ratification, together with articles 1-7 of the treaty, are reproduced in Robert L. Cord, *The Separation of Church and State* (New York, 1982), 262-263. Article 3 states:

> And whereas the greater part of the said tribe have been baptised and received into the Catholic church, to which they are much attached, the United States will give, annually, for seven years, one hundred dollars towards the support of a priest of that religion, who will engage to perform for said tribe the duties of his office, and also to instruct as many of their children as possible, in the rudiments of literature. And the United States will further give the sum of three hundred dollars, to assist the said tribe in the erection of a church.

[21] This action was upheld by the United States Supreme Court in Worcester v. Georgia, 31 U.S. (6 Pet) 515 (1832).

[22] Examples are given in Harold J. Berman, "Religion and Law: The First Amendment in Historical Perspective," *Emory Law Journal* 35 (1986): 777-778.

churches' own parishioners. Moreover, homelessness in America today is a large scale problem that can only be solved ultimately by government-supported housing and mental health programs. In recent years the churches, among other voluntary agencies, have stepped in chiefly to help meet a crisis that arose when government aid was reduced. Similarly, churches have given government substantial assistance in administering foreign aid in various countries, operating under essentially political guidelines.[23]

Perhaps the most important reversal in the roles of religion and government is in the area of family life. The urban family today is not, for the most part, a religious unit. Family law no longer reflects religious beliefs. The organization of the family—or rather the disorganization of the family—is now treated in practice as a problem to be regulated primarily by governmental rather than by religious norms. The economic and legal aspects of family life are treated independently of its spiritual aspects.

The same is true of urban crime. Criminal law has been almost wholly divorced from sin and penance. With some important exceptions, religion today has little to do with defining what is criminal or with determining what the punishment or other treatment of criminal offenders should be.

In short, religion has lost most of its importance as a way of addressing publicly the major social problems of our society. Religion has become increasingly a matter of the private relationship between the believer and God. Worship remains collective, and the churches continue to play an important part in the individual lives and the interpersonal relations of their members, but the occasional gatherings of fellow worshippers make only a minor contribution toward solving society's social needs.

As religion has become increasingly a private matter, the social responsibilities of government have become magnified. Society has become increasingly identified with government. Divorced from religion, government has become increasingly political, so that the words "government and politics," or "government and state," have become almost synonymous. The state, as the great Polish Nobel-Prize-winning poet Czeslaw Milosz has said, threatens to swallow up the civil society.[24]

The implications of the reversal.—How does, how should, this change in the roles of religion and government—indeed, this *exchange* of roles—affect

---

[23] See generally J. Bruce Nichols, *The Uneasy Alliance: Religion, Refugee Work and U.S. Foreign Policy* (New York, 1988).

[24] Milosz said, "[The] basic issue of the twentieth century . . . [is that] the state . . . has eaten up all the substance of society." Nathan Gardels, An Interview With Czeslaw Milosz, *New York Review of Books* (Feb. 27, 1986), 34.

our understanding of the religion clauses of the First Amendment? Must one draw the conclusion that the very words "religion" and "government" (or more exactly "Congress") in the First Amendment, and in parallel provisions of the state constitutions, have come to have fundamentally different meanings today from what they had not only in the 1780s and 1790s but also in the following century and a half? If that is true, does it follow that the "original intent" of the framers of the religion clauses is irrelevant to the interpretation of the words themselves?

The difficulty of interpretation remains acute if we look not to the intent of the framers as such but rather, as the leading framer himself recommended, to the intent of the people of the several states who ratified it.[25] That avoids the tortuous path of committee drafts, legislative debate, and contemporary polemics. Yet the broader question is equally intractable: how is the word "religion," as it was understood in 1787 or 1791 by a nation whose electorate was divided largely among Anglo-Saxon Protestant Christian denominations, to be interpreted for a nation whose electorate is divided not only among Protestants, Catholics, Jews, and Muslims, all theists, but also among many other non-theistic religious groups as well as agnostics and atheists, and then cross-divided not only among whites and non-whites but also among numerous ethnic subdivisions of both whites and non-whites?

Should we then disregard the historical dimension of the Constitution and attribute to the term "religion" in the First Amendment the meaning which it has in current usage? This, indeed, is what the courts have done when they have said that religion is the private affair of each individual, a matter of his or her personal choice, rather than a matter of the collective identity of a nation made up of religiously diverse communities.[26] On the basis of a purely individualist definition of religion, the theory of a

---

[25] Madison wrote to Thomas Ritchie in 1821 that,

the legitimate meaning of the Instrument must be derived from the text itself; or if a key is to be sought elsewhere, it must be, not in the opinions or intentions of the body which planned and proposed the Constitution, but in the sense attached to it by the people in their respective State Conventions, where it received all the authority which it possesses.

Writings of James Madison (Philadelphia, PA, 1865), 3: 228. See also B. Nelson Ong, "James Madison on Constitutional Interpretation," *Benchmark*, 3(1-2) (January-April, 1987): 17.

[26] In Wallace v. Jaffree, 472 U.S. 38, 52-53 (1985), Justice Stevens analogized the free exercise of religion to the right to speak or to refrain from speaking, stating that "the individual freedom of conscience protected by the First Amendment embraces the right to select any religious faith or none at all." Many religious believers, however, would deny that they once "selected" a religious faith and that their continued adherence to a religious faith is basically a matter of individual choice.

constitutional "wall of separation between church and state" might indeed be justified. The definition, however, is open to challenge. It remains for churches, synagogues, and other religious communities to demonstrate that religion does have a social dimension and that creative ways can be found to bring religion and government together.

If religious communities can, in fact, show that not only private belief but also social commitment is an integral part of what they mean by "religion," then the courts should begin to expand the "free exercise" clause of the First Amendment. If the social commitment of various religious groups is exercised in cooperation with government programs in ways that do not adversely affect other religious or non-religious groups, then the courts should begin to contract the "establishment" clause, thus reconciling the two clauses. In the words of the Williamsburg Charter, "In light of the First Amendment, the government should stand in relation to the churches, synagogues and other communities of faith as the guarantor of freedom."[27] That freedom should include not only the freedom to exercise inner belief but also the freedom to exercise social commitments intrinsically involved in such belief.

Such a reconciliation of the two clauses could also serve as a basis for reconciling twentieth-century constitutional law with the constitutional law of the eighteenth and nineteenth centuries.

There are already many examples of constitutionally permitted coopera-tion between religion and government. In addition to traditional examples such as government employment of chaplains in the armed forces and in legislatures, ceremonial prayers at the opening of legislative and judicial sessions, the pledge of allegiance to the flag, and the language of official patriotic songs, other equally important examples are those of cooperation between churches and government agencies in the building of low-cost housing and in other forms of poor relief, as well as in the treatment of alcoholism and drug addiction, in foreign aid, and in various other govern-mental activities that have a strong moral dimension. There can be no consti-tutional objection, surely, to the use of religious counselors by courts in resolving questions of family responsibility in cases of divorce and care of children.

Even with respect to the acute question of religion in the schools, there are ample opportunities within the Constitution for reciprocal aid by government to religion and by religion to government. Public schools may offer courses in the history of religion, in the Bible as literature, and in com-parative religion. Public school teachers at all levels are free to explain Jewish

---

27 *The Williamsburg Charter: A National Celebration and Reaffirmation of the First Amendment Religious Liberty Clauses* (Williamsburg, VA, 1988), 19.

beliefs relating to Chanukah and Christian beliefs relating to Christmas. Such instruction does aid religion without, however, constituting an establishment. Blatant discrimination against one or more belief systems might indeed rise to the level of a constitutionally prohibited preference of the majority faiths. Yet there is no reason to believe that conflicts among religions, as well as conflicts between theistic religions and various forms of so-called secular humanism, could not be presented in a classroom setting openly and fairly to all sides.

Similarly, the widespread use of government funds—especially at the municipal and state levels—to finance social welfare activities in which religious groups participate does indeed "aid" not only religion in general but also those religious groups in particular. Such aid should be, and for the most part is, understood, however, not as an establishment of religion but as part of government's responsibility to protect the free exercise of religion.

America today is groping for a public philosophy that will look beyond our pluralism to the common convictions that underlie our pluralism. We must come to grips with the fact that freedom of belief—which includes freedom of disbelief—rests, in the last analysis, on the foundation of belief, not on the foundation of skepticism. That is what John Adams meant when he said that the Constitution, with its guarantee of freedom to believe or disbelieve, "was made only for a moral and religious people. It is wholly inadequate to the government of any other."[28] It is not to be regarded as an instrument framed (in the words of a Missouri court in 1854) for a society "composed of strangers . . . each with a religion of his own, bound by no previous social ties, nor sympathizing in any common reminiscences of the past."[29]

At the same time, our public philosophy must also come to grips with the deep conflict in our society between orthodox religious belief systems and widespread indifference or opposition to such belief systems. We have in the past sought to resolve this conflict largely by trying to sweep it under the rug. We have pretended that all belief, both religious and non-religious, is the private affair of each individual. This has inhibited the articulation of a public philosophy grounded in our fundamental beliefs concerning human nature, human destiny, and the sources and limits of human knowledge.

Especially with regard to debate concerning the religion clauses of the First Amendment, there should be open discussion of the significance of its historical roots. More particularly, a reconsideration of Adams' and Madison's conception that religious freedom can only be secure if it is undergirded by

---

[28] *The Works of John Adams* (Boston, 1856), 9: 229.

[29] State v. Ambs, 20 Mo. 214, 216 (1854).

religious faith[30] could lead to a reinterpretation of the relationship between the "establishment" clause and the "free exercise" clause—a reinterpretation which would permit not only "religion" to cooperate with "government" but "government" openly to cooperate with "religion"—without discrimination for or against any belief system (and hence without establishment) and without coercion (and hence without restriction upon free exercise).

---

[30] Madison stated that the right to free exercise of religion is founded on the duty of every man

> to render to the Creator such homage, and such only, as he believes to be acceptable to him. This duty is precedent both in order of time and degree of obligation, to the claims of Civil Society. Before any man can be considered as a member of Civil Society, he must be considered as a subject of the Governor of the Universe. . . . We maintain therefore that in matters of Religion, no man's right is abridged by the institution of Civil Society, and that Religion is wholly exempt from its cognizance.

Hunt, ed., *The Writings of James Madison*, 2: 184-185. Madison's reference to the distinction between man as "a member of Civil Society" and man as "a subject of the Governor of the Universe" is an implicit reference to the Lutheran doctrine of Two Kingdoms—the heavenly and the earthly—as well as to the Calvinist doctrine of two covenants, one between God and man, the other between government and people. See Berman, "Religion and Law," 787.

Part Two

SOCIOLOGICAL AND
PHILOSOPHICAL THEMES

~~⟊~~ 10 ~~⟊~~

SOME FALSE PREMISES OF MAX WEBER'S
SOCIOLOGY OF LAW*

M ax Weber's sociology of law has received an enormous amount of acclaim among American legal scholars during recent decades,[1] and many of his ideas have become very widely accepted even by people who

---

   * Reprinted from *Washington University Law Quarterly* 65 (1987): 758-770, in a collection of essays dedicated to Gray L. Dorsey.

   [1] In a perceptive review of one of the earliest English translations of Weber's writings, Samuel E. Thorne, then Associate Professor of Law and Librarian at Yale Law School, noted that Weber's sociological works "have received little direct attention from English readers." Samuel E. Thorne, Book Review of *From Max Weber: Essays in Sociology*, eds. H. H. Gerth and C. Wright Mills (1946), *Yale Law Journal* 56 (1946): 188, 189. It was the appearance eight years later of *Max Weber on Law in Economy and Society*, ed. Max Rheinstein (New York, 1954) that first stimulated a rash of writings about Weber by American legal scholars. In 1986 David Trubek, John Esser, and Laurel Munger produced a bibliography entitled *Preliminary, Eclectic, Unannotated Working Bibliography for the Study of Max Weber's Sociology of Law* (Madison, WI, 1986). Today Weber is referred to as a "patron saint" of American legal thought concerning the relationship of law to society. See David Trubek, "Max Weber's Tragic Modernism and the Study of Law in Society," *Law and Society Review* 20 (1986): 573. In 1984 one writer called him "the premier social scientist of this century." Nancy L. Schwartz, "Max Weber's Philosophy," *Yale Law Journal* 93 (1984): 1386.

   Weber's enormous influence extends, of course, to other countries as well. John Finnis wrote in 1985 that "[a]mong the hidden streams nourishing jurisprudence at Oxford during the past thirty years, the work of Max Weber is among the most significant." John Finnis, "On 'Positivism' and 'Legal Rational Authority'," *Oxford Journal of Legal Studies* 5 (1985): 74.

have never studied his writings. His sharp distinctions between "charismatic," "traditional," "formal-rational" and "substantively rational" types of law, his characterization of modern Western law as formal-rational, capitalist, and bureaucratic, and more generally his identification of various types of law with various types of political domination—reflect theories of law which, when baldly stated, are controversial. Nevertheless, being embedded in the immense historical and legal scholarship which Weber commanded and in the complex and intricate analytical network which he elaborated, these theories have seemed to his numerous admirers to be validated almost beyond a doubt.

One reason for the acceptance of Weber's legal sociology is that few people have carefully reviewed his historical and legal scholarship but instead have merely assumed that since it is so immense it must be sound. Another reason is that the subtle interconnections which Weber draws between his theoretical models ("ideal types") and historical reality give an aura of plausibility to the former. When the ideal type fails to account for important elements of historical reality, Weberians fall back on its "analytical" or "heuristic" value. The fact that a given legal system falls within two or more ideal types is not disturbing to them: the ideal type is, for them, as real as the historical reality.[2] This confusion is aggravated by the fact that Weber does not always distinguish between an "ideal" type (like bureaucracy) and a "real" type (like the Protestant ethic).

A third, more important reason for the widespread acceptance of Weberian legal theory among contemporary legal scholars is the fact that underlying its central concepts, as Anthony Kronman has shown, are certain unstated philosophical assumptions which give it intellectual coherence;[3] and

---

[2] Alexander von Schelting, in his authoritative work on Weber's sociology of knowledge, states that it is impossible to remove from Weber's concept of ideal types "all its inherent obscurities, contradictions, and ambiguities." Alexander von Schelting, *Max Webers Wissenschaftslehre: Das logische Problem der historischen Kulturerkenntnis, Die Grenzen der Soziologie des Wissens* (Berlin, 1934; repr. ed., Aalen, 1975), 329. Schelting stresses that by definition ideal types are theoretical models which can exist only in the mind of the observer. Nevertheless, it would seem that if they are to serve as useful models they must correspond to some degree to that which is observed, and, in fact, Weber illustrates his ideal types with a wealth of data which he purports to draw from the real history of diverse societies. He also admits, however, historical "deviations" from the ideal type. As my colleague Frank Lechner has put it, Weber's ideal types are intended in part to describe and in part to distort historical reality. This would bear out the statement in the text.

[3] Anthony T. Kronman, *Max Weber* (Stanford, CA, 1983). Kronman writes: "In this book, I offer an interpretation of the *Rechtssoziologie* which is intended to show that it does have an overarching conceptual unity. . . . My interpretation . . . elaborates and emphasizes the common philosophical assumptions underlying Weber's treatment of many different topics in the Rechtssoziologie. . . . All reveal an implicit commitment, on Weber's part, to a

these assumptions are widely shared. First, Weber starts from a sharp distinction between fact and value: facts, in Weber's view, do not have any inherent meaning or purpose, and the meanings and purposes (values) attached to them by those who observe them are chosen by an exercise of will of those observers. Kronman rightly calls this a "positivistic theory of value," which rests on a "will-centered conception of personhood."[4] Second, Weber treats law as a fact, not a value, and states further that the social scientist should study law without himself evaluating the normative commitments of those who attach value to it.[5] In other words, the values which a given legal institution or set of legal institutions expressly or implicitly reflects or pursues are not values that inhere in the institutions but are values attributed to them by those who make or apply or respond to them; the scholar should study them

---

few simple philosophical ideas; it is these that provide the unifying link between what is otherwise likely to seem a jumble of sometimes brilliant but essentially unconnected insights." Ibid., 3. Cf. ibid., 4: "This book . . . attempts to demonstrate that the unstated philosophical assumptions that underlie [the] central concepts [of Weber's *Rechtssoziologie*] give the work as a whole a significant degree of intellectual coherence." I have quoted these passages to counteract the statement made by David Trubek that although Kronman "does . . . try to demonstrate the unity of Weber's thought [. . . his] ultimate conclusion is that Weber's theory of law and his ideas about the nature of society and social science were contradictory and reveal his apparent 'intellectual or moral schizophrenia'." Trubek, "Max Weber's Tragic Modernism," 575.

The consistency of Weber's "methodology" has been defended by Maureen Cain, "The Limits of Idealism: Max Weber and the Sociology of Law," *Research in Law and Sociology* 3 (1980): 53 and by Sally Ewing, "Formal Justice and the Spirit of Capitalism: Max Weber's Sociology of Law," *Law and Society Review* 21 (1987): 487.

Consistency in philosophical assumptions and in methodology does not necessarily lead, however, to consistency in factual and theoretical conclusions. As the present essay attempts to show, Weber's philosophical and methodological errors, consistently pursued, led him in some instances to contradictory results.

[4] Kronman, *Max Weber*, 36. Arnold Brecht has traced the emergence of the sharp distinction between fact and value to the writings of Simmel, Rickert, Jellinek, and Max Weber in the late nineteenth century. Its first expression was the doctrine of the logical "gulf" (Brecht calls it "the Gulf Doctrine") between the Is and the Ought. See Arnold Brecht, *Political Theory: The Foundations of Twentieth-Century Political Thought* (Princeton, NJ, 1959), 207-231. He states that this doctrine was reflected in the belief that values are essentially subjective and not capable of scientific proof or disproof. "Its inability morally to condemn Bolshevism, Fascism, or National Socialism in unconditional terms was to become the tragedy of twentieth-century political science, a tragedy as deep as any that had ever occurred before in the history of science." Ibid., 8. Yet Brecht himself defends "Scientific Value Relativism" as itself logically unassailable. Ibid., 488-490.

[5] Weber wrote that scholarship, science, should be "value-free" (*Wertfrei*). There has been some debate about what he meant by that. For a recent discussion see Cain, "The Limits of Idealism." Cain's defense against critics of Weber goes so far as to raise the question whether he meant anything at all by "value-free" other than that the scholar should make his own values "explicit and public."

empirically but should attempt to exclude his or her own values from such study. Third, what Weber calls formal-rational legal authority, namely, a system of politics in which domination is exercised by means of a logically consistent system of consciously made legal rules, corresponds to Weber's theory of value, which asserts the positivity of all norms. As Kronman has shown, formal-rational authority is the one form of political domination whose fundamental principle of legitimation expresses what Weber considered to be the truth about values; therefore he was inclined (Kronman says "bound") to make this form of authority the model against which he contrasted other types.[6]

Thus Weber's sociology of law is appealing to many contemporary legal scholars partly because it denies that the world, including the world of law, has any inherent meaning or purpose, that is, any value "that antedates the choices and commitments of individual human beings."[7] At the same time, Weber interprets social action, including law, in terms of dramatic contrasts among different civilizations and different eras of Western civilization, leaving the impression that history, including legal history, does indeed have a pattern and possibly even a direction, and that law in the West did indeed at one time have a historical mission. Weber's belief in the "disenchantment" of contemporary law and his own tragic view of modern man[8] reflect a nostalgia

---

[6] Kronman, *Max Weber*, 55. Finnis, "On 'Positivism'," 76-80, attacks Kronman's view that Weber "was bound" by a positivist theory of values to give a privileged position to legal rational authority. He agrees with Kronman, however, that Weber did in fact move from a positivist theory of values to a positivist theory of law. Finnis argues that a formal-rational model is also consistent with a theory of natural law. He points out that Weber himself stressed the influence of "natural law dogmas" on lawmaking in the past and called attention to the dangers involved in the contemporary "unmasking" of law as a mere instrument of power. Ibid., 80-83. Yet Finnis confirms the fact that Weber denied the objectivity of values and asserted that both values and law are essentially creatures of will.

[7] Kronman, *Max Weber*, 20-21. Kronman points out that "[a]ccording to Weber, there is and can be no such thing as a group idea, an idea grounded in something other than the consciousness of a single individual." Ibid., 25. This, of course, is consistent with, and perhaps essential to, the positivist theory that values do not inhere in factual reality but are willfully imposed upon it. Schwartz, "Max Weber's Philosophy," 1387 incorrectly concludes that Kronman is arguing that Weber believes that each individual is entirely free to choose among existing values or entirely free to choose new values. She combats this view by pointing out that Weber also believed very strongly in the "givenness of things," and that "our choices are situated in interpretive contexts which are historically given." Ibid., 1392. Schwartz misses the point that the givenness of things, for Weber, does not imply the givenness of the individual's own values, and that "interpretive contexts," for Weber, are only the values which numbers of individuals have attributed to things in the past.

[8] At the end of the First World War, Weber said that "the fate of our times is characterized by rationalization and intellectualization and, above all, by the 'disenchantment of the world'." "The ultimate and most sublime values," he declared, have "retreated"

that is appealing to those legal scholars who, although they may have little hope and even less faith, nevertheless find some comfort in the myths of an earlier age.

Finally, Weber's appeal is based in part on widespread acceptance of certain of his historiographical (as distinguished from philosophical) assumptions. Weber postulated that in the West, starting in the sixteenth century, an earlier "medieval" "feudal" "traditional" type of law was gradually superseded by a "modern" "capitalist" "formal-rational" type of law. To be sure, this conception was contradicted by some of his own historical insights (for example, the insight that the canon law of the "medieval" Roman Catholic Church was in fact "modern" and "rational" in his sense of those terms, and that the modern city—as we shall see below—also originated in the heyday of "feudalism"). Nevertheless, Weber associated the rise of capitalism and the rational bureaucratic state with Protestantism[9] and insisted on the "traditional" and "patrimonial" character of both feudalism and Roman Catholicism. This corresponded not only to the conventional historiography of the late nineteenth and early twentieth centuries but also to the left-wing socialist historiography of that era which postulated a historical evolution from feudalism to capitalism to socialism.

Respect for Weber is so great, and criticism of him has been on the whole so subdued, that to state bluntly that his sociology of law is generally wrong and that his influence has been generally harmful will strike many readers as perverse. At the same time, his scholarship is so massive and so complex that it would take far more than a single essay to expose the fallacies in it. What I propose to do here is to analyze one portion of Weber's work, namely, his sociology of the city,[10] to criticize its historiography, and to show some of the

---

either into mystical experience or into intimate personal relations. Although he deplored this "disenchantment of the world" (including the world of law), Weber nevertheless rejected any role for scholarship other than that of maintaining "plain intellectual integrity" and of meeting "the demands of the day." See Max Weber, "Science as a Vocation," in Gerth and Mills, *From Max Weber*, 155-156. This divorce between the vocation of science and the vocation of prophecy corresponds to the divorce between facts and values. It contributed to the defection of the German universities in the spiritual crisis of the 1920s and 1930s.

[9] Max Weber, *Gesammelte Aufsatze zur Religionsgeschichte*, vol. 1, part 1, translated by T. Parsons as *The Protestant Ethic and the Spirit of Capitalism* (New York/London, 1930).

[10] This analysis is drawn from Harold J. Berman, *Law and Revolution: The Formation of the Western Legal Tradition* (Cambridge, MA, 1983), 399-403. The references to Weber are drawn chiefly from Max Weber, *The City*, trans. and ed. Don Martindale and Gertrud Neuwirth (New York, 1958).

connections between its weaknesses and the weaknesses of his legal sociology as a whole.[11]

* * *

Weber's urban sociology starts with an analysis of the structural unity of the Western city as a community at the time of its historical origin in the eleventh to thirteenth centuries. He wrote that although the rudiments of the Western type of city may be found occasionally in other cultures, "an urban 'community' in the full meaning of the word appears only in the Occident." "To constitute a full urban community," he stated, "a settlement had to represent a relative predominance of trade-commercial relations, with the settlement as a whole displaying the following features: (1) a fortification, (2) a market, (3) a court of its own and at least a partially autonomous law, (4) a related form of association, and (5) at least partial autonomy and autocephaly, thus also an administration by authorities in the election of whom the burghers participated."[12] Such a peculiar system of forces, according to Weber, could only appear under special conditions and at a particular time, namely, late medieval Europe.[13]

Although cast in historical terms, Weber's theory of the city fails even to mention, much less to explain, the most striking and distinctive characteristic of the Western city, namely, its historical consciousness—that is, its consciousness of its own historical movement from past to future, its sense of its own ongoing, developing character. Partly as a result of that omission, the constituent elements attributed by Weber to the "full urban community" of the Occident reflect its structural integration, but they do not account for its dynamic character, its development in time. They do not explain why or how the twelfth-century city developed into the city of the sixteenth and the twentieth centuries, many of whose characteristics are identical to, or at least continuous with, those of the twelfth-century city, but others of which are substantially different in degree if not in kind.

A typical twentieth-century city has the following characteristics: (1) it is a corporation, endowed with legal personality, with capacity to sue and be sued, hold property, make contracts, purchase goods and services, employ labor, borrow money; (2) it is a political entity, usually governed by a mayor or city manager together with an elected council, which may employ officials, levy taxes, exercise the right of eminent domain, and perform other

---

[11] See also Berman, *Law and Revolution*, 546-554.

[12] Weber, *The City*, 54-55.

[13] Ibid.

governmental acts and functions; (3) it is an economic unit, which usually purveys or controls the purveyance of water, gas, electricity, and transportation, and regulates the construction and use of housing and the location of economic enterprises; (4) it is an agency for the promotion of social welfare, including education, health protection, poor relief, and public recreation.[14] Like their twentieth-century progeny, the cities of twelfth-century Europe were also corporate, political, economic, and social entities; however, the range of their activities in each of these roles was much more limited than that of a present-day city. Much of what a city does today was done then within the city, by guilds and by the church as well as by the extended family. Also the city today is much more integrated in, and much more representative of, the modern national state, an entity which was only beginning to come into existence in the twelfth century. Yet despite these differences, the present-day city developed, by a process of organic growth, out of the cities and towns that were created, or recreated, in the period of the Papal Revolution;[15] and that process of growth was part of its character as an urban community.

The process of growth of the Western city cannot be explained without reference to its historical self-awareness, its sense of its own historical continuity and development, its consciousness of its own ongoing character as a community, its own movement from the past into the future. Historically, this was connected, first, with the religious dimension of the Papal Revolution, and especially with the mission of the church gradually to reform and redeem the secular order. It was connected, second, with the political dimension of the Papal Revolution and especially with the belief in the coexistence of plural autonomous secular polities; it was this belief that made it both possible and urgent for citizens to form urban communes independent of royal, feudal, and even ecclesiastical authority—something that would have been unthinkable before the papacy desacralized kingship. It was connected, third, with the legal dimension of the Papal Revolution, and especially with the belief that the reformation and redemption of the secular order had to take place by the continual progressive development of legal institutions and periodic revision of laws in order to overcome the forces of disorder and injustice.

Strangely enough, Weber in a later chapter contradicted his own earlier statement of what constitutes the uniqueness of the medieval Western city.

---

[14] Cf. William Bennett Munro, *The Government of American Cities* (New York, 1926).

[15] The rise of the modern European city in the late eleventh and twelfth centuries, and its connection with other revolutionary social, economic, and political changes that accompanied the struggle of the Church under the papacy, to free itself from imperial, royal, and feudal control, is described in Berman, *Law and Revolution*, 357-403.

Without noticing the discrepancy, he attributed all five characteristics of a "full urban community"—which at first he had said "appears only in the Occident"—to the Asiatic and oriental city also. The latter, too, he stated, was a fortress and a market. It, too, contained farms held in socage (that is, in nonfeudal tenure), with land alienable without restriction, or hereditary in an unencumbered way, or obligated only with a fixed land rent. It, too, had its own "autonomous constitution," which presumably meant its own form of association and at least partial autonomy and autocephaly.[16] In all these respects, the differences between the medieval occidental city and its Asiatic counterparts were differences—Weber stated—only in degree. What "absolutely" distinguished the Western city, he finally concluded, was the personal legal condition, that is, the freedom, of the citizen.[17] Serfs emigrating to the cities had a common interest, he stated, in avoiding the imposition of military or other services by their erstwhile lords. "The urbanites therefore usurped the right to violate lordly law. This was the major revolutionary innovation of medieval occidental cities in contrast to all others."[18] Weber went on to say that the "cutting of status connections with the rural nobility" had been connected with the formation of municipal corporations—legally autonomous communes. "Similar preliminary stages of the constitution of a polis or commune may have appeared repeatedly in Asia and Africa," he added. (Note the cautionary words "preliminary" and "may".) "However, nothing is known [in Asia or Africa] of a legal status of citizenship."[19]

Thus Weber eventually recognized, albeit obliquely, that there was something about Western law that was of critical importance in the rise of the Western city. Also, it appears, there was something critically important about Western religion as well—which Weber also dealt with only obliquely. He pointed out that in the Asiatic cultures, including China and India, it was impossible to bring all the inhabitants of a city together into a homogeneous status group. "Foremost among the reasons for the peculiar freedom of urbanites in the Mediterranean city, in contrast to the Asiatic," he wrote, "is the absence of magical and animistic caste and sib constraints. The social formations preventing fusion of urban dwellers into a homogeneous group vary. In China it was the exogamous and endophratric sib; in India . . . it has been the endogamous caste."[20] Here Weber turned to Fustel de Coulanges's work to show that the ancient Greek and Roman cities did create a religious

---

16 Weber, *The City*, 91.
17 Ibid., 92, 93.
18 Ibid., 94.
19 Ibid., 96.
20 Ibid., 97.

foundation of citizenship by substituting the city cult meal for the cult meal of the family. Yet Weber offered no explanation of the relationship of the religious factor to the legal and political factor; more particularly, he did not confront the fact that ancient Greek and Roman cities rested on slavery and lacked that "peculiar freedom of urbanites" which was, in fact, characteristic not of "the Mediterranean city" as such but of the Western European city of the late eleventh century and thereafter. Thus Weber stopped short of saying that the emergence of urban liberties in the West was part of a revolutionary religious change, in which, on the one hand, the ecclesiastical polity declared its independence from all secular polities, and, on the other, the very concept of secular polities was for the first time created and secular polities were said to be reformable and redeemable by law.

Why did Weber misjudge the role played by law and religion in the origin and development of the Western city? And why did he miss entirely the role of Western historical consciousness, including the Western belief in the organic growth of legal institutions over generations and centuries?

Karl Marx had attributed changes in social consciousness, including religious and legal consciousness, to changes in technologies for meeting economic needs (the mode of production), and in the class struggle to control those technologies (relations of production). Weber, on the other hand, believed that in addition to the economic forces that determine social consciousness there are also political forces—in other words, that the drive for political power is an independent objective force and not (as Marx had thought) merely a reflection of economic conditions ("relations of production"). For Weber, therefore, the rise of the Western city in the late eleventh and early twelfth centuries was due not merely to the development of a new mode of production (artisan and craft industry), which drew the serfs from the manor in opposition to their feudal lords, but also to the development of new political relationships. Weber could see that the nobility, too, had political reasons to favor the creation and development of cities. He also introduced other factors into the causal chain, including legal factors. But Weber, like Marx, believed that the idea of creating cities, the growth of communal consciousness within cities, and the development of urban legal and religious concepts which manifested such consciousness—that all these constituted "values" attributed to "factual" (economic and political) developments.

Western legal institutions cannot, however, be explained satisfactorily in instrumental terms as an ideology or a superstructure based on economic and/or political foundations; nor can they be explained as essentially factual phenomena to which people attribute values. They can only be satisfactorily explained in terms that encompass and go beyond both values and facts.

Indeed, all given ("factual") legal institutions contain within themselves values, in the sense of meanings or purposes. They have, in other words, what Lon Fuller called their own internal morality.[21] This means that in interpreting a prevailing legal rule one cannot properly avoid treating it as both an "is" (it prevails, it has force) and an "ought" (it has a moral purpose, a *telos*). To take an obvious example, the legal requirement of a fair hearing cannot properly be understood as having either a "factual" content separate from the "values" it embodies or a "value" content separate from its "factual" existence.

Weber refuted Marxian historical materialism by showing that causal relations in history are more complex and more indeterminate than Marx and Engels had supposed. He wrote:

> "If we look at the causal lines we see them run, at one time, from technical to economic and political matters, at another from political to religious and economic ones, etc. There is no resting point. In my opinion, the view of historical materialism, frequently espoused, that the economic is in some sense the ultimate point in the chain of causes is completely finished as a scientific proposition."[22]

Nevertheless, Weber's fact-value distinction led him repeatedly to trace the derivation of legal institutions to political domination (*Herrschaft*). Both tradition and rationality were, for him, primarily sources of legitimation of political authority, whereby coercion could be more effectively exerted. His definitions of the state and of law were in terms of coercion. He defined the

---

[21] See Lon Fuller, *The Morality of Law*, rev. ed. (New Haven, CT, 1969).

[22] *Proceedings of the First Conference of German Sociologists* (1910), quoted in Max Weber, *Economy and Society*, eds. Guenther Roth and Claus Wittich (New York, 1968), 1: lxiv. Weber's *Protestant Ethic and the Rise of Capitalism* is sometimes cited as evidence of an idealist, as contrasted with materialist, interpretation of history. In it, however, Weber does not trace the effect of Protestant ideas and values on material economic and political developments as such but rather traces their effect on capitalist ideas and values, arguing that Protestant "asceticism" contributed substantially to the development of a capitalist vocational ethic (*Berufskultur*). As Wolfgang Schluchter has said, "It is true that Weber's analysis can illustrate the general manner 'in which ideas become effective in history'. For this purpose he deals not only with the doctrines but also with their practical consequences. But this does not turn his analysis into a plea for a spiritualist or idealist interpretation of history." Wolfgang Schluchter, *The Rise of Western Rationalism: Max Weber's Developmental History*, trans. Guenther Roth (Berkeley, CA, 1981), 142. Schluchter cites statements of Weber in which he repudiated both an idealist and a materialist interpretation of history as "foolish and doctrinaire" and argued that all culturally significant phenomena are subject to "both [ideal and material] causal relationships." Ibid. It should be noted, however, that Weber seems to identify materialism with economic materialism. His view of law as an instrument of political coercion, and of politial coercion as part of an objective factual reality distinct from subjective values, may properly be called a form of political materialism.

state as a "human community that (successfully) claims the *monopoly of the legitimate use of physical force* within a given territory,"[23] and he defined law as "an order . . . [which] is externally guaranteed by the probability that physical or psychological coercion will be applied by a *staff* of people in order to bring about compliance or avenge violation."[24] Thus his belief in the objectivity of facts and the subjectivity of values led him, in his sociology of law, to a political (as contrasted with an economic) materialism.

Weber's emphasis on the political foundations of law is associated with his neglect of the creative role of historical consciousness in the development of new legal institutions. He defined a "traditional society" as one in which legitimacy is based on "the sanctity of age-old rules and powers," and "traditional law" as law "determined by ingrained habituation." He stated that innovations in traditional law can be legitimized only by disguising them as reaffirmations of the past. Thus tradition, for Weber, refers to some point or points in the past, not to an ongoing continuity from past to future. It is (in Jaroslav Pelikan's phrase) not tradition but traditionalism, not the living faith of the dead but the dead faith of the living.[25] It is historicism, not historicity.[26] It is partly because he neglected the dynamics of traditional law that Weber overlooked the role of law (and of religion) in the revolutionary formation and gradual evolution of the European city.

Not only traditional authority (based on historicism) but also the other three types of authority postulated by Weber—the charismatic (based on inspiration), the formally rational (based on logical consistency of rules), and the substantively rational (based on fairness and equity)—are defined narrowly, so that they appear to be mutually exclusive.[27] In fact, however, the Western legal tradition, as it existed from the late eleventh to the twentieth century, combined—and thereby transformed—all four of these "ideal

---

[23] Max Weber, "Politics as a Vocation," in Gerth and Mills, eds., *From Max Weber*, 78 (emphasis in original).

[24] Max Weber, *Economy and Society*, 34 (emphasis in original).

[25] See Jaroslav Pelikan, *The Vindication of Tradition* (New Haven, CT, 1984), 65.

[26] See Harold J. Berman, "Toward an Integrative Jurisprudence: Politics, Morality, History," *California Law Review* 76 (1988): 779.

[27] Weber's definitions of his "ideal types" of law are summarized in Weber, *Law in Economy and Society* (1966 ed.). It should be noted that substantive rationality in law and economics, which emphasizes ethical considerations, utility, expediency, and public policy, does not, in Weber's concept, correspond to any historical type of society, although Weber saw it emerging in "the anti-formalist tendencies of modern legal development" and possibly in a future socialist society. See ibid., 63-64, 303.

types."[28] The Western city owes both its origins and its subsequent development to a considerable extent to this combination.

Weber's sociology of law has been generally harmful, in my opinion, because it has contributed substantially to the widespread belief that the basic reason for the existence of legal systems is to enable those who have "a monopoly of the legitimate use of physical force within a given territory" to effectuate their control over the people of that territory, and also because it has contributed substantially to the widespread tendency to label given legal systems in terms of specific ideological types, each associated with a specific type of political authority. Today, for example, it is common to characterize the American legal system as capitalist, individualist, and democratic, and to contrast it with the Soviet legal system, which is characterized as socialist, collectivist, and authoritarian—without recognizing that each of these legal systems combines all these characteristics and others as well. Weber's disenchantment, and his determination to distance his scholarship from the crisis of law which he saw coming, was reflected in his separation of legal systems into distinct and mutually exclusive "ideal" categories of the sacred, the historical, the logical, and the equitable. Both he and his followers were thus distracted from the constructive task of showing the ways in which, in any healthy legal order, these elements are made to interact.

---

[28] Weber's own formalism went so far that he denied the possibility of reconciling conceptualism ("formal rationality") and equity ("substantive rationality"). Thus he wrote that "the juristic precision of judicial opinions will be seriously impaired if sociological, economic, or ethical argument were to take the place of legal concepts." Weber, *Economy and Society*, 2:894. He is right, of course, if his proposition is read literally, with emphasis on the words "take the place of." What is missing is the recognition that ethical argument, certainly, and only to a slightly lesser extent economic and sociological argument, are not only implicit but often explicit in the body of formal rules developed in all Western legal systems and especially in the body of case law that developed in the English and American systems. Ewing, "Formal Justice and the Spirit of Capitalism" defends Weber against the charge that he underestimated the adaptability of the English common law to the need for a legal system which would protect contracts and property and thus achieve justice in the capitalist sense. She neglects to say, however, as Weber neglected to say, that the doctrine of precedent which was developed in England and the United States in the seventeenth, eighteenth, and nineteenth centuries probably produced more calculability than the system of codes and commentaries—the *Pandektenrecht*—of the Continental jurists. At the same time, the linking of formal rules with concrete fact situations, and thus the theoretical possibility of combining what Weber called formal and substantive rationality—and of combining both with tradition—is probably greater in the Anglo-American than in the nineteenth-century Continental system of legal thought.

$$\text{——} \quad \text{ᎧᏅ} \ 11 \ \text{ᎧᏅ} \quad \text{——}$$

INDIVIDUALISTIC AND COMMUNITARIAN
THEORIES OF JUSTICE:
AN HISTORICAL APPROACH*

Whether justice rests primarily on individualistic or primarily on communitarian foundations is a question that has exercised the minds of moral and political philosophers in the United States in recent decades. It is, of course, an age-old question; indeed, the main purpose of this chapter is to show that only by seeing it as such, that is, only by seeing the question in historical terms, can we resolve it satisfactorily. Nevertheless, I start with its contemporary formulation in the well-known debate between the moral philosopher John Rawls and the political philosopher Michael Sandel.

In his 1971 book *A Theory of Justice*, Rawls based his moral theory of justice on a concept of the primacy of individual rights which, in his view, are derived ultimately from individual liberty.[1] Rawls defined justice as a product

---

* Reprinted from *University of California at Davis Law Review* 21 (1988): 549-575, in a collection of articles dedicated to Edgar Bodenheimer in honor of his eightieth birthday.

[1] Rawls states that when people engage each other in a social contract (or "mutually advantageous cooperative venture"), each possesses the same liberty as every other, and none may be required to sacrifice more than any other. John Rawls, *A Theory of Justice* (Cambridge, MA, 1971), 11. From the postulate of equal liberty, Rawls draws a definition of "justice as fairness." Ibid., 60. The first principle of justice, he writes, is that "each person is to have an equal right to the most extensive basic liberty compatible with a similar liberty for others." Ibid., 112. "The principles of justice" are those that "free and

of the rational choice of individuals in giving up to society only so much of their liberty and equality as is necessary to prevent arbitrary interference in the liberty and equality of others. Replying to Rawls in his 1982 book *Liberalism and the Limits of Justice*, Sandel contended that any theory of justice must be based primarily on public rather than private ends, and that once the primacy of the community is recognized then justice itself is seen as only an intermediate and not, as in Rawls's theory, a final goal.[2] Although a number of legal scholars have found this debate to have relevance to jurisprudence,[3] the main participants themselves have avoided reference to law and legal institutions and have confined themselves almost exclusively to philosophical argument of a moral and a political character.[4]

The terms of the debate have been sharply criticized from the standpoint of both moral philosophy and political philosophy. From the former standpoint, Edgar Bodenheimer has shown that human nature contains both individual and social characteristics and that injustice will result unless a symbiosis of these two conflicting sets of characteristics is achieved.[5] From

---

rational persons concerned to further their own interests would accept in an initial position of equality as defining the fundamental terms of their association." Ibid., 150-151.

[2] Contesting Rawls's statement that "[j]ustice is the first virtue of social institutions, as truth is of systems of thought," Sandel argues that "justice can be primary only for those societies beset by sufficient discord to make the accommodation of conflicting interests and claims the overriding moral and political consideration. . . ." Michael L. Sandel, *Liberalism and the Limits of Justice* (Cambridge, MA, 1982), 15. Thus Sandel sees justice as arising not from an abstract initial position of the equal liberty of all individuals in society but rather from specific social circumstances of discord and conflict within a community. Ibid., 31.

[3] An impression of the intense interest and raging controversies which Rawls's work elicited may be gained from J. H. Wellbank, D. Snook & D. T. Mason, eds., *John Rawls and His Critics: An Annotated Bibliography* (New York, 1982). Citations to writings of legal scholars include items B8-B12 (Ackerman), B208 (Bickel), B348-B350 (Calabresi), B384 (Cavers), B481 (D'Amato), B607-B612 (R. Dworkin), B1496-B1503 (Michelman), B2215-B2217 (Stone), and many others.

[4] Rawls devotes some pages to a discussion of law, which he views as a system of restrictions of liberty necessary for the maximization of liberty. Rawls, *A Theory of Justice*, 235-253. Sandel addresses law in a footnote which refers to Alexander Bickel's designation of law as "the value of values," that is, "the principal institution through which society can assert its values." Sandel adopts Bickel's phrase "value of values" to define not law but justice. Sandel, *Liberalism*, 16.

[5] See Edgar Bodenheimer, "Individual and Organized Society from the Perspective of a Philosophical Anthropology," *Journal of Social and Biological Structures* 9 (1986): 207. Bodenheimer lists in some detail affirmative aspects of both the individual and social interpretations of human nature.

Defending Rawls against Sandel, C. Edwin Baker argues, in effect, that Rawls has undertaken a fundamentally different enterprise from the one that Sandel attacks. Rawls, according to Baker, "emphasizes people as rational and autonomous agents concerned with

the standpoint of political philosophy, Richard Rorty has shown that Rawls's concepts of individual rights and individual liberty are not based on a theory of human nature (as they seem to be at first reading) but rather (as Rawls himself has admitted in later writings) on the specific twentieth-century American experience of democratic individualism.[6] Rorty nevertheless defends Rawls's "American" definition of justice and challenges Sandel and others who espouse communitarian values to defend them in political terms and not to disguise them in arguments based on metaphysics or on philosophical anthropology.[7] Rorty, in short, proposes that the philosophers should turn from the search for a definition of justice based on universal moral values and a universal human nature and should confront the essentially political question whether in the United States today individual rights or community values should be treated as the ultimate foundation of justice.[8]

---

advancing their individual interests" *not* because he considers that "this conception of the person is empirically or historically accurate, or even that it is a relevant conception of the person for other purposes," but only because it is useful to view them as such in order to construct a theory of justice. C. Edwin Baker, "Sandel on Rawls," *University of Pennsylvania Law Review* 133 (1985): 895, 901. If that is so, one might ask, "What kind of theory of justice can be constructed on the basis of so abstract a theory of the person?" The answer must be, "A very abstract theory of justice." One might also ask, "Could we not construct a different theory of justice, equally valid, and equally abstract, by emphasizing the nonrational and communitarian aspects of human nature?"

[6] Richard Rorty, "The Priority of Democratic Politics to Philosophy" (1988) (unpublished manuscript on file with the author).

[7] Ibid., 38-40. Rorty writes: "I would urge that the communitarian make his or her point against the liberal on the liberal's own ground: in terms of history and sociology rather than philosophy. . . . What [communitarian critics of liberalism] propound is the *need* for. . . a theory [of the nature of the self]: something philosophical, we know not what, to set over against the Enlightenment vision of the self. We are told that 'individualism is bankrupt' and that we need something to put in its place—something more like what the Greeks or the medievals had—but nobody claims to know what that might look like. . . . I think that communitarian critics might avoid this tone of wistfulness, and make their arguments more relevant to our current problems, if they stuck to the political question 'How might we combine democratic institutions with some of the advantages in respect to a sense of common purposes which pre-democratic societies enjoyed?' and dropped the philosophical question 'What is wrong with the Enlightenment concept of the self?'"

[8] Ibid., 44-45. Rorty writes: "Communitarian critics tend to agree with Sandel that 'the deontological vision is flawed, both within its own terms and more generally as an account of our moral experience'. I have been arguing that it is not, as Sandel thinks, flawed in its own terms. It will seem that way only if one attributes to it a philosophical project which it self-consciously eschews. The question of whether it is flawed as an account of 'our moral experience' depends upon whether 'our' means 'human moral experience in general' or 'the moral experience of the Americans'. I have been arguing that there is no such thing as the former. The price for systematizing our own moral intuitions is to

Although the main protagonists have almost totally neglected the legal aspects of the question, the debate between philosophical liberalism and its opponents has strong overtones of the ancient jurisprudential argument between natural law theory and legal positivism. Classical natural law theory, as Lloyd Weinreb has recently shown, is based ultimately on a concept of either fate or providence; it presupposes that the universe itself, including human life, is not only existential but also normative and that it contains an objective standard by which the legality of positive laws are to be judged.[9] Classical legal positivism, in turn, rests ultimately on a concept of the absolute lawmaking power of government; like natural law theory, however, it presupposes the legitimacy of the state and, in addition, the fundamental objectivity and consistency of the body of laws through which the state exercises its authority.[10] Prior to the twentieth century, the conflict between these two classical schools of legal theory turned on the question of the ultimate source and the ultimate sanction of law: whether, in the last analysis, they are to be found in morality ("justice") or in politics ("order"). In recent generations, however, this issue has been reduced to much narrower terms. Contemporary legal theorists have divided over the question whether, as natural law theorists assert, a law that contravenes fundamental morality lacks the character of legality and is therefore not binding as law, or whether, as positivists assert, it remains a law, since it expresses the will of the sovereign.[11] To the credit of moral and political philosophers such as Rawls

---

give up the universalism of the Enlightenment, to drop the idea that human beings as such share some single 'moral experience', along with the idea that they share a single 'moral sense'. If one settles for a self-consciously ethnocentric sense of 'our moral experience', then I think the account Rawls provides is the best we have had so far."

[9] Weinreb traces shifts in natural law theory from Homer to the present. He shows that for the Greeks, natural law rested on a belief in a normative order in nature, and that today, as well, "[t]he vitality of contemporary natural law theories is due to their insistence on an objectively valid moral order." See Lloyd Weinreb, *Natural Law and Justice* (Cambridge, MA, 1987), 12.

[10] Current expositions of positivism assimilate the concept of the legitimacy of the state ("sovereignty") to the habit of rule and obedience and reduce the concept of the consistency of rules to the formalism of a closed system. See H.L.A. Hart, *The Concept of Law* (Oxford, 1961), 49 ("in every human society, where there is law, there is . . . to be found . . . this simple relationship between subjects rendering habitual obedience and a sovereign who renders habitual obedience to no one"); ibid., 253 (the term "legal positivism" designates the contention "that a legal system is a 'closed logical system' in which correct decisions can be deduced from the predetermined rules by logical means alone").

[11] Weinreb, *Natural Law and Justice*, 4 criticizes the reduction of the debate to a question of the source of the obligation to obey the law. In an earlier article Weinreb stated that at the merely ethical level "it is very hard indeed to explain the fuss that is made in legal philosophy about the debate between natural law and legal positivism." See Lloyd

and Sandel, it may be said that they have revived larger questions concerning the nature and interrelationship of liberty and equality, of remedial and distributive justice, and of what they call "the right" and "the good." Yet they, too, have narrowed the focus of the classical inquiry into these aspects of justice by reducing it largely to a debate concerning priorities among competing values.

Moreover, by omitting law from their inquiry into the nature of justice, philosophers such as Rawls and Sandel tacitly accept a positivist definition of law. That is, they assume that justice is essentially a moral category, to be defined by reason alone, and that the definition of justice which is provided by law itself, whether explicitly or implicitly, is immaterial and perhaps irrelevant to the definition offered by reason. This assumption carries a strong negative implication that law is, as the positivists say, a body of rules laid down by the lawmaker, to be judged solely by a morality derived from outside itself; that it is essentially a product of will; and that reason is to be introduced from outside the law as a criterion by which to evaluate it. To this the natural law theorist would respond that law also consists of standards and purposes, that is, it has its own internal morality,[12] a meta-law,[13] and that

---

Weinreb, "The Natural Law Tradition: Comments on Finnis," *Journal of Legal Education* 36 (1986): 501. Of particular relevance to the present chapter is a penetrating essay by Frank S. Alexander in which he criticizes both legal positivists and natural law theorists for failing to deal with ontological questions concerning the purposes of law in the fulfillment of both individuality and community. See Frank S. Alexander, "Beyond Positivism: A Theological Perspective," *Georgia Law Review* 20 (1986): 1089, 1090.

[12] This was the argument of Lon L. Fuller, *The Morality of Law*, rev. ed. (New Haven, CT, 1969). Fuller, who died in 1974, did not regard himself as an adherent of a "system of natural law" but rather as a critic of legal positivism who used "the natural law method." Undated letter from Fuller to T. R. Powell, reprinted in Lon Fuller, *The Principles of Social Order*, ed. K. Winston (Durham, NC, 1981), 296. The letter was written to his colleague Powell in response to the latter's review of Fuller's 1940 book *The Law in Quest of Itself*. Fuller contended that laws must be understood in terms of their purposes, and also in terms of the purposes of the legal enterprise as a whole, and that those purposes include moral, and not only political, purposes. Thus a law or legal rule is to be interpreted in such a way as to fulfill its legitimate purposes. Conversely, a retroactive penal law or a law or procedure which condemns a person without a hearing may be said to lack inherent qualities of legality.

Perhaps partly because Fuller insisted on combining analytically what law (or a law) is with what it ought to be, and partly also because he wrote in a style generally accessible to all persons educated in law and not in the polemical style of contemporary professional legal philosophers, Fuller's writings have not been sufficiently understood or appreciated by those philosophers. This situation has been remedied to some extent by some recent articles. See Robert C.L. Moffatt, "Lon Fuller: Natural Lawyer After All," *American Journal of Jurisprudence* 26 (1981): 190; Anthony D'Amato, "Lon Fuller and Substantive Natural Law," *American Journal of Jurisprudence* 26 (1981): 202; Ian R. MacNeil, "Lon Fuller: Nexusist," *American Journal of Jurisprudence* 26 (1981): 219; Peter Teachout, "The Soul of

legal justice—justice based on law—is entitled to at least equal weight in determining the meaning of justice as that which the philosophers attach to such universal concepts as human nature, the social contract, and the interrelationship of the individual and the community. The natural law theorist acknowledges that different legal systems contain different concepts of justice, but insists that nevertheless they all share certain common moral features.

It is doubtful that the debate concerning the nature of justice, whether in its classical or in its contemporary forms, can be resolved, or can even make sense, without reference to the historical context, including especially the legal historical context, in which justice and rights, individual and community, occur. The answer to the question, "Which comes first, the individual or the community?" does indeed have a moral dimension (although Professor Bodenheimer is surely right in stressing that the fundamental moral problem is to maintain the proper balance between the two). It also has a political dimension (although Professor Rorty is surely right in stressing that the political answer depends on which type of polity is presupposed).[14] But it also has an historical dimension. A good deal depends on which did actually "come first," as well as on what happened thereafter and on what is anticipated for the future—since history includes not only material facts but also the hopes and fears that surround those facts. Both the moral need to strike the right balance between individualism and communitarianism and the political need to strike that balance in light of the prevailing institutions of a particular polity must be judged in the light of the long-range historical development of the society in which such moral and political questions arise. The introduction of a long-range time perspective into both the philosophical and the political arguments substantially changes their character.

The Fugue: An Essay on Reading Fuller," *Minnesota Law Review* 70 (1986): 1073; Alexander, "Beyond Positivism," 1113-22, 1124-26. See also Robert Summers, *Lon L. Fuller* (Stanford, CA, 1984)—an important book which, however, in my view, has not done justice to Professor Fuller's thought. John Noonan has referred to Fuller as "probably the most creative mind in modern American jurisprudence." John T. Noonan, "Hercules and the Snail Darter," *New York Times Book Review* (May 25, 1986): 12, col. 3 (reviewing R. Dworkin, *Law's Empire* (1986)).

[13] See Harold J. Berman, *Law and Revolution: The Formation of the Western Legal Tradition* (Cambridge, MA, 1983), 8 ("The law contains within itself a legal science, a meta-law, by which it can be both analyzed and evaluated") and 120-64, where the point is developed that law consists not only of legal institutions, legal rules, legal decisions, and the like, but also of legal science, that is, the legal scholarship of professors, judges, and others whose conceptualization and systematization of those institutions, rules, and decisions are often incorporated into the law and help to give it direction.

[14] This is implicit in the title of Rorty's essay, see Rorty, "The Priority of Democratic Politics."

It was precisely this point which in 1814 led the great German jurist Friedrich Carl von Savigny, inspired in part by the writings of Edmund Burke, to found a third school of legal theory, the historical school, in opposition to both natural law theory and legal positivism.[15] Unfortunately, the historical school has been greatly misunderstood and ultimately almost abandoned by almost all American legal theorists—though not by American courts—in the twentieth century. I have argued elsewhere that it is necessary to restore and revitalize the historical school and to combine it with natural law theory and with legal positivism in a new "integrative" jurisprudence, in which the virtues of each approach—the moral, the political, and the historical—would be maintained and its vices corrected.[16] I shall not repeat that argument here, but shall attempt to apply a historical method to the debate between adherents of an individualistic and a communitarian theory of justice.

To apply a historical method requires that a choice be made: whose history? what history? May one answer the question, "What is justice?" by reference to the history of China? And if so, would one choose the Ming dynasty? the Cultural Revolution? Undoubtedly the many ambiguities that lie in the term "history" contribute to the philosophers' inclination to reject it as a criterion of justice. Reason and/or power seem to them to be more certain criteria.

It should be noted that the Western philosophers have their own history, namely, the history of ideas, and they commonly analyze the meaning of justice by tracing similarities and differences among the various philosophical schools that have analyzed the meaning of justice in the past, starting with Plato and Aristotle. Although they might occasionally discuss concepts of justice found in the writings of Chinese or other non-Western philosophers, they basically write in a tradition which traces its lineage from ancient Greece across the "Middle Ages" to Spinoza, Hobbes, Locke, Hume, Kant, Hegel, and ultimately into the philosophical morass of twentieth-century Europe and America. That is *their* history.

Even from the viewpoint of intellectual history, this genealogy is far too limited. Western theories of justice must be traced not only to ancient Greek

---

[15] Friedrich Carl von Savigny, *Vom Beruf unsrer Zeit für Gesetzgebung und Rechtswissenschaft*, 2d ed. (Berlin, 1840), translated as Friedrich Carl von Savigny, *On the Vocation of Our Age for Legislation and Jurisprudence*, trans. A. Hayward (1831; repr. ed., New York, 1975). For a discussion of Savigny's contribution and the fate of historical jurisprudence in America in the nineteenth and twentieth centuries, see Harold J. Berman, "Toward an Integrative Jurisprudence: Politics, Morality, History," *California Law Review* 76 (1988): 779

[16] Berman, "Toward an Integrative Jurisprudence."

philosophy but also to ancient Hebrew moral and religious thought and ancient Roman law. It was the remarkable achievement of the European schoolmen of the late eleventh and twelfth centuries to have combined, for the first time, these three diverse and even mutually antagonistic outlooks—the Hebrew, the Greek, and the Roman—and to have founded on that combination the modern Western disciplines of theology, philosophy, jurisprudence, and political science.[17] Only in the seventeenth century did the latter three disciplines break off from theology, and only in the nineteenth and twentieth centuries did they break off from each other. To this day the concept of justice is a primary concern of each of them and although each attempts to impose its concept of justice on the others, each by the same token must reckon with the others.

At the same time they all must reckon with the fact that justice is not only a matter of intellectual inquiry. It is not an abstract concept, like beauty, which exists solely in the mind; it is also a profession, or calling, something which is practised, like art. Our Western concept of justice is ultimately derived less from the several scholarly disciplines which claim it than from the history of our political and legal and other social institutions.

The history that we must study, then, in order to find answers to the question, "What are the interrelationships between individual rights and community interests in a definition of justice?"—is *our* history, that is, Western history, since it is out of that history that the question has arisen among us. But it must be our entire history, and not only our intellectual history; and more particularly, it must include the history of those political and legal institutions which have purported to attempt to put justice into practice.

The particular parts of our history that we must study are those parts which are most relevant to the question. In a multi-volume historical study we would want to examine various periods in which critical conflicts arose between an individualistic and a communitarian concept of justice. In a short article such as this, a beginning might be made to such a multi-volume study, first, by focusing on a time when the peoples of Europe did not distinguish between a justice based on individual rights and a justice based on commu-

---

[17] The pioneers in theology include Anselm of Canterbury (1033-1109) and Peter Lombard (c.1100-c.1160); in philosophy, Abelard (1079-1142); in jurisprudence, Irnerius (c.1060-c.1125) and Gratian (dates unknown; his great treatise is usually dated 1140); in political science, John of Salisbury (1115-1180). Of these, the only controversial person is John of Salisbury, since contemporary scholarship in the history of political science prefers to trace the modern discipline to Machiavelli (1469-1527) or possibly Marsilius of Padua (c.1280-c.1343). On John of Salisbury and his significance to the history of political science, see Berman, *Law and Revolution*, 276-88.

nity interests; second, by focusing on the conditions and circumstances that eventually gave rise to that distinction; and third, by considering what light those conditions and circumstances shed upon the nature of the distinction.

More specifically, I propose to approach the question, "What is justice?" by asking the question, "What *was* justice in Europe in the year 1000 and how had it changed by the year 1200?" This more specific question is relevant because in Europe prior to the year 1000 a wholly communitarian conception of justice prevailed, whereas by the late eleventh and twelfth centuries the concept of individual rights was articulated for the first time and a legal order was developed in which individual rights were protected as essential parts of the system of community interests.

The best evidence of what justice *was* in Europe in the year 1000 is to be found in the type of law that prevailed at that time among the numerous tribal groups ("stems") which inhabited that continent.[18] Despite their

---

[18] Ibid., 49-84 (chapter on "The Background of the Western Legal Tradition: The Folklaw") from which the following pages are adapted and in which citations to sources may be found. On ibid., 81 a map illustrates the areas of Europe inhabited by the various tribes, of which the Germanic tribes were the most numerous. In this article, reference is made to the Germanic folklaw and the European folklaw more or less interchangeably.

Several reviewers of *Law and Revolution* have not dealt kindly with my treatment of the European folklaw, and although this is not the place for a detailed refutation of their comments it may, nevertheless, be appropriate to note several points that bear on an understanding of the following pages of this chapter. Four main types of criticisms have been made. (1) It has been charged that I underestimated the sophistication of the Germanic folklaw and depicted Germanic society in a condescending or patronizing way. I leave it to the reader of this article to judge whether the stress placed on the communitarianism of the Germanic peoples is condescending or patronizing. As far as the formalism of the Germanic folklaw is concerned, and especially of such features as trial by ordeal and by compurgation, these are explained in the book (as in this article) partly as a reflection of a belief system based on fate and honor and partly as an effective means, within that system, of peaceful settlement of conflict. (2) It has also been asserted that the Germanic peoples are erroneously treated in the book as homogeneous. In fact, at least two references are made in the book (ibid., 52 and 61) to the diversity and independence of the various tribes. It is true, however, as stated in those pages, that their *laws* were "nevertheless remarkably similar," and that there was among them "a common legal style." (3) It has been said that the history of the Germanic peoples over five centuries is presented in the book as static. In fact, a whole section of the chapter in question (ibid., 62-68) is devoted to "dynamic elements in Germanic law." To be sure, the dynamic elements affected chiefly the official law and only gradually and slightly the main features of the folklaw. Sir Frank Stenton, *Anglo-Saxon Law*, 3d ed. (New York, 1981) has been cited in opposition to this view. Yet Stenton states in that book: "In most of its details, the law observed by the Englishmen in 1087 was . . . the law of Cnut and Aethelred II [almost a century earlier]," and his treatment of "the laws observed by the Englishmen" under those kings does not show marked differences in general nature and style from the laws of two or three centuries prior thereto. Ibid., 686. (4) The thesis that Germanic folklaw was diffused in the entire political, economic, and social life of the community has also been criticized, and reference has been made in that connection to an article by Susan Reynolds, "Law and

independence from each other, and, indeed, the hostility which often existed among them, these Germanic, Celtic, Romance, and other peoples lived under legal institutions that were remarkably uniform. Moreover, European legal institutions in the year 1000 corresponded in many respects to those of other cultures in which tribal organization has prevailed. Thus legal historians have classified the European folklaw of the sixth to tenth centuries as a type of "archaic law," bearing some strong similarities to what cultural anthropologists have called "primitive law."

The European folklaw had the following features in common with other systems of archaic and primitive law:

(1) It was largely tribal and local.

(2) It was largely customary; that is, it was largely unenacted and unwritten. There were no professional lawyers or judges or other law enforcement officials. There were no legal scholars and no law books. Very rarely a strong king might issue a collection of laws, but such collections (of which there were perhaps a score or more throughout Europe in the course of five centuries) usually consisted chiefly of restatements of those customs that needed clarification or reinforcement.

(3) The community itself administered and enforced the law. Characteristic means of law enforcement were the judicial outcry which summoned the local community to pursue a criminal, collective group responsibility for offenses committed by a member, public assemblies in which the great people met to hear grievances and to administer the affairs of the tribe or region, and the ultimate sanction of outlawry. These elements of the folklaw were diffused in the entire political, economic, social, and religious life of the community.

(4) The folklaw was greatly concerned with controlling violence between households. Such violence often took the form of blood feud, which was controlled in part by a system of fixed tariffs (*wergeld, bot*) payable by the kin of the offender to the kin of the victim. The system aimed at the negotiation of a peaceful settlement among the feuding parties.

Communities in Western Christendom, c. 900-1140," *American Journal of Legal History* 25 (1981): 205. Yet that article supports, rather than negates, my point. It states that only in the twelfth century did the law become "more differentiated, less diffused," with the rise of a new legal learning which "threatened the supremacy of unlearned, collective judgment." In her book, *Kingdoms and Communities in Western Europe, 900-1300* (Oxford, 1984), Reynolds does, indeed, attack those who treat the law of the tenth and eleventh centuries as "rigid, formalist, and essentially irrational." Ibid., 13-14. But that in no way challenges the point that twelfth and thirteenth century jurists did in fact criticize the rigid, formalist, and irrational features of the earlier law.

5) Control of deviance also took the form of community judgments and community sanctions of a formalistic and ritual character appealing to a supernatural authority. Characteristic procedures for determining liability were the ordeals of fire and water and proof by formal oaths recited by supporters of the opposing parties (compurgation).

6) The folklaw had a sacred character. Especially among the Germanic peoples, who were the most numerous in Europe, a high value was placed upon honor, in the sense of getting even, as a means of winning glory in a world dominated by warring gods and by a generally hostile and arbitrary fate. The belief in fate underlay not only the ordeals but also compurgation, in which the oaths had to be repeated flawlessly, "without slip or trip," as well as noxal surrender, that is, the forfeiture of the instrument that caused an unlawful injury (for example, an offending beast), and even the trials that took place before public assemblies, in which the parties hurled oaths at each other instead of blows. The same word, "doom," meaning judgment, was used to refer to a decree of fate and to the outcome of a trial. In the words of Beowulf, "Often Fate saves an undoomed man, if his courage is good."[19]

(7) At the same time, Germanic law emphasized comradeship and trust, especially (but not only) within the extended household. Collective protection of the members of a household, in Anglo-Saxon law called *mund*, and preservation of the peace of the group, called *frith*, were highly valued. Also justice, called *riht* (Right), was highly valued, and was associated with comradeship and trust.

In addition to features characteristic of archaic or primitive law, the law of the European peoples of the sixth to the eleventh centuries contained certain unique features. Many of these were attributable to the introduction of Christianity. Others were attributable to the strengthening—partly under the influence of Christianity—of kingship, especially among the Franks and the Anglo-Saxons. These factors—the religious and the royal—introduced a dynamic element into the tribal and local folklaw.

Features of early European law attributable at least in part to the spread of Christianity include the following:

(1) In adopting Christianity rulers were transformed from tribal chiefs into kings, whose authority could extend to many tribes. Although they were no longer treated as descendants of gods, the kings nevertheless remained sacral figures. They were the supreme religious leaders of the peoples under

---

[19] Beowulf, lines 2140-2141. See also *The Icelandic Saga: The Story of Burnt Njal*, trans. Sir G. W. Dasent, ed. G. Turville-Petre (Edinburgh, 1957), in which the spirit of heroism and vengeance is exemplified in dramatic proceedings before the tribal judicial assembly.

their rule, appointing bishops and dictating liturgical and other ecclesiastical matters.

(2) Conversion to Christianity gave an impetus to the writing down of the tribal customs in primitive collections such as the Salic Law of Clovis, the first Christian king of the Franks and the Laws of Ethelbert, ruler of Kent, the first Christian king in England.[20] Writing, generally introduced by Christian missionaries, strengthened the incipient jurisdiction of public authorities to punish the most serious forms of crime. Also the writing down of customs gave authorities an opportunity to make some changes in them. The Christian clergy, who became the king's advisers, wanted protection. The Laws of Ethelbert begin: "Theft of God's property and the Church's to be compensated twelvefold."[21]

(3) Christianity introduced new moral elements into the folklaw. The Laws of King Alfred start with the Ten Commandments, and contain references to the monastic rules on penances for sins. They include such striking provisions as: "Doom very evenly; doom not one doom to the rich another to the poor, nor doom one to your friend another to your foe."[22] Gradually, between the sixth and the eleventh centuries, the European folklaw, with its overwhelming biases of sex, class, race, and age, was affected, if only slightly, by the Christian doctrine of the fundamental equality of all persons before God: woman and man, slave and free, poor and rich, child and adult. The Church also added to the system of oaths and oath-helping the doctrine that perjury was a sin and that one who perjured himself had the duty to confess the sin to his priest and be subjected to penitential discipline. Other obstructions of justice were also considered to be sins—for example, persistence in blood feud after a reasonable offer of satisfaction.

(4) Beginning in the sixth century, there developed alongside the tribal folklaw a system of private penance with secret confession by each individual to a priest and secret imposition of the duty to perform penitential acts. An elaborate system of penances was introduced for particular types of sins or

---

[20] Clovis issued the Salic Law shortly after his conversion to Christianity in 496. The Laws of Ethelbert were issued in about 600, a few years after Ethelbert's conversion. These are discussed in Berman, *Law and Revolution*, 53-54, 64-65, 565-566, 568-569.

[21] Laws of Ethelbert, sec. 1, translated in F.L. Attenborough, ed., *The Laws of the Earliest English Kings* (New York, 1922), 4-17, and B. Thorpe, *Ancient Laws and Institutes of England* (London, 1840), 1-25.

[22] The laws of Alfred are translated in Attenborough, ed., *The Laws of the Earliest English Kings*, 62-94, and Thorpe, *Ancient Laws and Institutes of England*, 44-101. They start with the Ten Commandments, and include the golden rule, do unto others what you would have them do unto you, followed by the statement, "From this one doom a man may remember that he judge everyone righteously; he need heed no other doom book." Alfred ruled from 871 to 900.

crimes (the two terms were used interchangeably). These were embodied in written codes, called "penitentials," which varied among the different monasteries and bishoprics.[23] The usual sanction was expressed in terms of a certain number of days, months, or years of fasting, but there were also many alternative types of atonement, including prayers and vigils, reading of psalms, and pilgrimages as well as compensation of victims and assistance of their relatives. The idea of punishment was subordinated to the idea of the cure of souls. All major secular offenses, such as homicide and robbery, were also sins to be atoned for by penance; and all major ecclesiastical offenses, such as sexual and marital sins, witchcraft, and breaking of vows by monks, were also crimes prohibited by the folklaw and subject to secular sanctioning. Thus the folklaw and the penitential law covered the same ground but in different ways. The writings of the period from the sixth to the eleventh centuries referred to the two ways as worldly law, or man's law, on the one hand, and God's law, on the other. Yet what are called today the state and the church were both equally concerned with each kind of law. For example, emissaries (*missi dominici*) sent by Charlemagne to check on local administration addressed his subjects as follows: "We have been sent here by our Lord, the Emperor Charles, for your eternal salvation, and we charge you to live virtuously according to the law of God, and justly according to the law of the world."[24] It was only through virtuous living according to the law of God that the Christian was to avoid eternal punishment in the world to come.

(5) Beginning in the eighth century, kings extended their household law (their "peace") beyond their own families, friends, servants, and messengers. More offenses became triable before the king. Treason, intentional homicide, and adultery were made capital offenses. In 973 King Edgar, in a coronation oath composed by Archbishop Dunstan of Canterbury, swore that "true peace" should be assured to all "Christian people" in his kingdom, that robberies and "all unrighteous deeds" should be forbidden, and that "justice and mercy" should govern all judgments.[25] The Frankish emperors had for some

---

[23] The penitentials are analyzed in some detail in Berman, *Law and Revolution*, 68-75.

[24] Quoted in Christopher Dawson, *The Making of Europe: An Introduction to European Unity* (1932; repr. ed., New York/Cleveland, OH, 1956), 218. Charlemagne reigned from 768 to 814. He had himself crowned emperor by the pope in 800. His authority as ruler was derived partly from his military leadership of the various peoples over whom he reigned, whose armies he mobilized to resist invasions from Arabs, Saxons, Danes, and Slavs, and partly from his religious role as head of the church and deputy of Christ. As Dawson writes, "Charles regarded the Pope as his chaplain, and plainly tells Leo III that it is the King's business to govern and defend the Church and that it is the Pope's duty to pray for it." See Berman, *Law and Revolution*, 66-67.

[25] 8 Aethelred 2, in Agnes J. Robertson, ed., *The Laws of the Kings of England from Edmund to Henry I* (1925; repr. ed., New York, 1974), 119.

time sworn similar oaths. Eventually, royal officials were appointed to supervise local assemblies and other administrative devices were used to maintain royal influence over the tribes and the localities. Royal delegates summoned inquests and interrogated witnesses. An official law grew up alongside the folklaw. The official law drew on some of the rules and some of the terminology that had survived from the Roman law as it had existed in the territories conquered by the invading Germanic people. There was, in effect, a reception, and at the same time a vulgarization, of Roman law.[26] Yet the official law was extremely weak, if only because prior to the late eleventh century the European economy was almost entirely local, and the monarch had to travel with his household continually throughout his realm to hold court. Royal delegates tended to be swallowed up by the localities which they were supposed to administer in the king's behalf or else they became their own masters. There was virtually no royal law of contract, or of property, or of landlord and tenant, and very little royal law of crime and tort. The written collections of laws which kings occasionally promulgated, setting forth customs that needed to be better known or more firmly established, were not legislation in the modern sense but were rather exhortations to keep the peace and do justice and desist from crime. The king had to beg and pray, as Maitland put it, for he could not command and punish. Indeed, Germanic laws contain provisions stating that when a person has exhausted his opportunities in the local courts, he should not go to the king for a remedy.

(6) Christianity attacked the pagan myths, with their emphasis on honor and fate. It brought to Germanic man a positive attitude toward life and toward death, a larger purpose into which to fit the tragedies and mysteries of his existence. In the "Addition" to his translation of the sixth-century Roman philosopher Boethius, King Alfred wrote, "I say, as do all Christian men, that it is a divine purpose that rules, and not fate." But Germanic Christianity did

---

[26] Several reviewers of *Law and Revolution*, from which the present section of this article is adapted, criticized the book for failing to emphasize that Roman law survived in the West after the fall of the Western Roman Empire. In fact, the survival of some of the terminology and concepts and many individual rules of Roman law, both in the canons of the church and in the folklaw and official law of some of the Germanic peoples, is fully acknowledged and discussed in various parts of the book (see e.g., ibid., 3, 67-68, 122, 471, 565). Nevertheless, the point is also stressed that Roman law did not survive as a living body of law by which the peoples of Western Europe were governed. It survived, so to speak, in bits and pieces. If that fact is not accepted, it is foolish to attach to the work of the glossators and canonists of the twelfth century the great importance that everyone agrees it had in the development of new legal systems. One cannot have it both ways: either the "vulgar" Roman law of the sixth to eleventh centuries was of much less importance than some scholars suppose or the revival of Roman law in the twelfth century was of much less importance than those same scholars acknowledge.

not openly challenge Germanic social institutions. Its message was other-worldly. It was concerned above all with preparation for the life to come—heaven and hell—through prayer, personal humility, and obedience. Its ideals were symbolized above all in the lives of holy men and in monasticism, with its emphasis on spiritual withdrawal from the temporal world. It did not oppose ordeals, compurgation, *wergeld*, and other features of the European folklaw; it only said that they could not bring salvation. Outside the monastic orders, the majority of bishops and priests of the church became, in fact, wholly involved in the corruption and violence that characterized the age; this was inevitable because they were generally appointed by leading politicians from among their friends and relatives. Christianity was Germanized at the same time that the Germanic peoples were Christianized.

In summary, we may say that in the year 1000 all of the peoples of Europe had similar legal orders, each with its own customary rules and procedures for governing, for punishing offenses, for compensating for harm, for enforcing agreements, for distributing property on death, and for dealing with many other problems related to justice. But none had a consciously articulated and systematized structure of legal institutions clearly differentiated from other social institutions and cultivated by a corps of persons specially trained for that task. As in many non-Western cultures, the European folklaw was not a body of rules imposed from on high but was rather an integral part of the common consciousness of the community. The people themselves, in their public assemblies, legislated and judged; and when kings asserted their authority over the law it was chiefly to guide the custom and the legal consciousness of the people, not to remake it. The bonds of kinship, of lordship units, and of territorial communities were the law. If those bonds were violated, the initial response was to seek vengeance, but vengeance was supposed to give way—and usually did—to negotiation for pecuniary sanctions and to reconciliation. Adjudication was often a stage in the reconciliation process. And so peace, once disrupted, was to be restored ultimately by diplomacy. Beyond the question of right and wrong was the question of reconciliation of the warring factions. The same can be said also of the law of many contemporary so-called primitive societies of Africa, Asia, and South America, as well as of many ancient civilizations of both the past and the present.

Before the professionalization and systematization of law, more scope was left for people's attitudes and beliefs and for their unconscious ideas, their processes of mythical thought. This gave rise to legal procedures which depended heavily on ritual and symbol and which in that sense were highly technical, but by the same token the substantive law was plastic and largely nontechnical. Rights and duties were not bound to the letter of legal texts but instead were a direct manifestation of community values. These characterizations, too, are applicable to the legal concepts and processes of many contemporary nonliterate cultures of Africa, Asia, and South America, as well as to complex, literate, ancient civilizations such as those of China, Japan, and India.

If a single designation can be used to characterize these various legal orders, it is customary law. In Sophocles' words, "these laws are not for now or for yesterday, they are alive forever; and no one knows when they were shown to us first" (*Antigone*). In this type of legal order, law is not something that is consciously and continuously made and remade by central authorities; there may be occasional legislation, but for the most part law is something that grows out of the patterns and norms of behavior, the folkways and the mores, of the community. Moreover, in this type of legal order, custom is not subjected to conscious and systematic and continuous rational scrutiny by jurists. It is simply unquestioningly and unquestionably respected.

Yet the European folklaw does not fit easily into the model or archetype of customary law—or, indeed, into any other model or archetype, including archaic law and primitive law—if only for the reason that it came under the influence of Christianity.[27] The emergence of Christianity and its spread across Europe was a unique event, which cannot be explained by any general social theory. By contradicting the Germanic world view and splitting life into two realms, Christianity challenged the ultimate sanctity of custom, including the ultimate sanctity of kinship, lordship, and kingship relations. It also challenged the ultimate sanctity of nature—of the water and fire of the ordeals, for example. It challenged their ultimate sanctity, however, without denying their sanctity altogether; on the contrary, the church actually supported the sacred institutions and values of the folk (including the ordeals). The church supported them and at the same time challenged them by setting up a higher alternative—the realm of God, God's law, the life of the world to come. When life was split into two realms, the eternal and the temporal, the temporal was thereby depreciated in value but not otherwise directly affected. The split took place not in the life of society but in the human soul. Yet social life was indirectly affected in important ways. The basic structure of the folklaw remained unaltered, but many of its particular features were strongly influenced by Christian beliefs.

If all traces of Christianity could be subtracted from the early European folklaw, it might well fall into one or more of the archetypes of legal orders

---

[27] This and the following paragraph are taken from Berman, *Law and Revolution*, 82-83.

which have been offered by social theorists. It would fall squarely into archaic law, together with the Roman law in the time of the Twelve Tables, early Hindu law, and ancient Greek law. It would fall less squarely into primitive law. It might be viewed as a type of law characteristic of an incipient feudalism. It would surely be an example of customary law. Such models as these, however, are only partly applicable to the legal institutions of the Frankish, Anglo-Saxon, and other peoples of Europe in the sixth to eleventh centuries. They make no place for the penitential law of the monasteries, or the religious and other laws occasionally issued by kings, or the central role of the clergy in all phases of government. Above all, Christianity attached a positive value to law which is in sharp contrast to attitudes toward law that are characteristic of religions or philosophies of other societies whose general institutional structure is comparable to that of the Christianized peoples of Europe. The Christian faith of that time accepted the world's law as just and even sacred. Yet the world's law had little value when compared with God's law, which alone could save the wicked from hellfire.

European concepts of justice changed dramatically in the late eleventh and twelfth centuries. At that time a great revolutionary upheaval took place in both the ecclesiastical and the secular spheres.[28] The Roman Catholic

---

[28] Historians of the eleventh and twelfth centuries are virtually unanimous in saying that in the period roughly from 1050 to 1150 the papacy established for the first time its political and legal independence of emperors, kings, and other secular rulers as well as its supreme political and legal authority over bishops, priests, and other clergy. Also it is undisputed that secular royal power and secular royal legal institutions underwent substantial expansion in the twelfth century, especially in the Norman Kingdom of Sicily, England, France, and the German principalities; and further, that in that period some thousands of cities and towns came into existence in Europe and the urban population increased from a tiny fraction of the total to a sizable percentage. What the book *Law and Revolution* did that was new was, first, to show the interrelationships of these various phenomena as parts of a total revolutionary upheaval; second, to trace to that upheaval the origin of modern legal systems (especially canon law, royal law, urban law, and mercantile law); and third, to view the political, philosophical, and religious underpinnings of those systems as a source of the Western legal tradition.

The contention that in the period from 1075 to 1122 a "revolution" occurred within the Roman Catholic Church ("the Papal Revolution") has met some resistance from reviewers of the book, although it was endorsed by the two leading American scholars of church history during that period, Brian Tierney and George Williams. Recently, in opposition to my characterization of Pope Gregory VII as a "revolutionary," the author of an article discussing the same period quoted Walter Ullmann's characterization of Gregory as "a conservative." David S. Clark, "The Medieval Origins of Modern Legal Education: Between Church and State," *The American Journal of Comparative Law* 35 (1987): 653, 668-669. Ullmann's views are reported in *Law and Revolution*, where I state that "[e]ven so strong a believer in the unbroken continuity of Roman Catholic history as Walter Ullmann, who wrote that Gregory VII was only attempting 'the translation of abstract

Church, under the papacy, established itself for the first time as a visible, corporate, legal entity, independent of imperial, royal, feudal, and urban authorities. It created the first modern legal system, the modern canon law, which had a wide jurisdiction not only over clergy but also over laity. Partly in rivalry with the canon law, partly in emulation of it, the secular polities began to introduce modern legal institutions. New legal systems were needed to maintain the cohesion of each polity, to achieve the reform of each, and to keep equilibrium among them all.

In sharp contrast with the earlier folklaw, the new law was not diffused in a more or less undifferentiated customary political, economic, and social order but formed a distinct and autonomous institutional structure. A class of professional jurists arose, many of them trained in the first European universities, founded in the late eleventh and twelfth centuries. Full-time professional judges appeared for the first time in Europe to staff newly established papal and royal courts. Statutes were enacted under papal and imperial or royal authority, and for the first time scholars produced a body of legal literature. The new systems of canon and royal law were analyzed and summarized in treatises such as Gratian's *Concordance of Discordant Canons* of 1140 and Glanvill's *Treatise on the Laws and Customs of England* of 1187.[29]

Despite these radical changes, it should not be thought that the older law was simply abolished. On the contrary, it survived, but it was gradually reformed. The learned law taught in the universities was based chiefly on the Digest of Justinian, which was conveniently rediscovered in the late eleventh century after five centuries of oblivion in the West, but the law applied in day-to-day life as well as the law applied in the courts, although influenced by the revival of Roman law, necessarily built on the older law. At the same time it sought to overcome the essential formalism and conservatism of the older law. New "rational" modes of proof were gradually substituted for the ordeals and compurgation. Negotiation and composition of blood feud through *wergeld* and *bot* were replaced by criminal and civil adjudication. Custom was

---

principles into concrete government actions', nevertheless characterized the Gregorian Reform as 'the first concrete application of these principles'." Berman, *Law and Revolution*, 575. Ullmann argues, in effect, that what the papacy did in the last half of the eleventh century was to put into practice *for the first time* the "hierocratic tenets" (as he put it elsewhere) implicit in the foundation of the Church of Rome by Christ himself. Walter Ullmann, *The Growth of Papal Government in the Middle Ages* (London, 1955), 262. This is to be a conservative in the same sense that Luther was a conservative in going back to Scripture as a basis for overthrowing Roman Catholicism and the seventeenth-century English Puritans were conservatives in going back to Magna Carta as a basis for overthrowing royal absolutism.

[29] On Gratian's treatise, see Berman, *Law and Revolution*, 143-148. On Glanvill's treatise, see ibid., 457-459.

no longer treated as sacred but was subjected to tests of reasonableness. The canonists attacked the formalism of the penitentials; they also developed a whole new system of criminal law, applied in the church courts, requiring proof of a criminal act (and not only a sinful state of mind), and of a close causal connection between the act and the injury, and defining intent and negligence not only in subjective but also in objective terms.[30]

It was in this period that the concept of individual rights was first developed. In the earlier Roman law the word "right" (*jus*) meant "law"—in a variety of senses, including the law as a whole, legal justice, and sometimes an individual legal doctrine or remedy. It did not refer to a *subjective* right, such as the right of a person to acquire or possess something or to require another person to do or refrain from doing something; but only to *objective* right, or law, *under* which acquisition or possession or some act was legally permitted or required.[31] Roman law recognized subjective duties (obligations) but not subjective rights. The same was true, incidentally, of Greek law and of Jewish law. Like the ancient Latin, the ancient Greek and Hebrew languages did not have any word for a right or rights; but only a word for a duty, or duties.

Jurists of the late eleventh and twelfth centuries, including both Romanists and canonists, not only developed the terminology of subjective rights—that *A has a* right against *B* (and not only that *under* objective right, that is, law, *B* has a duty to *A*), but also introduced into objective right the classification and analysis of subjective rights. Historians have discussed the effects of this shift in terminology, classification, and analysis upon the law of procedure, property and obligations, and other branches of private law, but have not paid sufficient attention to its effects on public law and, eventually,

---

[30] See ibid., 185-198.

[31] Cf. Michel Villey, "Les origines de la notion du droit subjectif," in *Leçons d'histoire de la philosophie du droit* (Paris, 1962), 221-250; id, "Le 'jus in re' du droit romain classique au droit moderne," *Publications de l'institut de droit romain de l'université de Paris* 6 (1950): 187-225; Helmut Coing, "Zur Geschichte des Begriffs 'subjektives Recht'," in Helmut Coing, *Gesammelte Aufsätze zur Rechtsgeschichte, Rechtsphilosophie und Zivilrecht* (Frankfurt am Main, 1982), 245.

Professor Villey's argument that the modern idea of subjective rights was first developed by the fourteenth-century nominalist William of Ockham has been refuted by Brian Tierney, who shows that the doctrine of individual rights "was a characteristic product of the great age of creative jurisprudence that, in the twelfth and thirteenth centuries, established the foundations of the Western legal tradition." See Brian Tierney, "Villey, Ockham and the Origin of Individual Rights," in John Witte, Jr. and Frank S. Alexander, eds., *The Weightier Matters of the Law: Essays in Law and Religion* (Atlanta, GA, 1988), 1, 31. Cf. Peter Landau, "Zum Ursprung des 'ius ad rem' in der Kanonistik," in Stephan Kuttner, ed., *Proceedings of the Third International Congress of Medieval Canon Law* (1971): 81-102; R. Tuck, *Natural Rights Theories: Their Origin and Development* (Cambridge, 1979), 5-31.

political theory. In fact, the idea of subjective rights (or, in contemporary · terminology, individual rights) was reflected in repeated demands made by groups of persons for protection of their rights and liberties against invasion by superior authorities, and in numerous charters of liberties and other compacts agreed upon between subordinates and superiors.

I shall give one example chosen from among hundreds. In Beauvais, in Picardy, the citizens (*bourgeois*) of the town assembled in the last years of the eleventh century, after four decades of sharp conflict between them and a succession of bishops, and instituted a sworn commune, that is, an autonomous city polity constituted by oath of the citizens. Eventually, King Louis VI of France (1108-1137) issued a charter recognizing the authority of the commune. The charter was confirmed in 1144 by Louis VII and (with some additions) in 1182 by King Philip Augustus. The seventeen articles of the charter included the following provisions:[32]

> all men within the walls of the city and in the suburb shall swear the commune;
>
> each shall aid the other in the manner he thinks to be right;
>
> if any man who has sworn the commune suffers a violation of rights, and a claim comes before the peers of the commune [in French, *pairs*, literally "equals," referring to leading citizens generally], they shall do justice against the person or property of the offender, unless he makes amends according to their judgment; and if the offender flees, the peers of the commune shall join in obtaining satisfaction from his property or person or from those to whom he has fled.
>
> similarly, if a merchant comes to Beauvais to the market and someone within the city violates his rights, and a claim comes before the peers, they shall grant the merchant satisfaction;
>
> no one who has violated the rights of a man of the commune shall be admitted to the city unless he makes amends according to the judgment of the peers; this rule may be waived, by advice of the peers, in the case of persons whom the Bishop of Beauvais has brought into the city;
>
> no man of the commune shall extend credit to its enemies and no man shall speak with them except by permission of the peers;
>
> the peers of the commune shall swear that they shall judge justly, and all others shall swear that they will observe and enforce the judgment of the peers.

---

[32] The seventeen articles of the charter, reproduced below, as well as the following discussion are drawn from Berman, *Law and Revolution*, 366-367. See also ibid., 380-386, analyzing the charter of Ipswich and describing the procedure of its adoption. The population assembled in the town square for many days to hear the charter read to them as they held hands and swore oaths to approve and observe it. Talk about social contract!

Other provisions dealt with regulation of mills, collection of debts (no person was to be taken as security for a debt), communal protection of food, equal measures of cloth, and restrictions on various feudal labor services still owed to the bishop.

The charter did not specify the form of government of the commune but only provided that its peers were to render judgment and to secure the life and property of the members. Indeed, the charter added nothing to what had been established at least one or two decades before, except that its final provision stated that "we [the king] do concede and confirm the justice and judgment which the peers shall do." In short, the charter was a recognition of a *fait accompli*: the uprising—at the height of the Papal Revolution—of the bourgeois of Beauvais, the formation by them of a sworn commune, and the restriction of the political and economic power of the bishop, who had previously been not only the chief ecclesiastic but also the chief feudal lord of the place, wholly involved in local and interfamily politics. Although the charter itself was laconic in the extreme, it clearly implied that seignorial rights in the town of Beauvais were to be severely restricted.

The provision that "all men" were to swear the commune and be subject to its jurisdiction was not intended to include clergy or nobles, whether or not they lived within the walls. In fact, the new urban communities of Europe were in competition with clerical and feudal authorities. In the background, central royal and papal authorities helped to regulate this competition.

Western philosophers who define justice in terms of individual rights, and individual rights in terms of liberty and equality, and liberty and equality in terms of a fictitious social contract, should, at the very least, take note of the fact that in hundreds of cities of Europe, founded in the late eleventh and twelfth centuries, an actual compact was entered into among the citizens, and between them and superior authorities, providing for the individual rights of citizens, their liberties, and their equality. Similar compacts also were entered into between superiors and subordinates in the royal and feudal regimes of Europe from the twelfth century on.[33]

In terms of the relationship between individualistic and communitarian concepts of justice, what is most striking about these compacts is the combination of the two concepts. But if one asks about the historical derivation of these compacts, that is, about the conditions and circumstances that produced them, one must start with their heritage in the European folklaw of the sixth to the eleventh centuries. The twelfth-century juxtaposition of individualistic and communitarian concepts arose on the wholly communitarian

---

[33] Examples include the Magna Carta (1215) and the Hungarian Golden Bull (1222). See ibid., 293-294.

foundations laid in the earlier period. Indeed, the entire revolutionary upheaval that occurred throughout Europe beginning in the 1050s, reaching a climax in 1075, and culminating in 1122,[34] presupposed the previous existence of an integrated *populus christianus*, a Europe united by an otherworldly faith, in which there was neither a separation of church from state nor a separation of law from other modes of social control. From a sociological and historical point of view, the existence of such a universal faith, in a political and economic and social culture that was predominantly tribal and local, was a necessary basis for the subsequent creation of diverse, autonomous, competing systems of law, ecclesiastical and secular. The tension, introduced by Christianity, between God's law and worldly law was a factor of critical importance in the ultimate overthrow of Germanic legal institutions. Yet without the prior types of communitarian integration in both spheres, the new legal systems would have had no social or spiritual foundation and would have been incapable of achieving their ultimate purposes of cohesion, reform, and equilibrium.

In arguing (like Sandel) for an essentially political resolution of the Rawls-Sandel debate, but (like Rawls) for one which favors the priority, in a democratic society, of individual rights over communitarian values, Richard Rorty has touched briefly on the historical dimension of the subject.[35] He found in Rawls' *A Theory of Justice* a passage in which the author purported to take a middle position between universal moral sentiments, on the one hand, and the existential situation in which people express their personal preferences, on the other. In that passage Rawls acknowledged that the individual with whose rights and liberties he is concerned is a person living in the political culture of twentieth-century America, and that the justice which is based on those rights and liberties is not derived from an abstract theory of moral sentiments but rather on the moral sentiments of persons living in that culture.[36] Nevertheless, Rawls wrote, "[J]ustice as fairness is not at the mercy, so to speak, of existing wants and interests."[37] Between universality and relativism, Rawls postulated "an Archimedean point" for judging conflicts

---

[34] In 1058, the college of cardinals was founded, thereby challenging for the first time the power of the emperor to name the pope. In 1075, Pope Gregory VII declared the *Dictates of the Pope*, announcing Papal legal supremacy over emperors and kings as well as over all bishops. In 1122, the Concordat of Worms was signed by the Pope and the emperor, whereby power to invest bishops and priests was divided between them. See Berman, *Law and Revolution*, 94-99.

[35] See Rorty, "The Priority of Democratic Politics," 16.

[36] Quoted in ibid., 13.

[37] Ibid., 23.

between the existing social system and the existing preferences of individuals. "The long range aim of society," he wrote, "is settled in its main lines irrespective of the particular desires and needs of its present members. And an ideal conception of justice is defined since institutions are to foster the virtue of justice and to discourage desires and aspirations incompatible with it."[38] "The long range aim of society" and "institutions" are such, Rawls added, that no matter what, at a given time, men's desires or perceptions might be, it would be a violation of justice to establish autocratic institutions or repress liberty of conscience.[39]

Thus Rorty has discovered in Rawls "an historical outlook,"[40] which underlies the individualism and pluralism that he espouses. Although Rawls gives only the slightest hints of his own conception of that historical outlook ("the long range aim of society"), Rorty supplies some evidence of it: "The sixteenth and seventeenth centuries," Rorty writes, "—the centuries in which religious toleration and constitutional democracy began to seem like live options for European society—were the times in which the Europeans developed a sense of themselves as plural."[41] Although Rorty acknowledges that this interpretation of the events of the sixteenth and seventeenth centuries "is a cliché of intellectual history," he adds that "the tiresome familiarity of talk about the connections between Lutheran protest, Cartesian subjectivity, and the Rise of the Bourgeoisie should not blind us to the fact that something did happen in those centuries which opened up both political and philosophical options."[42]

In this passage Rorty has effectively exposed the historical perspective that underlies much of the contemporary debate—on both sides—between an individualistic and a communitarian theory of justice, and has thereby undermined the debaters' pretensions to philosophical universality. Let us "drop the idea," Rorty proposes,[43] "that human beings share some single 'moral experience' . . . [or] 'moral sense.'" Instead, let us "settle for a self-consciously ethnocentric sense of 'our moral experience' . . . ."[44] This proposal has the merit that individualists and communitarians alike, in *our* "ethnocentric" tradition, have a common ancestry and a common tradition. In Rorty's view, that ancestry and tradition is found in the sixteenth-century

---

[38] Ibid., 23-24.
[39] Ibid., 24.
[40] Ibid., 29.
[41] Ibid.
[42] Ibid.
[43] Ibid., 45.
[44] Ibid.

struggle for religious toleration, the seventeenth-century scientific method, and eighteenth-to-twentieth century democratic ideas. Thus, the debate as to the final end, the moral goal—is it individual liberty or is it community welfare?—can be resolved, and can only be resolved, on historical grounds. Either the individualists are right in saying that in our sixteenth-to-twentieth century tradition the advancement of community interests is essentially a means to the final end of enhancing individual rights, or the communitarians are right in saying that in the same tradition the enhancement of individual rights is essentially a means to the final end of advancing community interests. The debate is over the nature of the tradition, which includes its meaning for today.

Rorty's admittedly "clichéd" history has two major defects. First, it is basically intellectual history; despite his reference to Protestantism, constitutional democracy, and the "rise of the bourgeoisie," Rorty shows no interest in the context of political, economic, and social institutions, including legal institutions, which gave experiential content to what came to appear—only in the nineteenth century—as an individualistic concept of justice. In fact, Western society, until the twentieth century, was intensely communitarian in its practices and valued certain kinds of community as ends and not only as means to individual self-fulfillment. It is only in the twentieth century that Western society has begun to experience a kind of justice which exalts the individual over the family, the church, the local community, the guild, the profession, ethnic groups, and the nation. Legal justice, especially, has not traditionally treated community as a means of fostering individual rights but on the contrary, where the two have conflicted, has usually treated individual rights as subordinate to community ends.

A second defect of the conventional historiography of contemporary philosophical discussions of justice is that they tend to neglect or else to disparage the roots of modern Western thought and Western institutions in the so-called Middle Ages. I have tried to make a start toward correcting that defect.

It goes without saying that it is important for philosophers to know where their ideas have come from, including their sources in political, economic, and other social conditions and circumstances, both past and present. The relevant question, however, is whether such historical knowledge has philosophical meaning. If history were merely part of the factual experience about which philosophers are philosophizing, then their failure to take adequate account of it would be only a technical weakness, a weakness of erudition. But if the philosophical inquiry concerns a topic such as justice, which is itself defined by history, and in the case of Western justice by Western history, including the Western legal tradition—then the historical definition has philosophical meaning not only in the descriptive or logical sense but also in the prescriptive or normative sense.

Concerning the relationship between individualistic and communitarian concepts in a definition of justice, Western history tells us that historically the community came first and that the "discovery of the individual" (as it has been called) in the late eleventh and twelfth centuries,[45] and the appearance at that time of the concept of individual rights and liberties, were rooted in the coexistence and competition of a single corporate church and diverse secular communities, with overlapping political and legal jurisdictions. The social contract securing individual rights originated at the same time as a political reality, and only centuries later was transformed by political philosophers into a theoretical construct.

Among the philosophical implications of that history, insofar as it concerns individualistic and communitarian concepts of justice, the following may be mentioned:

- that justice, in the Western tradition, is itself a shared concept, presupposing a community in which people not only wish to act justly toward each other but also wish to have common beliefs concerning what justice is;
- that in the Western tradition individual liberty and individual rights have always depended for their validity on community solidarity;
- that the widespread contemporary American view that individual liberty and individual rights are in some sense superior to social interests and social values is, from the perspective of the Western tradition of justice, an illusion and possibly itself a social myth whose primary function it is to protect community interests;
- that justice, in the Western tradition, seeks a symbiosis (in Bodenheimer's phrase) of individual and community interests;
- that in the Western tradition theories of moral justice and political justice cannot legitimately be dissociated from concepts of legal justice;
- that theories of legal justice must take into account the fact that, in the Western tradition, law contains within itself its own theories of justice, its own meta-law, by which law itself is to be judged.

Of course, propositions concerning the nature of justice cannot be proved by history alone. In an integrative jurisprudence, history without philosophy is meaningless, and history and philosophy without politics are inconclusive. Together, however, history, philosophy, and politics are persuasive; and when they come together there is no point in arguing which has primacy.

---

[45] Cf. Colin Morris, *The Discovery of the Individual, 1050-1200* (New York, 1972).

The chief normative significance of that part of the history of justice which is recounted in this article derives from the implication, stated above, that justice, in the Western tradition, seeks a symbiosis of individual and community interests. This historical, political, and philosophical truth gives rise to a norm requiring that excessive protection of the community against the individual should be corrected, and that excessive protection of the individual against the community should be corrected. Such a norm is especially significant in a time, like our own, when Western societies are experiencing the fragmentation and uprooting of smaller communities such as the family, the local church, the neighborhood, and the workplace, and the subordination of larger religious, ethnic, and national loyalties to individual self-realization.

Professor Bodenheimer has defined the symbiotic society as one that "gives credit to the affirmative aspects of both the individual and social theory of human nature." Symbiosis, as he points out, means the coexistence in close union of two dissimilar organisms.[46] In this article, I have sought to add a necessary historical dimension to his thesis.

---

[46] Bodenheimer, "Individual and Organized Society," 223.

12

LAW AND RELIGION IN THE DEVELOPMENT OF A WORLD ORDER*

That mankind, in the aftermath of two World Wars, has reached a turning point in its history, that the world has entered a new era of global interdependence, that all inhabitants of Planet Earth share a common destiny, is a historical fact, a political fact, an economic fact, and a sociological fact, that has finally penetrated the consciousness of most people, including the political leaders of most countries. I know of no better short description of this new world situation than that of the astonishing new Soviet leader Mikhail Gorbachev, first in his November 1987 address commemorating the seventieth anniversary of the Bolshevik Revolution and then in his remarks made in connection with President Reagan's visit to Moscow in May of 1988. These statements of Gorbachev can serve as a text for the first part of this chapter: "Despite the profoundly contradictory nature of the world today," he said in the November address, "and the fundamental differences among the states making it up, it is interconnected and interdependent and constitutes a definite integral whole. This is a function," he continued,

---

* Reprinted from *Sociological Analysis: A Journal in the Sociology of Religion* 52(1) (1991): 27-36. Delivered as the Paul Hanley Furfey Lecture at the Fiftieth Anniversary Meeting of the Association for the Sociology of Religion, 1988.

of the internationalization of world economic ties, the all-encompassing nature of the scientific and technological revolution, the fundamentally new role played by information and communication media, the state of the planet's resources, and the glaring social problems of the developing world, which affect everyone. But the main thing is the emergence of the problem of survival of the human race, because the appearance of nuclear weapons and the threat of their use has called man's very existence into question.[1]

In his toast at the banquet welcoming President Reagan, Gorbachev spoke again of a new age of global interdependence. "At the turn of two millennia," he said, "history has objectively bound our two countries by a common responsibility for the destinies of mankind." And later:

> Here within the walls of the ancient Kremlin, where one feels the touch of history, people are moved to reflect on the diversity and greatness of human civilization. So may this give greater historical depth to the Soviet-American talks to be held here, infusing them with a sense of mankind's shared destiny.[2]

At the conclusion of the Reagan visit, Gorbachev once more spoke of "the entire world public, the entire world community," which, he said, welcomed the arms reduction agreement reached by the two leaders as "a door . . . leading . . . towards a . . . non-violent world. . . ."[3]

Gorbachev's references to the history of mankind are in the Marxist tradition, and his stress on global interdependence builds on the rhetoric of his predecessors since the late 1950s. And, of course, one can find parallel statements, though not always as eloquent, by Western political leaders since the end of World War II. But for a confirmed Leninist to speak of "the turn of two millennia" is indeed remarkable. He did not speak of human progress from feudalism to capitalism to socialism. Instead, he implied that mankind is entering the third millennium of the Christian era.

The fact that all mankind shares a common destiny, that we live in "one world," is a truth that has finally penetrated the consciousness of most of the earth's inhabitants. But this truth has had a harder time penetrating the social sciences and humanities as they are taught in our universities. It surely has not penetrated either the legal scholarship or the curriculum of our law schools.

---

[1] Mikhail Gorbachev, "The Nation's Road From 1917 to Now: The Leader Takes Stock," *New York Times* (Nov. 3, 1987): A11-13.

[2] "Transcript of Reagan and Gorbachev Remarks," *New York Times* (May 30, 1988): A6.

[3] "Gorbachev's Words: 'Soviet-U.S. Relations on Healthy Track'," *New York Times* (June 2, 1988): A18.

Our law teaching and our legal literature—let me start with that—is, for the most part, incredibly provincial. When we teach and write about criminal law and contract law and constitutional law and administrative law and the various other branches into which the subject of law has been subdivided, we teach and write almost exclusively about American criminal law, American contract law, American constitutional law, as they exist today. At the periphery there are, to be sure, in the leading law schools some courses in French and German law, Soviet law, Chinese law, Japanese law, and occasionally other national legal systems, but even in those areas only a few brave souls have ventured to compare the various national legal systems with each other in a systematic way and to determine what they have in common and where they diverge—and why—and with what consequences for the world. The study of what might legitimately be called the law of mankind, or world law, is confined for the most part to various subdivisions of international law; but these subdivisions are quite specialized, and the insights to be derived from them concerning the nature of law in the emerging world order have not yet penetrated law teaching and legal scholarship as a whole. Moreover, international law is usually approached largely from an American point of view, with emphasis on how American interests are affected by it. Such courses are thus only harbingers of a future time when law schools in America—and the same can be said, *mutatis mutandis*, of law schools in other countries—will become schools not of "American law" but of "law;" and "law" will be understood to be the law of mankind, including, to be sure, American law but transcending it.

Similarly, I anticipate a time when history will cease to be understood and studied only as national history and will be seen to be the history of mankind, including, of course, national histories but transcending them.

Sociology has already made a beginning in this direction, first with social theory, which attempts to find and explain patterns of social change that are common to diverse societies, and more recently with the sociology of the world system. I look forward to a time when these two disciplines—social theory and sociology of the world system—will be combined, and when together they will focus, more than either of them now does, on the emerging law of mankind as well as on the fundamental beliefs from which any such law must derive motivation and support.

Unfortunately, social theory, which if I am not mistaken is one of two disciplines of sociology that have dealt systematically with the nature of law, the other one being sociology of law, has been dominated by a Weberian concept of law that is ill-adapted to an analysis of the emerging law of a world order. It is perhaps partly for that reason that those sociologists who have begun to apply systems theory to the world order, and who speak of the sociology of the world system, have hardly addressed the question of the legal aspects of the world system.

Let me say just a few words about what I consider to be the fallacies of prevailing concepts of law. This will lead me to a discussion of religion— since the omission of the religious dimension of law is close to the heart of the fallacies of which I speak. Then, finally, I shall be able to address the question of law, properly conceived, and religion, properly conceived, in the development of a world order—properly conceived!

Prevailing concepts of law, including prevailing sociological concepts of law, start with a definition of law as a body of rules, and they generally find the ultimate source of those rules in the will or policy of the political authority that makes the rules and enforces them by coercive sanctions. This is the definition of the so-called positivist school of legal theory, and it was adopted by Max Weber. Weber defined the state as a "human community that (successfully) claims the *monopoly of the legitimate use of physical force* within a given territory,"[4] and law as "an order . . . [that] is externally guaranteed by the probability that physical or psychological coercion will be applied by a *staff* of people in order to bring about compliance or avenge violation."[5] He defined the type of law that prevails in contemporary society as a system of formal rules, imposed by the state, having rational consistency and thus fostering predictability and calculability in a bureaucratic economic and political system. This concept of law makes it only barely possible even to imagine a world society governed by law; indeed, a world society governed by Weber's formal rational type of legal order would be a scourge and a horror.

Let me refer in this connection to Niklas Luhmann's important book, *A Sociological Theory of Law*. Luhmann defines "the law of a social system" as "congruently generalised normative behavioural expectations." He discards Weber's requirement of a coercive order but he retains, as the central requirement, normative generalizations that have the function of facilitating and securing expectations.[6] Omitted from this definition is the legal process, in which legal actors—legislators, judges, administrators and, on the unofficial level, parties to contractual and other forms of legal relations—allocate rights and duties and thereby resolve conflicts and create channels of cooperation. Law consists not only of rules, or "normative generalizations," but also of application of rules; and as Immanuel Kant once said, "There is no rule for applying a rule." Two countries with quite similar formal legal rules may have

---

4 Max Weber, *From Max Weber* (New York, 1958), 78.

5 Max Weber, *Economy and Society* (Berkeley, CA, 1978), 34.

6 Niklas Luhmann, *A Sociological Theory of Law* (Boston, MA, 1985), 77-78.

very different legal systems. Omitted also from Luhmann's definition is the ideal of legal justice, an ideal which, in one form or another, has been proclaimed by every legal order known to history.

It is not surprising that Luhmann, working from so narrow a concept of law, finds little role for law in a world society. He describes the emergence of a world society in lucid terms, deploring the fact that sociologists have generally overlooked it. His list of factors that constitute the new global society is similar to that of Gorbachev, including global economic interdependence, global channels of communication, universal science and technology, and the possibility of the common death of all humankind. "An interlinked world history," he writes, "has come into being." Yet this cannot lead, he argues, to political unification, and "those problems that can only be solved at the level of a global society . . . can therefore no longer be resolved in the form of law."[7] I consider this to be an extraordinary and even a ridiculous statement. Luhmann devotes several pages to the attempt to show that politics and law, which in Europe were "until recently the most important risk carriers of societal evolutions," cannot play a significant part in the evolution of a world society.[8] But his whole argument is based on a positivist definition of law as a body of rules designed to promote predictability and calculability of expectations in a unified political state.

Neither the classical Weberian nor Luhmann's modified Weberian concept of the nature of law adequately explains the actual development of world law. It does not explain, for example, the fact that the state itself, which is viewed by legal positivists as the only source of legal rules within its jurisdiction, derives its character as a state from its membership in the international community of states. Any association of people that is in possession of weapons can, if it chooses, use those weapons to attack others or to defend itself as well as to maintain a system of domination within its own confines. But to claim the *right* to govern and the *right* to defend or attack—to claim the authority of a "state"—is to acknowledge participation in a legal order which transcends the state and which defines statehood.

Public international law is not only a precondition of the world order; it is also part of a process of creating and re-creating the world order. States are continually negotiating with each other to establish legal relationships of mutual advantage and mutual responsibility: that in itself is "law," in the sense of a "law way," as contrasted with a "force way" of resolving conflicts. More than 20,000 international treaties and conventions are registered with the United Nations. Despite the weakness of international judicial and

---

7 Ibid., 256.

8 Ibid., 259-264.

enforcement powers, such treaties and conventions are generally recognized as constituting international law in every sense of the word "law."

Also the United Nations now has some five hundred intergovernmental organizations charged with the responsibility of administering what may properly be called United Nations law. This body of law is derived indirectly from treaties and agreements among states, but in addition it is derived directly from what may be called the corporate law of the United Nations itself. This is a kind of world government, not in the sense of a unitary world state with a world police force or a world army, but more like the weak federal government established after our Revolutionary War by the Articles of Confederation.

If we view international treaties and conventions as a kind of international legislation, and the United Nations as a kind of international executive and administrative branch, and the International Court of Justice as an international judiciary, then we may say that the world order that is developing at the end of the twentieth century does have legal institutions, albeit weak ones. We may view these institutions as positive law, law enacted by the representatives of the nation-states that comprise the world order.

The world order also has legal principles whose ultimate source is universally shared conceptions of justice. Perhaps the best example of such principles are to be found in the human rights covenants—the United Nations Covenant on Civil and Political Rights and the United Nations Covenant on Economic, Social, and Cultural Rights. As international treaties, these are positive law. But their content is natural law: they enact broad principles of liberty, equality, and welfare, principles whose meaning cannot be derived from the documents themselves but only from the universally shared conceptions of justice that inform the documents. Once again, as with world law generally, enforcement is weak. Nevertheless, enforcement exists. In July 1988, for example, the Interamerican Court of Human Rights, sitting in Costa Rica, in a suit brought by private persons, handed down a judgment against the Government of Honduras requiring that government to pay compensation to the relatives of a victim of the Honduran government's previous policy of so-called "disappearances." The Honduran government defended the action, and lost. It promised to abide by whatever decision the Court handed down.[9] Many other important examples of enforcement of the international law of human rights could be cited—together with many more examples, to be sure, of non-enforcement. The point I would stress is that implicit in the Human Rights Covenants is the recognition that the entire world, all mankind,

---

[9] See Stephen Kinzer, "O.A.S. Tribunal Finds Honduras Responsible for a Political Killing," *New York Times* (July 30, 1988): A1,6.

despite its many diversities, not only shares some common beliefs concerning human dignity but also has a common concern to protect human dignity by a law that stands above the law of individual states.

Even more important than positive law and natural law as an indicator, in the long run, of the importance of law in the development of a world order, is customary law. By transnational customary law, I have in mind particularly, though not exclusively, the gradual growth of universal bodies of legal rules, legal procedures, and legal institutions, and even a common worldwide legal consciousness, out of the practices and behavioral norms of unofficial transnational communities. Of the many examples that could be cited, I shall single out the growth of a body of transnational commercial law relating to export-import contracts, bills of lading and other negotiable documents of title, marine insurance policies and certificates, bills of exchange, letters of credit, and similar commercial instruments. Based chiefly on custom and contract, this body of law is more or less uniform throughout the entire world. It is the law of the transnational community of exporters and importers, shipowners, marine insurance underwriters, bankers, and others—a community which has a European history dating from the twelfth century and which in the twentieth century has become not merely a Western but a worldwide community, held together by innumerable negotiations and transactions among its participants as well as by its own processes of self-government, including its own procedures for mediation and arbitration of disputes. Here is a world law, governing world trade, which has developed not primarily on the basis of the collective political will of nation states (as positivist theory would require), and not primarily on the basis of a moral order expressing universally accepted standards of procedural and substantive justice (as natural law theory would postulate), but primarily on the basis of an ongoing shared historical experience of a community. To quote the language of the founder of the historical school of jurisprudence, the great nineteenth century German jurist Friedrich Karl von Savigny, this is a body of law that is developed "first by custom and by popular belief, then by juristic activity—everywhere, therefore, by internal, silently operating forces, not by the arbitrary will of a legislator."[10]

Perhaps I should add that in the later stages of the development of customary commercial law it has sometimes been codified by national states and sometimes, where the laws of national states have come to differ too widely from each other, by international conventions.

---

[10] Friedrich Karl von Savigny, *Vom Beruf unsrer Zeit für Gesetzgebung und Rechtswissenschaft* (Heidelberg, 1814), 13-14.

But the reader will ask—I *hope* the reader will ask—What has this to do with religion?

If we think of law only in positivist terms as a body of rules laid down by political authorities and backed by coercive sanctions, we will not naturally be led to connect the law of the world community with religion. From that point of view, it is even hard to connect most *national* law with religion, even in national states that have established churches or that claim to have a religious mission.

Sociologists of law have generally stated that connections between law and religion that existed in earlier societies have been severed in modern times. They have linked the Weberian "rational" model of law with a "secular" model. The law of the modern state, they have said, does not reflect any sense of ultimate meaning and purpose in life; instead its tasks are finite, material, impersonal—to get things done, to make people act in certain ways. Legal man, like his brother economic man, has been portrayed in sociological literature, as well as in other literature, as one who uses his head and suppresses his dreams, his convictions, his passions, his concern with ultimate purposes. Likewise the legal system as a whole, like the economic system, is seen as a huge complex machine, a Weberian bureaucracy, in which individual units perform specific roles according to specific incentives and instructions, independently of the purposes of the whole enterprise.

Yet law itself, *in all societies*, encourages the belief in its own sanctity. It puts forward its claim to obedience in ways that appeal not only to the material, impersonal, finite, rational interests of the people who are asked to observe it but also to their faith in a truth, a justice, that transcends social utility—in ways, that is, that do not easily fit the image of secularism and instrumentalism presented by the prevailing theory.

To say that law is closely linked with religion, that each is a dimension of the other, that they interact, requires not only a broad definition of law but also a broad definition of religion. If religion is viewed merely as a set of doctrines and practices relating to the supernatural, it, too, can easily be isolated from other aspects of social life, including law. If, however, one defines religion in terms of shared intuitions and convictions concerning the purpose and meaning of life, shared emotions (as well as shared thoughts) concerning creation and redemption, concerning transcendent values, concerning the nature and destiny of mankind—then it is much harder to exclude legal relations, legal processes, and legal values from its purview.

In modern legal systems, the interaction of law and religion is reflected, first, in the *rituals* of law—its solemn language, the formalities of legal procedure, its reliance, in our tradition, on oaths; second, in its reliance on *tradition*, its continuity with the past and its sense of ongoingness into the future; third, in its appeal to *authority*, whether it be the authority of the court or of the ruler, of precedent or of statutes, or as in our case, of a written constitution; and fourth, in its *moral universality*, its justification of itself in axiomatic, *a priori* terms—that crime should be punished, torts should be compensated, contracts should be kept, government should respect personal integrity, and the like, *not* merely for pragmatic or utilitarian or philosophical reasons, but for religious reasons, that is, because of an all-embracing moral reality, a purpose in the universe.

Thus sanctity is attributed to law, and without such sanctity law loses its force. Without sanctity no coercion will be effective, since the agencies of coercion will themselves be corrupted. That sanctity *is* the religious dimension of law.

In the Christian West, in the Muslim world, in the Jewish tradition, such sanctity has been reinforced by theological doctrines and by ecclesiastical authority. This is true in some other cultures as well. But in the emerging world order, there is no common worldwide theology and no global church. What, then, is the source of sanctity of world law?

One answer is that the various existing historical religious traditions of the world, in all their multiplicity, are a principal source of the sanctity of world law, just as the existing national states are a principal source of the legitimacy of world law as a political matter. Another answer is that religion in a broader sense exists on a world scale as well. Most religions share some sense both of the lawfulness of the universe and of the unity of mankind. The Golden Rule—which is a rule of equality, to treat all others with equal respect—has parallels in most religions. There is a universal revulsion against—and not merely a rational disapproval of—disobedience of legitimate authority, unlawful killing, stealing, violation of sexual mores, perjury, and fraud.

To say that religion is a source of world order is not to deny that it is also a source of world *disorder*. Religious fanaticism is destructive of world order; there is no need to cite examples. Nonfanatical religious faith may obstruct what appear to be rational solutions of political problems. Religion is not necessarily good. Law is not necessarily good. World order is not necessarily good. But if we ask, "What are the respective roles of law and religion in the development of a world order?" it seems clear, that for better or for worse, the emerging world order needs, and to some extent is receiving, the support of both law and religion; that is, it needs, and to some extent is receiving, a structure, a process, for allocating rights and duties and, connected to that, a shared intuition of and commitment to transcendent values. And second, that these needs can only gradually be met as communities are formed—communities of all kinds, economic, cultural, political—that transcend national boundaries and form an infrastructure for the gradual transition, over many generations, from a world order to a world society to a world community.

The world society will be, and is, made up in part of a large variety of diverse communities and interests—often hostile to each other. National, racial, political, religious, ideological, class-based, gender-based, and other hostilities will undoubtedly continue to exist. What is new in the twentieth century is that we are all inextricably locked together in one Planet Earth. So the questions become, How can we reconcile the hostilities? How can we create a common future? Can each borrow from others the qualities that are needed to compensate for its own deficiencies?

Here law and religion, separately and together, play a crucial role. I do not suggest for a moment that the existing multiplicity of national legal systems can be, or ought to be, eliminated, or that the existing multiplicity of religions will or should give way to an established world religion. I believe that would be the worst possible outcome. As between tyranny and anarchy, I prefer anarchy. Our one world is and must remain a pluralist world, a world of many diverse nations, races, creeds, and social systems. It must also, however, be one world. *E pluribus unum.* Both plural and one.

The choice that confronts us is between remaining in a precarious international balance of forces, with relatively primitive legal and religious resources of a universal character, on the one hand, or, on the other, gradually reshaping and reconciling the diverse conflicting groups, the diverse interests, that now exist in the world.

Time and World Order.—We are indeed, as Gorbachev said, at a turning-point in the history of mankind, a third millennium. A world order has come into being and is developing. The world has entered a new age, the age of what was called, over forty years ago, by one of its prophets, Eugen Rosenstock-Huessy, the age of Planetary Man.[11] The crucial question is, what kind of Man he and she are to be.

Sociologists who apply systems theory to the emerging world order have neglected its dynamic elements, and particularly its time dimension, especially its ongoing character, its future development. This is due partly, in my opinion, to their failure to put themselves into the society they are analyzing. They objectively weigh, measure, and count the factors that make up the world order as it now exists, without reference to the world society, of which

---

[11] See George A. Morgan, *Speech and Society: The Christian Linguistic Social Philosophy of Eugen Rosenstock-Huessy* (Gainesville, FL, 1987), 70.

they themselves are a part, that is in process of becoming and the world community that is its final destiny. They are victims of Cartesian assumptions that have in fact been disproved not only by philosophy but by the natural sciences themselves. This has contributed, in my view, to their neglect of the role both of law and of religion—which I would call *time* sciences—in the development of a world order. An analysis of the respective roles of law and religion helps us to understand, on the one hand, the ways in which conflicts among constituent elements of the world order can, *in time*, be regulated and resolved, which is law, and on the other hand, the fundamental beliefs about the ultimate purpose and meaning of our ongoing experience, *in time*, the ultimate purpose and meaning of history itself, with its deaths and rebirths, which is religion.

I have criticized sociologists—that is, *some* sociologists. I must add by way of qualification that in a forthcoming article Frank Lechner has recognized and deplored the fact that law has been neglected in the sociology of the world systems; and further, that in sociological "reflection about global order" one must take into account not merely the synchronic but also "the diachronic dimension, the existence of a tradition, however conflict ridden, of global *thought and practice*." He concludes, finally, that "To think, and to try to show, sociologically, that a global open society is a possible world order, may well be an act of faith."

I would like to refer also to the work of one of the great *older* sociologists, Alexis de Tocqueville who, in his *Democracy in America*, stressed repeatedly the importance of law and of religion in holding the diverse peoples of the vast American continent together and in giving them both a vision of their future and a way of realizing that vision. Tocqueville studied and interpreted American society in terms of its long-range future, and indeed in terms of the long-range future of the world. I think we must do the same in studying and interpreting the new planetary age, in which the nation-states and peoples of the world face some of the same types of problems that were faced by the early nineteenth-century Americans.

Is one wrong in thinking that both law and religion have a time dimension, including both past times and future times, built into them? If that is not wrong, then I think one is safe in saying that in approaching the study of the development of a world order, both the sociology of law and the sociology of religion can benefit from mutual contact with each other; and further, that both must become sensitive to the time factor, including not only the immediate past and the long-range past, but also the immediate future and the long-range future, of mankind.

TOWARD AN INTEGRATIVE JURISPRUDENCE: POLITICS, MORALITY, HISTORY*

Without philosophy, history is meaningless.
Without history, philosophy is empty. —Anon.

I ntegrative jurisprudence is a legal philosophy which combines the three classical schools: legal positivism, natural-law theory, and the historical school. It is premised on the belief that each of these three competing schools has isolated a single important dimension of law to the exclusion of the others, and that it is both possible and important to bring the several dimensions together into a common focus.[1]

---

* Reprinted from *California Law Review* 76 (1988): 779-801.

[1] For some years I used the term "integrative jurisprudence" without knowing that it was first used by Jerome Hall. I am glad to have the opportunity now to apologize for this substantial oversight. My usage differs somewhat from Professor Hall's but contains some of the same basic characteristics. See Jerome Hall, "Integrative Jurisprudence," in Paul Sayre, ed., *Interpretations of Modern Legal Philosophies: Essays in Honor of Roscoe Pound* (New York, 1947), 313-331 (combining positivism and natural law theory with a sociological jurisprudence); Jerome Hall, *Studies in Jurisprudence and Criminal Theory* (New York, 1958), 37-47 ("Toward an Integrative Jurisprudence"); Jerome Hall, "From Legal Theory to Integrative Jurisprudence," *Cincinnati Law Review* 33 (1964): 153; Jerome Hall, *Foundations of Jurisprudence* (Indianapolis, IN, 1973), Chapter 6 ("Towards an Integrative Jurisprudence"). See also Edgar Bodenheimer, "Seventy-Five Years of Evolution in Legal Philosophy," *American Journal of Jurisprudence* 23 (1978): 181, 204-205, in which Professor Bodenheimer writes of "The Need for an Integrative Jurisprudence," citing, in addition to Hall, E. Fechner, *Rechtsphilosophie: Soziologie und Metaphysik des Rechts*, 2d ed.

The Main Differences Among the Three Classical Schools.—The positivist school treats law essentially as a particular type of political instrument, a body of rules laid down ("posited") by the state, having its own independent self-contained character separate and distinct from both morality and history. The natural-law school treats law essentially as the embodiment in legal rules and concepts of moral principles derived from reason and conscience. The historical school treats law as a manifestation of the historically developing ethos, the traditional social representations and attitudes, of a people or a society. Thus positivists analyze the rules of law existing in a given polity at a given time independently of principles of right and wrong and independently of the history or social consciousness of the given polity; only after it is established what the law is, they argue, is it legitimate to ask what the law ought to be or how it came to be what it is. Naturalists, on the other hand, believe that one cannot know what the law is unless one considers at the same time what it ought to be, since (they argue) it is implicit in legal norms that they are to be analyzed, interpreted, and applied in the light of the moral purposes for which they exist. Indeed, it is a tenet of natural-law theory that governmental acts or commands that grossly contravene fundamental principles of justice do not deserve to be called law at all. The historicists impose limitations both on the sovereignty of the lawmaking power and on the authority of reason and conscience: they argue that what the law "is" politically and "ought to be" morally is to be found in the national character, the culture, and the historical ideals and traditions of the people or society whose law it is.

(Frankfurt am Main, 1963). For earlier expressions of my views see Berman, *Law and Revolution: The Formation of the Western Legal Tradition* (Cambridge, MA, 1983), vii ("We need a jurisprudence that integrates the three traditional schools and goes beyond them."), and 44 ("A social theory of law . . . should bring the three traditional schools of jurisprudence—the political school (positivism), the moral school (natural-law theory), and the historical school (historical jurisprudence)—together in an *integrative* jurisprudence." In earlier works I did not use the phrase "integrative jurisprudence," but did express some of its basic concepts. See Berman, *Justice in Russia: An Interpretation of Soviet Law* (Cambridge, MA, 1950), 4 ("We might view the whole Soviet legal system analytically, in terms of the needs and interests of a socialist state, [or] historically, in terms of the characteristic features of Russian society over the past thousand years of its development, [or] philosophically, in terms of the parental concept of law and of man implicit in it. It has seemed more fruitful to use these three methods—the analytical, the historical, and the philosophical—as three screens to be placed sucessively over Soviet law. . . . Together they may suggest the main outlines of the Soviet legal system as a whole, and its main implications not only for an understanding of Soviet Russia but also for an understanding of law."); Berman, *The Nature and Functions of Law* (Mineola, NY, 1958), 29 ("Once one juxtaposes the three schools of jurisprudence which have been described, it becomes apparent that what is needed is not a choice of one to the exclusion of the others but rather a synthesis which will build on what is valid in all three.").

Each of these three main schools of jurisprudence has developed in various directions. Some positivists, especially those of the Kelsen school, have adopted an extreme conceptualism: consistency of legal norms is for them the only criterion of legality, once a sovereign lawmaker is postulated. At the opposite pole of positivist jurisprudence, self-styled "American legal realists" and many adherents of the more recent "Critical Legal Studies Movement" treat legal rules as rationalizations of empirical behavior of legal officials and find the sources of that behavior in economic, political, and other non-legal factors.[2] Natural-law theory has also moved in various directions. Some Roman Catholic theorists, building on Thomistic premises, have found in an elaborately constructed set of moral principles the criteria for judging the validity of legal rules, and for analyzing, interpreting, and applying them. Other naturalists have found such criteria in broad conceptions of procedural and substantive fairness. Still others have looked to an "oughtness" or "purposiveness" presupposed in the very nature of legal rules and in the very enterprise of making and interpreting them. The historical school has also undergone division, some of its adherents emphasizing the specific historical traditions of given national legal systems, others turning to sociological concepts of the relation of law to custom, to class structure, and to other empirical social and economic factors.

These three competing approaches can only be brought together by giving a broader definition to law from that which is usually adopted by each of the schools. Most positivists define positive law (which is the only law they recognize) as official rules or, in the case of the American legal realists, as official conduct rationalized or disguised in rules. Most naturalists also define positive law as rules but they test the rules of positive law by moral principles or standards, which they consider to be equally part of law. The historicists also define law in terms of both rules and moral principles but, unlike the positivists, they are apt to be more concerned with the rules of customary law than the rules of enacted law and, unlike the naturalists, they are apt to be concerned not with universal moral principles but rather with those specific moral principles that correspond to the character and traditions of a given people or a given society. Professor Jerome Hall, who invented the term

---

[2] It has been argued that Critical Legal Studies is an "anti-positivist phenomenon," but this characterization refers to its ultimate purpose of undermining law rather than to its definition of the nature of law. Cf. J. A. Standen, "Critical Legal Studies as an Anti-Positivist Phenomenon," *Virginia Law Review* 72 (1986): 983. Similarly, American Legal Realism, although it is sometimes said to be opposed to positivism, rests on the premise that the law which it realistically "sees through" consists of rules laid down by legislators, judges, and administrative officers.

integrative jurisprudence,[3] respects each of these definitions of law, but he goes beyond them all. He defines law as a type of social action, a process, in which rules and values and facts—all three—coalesce and are actualized.[4] It is, in my view, the actualizing of law that is its most essential feature. If law is defined as the activity, the enterprise, of legislating, adjudicating, administering, and otherwise—through unofficial as well as official conduct—giving a legal order to social relations, then its political, its moral, and its historical aspects can be brought together.[5]

The Search for Primacy.—What has divided the three traditional schools most sharply has been the assertion by each of its own primacy. The question of primacy only became critical in the eighteenth and nineteenth centuries when legal philosophy in the West was first divorced from theology. Prior to that time it was believed that ultimately it is God who is the author of law—indeed, in the words of the thirteenth century German law book the *Sachsenspiegel,* "God is himself law and therefore law is dear to him;"[6] it was therefore possible to integrate in theological terms the political, the moral, and the historical dimensions of law. Pre-Enlightenment Christian writers such as Aquinas, Grotius, Locke, and others who, despite their diversity, are often characterized as natural-law theorists were in fact also positivists and historicists—all three. They believed, to be sure, that God implanted reason and conscience in the minds and hearts of men. But they also believed that God ordained earthly rulers with the power to make and enforce laws, and in addition that the history of law represents the providential fulfillment of God's plan. They resolved the tensions among these three aspects of the human condition—the political, the moral, and the historical—by finding their common source in the triune God, who himself is an all-powerful lawmaker, a just and compassionate judge, and the inspirer of historical change in legal as in other social institutions. Prior to the eighteenth century positivist, naturalist, and historicist theories were not separate "schools" but rather three complementary perspectives on law.

---

[3] See Hall's writings cited in note 1 above.

[4] Jerome Hall, *Comparative Law and Social Theory* (Baton Rouge, LA, 1963), 78-82. Cf. Jerome Hall, *Law, Social Science and Criminal Theory* (Littleton, CO, 1982), 124.

[5] This definition is expanded in Berman, *Law and Revolution,* 4-5; Harold J. Berman, *The Interaction of Law and Religion* (Nashville, TN), 24. It takes one step further Lon L. Fuller's definition of law as "the enterprise of subjecting human conduct to the governance of rules." Lon Fuller, *The Morality of Law,* 2d ed. (New Haven, CT, 1964), 106.

[6] Karl August Eckhardt, ed., *Sachsenspiegel V: Landrecht in hochdeutscher übertragung* (Hannover, 1967), prolog.

With the Enlightenment, Western legal philosophers sought a new ultimate authority. Some found that ultimate authority in politics, others found it in morality, still others found it in history. The positivists say that the ultimate source of law is the will of the lawmaker and its ultimate sanction is political compulsion: they deify the state. The naturalists say that the ultimate source of law is reason and conscience and its ultimate sanction is moral condemnation: they deify the mind. The historicists say that the ultimate source of law is national character, the historically developing traditions of the people, what in the United States is sometimes called the unwritten constitution, and that its ultimate sanction is acceptance or repudiation by the people: they deify the people, the nation.

The Complementarity of Positivism and Natural-Law Theory.—The rich classical dialogue between positivist and naturalist theories of law, whose roots lie in ancient Greek philosophy and religion, in Roman Catholic and Protestant theology, and in the early Enlightenment, has for the most part degenerated in twentieth-century English and American jurisprudence to a debate about two questions: first, does law have an inherent moral character so that commands or rules issued by political authorities which lack that moral character do not deserve to be called laws? and second, should particular laws be interpreted and applied solely according to the will and intent of the lawmaker, whether broadly or narrowly construed, or also according to the moral purposes which are implicit in the particular laws as well as in the legal system as a whole?

I say "degenerated," not only because the questions are not the most important questions that can be asked about the nature of law[7] but also because they cannot be answered adequately in terms of either of the two opposing theories.

It is of some interest that positivists and naturalists have begun to soften their opposition to each other in recent decades. Each side has shown itself

---

[7] Lloyd L. Weinreb has criticized the reduction of natural law to an ethical as constrasted with an ontological theory, and has stated that at the merely ethical level "it is very hard indeed to explain the fuss that is made in legal philosophy about the debate between natural law and legal positivism." Weinreb, "The Natural Law Tradition: Comments on Finnis," *Journal of Legal Education* 36 (1986): 501. In his important book, *Natural Law and Justice* (Cambridge, MA, 1987), Professor Weinreb shows that classical natural-law theory is based on a concept of either fate or providence, and that it presupposes that the universe itself, including human life, contains an external standard of judgment of human conduct. See also Frank S. Alexander, "Beyond Positivism: A Theological Perspective," *Georgia Law Review* 20 (1986): 1089. Professor Alexander criticizes both positivists and naturalists for failure to deal with ontological questions concerning the purposes of law in the fulfillment of individuality and community.

more willing than in the past to accept, in modified form, certain doctrines propounded by the other. It is doubtful, for example, that a positivist would say today what Oliver Wendell Holmes, Jr., once said: "I hate justice, which means that I know if a man begins to talk about that, for one reason or another he is shirking thinking in legal terms." Today even ardent defenders of the positivist position concede that it is a legitimate function not only of the law student and law professor, but also of the judge and, above all, the legislator, to ask of a legal rule, *once it is determined analytically what it says and what it means*, "Is it just?"[8]

Moreover, positivists acknowledge that a legal system may expressly include certain ethical norms, such as the due process and equal protection clauses of the United States Constitution, which govern the application of legal rules. Even apart from such basic constitutional provisions, positivists acknowledge that there are "principles, policies, and values which lie behind legal rules" and which "impart at least a partial element of the moral into any legal system's operation." Indeed, the positivist definition of law as a body of general rules itself presupposes the moral principle that like cases should be decided alike. Such moral principles are, to be sure, viewed by the positivist not as speaking directly to the mind of the interpreter of the rule but rather as "express[ing] what those empowered to implement the rules see as being justifying rationalizations of the valid rules."[9]

As positivists have increasingly taken account of the effect of morality on law, so naturalists have increasingly taken account of the political elements in law. It has always been understood by naturalists that the morality by which law is to be tested includes the moral duty to preserve the legal order, including the system of legal rules imposed and enforced by the state. From this point of view, the role of reason and conscience, whose objectivity the positivists tend to doubt, is more limited in much natural-law theory than many positivists have supposed. One need only read the brilliant essay by Lon L. Fuller, entitled "Reason and Fiat in Case Law," to realize how close the two sides are to each other in that respect. In Fuller's words, "Law . . . is compounded of reason and fiat, of order discovered and order imposed, and . . . to attempt to eliminate either of these aspects of the law is to denature and to falsify it."[10]

---

[8] This is essentially the position taken in H.L.A. Hart, *The Concept of Law* (Oxford, 1961), 181-207 ("Law and Morals"). Hart does not discuss the historical school but concentrates on the opposition between positivism and natural-law theory.

[9] Neil MacCormick, "A Moralistic Case for A-Moralistic Law?" *Valparaiso Law Review* 20 (1985): 1, 8.

[10] Lon L. Fuller, "Reason and Fiat in Case Law," *Harvard Law Review* 59 (1946): 376, 382.

Ultimately, however, naturalists and positivists draw apart from each other at two points: first, and most obviously, when the sovereign enacts a law, or supports a procedure, which is grossly and fundamentally contrary to reason and conscience; second, when a court or other law enforcement agency interprets a law, or a legal rule, without sufficient regard to the moral purposes for which it exists. In these two types of situations, the positivist denies the legal relevance of the categories "reason," "conscience," and "moral purpose." He doubts that these categories reflect universal and time-less truths from which the positive law itself is derived. He asserts that the legal issues to be resolved are not universal but local and not timeless but contingent. Whereas the naturalist, in interpreting law, accepts the ultimate supremacy of reason, or conscience, the positivist accepts the ultimate supremacy of the will, or desire, or intent, of the lawmaker, as revealed, in the first instance, in the language of the rule itself. In current terminology, the issue is whether the Right is prior to the Good or the Good is prior to the Right.[11]

---

[11] Cf. John Rawls, *A Theory of Justice* (Cambridge, MA, 1971), chap. 68 ("The Right and the Good Contrasted"). Ronald Dworkin deals with the same problem in terms of individual "rights" versus collective "interests." He defines the "anti-utilitarian concept of a right," which he calls characteristic of U.S. constitutional theory, as follows: "If someone has a right to something, then it is wrong for the government to deny it to him even though it would be in the general interest to do so." Ronald Dworkin, *Taking Rights Seriously* (Cambridge, MA, 1977), 269. Cf. ibid., xi and xv, where he speaks of rights as "trumps" over collective goals. See also Ronald Dworkin, *Law's Empire* (Cambridge, MA, 1986), 160 and 223.

Dworkin seems to be groping towards an integrative jurisprudence as he struggles to reconcile the general interests of the state with the fundamental rights of individuals. On the one hand, he refers to law in positivist terms, as "the rights and duties that flow from past collective decisions and for that reason license or require coercion. . . ." Ibid., 227. On the other hand, he follows a natural-law approach in suggesting that the "right to concern and respect" is fundamental, and that "the idea of a collective goal may itself be derived from that fundamental right." Dworkin, *Taking Rights Seriously*, xv and 272ff. He does not, however, recognize the specific virtues of historical jurisprudence. He writes of "histori-cism" (Dworkin, *Law's Empire*, 167 and 227), which he sees, in positivist terms, as closely linked both with the interpretation of the intent of the lawmaker and with the desire for certainty (ibid., 359ff.). Discussing United States constitutional law, Dworkin distinguishes between what he calls weak historicism, which asks judges to follow the concrete opinions of the framers, "so far as these concrete opinions can be discovered," and strong histori-cism, which requires judges to treat "historical concrete intentions even more firmly: it requires them to treat these intentions as exhausting the constitution altogether." Ibid., 368-9. Although he concludes (ibid., 413) that law "aims . . . to show the best route to a better future, keeping the right faith with the past," he rarely discusses the specific historical background in which constitutional problems have arisen. For example, in dealing with the religion clauses of the First Amendment, Dworkin's judge Hercules "must develop a theory of the constitution, in the shape of a complex set of principles and policies that justify that scheme of government. . . . He must develop that theory by

Yet in practice these are not genuine antinomies, but only opposite sides of the same coin. The naturalist, or moralist, is also taking a political position; the positivist, or politicist, is also taking a moral position. In real life, other things being equal, they reach the same practical results.[12] In real life, that is, in history, the universal and the local, the timeless and the timely, interact. So do reason and will, values and rules, justice and order.

The jurisprudential debate is closely related in these respects to current controversies in the fields of moral philosophy and political theory. The word "justice" is, after all, common to all three disciplines. In all three, the heirs of Immanuel Kant contend with the heirs of Jeremy Bentham. Nevertheless, the moral philosophers and political theorists hardly deal with law, and the jurisprudes deal only casually with moral philosophy or political theory. Thus John Rawls' book, *A Theory of Justice*, which has attracted such an enormous amount of attention during the past fifteen years, barely mentions law.[13] Similarly, Michael Sandel's powerful rebuttal of Rawls, *Liberalism and the*

---

referring alternately to political philosophy and institutional detail." See Dworkin, *Taking Rights Seriously*, 107. Nothing is said about the fundamental changes in the character of American society as well as of American law which took place during the period from 1868, when the Fourteenth Amendment was adopted, and 1940, when the Supreme Court held that it incorporated by implication the religion clauses of the First Amendment. Cf. Harold J. Berman, "Religion and Law: The First Amendment in Historical Perspective," *Emory Law Journal* 35 (1986): 777.

[12] Cf. Ruth Gavison, "Natural Law, Positivism, and the Limits of Jurisprudence: A Modern Round," *Yale Law Journal* 91 (1982): 1250, 1274, 1283; Deryck Beyleveld and Roger Brownsord, "The Practical Difference Between Natural-Law Theory and Legal Positivism," *Oxford Journal of Legal Studies* 5 (1985): 1, 22: "(1) since neither natural-law theory nor positivism is tied to any specific ethical position there would be nothing in principle to prevent rival conceptual protagonists holding an identical view of ethics; in which case. . . . (2) there would be no necessary practically significant disagreement between such conceptual rivals."

Gavison argues more generally that positivism and natural law are "complementary and equally necessary approaches" to law, and calls for an integration of their perspectives. See Gavison, "Natural Law, Positivism," 1250. It is not clear from her article, however, what the basis of such integration is to be, other than her insight into the areas of agreement between the two schools (especially as represented in the work of the positivist Joseph Raz and the natural law theorist John Finnis). She makes no mention of the historical school of jurisprudence.

Needless to say, the fact that positivists and naturalists may agree on the solution of specific ethical questions and that there are large areas of agreement between them on the nature of law itself does not negate the fact that there are important differences between them in theory and in outlook.

[13] See Rawls, *A Theory of Justice*. Except for the phrase "law of nations," such terms as "law" and "legal" do not appear in the index and there is no substantial discussion of them in the text.

Limits of Justice, avoids any discussion of law.[14] Yet Rawls, in arguing for the primacy of individual liberty and individual rights as the basis of justice, and Sandel, in arguing for the primacy of the community and of public ends, carry on a debate which is strikingly parallel to that which is carried on between those legal philosophers who argue that positive law is founded on natural law and those who argue that positive law is founded on the will of the lawmaker. The naturalists defend the primacy of the moral order, which they translate into the language of legal rights. The positivists defend the primacy of the political order, which they translate into the language of social utility. Yet it can be said of the Right and the Good, as it can be said of reason and will, or of moral values and political rules, that—despite tensions and even contradictions between them—in real life, in history, they interact.

What is missing, above all, from the debate between the naturalists and the positivists is precisely the historical dimension of law. Law is more than morality or politics and more than morality and politics combined. Law is also history. What is morally right in one set of historical circumstances may be morally wrong in another; likewise what is politically required in one set of historical circumstances may be politically objectionable in another. More important, the apparent conflict between a moral and a political approach to law may be resolved in the context of historical circumstances: history, the experienced life of the community, may bring morality and politics together, permitting and even compelling an accommodation between the two. Law, indeed, may be defined as the balancing of justice and order in the light of experience.[15]

---

[14] Michael J. Sandel, *Liberalism and the Limits of Justice* (Cambridge, MA, 1982). Sandel mentions law in passing (see ibid., 16) and discusses Locke's theory of the Law of Nature and of God (see ibid., 116-117).

[15] Holmes is sometimes misrepresented as an exponent of historical jurisprudence, and in that connection his famous aphorism is quoted, "The life of the law is not logic but experience." Oliver Wendell Holmes, Jr., *The Common Law*, ed. Mark Howe (Cambridge, MA, 1963), 1. Holmes did, indeed, pay great attention to the historical development of legal concepts and rules, and he attributed their development to unarticulated political and social premises. "Behind the logical form lies a judgment as to the relative worth and importance of competing legislative grounds," he wrote in "The Path of the Law," *Harvard Law Review* 10 (1897): 457, 466. Nevertheless, as Martin Golding has said, "He remained a positivist to the last, since he viewed the value judgments which inevitably shape the law as being themselves *extra*-legal." See Martin P. Golding, "Jurisprudence and Legal Philosophy in Twentieth Century America: Major Themes and Developments," *Journal of Legal Education* 36 (1986): 441, 445. "Experience," for Holmes, was not the law itself, which he conceived as rules applied to cases ("a prediction of what courts will do"), but rather the hidden source of its vitality. Holmes's emphasis on the historical development of legal doctrine derived from his recognition of the importance of judge-made law in England and America; since the judges in that tradition explain their decisions in terms of precedent, it was necessary for Holmes, as a positivist, to analyze the meanings attributed to the rules at

Let me give the example of a statute which deprives certain races of basic political and civil rights, of which a positivist might say that it is in fact a law, albeit an unjust law, a bad law, which, although a law, should, as a purely moral matter, be disobeyed; and a naturalist might say that, in view of its fundamentally immoral character, it lacks essential features of legality and is no law at all. Both are right and both are wrong. Only under given historical circumstances can either of these arguments make a substantial practical difference. Thus to say that such a statute is no law at all may be quite important in a revolutionary situation, when the very lawfulness of the political regime that enforces it is being challenged (as may become the case in Mandela's South Africa). To say, on the contrary, that it is a bad law, an unjust law, but nevertheless a law, might be quite important in a time of reform, when there is a chance of amending it to reduce its injustice (as was indeed the case when Martin Luther King, Jr. wrote his Letter From Birmingham City Jail).[16]

The Historical School.—It is characteristic of the historical school that it itself was founded in response to historical events.[17] In 1814 an eminent German jurist named Thibaut published a plan for a code of laws for all the states that comprised the German confederation, to be drawn up by an inter-state committee of legal scholars and practitioners. (This was before the establishment of Germany as a unified national state.) Another German jurist, Friedrich Karl von Savigny, responded in the same year with an essay entitled, in English translation, "On the Calling of Our Time for Legislation and Jurisprudence." In it the thirty-five-year-old Savigny, who was to become the most important German legal figure of the nineteenth century, set forth a theory of what law is, how it is related to the social life and the beliefs and values of the community of which it is a part, and how it develops over time; and he argued that to attempt to codify German law in the year 1814 would be to freeze it and to threaten its historical foundations—its rootedness in the past and its calling for the future.

---

various times. In Holmes's view, history explained but did not justify the rules and the chief value of a historical explanation was, in fact, to remove the veil that concealed their essentially political character. Once the historical derivation of the legal rules was established, their application was for Holmes analytical and logical. See Roscoe Pound, *An Introduction to the Philosophy of Law*, rev. ed. (New Haven, CT, 1954), 62.

[16] Martin Luther King, "Letter from Birmingham City Jail (April 16, 1963)," reprinted in J. Washington, ed., *A Testament of Hope: The Essential Writings of Martin Luther King, Jr.* (San Francisco, CA, 1986), 289-302.

[17] For an exposition and critique of the historical school of jurisprudence, see Julius Stone, *The Province and Function of Law*, 2d ed. (Stanford, CA, 1950), 421–448.

Savigny's theory of law was directed in part against ideas that had come to prevail in France after the French Revolution and that had spread throughout Europe: that legislation is the primary source of law, and that it is the primary task of the legislator to protect the "rights of man" or the "greatest good of the greatest number," or both, without deference to the traditions of the past, with their prerogatives and prejudices. In opposing these views, Savigny was influenced by Edmund Burke's conception of the nation as a partnership of the generations in time. Like Burke, Savigny considered law to be an integral part of the common consciousness of the nation, organically connected with the mind and the spirit of the people. Law, wrote Savigny, "is developed first by custom and by popular belief, and only then by juristic activity—everywhere, therefore, by internal, silently operating powers, not by the arbitrary will of the lawgiver."[18] As a people becomes more mature, Savigny wrote, and as its social and economic life becomes more complex, its law loses some of its simplicity, it becomes less symbolic and more abstract, more technical, requiring administration and development by a professional class of trained jurists. Nevertheless, it must never become merely a body of ideal propositions or a mere system of rules promulgated by the state. It must always remain a particular expression of the social and historical consciousness of a people at a given time and place. The professional or technical element must never become divorced from the symbolic element or from the community ideas and ideals which underlie both the early and the later stages of legal development.

Those who rallied to Savigny's banner called themselves "the historical school" of jurisprudence. They succeeded in postponing codification of German civil law for some eighty-five years. At the same time they succeeded in making the civil code that was eventually adopted a far better code than could have been drafted in 1814.[19] As Savigny wrote in his famous essay of that year, the very language of German law had so deteriorated in the eighteenth and early nineteenth centuries that any code drafted at that time would inevitably have been a failure.[20]

Critics of the historical school have focused on its conservatism and romanticism in opposing legislative reform in the name of the *Volksgeist*, the

---

[18] Friedrich Karl von Savigny, *Vom Beruf unsrer Zeit für Gesetzgebung und Rechtswissenschaft* (1814; 2d ed. Berlin, 1840). The first edition was translated by A. Hayward as *On the Vocation of our Age for Legislation and Jurisprudence* (1831; repr. ed., New York, 1975).

[19] See Arthur T. von Mehren and James R. Gordley, *The Civil Law System*, 2d ed. (Boston, 1977), 75-79, for an account of the drafting of the German Civil Code, which was enacted on July 1, 1896, to take effect on January 1, 1900.

[20] Savigny, *Vom Beruf unsrer Zeit*, 2d ed., 25; A. Hayward, trans., *On the Vocation of our Age*, 64-65.

"spirit of the people." The issues, however, were much deeper. Savigny did not oppose all legislative reform; on the contrary, he worked actively for such reform.[21] And the concept *Volksgeist*, which translates so awkwardly into English, corresponds in some ways, as I have suggested earlier, to the American concept of "the unwritten constitution;" it could be translated "national ideals," or even "community values." The deeper issues involved the conflict between what can accurately be called the German "common law tradition" and the new rationalism that was associated with the Enlightenment and the French Revolution. That new rationalism emphasized the ultimate source of law in public opinion and the will of the legislature. Savigny's historical school emphasized the ultimate source of law in the older Germanic (*germanische*) tradition of popular participation in lawmaking and adjudication as well as the more modern German (*deutsche*) tradition of professional scholarly interpretation and systematization of the *jus commune*, the common law, which had been developed over the centuries out of the texts of the Roman law of Justinian and the canon law of the Church. Prior to the nineteenth century the Romano-canonical *jus commune* of the nations of Europe had been customary law in the same sense that the English common law was customary law; that is, it was traditional law, unenacted law. The *jus commune* of the continental European nations was derived, however, not primarily from judicial decisions, as in England, but primarily from scholarly glosses and comments on treatises and ancient texts. Just as the English common law was supposed to reflect the common sense of the English people, as it has developed over time, so the German *jus commune* was supposed to reflect the common consciousness of the German nation, as it has developed over time.

I should like to give two examples, of which I have personal knowledge, of the application of historical jurisprudence to specific legal problems in Germany today. The first is the example of the abolition of capital punishment. The German social philosopher Jürgen Habermas was asked in October 1986, at a meeting in Cambridge, Massachusetts, what he thought of capital punishment. He might have answered in natural-law terms: "It violates the

---

[21] Savigny was a professor at the University of Berlin from 1810 until his death in 1861. He was made a member of the Prussian Privy Council in 1817, and was appointed to the Berlin Court of Appeal for the Rhine Provinces in 1819. He became a member of the commission for revising the Prussian code in 1826, and served from 1842 through 1848 as head of the department for revision of statutes. See Stone, *The Province and Function of Law*, 421–422; Hans Kiefner, "Savigny, Friedrich Karl von," *Encyclopaedia Brittanica* (New York, 1984), 16: 289. Although he opposed imposing a codification on the entire German federation, Savigny expressed himself strongly in favor of legislative reform. Further, he and his followers elaborated a systematic method of analysis of Roman law, which eventually served the cause of national codification when the time came.

sanctity of life, it violates the Kantian categorical imperative," or alternatively, "It is the just desert of the murderer or traitor." He might also have answered in positivist terms: "It should be retained because it is useful in deterring murder and treason," or alternatively, "It should be abolished because it is not useful in deterring the crimes to which it is made applicable." Habermas did not, however, give either of these answers. Instead he said, "You must understand that after what Germany lived through under Nazism, it would have been impossible to restore capital punishment."

The second German example is like the first. Several American pro-life organizations sponsored a visit to the United States some years ago by the President of the German Constitutional Court, which in 1975 had handed down a decision declaring a German statute permitting abortion virtually on demand during the first twelve weeks of pregnancy to be in violation of the "fundamental law" (*Grundgesetz*) of the German Constitution. The distinguished German judge spoke in various cities, including, once again, Cambridge, Massachusetts. To the dismay of his audience, he announced in his lecture that he personally did not oppose abortion—he did not consider it to be in itself immoral. He also said that he considered it to be the responsibility of his court to uphold statutes unless they clearly violate the Constitution. Nevertheless, he said, it is perfectly clear that after the Nazi experience of genetic engineering and racial extermination the German Constitution could not possibly be interpreted as permitting abortions.[22]

Incidentally, Habermas expounded in his lectures in Cambridge a natural-law theory, based on Kantian premises, and the President of the German Constitutional Court expounded in his lecture a positivist theory, based on the supremacy of the enacted law. Nevertheless, in the crucial matters of capital punishment and abortion they followed, in effect, an historical jurisprudence.

---

[22] This was the reasoning of the court itself. See Decision of the Federal Supreme Court, Feb. 25, 1975, 39 B Verf E. 1. The Court stated: "The express incorporation into the Basic Law of the self-evident right to life . . . may be explained principally as a reaction to the 'destruction of life unworthy of life', [and] to the 'final solution' and 'liquidations' which were carried out by the National Socialistic Regime as measures of state." Robert E. Jonas and John D. Gorby, "Translation of the German Federal Constitutional Court Decision," *John Marshall Journal of Practice and Procedure* 9 (1976): 605, 637. And again: "Underlying the Basic Law are principles for the structuring of the state that may be understood only in light of the historical experience and the spiritual-moral confrontation with the previous system of National Socialism." Ibid., 662. Cf. George Fletcher's perceptive article on the relation of law to national character, in which, referring to the above case, he writes that "by the court's own admission it is 'the historical experience and the moral, humanistic confrontation with National Socialism' that makes a difference in Germany." See George P. Fletcher, "Lawmaking as an Expression of Self," *Northern Kentucky Law Review* 13 (1986): 201, 209.

In the nineteenth and twentieth centuries Savigny's historical school went in various directions in various countries. It remained always concerned with instruments and processes of legal development and with stages in the growth of law. Nevertheless, it was not always concerned primarily with the relation of legal change to the national character of a single people. It increasingly took on the character of an empirical sociology of law, or else simply technical legal history; insofar as it did so, it lost its normative character and became, for the legal philosophers, a mere datum, an explanation but not a justification.[23]

In England and America, however, the judges, as contrasted with legal philosophers, sociologists, and historians, have traditionally applied and sometimes expounded an historical jurisprudence in the normative sense in which Savigny first articulated it. In fact, historical jurisprudence is embodied in the Anglo-American common law, together with positivism and natural-law theory. That is, in the Anglo-American tradition of adjudication judges, in deciding cases, analyze the rules of positive law in order to determine their meaning, having in mind the will and intent of the legislature or court or other agency that made them; in addition, they interpret the rules in terms of reasonableness and fairness; and finally, they determine both the will of the lawmaker and the applicable principles of reason and fairness in the light of the history, and especially the legal history, of the nation. In having recourse to legislation, to equity, and to precedent, judges have traditionally applied, in fact, an integrative jurisprudence. Occasionally a judge who is also a legal scholar gives literary expression to such a jurisprudence. An outstanding example of such a judge in this century was Benjamin Cardozo.[24] An outstanding example in the nineteenth century was Joseph Story.[25]

---

[23] The work of the late Alexander Bickel is exceptional in this respect. Bickel drew on the philosophy of Edmund Burke, stating that "civil society is a creature of its past, of 'a great mysterious incorporation', and of an evolution which in improving never produces anything 'wholly new', and in conserving never retains anything 'wholly obsolete'." Bickel wrote: "The values of . . . a society evolve, but as of any particular moment they are taken as given. Limits are set by culture, by time- and place-bound conditions, and within these limits the task of government informed by the present state of values is to make a peaceable, good, and improving society. . . . Law is the principal institution through which a society can assert its values," Alexander Bickel, *The Morality of Consent* (New Haven, CT, 1975), 20. According to Bickel, "We find our visions of good and evil and the [moral] denominations we compute where Burke told us to look, in the experience of the past, in our tradition, in the secular religion of the American republic." Ibid., 24. Professor Anthony T. Kronman notes the "puzzling" fact that "despite the high regard in which his work is held, Bickel has few contemporary followers." Anthony T. Kronman, "Alexander Bickel's Philosophy of Prudence," *Yale Law Journal* 94 (1985): 1567, 1568.

[24] In *The Growth of the Law* (New Haven, CT, 1924), 62, Cardozo wrote of his "fourfold division separat[ing] the force of logic or analogy, which gives us the method of

Such integration of the three principal schools of legal philosophy has suffered greatly in recent decades from the decline of the historical method in adjudication and from the decline of the historical approach to law in legal scholarship and in legal education generally. This is not the place to elaborate this point. It is sufficient to remark on the well-known fact that our judges are increasingly torn between so-called judicial activism, which is usually defended in terms of a natural-law theory, and so-called judicial self-restraint, which is usually defended in terms of a positivist theory. And our legal philosophers are increasingly taking sides in this conflict, and increasingly devoting their writings to it. Each side, to be sure, bolsters its position with references to history. The belief that law is essentially the will of the lawmaker often takes the form of a return to what was said and meant by lawmakers of an earlier time—"the original intent of the Founding Fathers." Similarly, the belief that law is to be understood in terms of fundamental moral values often takes the form of a return to past proclamations of the spirit of freedom and equality. These are examples of blind historicism—a futile attempt at repetition of the past. They should be called historical positivism and historical moralism, respectively. In fact they feed the widespread antipathy toward a genuine historical jurisprudence, which is considered by

philosophy; the force of history, which gives us the historical method, or the method of evolution; the force of custom, which yields the method of tradition; and the force of justice, morals and social welfare, the *mores* of the day, with its outlet or expression in the method of sociology." What Cardozo called "the method of philosophy" is characteristic of traditional positivism; what he called "the method of sociology" is characteristic of traditional natural-law theory; and what he called "the method of evolution" and "the method of tradition" are characteristic of traditional historical jurisprudence.

An excellent example of Cardozo's integration of the three jurisprudential schools is to be found in his decision in the famous case of MacPherson v. Buick Mfg. Co., 217 N.Y. 382 (1916), in which he relied on the holdings of previous decisions (positivism), the equities of the case (natural law), and the social and economic evolution of the United States during the previous half-century (historical jurisprudence) as interlocking grounds for declaring a new doctrine of manufacturer's liability.

[25] In the twentieth century Story has been characterized as an adherent of natural law theory. In fact, however, both in his judicial opinions and in his numerous scholarly writings, he combined natural law theory with positivism and historical jurisprudence. Thus R. Kent Newmyer writes of his decision in the 1822 case of U.S. v. La Jeune Eugenie that Story relied upon "the universal morality of natural law," which, however, "rested on a firm foundation of positive law and history." R. Kent Newmyer, *Supreme Court Justice Joseph Story—Statesman of the Old Republic* (Chapel Hill, NC, 1985), 350. Newmyer points out that Story conceived the common law to be not only a body of principles and not only a moral code but also an ongoing process of adaptation to the "actual concerns of life" viewed in a historical context. Story's legal system, Newmyer writes, "would accommodate historical change. History, in turn, would inform law." Ibid., 245. Story's scholarly treatises on commercial law and on conflict of laws strongly reflect this three-dimensional quality of his legal philosophy.

most American legal philosophers to be at best a form of practical wisdom or common sense that leads to no genuine philosophical truths.

The Revival of Historical Jurisprudence.—The historical school has been almost universally disparaged and has virtually disappeared from almost all jurisprudential writings in the twentieth century, at least in England and the United States.[26] Indeed, the almost total neglect of historical jurisprudence during the past generation—the failure even to acknowledge its existence—has crippled English and American legal philosophy. Even Professor Hall in his jurisprudential writings has turned toward empirical sociology and away from the emphasis of the historical school on cultural factors and on the role

---

[26] Roscoe Pound wrote that "the historical school in one form or the other was dominant in Continental Europe and in America in the last half of the nineteenth century." Roscoe Pound, *Jurisprudence* (St. Paul, MN, 1959), 1:63. Nevertheless, the historical school is not even mentioned in most of the leading jurisprudential works of the 1950s to 1980s. In an excellent short summary of legal thought in the United States since 1880, Martin Golding has nothing to say about historical jurisprudence (except that Holmes was *not* an exponent of it), and in the symposium on "Contemporary Legal Theory" which his article introduced, the historical school was not represented. See Golding, "Jurisprudence and Legal Philosophy in 20th Century America." In 1951, Harold Gill Reuschlein reported on the theories of some fifty contemporary American legal philosophers. He did not identify any among them as adherents of the historical school. See Harold G. Reuschlein, *Jurisprudence—Its American Prophets, A Summary of Taught Jurisprudence* (Indianapolis, IN, 1951).

Savigny's school had come under heavy attack in the decades after World War I. Writing in 1946, Julius Stone stated that the "creative force" of the historical school "disappeared as the [19th] century proceeded." Stone, *The Province and Function of Law*, 301. He proposed that historical jurisprudence should now itself "disappear" as a separate branch of legal philosophy, and should be merged into sociological jurisprudence. Ibid., 34-35.

Hermann Kantorowicz also took the view that Savigny's work was essentially a "sociological description." Kantorowicz wrote that Montesquieu had listed fourteen "natural and social factors" on which law depended, including "l'esprit de la nation." "Savigny accepted this one alone and made it the one source of all law, obviously because it was more mysterious and therefore more romantic than climate, economic system or density of population, which Montesquieu had recognized and studied, though in a very aphoristic and rather journalistic spirit." Hermann Kantorowicz, "Savigny and the Historical School of Law," *Law Quarterly Review* 53 (1937): 326, 335.

In lectures delivered in 1921-22 at Yale Law School, Roscoe Pound criticized "the historical school which ruled in our law schools in the last quarter of the nineteenth century and taught us to think that growth must inevitably follow lines which might be discovered in the Year Books." See Pound, *An Introduction to the Philosophy of Law*, 156. Lecturing at Trinity College, Cambridge in 1922, Pound stated that "[i]n the reaction from the law-of-nature theory the historical school went too far in the other direction and sought to exclude development and improvement of the law from the field of conscious human effort." Roscoe Pound, *Interpretations of Legal History* (Cambridge, MA, 1923), 68.

of specific traditions in the development of specific types of legal institutions.[27]

If historical jurisprudence is to be revived, it must be clearly differentiated not only from romantic nationalism but also from the blind historicism to which positivism and natural-law theory have sometimes resorted. The essence of historical jurisprudence is not historicism but historicity, not a return to the past but a recognition that law is an ongoing historical process, developing from the past into the future. At the same time, historical jurisprudence is not merely a sociological statement; it starts from, but goes beyond, the general truths that law is a product of history, that the life of the law is experience, and that the legislator or judge finds in past history sources for adaptation of the law to new circumstances. A genuine historical jurisprudence—such as Savigny's or Story's—rests on the premise that certain long-term historical experiences of a given people lead it in certain directions; and more particularly with respect to law, that the past times through which the legal institutions of a given people have developed help to determine the standards according to which its laws should be enacted and interpreted, and the goals to which its legal system strives. Historical jurisprudence, in its initial form, was Savigny's explanation of why the time was not ripe in 1814 for a federal codification of German law. Historical jurisprudence helps to explain, for example, what had to happen in the United States in the twentieth century, legally and otherwise, before racial desegregation could become an effective constitutional principle. It also helps to explain—and to justify—the connections which are now being made between racial desegregation and racial equality in employment, as constitutional principles.

Of course, history alone—and especially national history alone—is as futile and as demonic as politics alone or morality alone. "National ideals," "community values," and "the unwritten constitution" cannot justify political arbitrariness or moral depravity. Indeed, history without political and moral philosophy is meaningless. Yet those philosophies without history are empty. In American jurisprudence the time is ripe to restore the historicity of law to its proper role alongside political principles of legal order and moral principles of legal justice.

The argument has been made that history is too vague or too subjective a concept to serve as a basis for jurisprudence. The same argument is

---

[27] Professor Hall's classic study *Theft, Law and Society* (Boston, 1935; 2d ed., Indianapolis, IN, 1952) effectively combines the historical and the sociological methods. In his jurisprudential writings of the 1960s and 1970s the historical method was not stressed. In his *Foundations of Jurisprudence*, 143 he writes that historical jurisprudence "is the bridge between the traditional legal philosophies [natural-law theory and positivism] and the new [empirical sociological] perspective."

applicable, however, to morality and politics. All three are to be seen as complementary approaches and methods, not as scientific formulae or philosophers' stones. Even the positivist method, which makes the strongest claim to precision and objectivity, has to acknowledge the indeterminacy of legislative intent divorced from moral purpose and historical significance.

The neglect of historical jurisprudence in the twentieth century is surely connected with a decline of the sense of history, the sense of destiny, the sense of mission, in America and throughout the West. Indeed, it was the Western sense of history as destiny and as mission that gave rise to historical jurisprudence.

It was in the West, and I believe it was only in the West, that the belief in the ongoing character of law was conceived and came to prevail: the belief, that is, in the capacity of the body of law, the *corpus juris*, to grow over generations and centuries. Moreover, in the West, and in the West alone, the belief was conceived and came to prevail that the growth of law has an internal logic, that changes that are made in law over generations and centuries are part of a pattern of changes, that law is not merely ongoing, it has a history, it tells a story.

The historicity of law in the West (and here I speak of Roman Catholic Christendom from the late eleventh to the sixteenth century, and of Catholic and Protestant Europe and America from the sixteenth to the early twentieth century) was linked with the concept of its supremacy over the political authorities who made it. The developing body of law, whether at a given moment or in the long run, was considered to be binding on the state itself. The ruler could make law, but he could not make it arbitrarily, and until he remade it—lawfully—he was bound by it.

Of course Western rulers did make law arbitrarily, and they did disregard and subvert the law that they made, and the destiny and the mission were not realized. Periodically, there were revolutionary upheavals, which sought to overthrow the *ancien régime* which had betrayed the vision and to replace the old positive laws with new laws. Every Western nation traces its legal system back to such a national revolution—and beyond that, to the 11th century revolution of the Roman Catholic Church which established the canon law as the first modern legal system and which gave rise to the rationalization and systematization of secular legal systems.[28]

If it is to reestablish its credentials, historical jurisprudence must recognize the revolutionary as well as the evolutionary element in the development of the Western legal tradition, its discontinuities as well as its continuities. By

---

[28] This is a main theme of Berman, *Law and Revolution*.

the same token it must recognize the times in which we now live, the direction in which we are moving, the alternative paths that lie ahead of us. It must combine historical insights into law with the political insights of legal positivism and the moral insights of natural-law theory.

Integrative Jurisprudence as a Key to Understanding the Development of World Law.—Only by means of an integrative jurisprudence can the development of law in the world community in the latter part of the twentieth century be properly explained, justified, and guided.

In speaking of law in the world community, I have in mind not only public international law, as it is traditionally defined, that is, the law governing relations among national states, and not only United Nations law, that is, the law governing international organizations, but also the enormous body of contractual and customary legal norms that govern relations, not among states, but among persons and enterprises engaged in economic and other activities that cross national boundaries.

Positivist jurisprudence once took the position that in the absence of an international sovereign, with powers of enforcement, there could be no such thing as international law. Since World War II, however, positivist jurisprudence has generally accepted the reality of international law as law and has played a significant role not only in explaining and analyzing it but also in contributing to its development. Today more than 20,000 international treaties and conventions are registered with the United Nations; these constitute legislation not only of the individual states that have ratified them but also of the international community of states. Despite the weakness of international judicial and enforcement powers, such treaties and conventions are generally recognized as constituting international law in the positivist's sense of the word "law." Also the United Nations now has 500 intergovernmental organizations charged with the administration of United Nations law. Positivist jurisprudence has contributed techniques of making, interpreting, and applying this body of international legal rules and procedures in a consistent and effective way.

Similarly, natural-law theory has also played a significant part in the development of world law. It has emphasized the rootedness of international law—the *jus gentium*—in universal principles of justice. A striking example of its contribution is the international law of human rights. Fundamental moral principles have been embodied in the two great human rights covenants—the U.N. Covenants on Civil and Political Rights and on Social, Economic, and Cultural Rights. The doctrine has been established that the international community of states, and even in some cases individuals, may take legal action to protect citizens of a foreign state against certain forms of oppression by their own government. Implicit in these legal instruments and procedures is the recognition that the entire world, all mankind, despite its many diversities, not only shares some common beliefs concerning human dignity but also has a common concern to protect human dignity by a body of law that stands above the law of individual states.

The political and moral aspects of the development of a world law need to be viewed, however, in the historical context of the gradual formation of a world community.[29] This has started primarily in the economic and cultural spheres. In the transfer of goods and services and capital, in transportation, in finance, in communications—the world is experiencing the rapid development of a common language and a common law. The exporters and importers of the world, the shipowners, the marine insurance underwriters, the bankers—have their own law: a c.i.f. contract, a bill of lading, a marine insurance certificate, a bill of exchange, or a letter of credit has the same legal character in Paris, Moscow, Beijing, Buenos Aires, New York, and Timbuktu. This body of mercantile law, which had its origins in the rapid development of European trade after the First Crusade, has developed during more than eight centuries into a world-wide system as the economies of all countries are gradually coming to form a single market.[30] Similarly, the world is becoming united by science and technology, by scholarship in other fields, by literature and the arts, by medicine, by tourism, by sports, and by much else; and in the process of such unification there is gradually developing a universal body of legal norms and processes, and even a common world-wide legal consciousness, connected with these types of activities. The body of law governing such international economic and social intercourse has emerged in the form not only of an expanded public international law but also, and primarily, in the form of mutual understandings among the participants, built up out of

---

[29] Some sociologists have undertaken to study political and cultural aspects of what they call "the modern world-system." Niklas Luhmann wrote in 1972 that "the fact of a context of interaction which extends over the whole globe is evident. The universal possibility of communications (with periodic and regional exceptions) and universal peace has been factually established. An interlinked world history has come into being. The common death of all humankind has become possible. Commercial traffic connects all parts of the world. . . ." Niklas Luhmann, *A Sociological Theory of Law* (Boston, 1985), 256. Cf. John W. Meyer, "The World Polity and the Authority of the Nation-State," in Albert Bergesen, ed., *Studies of the Modern World-System* (New York, 1980), 109-137; Roland Robertson and Frank Lechner, "Modernization, Globalization and the Problem of Culture in World-Systems Theory," *Theory, Culture and Society* 2 (1985): 103.

[30] See Harold J. Berman, *The Law of International Commercial Transactions* (*Lex Mercatoria*), 2d ed., Part III, Folio 3, of "A Lawyer's Guide to International Business Transactions," 1983. Cf. Berman, *Law and Revolution*, chap. 11 ("Mercantile Law").

negotiation and agreement and informal methods of dispute resolution. It is a law based on custom and contract, with transnational nongovernmental associations playing an important part in its development. Only in later stages has it sometimes been codified—in some instances prematurely—by intergovernmental organizations. The law of the world community "is developed," in Savigny's words, "first by custom and by popular belief, and only then by juristic activity—everywhere, therefore, by internal, silently operating powers, not by the arbitrary will of the lawgiver."

Thus the emerging law of the world community is explained, justified, and guided not only by the collective political will of national states, expressed in international legislation and administration, and not only by a moral order, expressed in universally accepted standards of procedural and substantive justice, but also by an ongoing long-term shared historical experience, namely, the growth of a body of transnational customary law, which may be understood as constituting an early stage of a new era.

This, indeed, is the crisis of our legal tradition: that we are at the end of one era and at the beginning of another. We are at the end of an era in which *world* history was centered in *Western* history and at the beginning of an era in which *Western* history is centered in *world* history. With respect to law, the sense of ongoingness, of progress, of destiny and mission, which has characterized the Western legal tradition for some nine centuries, and which has given the political and moral aspects of that tradition their dynamic impulse, has diminished substantially. At the same time, a new global legal tradition is emerging which in some ways threatens the Western legal tradition at the same time that it, in some ways, builds upon it. This is a crisis in the Greek sense of that word—a *krisis*, a choosing—and at the same time in the Chinese sense, which I am told is called *wei-ji*, represented in two characters signifying respectively "danger" and "opportunity."

As Jürgen Moltmann has emphasized, our sense of history is based on hope.[31] When we say "history" we mean something more than chronology; we mean not merely change but patterns of change, implying direction in time, which in turn implies either purpose or fate. We mean either Hebrew linear history from Creation to the coming of the Messiah, or Greek cyclical history, or Enlightenment progress, or Christian history of fall and rise, decline and regeneration, death and rebirth. "History" does not mean "the past," nor does it mean "time" in some abstract Kantian sense. It means, rather, "the times," and especially "our times," including times which

---

[31] Jürgen Moltmann, *Theology of Hope: On the Ground and the Implications of a Christian Echatology*, trans. J. Leitch (London, 1967), 230ff.

separate our past times from our future times. It inevitably contains a prophetic element.

The Western belief in a providential history is built into the Western concept of historical jurisprudence. It also lies at the base of the belief that we are living in a time of global crisis, a time of global choices having to do with the preservation of the environment, the reduction of racial conflicts, the elimination of hunger, and, above all, the establishment of peace among the nations. That a body of world law is emerging to help us make these choices constitutes the historical context in which the politics and the morality of law is to be determined.

The legal positivist and the legal moralist will say, "This may—or may not—all be true, but what does it teach us about the nature of law? How does it answer the philosophical questions, 'What *is* law?' and 'What is its relation to politics and to morality?'" An integrative jurisprudence does not deny the validity of those questions. It affirms, however, that in national legal systems, as in the developing body of transnational law, the tensions that exist between a political and a moral answer to those questions cannot be resolved unless they are viewed in the context of another set of questions: "What is a legal tradition? How does it come into being and how does it develop? To what extent are the analytical concerns of the positivist and the moral concerns of the natural-law theorist not only conditioned and structured but also directed and resolved by the long-term historical concerns of the community whose law it is?"

This is not to say that in law history "trumps" morality and politics. The issue is not the primacy of one or another of these three aspects of the legal enterprise but rather their integration. In situations where they appear to conflict with each other, the right solution can only be reached by prudential weighing of the particular virtues of each against the particular virtues of the others. What are trumps depends on what is bid; and sometimes the bid is "no trump." Indeed, all that needs to be subtracted from each of the three major schools of jurisprudence, in order to integrate them, is its assertion of its own supremacy. All that needs to be added is a recognition of their mutual interdependence.

Part Three

THEOLOGICAL, PROPHETIC, AND EDUCATIONAL THEMES

—⊸ 14 ⊸—

LAW AND LOVE*

I would contend that law, understood in a Christian perspective, is a process of creating conditions in which sacrificial love, the kind of love personified by Jesus Christ, can take root in society and grow.

Perhaps some of you will be angry at such a definition of law. You will perhaps reproach me in Jesus' words: "Woe to you lawyers also, for you load men with burdens hard to bear, and you yourselves do not touch the burdens with one of your fingers."[1] Carl Sandburg puts it this way: "'A lawyer,' hiccupped a disbarred member of the bar, 'is a man who gets two other men to take off their clothes and then he runs away with them'."[2]

If we think of the law of which Jesus spoke, we think of the Ten Commandments, the Torah, and also the rules of criminal law, family law, contract, property, procedure, administrative law, and the like, which the priests and the rabbis spun out of those sources, especially in the Talmud. Jesus had the greatest respect for that law. Indeed, he identified it with justice, with mercy, and with good faith. He said that the summary of the law, the gist of it, is love of God and of neighbor. And he berated the Pharisees for abusing it. He said that they singled out the techniques and neglected the essence: "Woe unto you, scribes and Pharisees, hypocrites," he said, "for you

---

* Delivered as the Matriculation Address, Episcopal Theological School, Cambridge, Massashusetts, November 4, 1963. Reprinted in abridged form from *Episcopal Theological School Bulletin* 56 (1964): 11-14.

[1] Luke 11:46 (RSV).

[2] Carl Sandburg, *The People, Yes* (New York, 1936), 69.

tithe mint and dill and cummin, and have neglected the weightier matters of the law, justice and mercy and good faith; these you ought to have done, without neglecting the others."[3] Notice that Jesus here also insists on the necessity of preserving the *less* weighty matters of the law, the techniques, the tithes of mint and dill and cummin.

Some modern theologians have drawn a contrast between law and love which is entirely contrary to Jesus' teaching. They have said that law is abstract, impersonal, objective, deliberate, whereas love is concrete, personal, subjective, spontaneous.[4] But such a notion is a caricature both of love and of law. It makes love sentimental and romantic, and law wooden and sterile. Law, by which I mean society's effort to establish just relations among people, to resolve conflicting interests, to regulate social life, and love, by which I mean the sacrificial sharing of one's whole life with God and with one's fellow men, stand in a complementary relationship to each other. Love needs law to give it structure; law needs love to give it direction and motivation.

Of course there are situations in which love requires that we go beyond the requirements of the law. The law forbids us to steal, or kill, or commit adultery, while love requires us to try to overcome even the desire to do these things. And in a still deeper sense, Christianity denies to the existing body of law the ultimate value, the sacredness, which the Jewish tradition ascribed to it. Thus it may even be necessary to break the law, for the sake of the love which law serves. But to say this is far different from saying that love and law are opposed in some ultimate sense. Indeed, as soon as love extends beyond the most intimate relationships of a few people, it requires procedures and rules to make it work. The hypocrisy of the Pharisees is matched by that of the sentimentalists who have compassion for the poor but are indifferent to legislation which would improve their lot.

The theological fallacy which draws a sharp contrast between law and love is matched by a jurisprudential fallacy which tries to separate law and morals. Certain legal philosophers—indeed, in the 1920s and 1930s they were predominant and in the 1970s and 1980s they reasserted themselves— deny that law has any moral content. They treat law as a fact, an "is," without any dimension of "oughtness." They define law simply as the will of the stronger, or the will of the state, embodied in a system of rules which is held together by its own internal logic and is only indirectly related to the moral or ethical values of the community.

---

[3] Matt. 23:23 (RSV).

[4] See, e.g., Emil Brunner, *Justice and the Social Order*, trans. Mary Hottinger (New York and London, 1945), 21-22.

Legend has it that many years ago a law student asked the professor during a classroom discussion of a case, "But sir, is that just?" The professor replied, "If it is justice you are looking for, you should have gone to the divinity school." Today such a reply would be preposterous—for two reasons: first, the law schools have recognized that it is impossible to speak of legal rules independently of the social purposes for which they exist, and, secondly, many of the divinity schools have changed. Indeed, I could well imagine a student in some divinity schools being told today, "If it is justice you are interested in, you should have gone to law school!"

In the law schools, at least, we have come to understand law not solely in terms of general rules but also in terms of the values which those rules protect. As A.P. d'Entrèves has said, "[l]aw is not only a measure of action. It is a pronouncement on its value."[5] More than that, law is not a set of abstractions to be found in books; it is a set of practices engaged in by people. It is a living social institution, which is just as concrete, subjective, and personal as any other social experience. There is nothing abstract or impersonal about putting a man in jail because he committed a robbery, or directing a school board to integrate the schools, or deciding which of two parents should have custody of a child. Law is not only rules and concepts; law is also, and primarily, a type of relationship among people. Love in the Christian sense is not more excluded from legal relationships than from any other type of human relationships.

Of course law may be *immoral* and much of our law *is* immoral (an example is the law of many of our states requiring hospitals to keep a body alive for years after the soul has gone out from it). And morality may be without love (an example is the morality which permits a person to avoid certain contractual obligations on purely technical grounds). What I am saying is that Christianity requires us both to exert every effort to conform our legal system to morality, and to make both law and morality a vehicle of love.

Let me give, very briefly, three types of examples of how our legal system can foster Christian love:

First, law creates conditions in which the ecumenical church—the community of believers—may carry on its work, and in which secular society may also carry on the work of the church. Thus the United States Constitution provides for freedom of religious worship and religious teaching. The tax laws permit charitable deductions from income and thus encourage financial contributions to churches and to charities generally. School laws make

---

[5] A.P. d'Entrèves, *Natural Law: An Introduction to Legal Philosophy* (New York, 1951), 80.

education compulsory and thus promote literacy and make possible the reading of the Scriptures. Family law prohibits polygamy and thus helps to prevent the oppression of women. A host of similar instances could be given, indeed the whole legal system exists, from a Christian point of view, in order to maintain conditions favorable for the operation of love. Without law, love would be forced to operate in a social chaos.

Secondly, the standards of law reflect a secular morality which I believe is derived from a higher morality, but which, in any event, helps to keep alive that higher morality. The fact that the judge is impartial, that he listens to both sides of a case, that he opens his mind and heart to both plaintiff and defendant, is designed to exclude prejudice, hatred, as a factor in deciding. This in turn suggests, at least, that it is love that requires the elimination of prejudice. The recognition of the binding force of promises in contract law, the punishment of wrongdoing, the compensation for harm caused by negligence, the enforcement of obligations of trust and confidence—these are all directed toward the maintenance of minimum standards of good will in society—not, it is true, the maximum standards of self-sacrifice which Christianity requires of us; yet these minimum standards are important means of keeping alive our belief in the maximum standards.

I can illustrate this by reference to a rule of American law called the "Good Samaritan rule," which states that a man is *not* required to help another whom he finds in distress. It should really be called the "Priest and Levite rule." A person is said to be under no legal duty to come to the aid of another who is lying helpless and in danger by the wayside, or of a child who is drowning, even though a rescue could be effected without any risk to the rescuer. The heartless passerby is guilty of no crime and is not liable civilly.

The rule seems at first to clash with common decency. Yet let us look at it more closely. In the first place, there are many exceptions to it. Of course, if one has negligently placed another in a position of peril then one is liable for not acting to rescue him from that position; the so-called "Good Samaritan rule" is applicable only in situations which have arisen without the fault of the non-rescuer. Beyond that, if the non-rescuer has innocently contributed to the plight of the victim he may have a duty to rescue; for example, one cannot simply run away from an automobile accident in which one is involved, even though the fault is entirely that of other people, and if one owns a business establishment and a customer on the premises is in danger— let us say, a child's hand is caught in a moving escalator—one is liable for not acting with due care to rescue him. Also, where two or more people are engaged in a joint venture, where they enter into a relationship of mutual dependence, each may be under a legal duty to come to the aid of the others.

In modern times the courts are finding such mutual dependence—and hence legal liability—in more and more types of activities. These exceptions cast new light on the rule; indeed, one must reformulate the rule in the light of them. There is a duty to rescue—though not in all cases. The duty, however, like all legal duties, presupposes a right on the part of the person to be rescued. The legal relationship rests on reciprocity of rights and duties.

If a poor man asks for alms, he does not claim them as his right; he invokes the graciousness of his benefactor, and if the benefactor believes that he is legally bound to make the donation then the act loses something of its character as a free gift.

It seems to me to be right that the law does not require heroism or self-sacrifice, for these must come not as the result of legally enforceable claims made upon us by others, but as free gifts. Yet our insistence, in the law, upon the enforcement of reciprocal rights and duties, and our extension of the concept of mutual dependence, suggest, and teach, the higher duty that needs no legal claim as its correlative. It is more blessed to give than to receive; but it may also be blessed to receive, and the reciprocity of giving and receiving helps to teach the blessedness of each.

It is this law, the law of reciprocity of rights and duties, which Christ came not to destroy but to fulfill—by inspiring us to go beyond it. Yet not only Christ but the law itself gives such inspiration.

I have chosen one illustration of how the law, in helping to maintain minimum standards of good will in society, at the same time and by the same token helps to keep alive our belief in the maximum standards imposed by God. In many ways law imposes higher duties upon us than social morality, the existing moral sense of the community, imagines; indeed, it is one of the tasks of law to lead the community to higher moral standards. Under the law of trusts, for example, a trustee owes to the beneficiary of the trust a duty of care higher than that which he would apply to himself. He must love his neighbor, the beneficiary of the trust, *more* than himself. Yet it is not for the community, through law, to play God; at a certain point, law is helpless. This fact, however, should not obscure the importance of law in leading us to that point—and in showing us what is beyond.

Finally, I would speak of the courage, the self-sacrifice, of the lawyer or judge who is responsible for maintaining what I may perhaps now call the middle standards of the law. The conscientious lawyer who is torn between his duty to his client and his duty to the court—for he is both the representative of his client and an officer of the court—has need of great strength of mind and of heart. Whatever judgment one may make as to the legal profession as a whole, it is important that we recognize the devotion of those lawyers who take their responsibilities seriously and who sometimes find themselves in intolerable spiritual dilemmas not of their own making. Similarly, we should sing the heroism of those judges who risk the opprobrium and scorn of their communities by their adherence to law: I am thinking especially of many judges in the South who in the 1950s and 1960s conscientiously applied high legal principles which their local communities rejected.

Thus the study of law cannot be treated by us as a purely "academic" matter. When we approach law as believers we must understand it as part of God's plan of salvation. We know that our mission goes beyond the law, but we also know that by this faith we do not overthrow the law. "By no means; on the contrary, we uphold the law." We uphold it as a means of preparing our hearts and minds to receive faith and to grow in hope and love.

—∽ 15 ∾—

JUDAIC-CHRISTIAN VERSUS
PAGAN SCHOLARSHIP*

T he founders of Harvard University were convinced that the pursuit of scholarly knowledge would lead to the discovery of truth, not merely in the secular sense but also in the Christian sense, that is, truth which discloses the glory of God. They believed that God reveals himself both in nature and in man, and that therefore the study of natural and human phenomena will disclose God's purposes. For over two hundred years the Harvard motto *Veritas* was followed by a reference to the Gospel According to St. John 8:32, "You shall know the truth and the truth will set you free."

In the past century we have moved very far from that vision of the purpose of scholarship. Today the books assigned in the various sciences and humanities, the lectures offered by the faculty, and the class discussion, give little if any recognition that God even exists, much less is glorified. Our intellectual life, our thinking, has been largely divorced from our religious faith.

Faculty, students, and administrators now think of themselves as members not of a religious community but of an academic community, named for the Greek hero Academus. It was in a grove dedicated to Academus—I think

* Reprinted from *Veritas Reconsidered*, September 1986 (Special Edition), 12, 73-74, a publication privately printed for circulation at the alumni celebration of the 350th anniversary of the founding of Harvard College. The chapter combines several talks given at the Harvard University Chapel during the period 1948 to 1984. It is scheduled to be published in more or less its present form in Kelly K. Monroe, ed., *God and the Harvard Experience.*

we may call him the unknown god of our universities—that Plato in about 390 B.C. founded his famous school, dedicated to the pursuit of wisdom.

The academic community stands in sharp contrast with Jewish and Christian communities, which are dedicated to the worship of the *known* God,—the God who, we are told, has confounded wisdom and made it foolish.

"The Lord knoweth the thoughts of the wise, that they are vain." The Lord knoweth the thoughts of the eminent historian Professor X, that they are vain. God has made foolish the writings of the distinguished economics Professor Y. Where is the scribe, Professor A. of the Divinity School? Where is the disputer of the world, Professor B. of the Law School? "Hath not God made foolish their wisdom?"

What is the difference between the wisdom of God and the wisdom of the world?

The wisdom of the world assumes that God's existence is irrelevant to knowledge, and that truth is discoverable by the human mind unaided by the Holy Spirit. Jewish and Christian wisdom, on the other hand, seeks God's guidance, the guidance of the Holy Spirit, in order to discover the relationship between what we know and what God intends for us.

The pagan scholar says, "Facts are facts." He treats nature and society as objects, as things, to be dissected and analyzed by his brain. The Jewish or Christian scholar sees not merely nature and not merely society but God's creation; he sees nature and society as creatures of God bearing witness to their creator. Heaven and earth are his handiwork and declare his glory. They reflect his purposes for mankind. The Jewish or Christian scholar attempts to see this reflection—and not only to see it but to participate in it and be committed to it.

But isn't a fact a fact? Are not the facts which we seek to discover, as natural and social scientists—the facts about the moon, or about history, or about law—the same facts to a believing Jew or a Christian as to a pagan? In one sense, of course, they are. That the sun rose this morning is a fact recognized by Agnostic, Atheist, Polytheist, Hindu, Moslem, Jew, or Christian. But in another sense, that is not so. For a fact is never seen in isolation from other facts. The phenomena of space and time may be seen from many different perspectives. As a matter of fact, the sun, of course, did not rise; the earth turned.

A Judaic-Christian perspective reveals certain facts that otherwise cannot be known. It reveals that human history is part of God's plan of the universe, and that every *fact* of the universe is an *event* in the life of God. The believing Jewish or Christian scholar strives to find God's purposes, God himself, in the subject of his scholarship. He must therefore be a prophet, and more than that, an apostle.

Pagan scholarship assumes that truth is discoverable by human reason alone. Judaic-Christian scholarship denies that that is so. God is the Lord of our minds as much as he is the Lord of our hearts. Nothing is discovered without his help. I believe that if we open our minds to the inspiration of the Holy Spirit and pray for his guidance in intellectual matters, we shall discover new truth which will astound those who believe that God's existence is irrelevant to scholarship.

It is customary to treat the conflict between science and religion as a dead issue—and it is, in the old sense. We are no longer troubled by the claim that science disproves religious truth. But there is a far more serious conflict between science and religion which *should* trouble us: that is the conflict between the secularism of modern scientific thought, especially in the social sciences, and the Judaic-Christian insight that man is more than a natural phenomenon, more even than an observer of natural phenomena, that man is rather a creature of God who partakes also of God's creative powers. Man—including scholars—is a creature who is also a creator.

There is need among believing Jews and Christians to cultivate Christian methods of thinking about life—Jewish and Christian modes of analysis of society, of history, of economic life, of the human psyche. The modes of analysis which dominate our intellectual life today are essentially pagan modes of analysis. They are inherently skeptical modes of analysis, rather than faithful modes of analysis. They stress causation rather than creation. They stress the role of forces rather than the role of spirit. They stress facts rather than acts. They look only at the temporal things which are seen and not at the eternal things which are unseen. They deny the reality of God's self-revelation in the intellectual process itself. Underlying these pagan modes of analysis is the tendency of the analyst—the social scientist in particular—to arrogate to himself a power to treat men as objects, a tendency to "play God" with his intellectual systems. Pride of intellect is the besetting sin of the modern university, whether it take the form of the professor's skepticism or the student's idle curiosity.

Thus knowledge, intellectual understanding, is, from a Judaic-Christian standpoint, intimately connected with faith, with hope, and with love. There is a faithful, a hopeful, and a loving mode of scholarship which it is the task of Jewish and Christian scholars to cultivate. Though such a mode of scholarship may be classified as "unscientific" by the unbeliever, it will come much nearer the truth about human nature and social life. For the truth is that God does not call us to be merely observers of life; rather he calls all of us—even the scholars—in all that we do—to participate with him in the process of spiritual death and rebirth which is the fundamental religious experience.

──── ᷗ 16 ᷙ ────

LAW AND HISTORY AFTER
THE WORLD WARS*

E ugen Rosenstock-Huessy was a bitter critic both of contemporary academic scholarship and of the contemporary university. Yet he encouraged me—and some others—to enter academic life. He was also a bitter critic of law, which, like Martin Luther, he considered to be opposed to grace. Law he said, was concerned with the mundane, the repetitive, the fixed and stable aspects of life, not with creativity, not with spontaneity, not with inspired speech and inspired actions that defy routine and regularity. Yet he encouraged me to become a legal scholar. And he himself was trained as a legal scholar and was a professor of law both before and after the first World War. He fought legalism but he believed strongly in both order and justice. And although he fought the academy, he lived and worked in the academy. He was incredibly learned—he read more widely and more deeply, and he knew more, than any other person I have ever known; he believed in learning, and his writings cannot be easily grasped by readers who are not steeped in learning. He understood that if a scholar is not a teacher, his scholarship will be sterile; but he also understood that if a teacher is not a scholar, his teaching will be superficial.

---

* Opening Address at a Conference Marking the Hundredth Birthday of Eugen Rosenstock-Huessy (1888-1973), Hanover, New Hampshire, August 15, 1988. Reprinted with some changes from *Jahrbuch der Eugen Rosenstock-Huessy Gesellschaft* 3 (1990): 46-59.

Rosenstock-Huessy would, of course, be gratified, if he were here, that we have assembled to honor his life and his work. But he would excoriate us bitterly if he thought we were simply analyzing and summarizing and system-atizing what he said and wrote. He expected his listeners, his followers, his readers, to respond to him in their own language, with their own ideas—not merely to repeat or summarize his language and his ideas. He did not expound a finished system of thought, with its own definitions, its own methodology. Instead, he engaged the listener, or the reader, and asked for a creative response. He spoke with authority, and not as the scribes. He reminded me of Coleridge's Ancient Mariner and I sometimes thought of the lines: "By thy long grey beard and glittering eye, now wherefore stopp'st thou me?"

Paul Tillich said of Rosenstock-Huessy, "When he speaks it's like light-ning." That means he expected his words to be followed by thunder—and more lightning. The proof of the validity of his prophetic scholarship must rest first and foremost on its power to inspire others to respond with their own prophetic scholarship.

Let me respond, then, to the Rosenstockian challenge that we draw from our collective experience, from history, which he defined as "group memory," lessons, first, concerning history itself, that is, the times in which we live, past and future, and second, concerning the social structures of the historical group, the historical community, its processes of ordering and of doing justice, which I call law.

By "the times in which we live" I mean—and here I am a complete Rosenstockian—the new era of human history introduced by the two World Wars. In his lifetime he had two different visions of that history. One was born in the trenches of Verdun: it was a vision of European history in terms of a series of six Great Revolutions, from the eleventh to the twentieth cen-turies, culminating in the World War, and it led him to seek a revitalization of the nations of Europe, a regeneration of Europe itself. In the years before Hitler he remained a good German and a good European, committed to a vision of national solutions within Europe and of cooperation among the nations of Europe, especially in response to the challenges posed by America and Russia. As late as 1938 he hoped for a partnership of the European nations in developing Africa as a means of reducing the threat of another European War.

His second great vision of history was born in the Second World War, which he had sought for two decades to prevent and which as late as 1938 he thought would not—and perhaps could not—happen. His second vision, about which he wrote at the close of the Second World War, was a vision of what he called "Planetary Man." He saw in the existence, for the first time in human history, of a world-wide economy a foundation for the emergence of a global society. Yet he understood that the mere economic interdependence of all countries on the planet earth is not a sufficient basis for overcoming the deep hostilities among the multiple political and cultural creeds and loyalties. Ultimately, he believed, it is only speech itself, language, that can overcome those hostilities and can bring people into relationships of community. By "speech" and "language"—and we must remember that in German the two words are one, *Sprache*—he meant, of course, not any speech or language but language spoken in good faith, genuine speech, the kind of language that reaches out to others and responds to others. The unity of mankind, he wrote, is evoked by our belief in language. What he meant was the belief in the power of speech to draw people together into a common future. He believed that by listening and responding to each other, with the right words, all mankind could be brought eventually into community.

Others at this Conference will speak more fully about Rosenstock-Huessy's ideas concerning both language and history. I only want now to stress that I share his conception of the Christian era as one in which mankind consciously strives toward unity and universality. When St. Paul declared that God made of one blood all the nations of the earth, neither he nor the readers of his epistle had any knowledge of all the nations of the earth or indeed any knowledge of the geography of the earth beyond the Roman Empire and perhaps India. Yet in the first millennium of the Christian era the numerous pagan tribes of Eastern and Western Europe were converted to a belief in one God; and during the second millennium of the Christian era the Western Europeans created a political-legal order which was founded on a belief in one world of nature and which ultimately, through religious and military and economic colonization, and above all through science and technology, brought that one world of nature to all parts of the globe. The task of the third millennium of the Christian era, Rosenstock-Huessy taught us, is to create one human society. "Church, State, and Society," he wrote, "are the three Gestalts of the [three millennia of the] Christian era."

But the task of realizing the third millennium, the millennium of Planetary Man and of what he sometimes called "the Great Society," is not just a European or a "Western" task. It is primarily a task which is shared by all the cultures, all the creeds, all the political systems into which our planet earth is divided. Rosenstock-Huessy had no program for accomplishing this. He did not address, so far as I know, the practical political side of it. He did write, however, that in the planetary age that we are now entering, different "religions, races, and countries live in a single, common time-space and borrow traits from each other: Islam, India, China, Eastern and Western Churches."

Here I would like to draw on another, closely related, main theme of Rosenstockian historiography, namely, the transition from an age dominated by scientific rationalism and objective quantification, appropriate to the conquest of nature in all its forms, appropriate to the measurement and control of the manifold spaces in which we live, to a new age which will be dominated by social thought rather than by natural-scientific thought. This, of course, is the theme to which the motto of this Conference refers: *Respondeo etsi mutabor*, or, as Rosenstock-Huessy translated it "I respond though I have to change." Not merely "will change" but "have to change."

I shall return to the relationship of this motto to "law and history after the World Wars," but I cannot refrain from saying something first about the motto itself. It was intended to supersede Anselm's *credo ut intelligam* ("I believe and so I may understand") of the late eleventh century, and Descartes' *cogito ergo sum* ("I think therefore I am") of the early seventeenth century. The first formula dealt with the tension between faith and reason. Anselm said, "Because I have faith in God, I am able to know truth—and especially truth about God—with my intellect." This formula distinguished understanding from believing. It led Anselm to his famous proof, by reason alone, independently of faith, independently of revelation, that God exists and that he was incarnate in Christ. Descartes could accept Anselm's postulate that *theological* truths are capable of rational proof; the problem that tormented him was how to prove the *secondary* truths of physical existence, the truths of matter and motion. His formula was designed to resolve the tension between reason, on the one hand, and faith not in God but in nature, on the other, including faith in the natural fact of one's own existence. Thus Descartes separated the subjective thinker from the objective thing which he thought *about*. His formula stated that doubt, "cogitation," which he considered to be the necessary precondition of all observation and calculation of natural phenomena, could yield objective truth concerning natural phenomena. Starting from absolute skepticism, including doubt about his own existence, Descartes showed by his formula that such doubt in fact proved his own existence, since if he did not exist he could not doubt. And so while Anselm said "I believe and therefore I am able to understand," Descartes said, "I doubt and therefore I know that I exist." In the same work in which he uttered his famous formula, Descartes laid it down that by skeptical reasoning, and especially by mathematical reasoning, all aspects of human observation and human experience could be measured and explained; in other words, that all existence can be translated into numerical data.

Rosenstock-Huessy prophesied a third millennium in which not the intellectual understanding of Anselm, which presupposed faith, and not the mathematical measurement of Descartes, which presupposed doubt, must become
the key to truth but, instead, human interaction, mutual responsiveness,
especially through speaking and listening. Rosenstock-Huessy sought a
formula which would resolve not the tension between objective faith and
subjective reason in a world of spirit, a world of minds, or between objective
reality and subjective knowledge in a world of nature, a world of spaces, but
rather the tension between thou and me and the tension between past and
future in a social world, a world of times. He substituted, I would say, a *social*
axiom for an *intellectual* or *scientific* axiom. He substituted *social* truth for
intellectual or *scientific* truth. In the new age of global society, truth, he said,
must be socially represented. Indeed, it is now widely accepted that science
itself is a kind of discourse among scientists in which each seeks to teach and
learn, persuade and be persuaded, and the community of scholars sets the
rules of the discourse and decides who must change. Thus "I respond" means
"I respond to others" and "I respond to the challenge of the times." "Although
I shall have to change" means "although I may have to sacrifice my economic
security, my social position, my political success, my prestige, my loyalties, or
even, most difficult of all, my previous ideas." (I think of William James's
poignant statement, "There is no pain like the pain of a new idea.")

Incidentally, much confusion can be avoided if we recognize that Rosenstock-Huessy did not deny the validity of Anselm's belief that faith in God is a
necessary precondition of theological science and Descartes' belief that intellectual doubt is a necessary precondition of the natural sciences. The mistake,
he said, is to apply either the method of theology or the method of natural
science to society. *Social* truth cannot be achieved by any analysis which
separates the truth-seeker from the society of which he is an integral part.
Every scholarly analysis of society is a self-analysis. Every historical narrative
is autobiography. "I respond—I change" includes but goes beyond Anselm's
"I believe—I understand" and Descartes' "I think—I am." It includes but goes
beyond the separation and reconciliation of faith and reason as well as the
separation and reconciliation of existence and knowledge.

A genuine response represents a willingness to change. And change
means future. As Rosenstock-Huessy wrote, "There is no future except that
future which is able to make a man give up his present benefits." Future is
"that for which it is right to sacrifice the present." Sacrifice was a key word
for Rosenstock-Huessy. He complained bitterly that, as he put it, "[t]he word
'sacrifice' has been tabooed. It has been eliminated from thought and teaching
and public discussion." For Rosenstock-Huessy, "change" meant death and

resurrection. Indeed, when I was at Dartmouth I heard him give an earlier and even more dramatic version of the saying: *Respondeo etsi morior*—"I respond although I must die."

Now what has that to do with law and history after the World Wars? Everything!

To speak first of history, it is now clear as a factual matter that Planetary Man has become a reality in the twentieth century. But the crucial question remains, What kind of Man is he? Or perhaps I should say, What kind of Person is she?

He—she—is surely an economic person. The economies of all countries of the world have already begun to form a single market. Not only transfer of goods but also transfer of capital and even transfer of labor—transfer of persons—have increasingly transcended national boundaries. There is a world system of transportation, finance, and communications.

Not only the economy but also science and technology, literature and the arts, tourism, sports, and, above all, news—are now tending increasingly to be supranational and world-wide in character. People in all parts of the globe are in contact with each other. If an industrial plant explodes in Bhopal it will be on the T.V. screens the same day—or the next day—in Baghdad, in Belgrade, in Boston, in Bogota, in Beijing.

A world system has come into existence. It is, however, chiefly a technological system. Its chief symbol is the computer, which embodies the power, by mathematical quantification, to store and transmit infinite amounts of information. At its worst, the world system is represented by the capacity of the computer to digitalize all human experience.

Planetary Man is torn by the tension between the Cartesian presuppositions of our technology and what I would call the Rosenstockian presuppositions of true community. The technological multiplication of interactions trivializes them. Lasting personal relations are crowded out. Time is reduced to instantaneous reactions. This leads to isolation, to anomie, to dehumanization.

In contrast to technology, science itself, that is, scientific theory, has finally overcome the Cartesian postulates which dominated it for three centuries. Pure science, at least since Heisenberg and Einstein and Goedel, has surpassed Cartesian rationalism, with its subject-object dualism. In addition, contemporary philosophy has inclined more and more to recognize the power of speech to shape thought. Indeed, although Rosenstock-Huessy's writings have been largely ignored, his basic insights into the fallacy of applying the methods of mathematics and the natural sciences to the social sciences and humanities are today widely shared, as are many of his basic insights into the nature of language. Nevertheless, the *practice* of the social sciences and humanities, in contrast to the best of their *theories*, remains Cartesian. The practice of economics has become increasingly mathematical in its techniques, although writers about economics recognize that in actuality the economy does not and cannot operate according to the mathematical constructs which the economists use. Similarly in sociology and political science, while the best theoreticians—those who write *about* these subjects—attack the concept of value-free scholarship, the majority of practitioners, those who *do* the detailed research, continue to present their analysis in value-free terms.

Likewise in historiography, the writers *about* history are increasingly Rosenstockian in their emphasis on the deficiencies of so-called scientific history, or realist history, and in their awareness of the importance of passions and of traditions in shaping the larger patterns of change. But the writers *of* history, that is, the writers of Ph.D. dissertations and of history textbooks and of authoritative monographs, remain Cartesian in their skeptical analysis of historical detail and their mechanical explanations of historical development.

The study of the emergence of a world system has now become a special sociological discipline. However, because—once again—of Cartesian presuppositions, the sociologists engaged in this discipline claim that the social relations of the societies that participate in the world system are dominated by intense nationalism. They portray nationalist emotions and loyalties as the motive force in an essentially mechanical world order.

What is not yet observed by the world-system sociologists is the movement toward integration of beliefs within the world system, the interaction and mutual influence of the different world religions, and the global cultural and political context in which the different conflicting orientations and values co-exist, and not only co-exist but also interact, and respond to each other, and change.

In law as well, the reality of new global developments transcends the general awareness of the scholars and also of the general public. The emerging world community is developing new legal institutions and new legal processes, although this root fact has not sufficiently penetrated our consciousness. I have in mind not only public international law as it is traditionally defined, that is, the law governing relations among national states, and not only United Nations law, that is, the law governing international organizations, but also the enormous body of contractual and customary legal norms that govern relations not among states, as such, but among persons and enterprises engaged in a myriad of economic and cultural activities that cross national boundaries. Despite the terrible ethnic and territorial conflicts that divide mankind, we are experiencing for the first time an emerging law of an emerging world community.

Peace, as Rosenstock-Huessy wrote, is the one word that commands universal understanding and universal respect, even in—especially in—times of war. Peace has two dimensions: an inner and an outer. It means both social peace, peace within the group, including racial peace and peace between the sexes, and also political peace, external peace between and among groups that are in an adversarial relationship with each other. In the world society that has emerged after the World Wars, these two types of peace, the inner and the outer, are inseparable from each other.

But there are also, in Rosenstockian terms, two other dimensions to peace: a past dimension and a future dimension. The world peace which we are now struggling to create must build on the experience of the past. And here I think the example of the development of customary international law over a period of centuries, especially at the level of mutually beneficial economic relations among economic entities whose activities transcend national boundaries, is of crucial importance. Living, as we now do, in the early stages of the formation of a world law, we must rely heavily on the emergence of transnational communities which will gradually, through both tacit and explicit agreements, develop their own institutional structures and processes. Only in that way will we be able to lay a foundation for solving the problems that threaten our unity, including such crucial problems as that of the impending destruction of the environment.

Law must be understood as language, as speech. Unfortunately, it is still widely understood in terms of rule formalism, on one hand, and political power on the other. And here I must take issue with the neo-Lutheran emphasis on the sharp separation of Law and Gospel, law and grace, law and creativity, which led in nineteenth-century Germany to extreme legal conceptualism and to the positivist reduction of law to a system of rules enacted by the state.

Rules of law are, to be sure, general by nature, and therefore do not meet the unique characteristics of individual persons and individual situations. Also, when they are codified their language and their relationship to each other may be fixed. But rules of law are only one aspect of law. The rules are intended to be applied, and in their application the unique circumstances are presented by opposing parties to an impartial tribunal. Here creativity and inspiration enter in. Here law is spoken—with passion, albeit controlled passion. Immanuel Kant once wrote, "There is no rule for applying a rule."

And it is to law in application, law in action, and not merely law in books, that Jesus referred when he charged the lawyers, saying "Woe unto you, for you tithe mint and anise and cummin and neglect the weightier matters of the law, which are justice, and mercy, and good faith. These you should do without neglecting the others." In other words, the rules, the fine print, the techniques, are necessary, but the heart of them is in their just and merciful and honest application.

When Jesus spoke of the weightier matters of the law, he was referring primarily, of course, to the Ten Commandments, which at another time he summarized (quoting two passages from Leviticus and Deuteronomy) as "Love the Lord your God" and "love your neighbor as yourself." If we are to take seriously the role of law in the gradual development of a world society it is important to recognize that the last six of the Ten Commandments reflect fundamental legal principles that are embodied in the legal systems of all peoples. Respect for parental authority, prohibition of murder, prohibition of incest and other sexual taboos, prohibition of stealing, prohibition of perjury, and respect for property rights of others—these constitute one basis of a common law of mankind, applicable among all peoples, including those who do not accept Judaic-Christian monotheism.

Morality alone, however, or what the philosophers call natural law, will not save us. Politics is also necessary, and politics involves relations not only of reason and equity but also of will and power. A common law of mankind requires not only natural law but also positive law, political law. But in the political realm mankind is torn by raging conflicts.

There is, however, a third element, in addition to morality and politics, in the development of law, and that is, as I have stressed in this talk, the element of history, of group memory. Our collective universal memory of the experience of the two World Wars is the historical foundation upon which the moral and political elements of the emerging law of mankind are being built. It is, I believe, that historical experience, which ended an entire era, that enables us to speak—however cautiously—of the beginning of a new era of world law and world peace.

17

THE CRISIS OF LEGAL EDUCATION
IN AMERICA*

A dedication such as this is an historic occasion, in a double sense of the word "historic." It looks both to the future and to the past. As teachers and students, officers, alumni, and friends of Boston College Law School, you are here partly to celebrate a renewal of your own community, your own common purposes. Even an outsider can sense the pride and joy of this occasion, when a community comes together and, in the name of dedicating a building, re-dedicates itself.

Such a re-dedication looks not only to the future but also to the past. Someone has said that a historian is a prophet in reverse. By the same token, a prophet is a historian in reverse: he is concerned with the historical significance of the new age that he proclaims. In reading the signs of the times, he divides the future from the past and thereby helps to orient us toward both.

And so those who wish to dedicate an important new building give it a name, and the choice of that name may tell something about the direction, from past to future, that the community is taking.

I regret very much that I did not have the privilege to know James Warren Smith personally. I know that he was a beloved and a gifted teacher. I know also that he was a person of great public spirit who made many

* Reprinted from *Boston College Law Review* 26 (1985): 347-352. Delivered as the Address at the Dedication of the James Warren Smith Memorial Wing of Stuart Hall, Boston College Law School, April 28, 1984.

contributions to the Commonwealth and to its legal system. He was devoted to the law—both the law in action and the law as a system of thought. And finally, he was a deeply religious person whose professional life and work, including his teaching, were strongly motivated by his religious faith.

James Warren Smith serves as a source of inspiration, not only in a general sense, but more specifically as a source of strength in meeting the critical problems that have confronted legal education in the United States for the past forty years, and have now brought it, in my view, to a real crisis.

When I speak of a crisis of legal education in America, I do not mean that law students are not studying hard; nor do I mean that law teachers are less diligent or less able than they ought to be or than they were. So far as I can judge, the law students who graduate in 1984 will not be noticeably less skillful or knowledgeable in the practice of law than their predecessors.

Nor am I referring to the criticism that law students today are not receiving sufficient training in how to serve the public interest. It may be true, as President Bok of Harvard University has written, that we need more educational programs that would prepare prospective practitioners and legislators to expand the delivery of legal services to the poor, to develop new, less expensive and less acrimonious methods of dispute resolution, and to explore new ways to finance efforts to raise industrial productivity and combat pollution, crime, poverty, and other social ills. Nevertheless, our inadequacies in these respects hardly constitute a genuine crisis of American legal *education*, since ultimately the law schools can only play a relatively small part in the achievement of needed reforms in these areas.

The crisis of which I speak is a crisis of attitudes toward law and a crisis of legal thought. Law teachers and law students of 1984 are more one-sided, and more mistaken, in their view of the nature of law than were their predecessors in any other period of American history.

We have been overwhelmed by the belief that law is politics—and politics in a rather narrow sense: not in the sense that Aristotle meant when he said law is politics, but more in the sense that Max Weber and V.I. Lenin meant when they said that law is politics, namely, domination. It is widely accepted in our law schools that law is essentially something that is made by political authorities, including legislators, judges, and administrators, to effectuate their policies; that law is essentially a means of social engineering; that law is essentially a pragmatic device, an instrument, used by those in power to accomplish their will. Of course law *is* all that. But it is not *solely* that—it is not *essentially* that. What is omitted from the prevailing view is a belief that law is rooted in something bigger than the people who hand it down—that law is rooted in history and in the moral order of the universe.

Of course, law is politics. But law is also morality. And law is also history. Law is not only something that is *made* by those who are in power; law is also something that is *given*. The legislators and judges are not only its masters. They are also its creatures.

In American law schools today, reference is rarely made to the sources of our legal tradition in the religious convictions of our ancestors, both Jewish and Christian. It is simply not mentioned that, historically, all the legal systems of the West emerged in response to a belief in the lawful character of the universe and in the fundamental purpose of law to guide men and women to salvation. The king, said Bracton in the early thirteenth century, is under the law, and both are under God. At about the same time, in the first lawbook ever written in the German language, the *Sachsenspiegel*, it was said, "God is himself law, and therefore law is dear to Him." Without the fear of purgatory and the hope of the last judgment, the Western legal tradition would not have come into being.

Admittedly these historical truths, which are not taught today, were also not generally taught in American law schools one hundred or one hundred and fifty years ago. But then they were taught in the homes and in the churches. They were taken for granted. They were part of the public philosophy. Indeed, throughout the nineteenth and into the first decades of the twentieth century American lawyers learned their law chiefly from Blackstone, who wrote that "[T]he law of nature . . . dictated by God himself . . . is binding . . . in all countries and at all times; no human laws are of any validity if contrary to this; and such of them as are valid derive all force and all their authority, mediately or immediately, from this original."

Only in the past two generations, in my lifetime, has the public philosophy of America shifted radically from a religious to a secular theory of law, from a moral to a political or instrumental theory, and from a historical to a pragmatic theory. Law is now generally considered to be simply a device for accomplishing specific political, economic, and social objectives. The tasks of law are thought to be finite, material, and impersonal—to get things done, to make people act in certain ways. Rarely does one hear it said that law is a reflection of an objective justice or of the ultimate meaning or purpose of life. Usually it is thought to reflect at best the community sense of what is expedient; and more commonly it is thought to express the more or less arbitrary will of the lawmaker.

The shift in public philosophy has changed the context in which law is taught. Even when we teach the same cases, the same rules, the same theories, that were taught sixty or a hundred years ago, they have a different meaning. For example, Christopher Columbus Langdell, who in the 1870s collected for the first time cases on contracts, combining the actions of debt, assumpsit, and various other forms of action and developing a set of principles of general contract law, taught his students that his science of law had nothing to do with justice. If it was justice they were interested in, one of his followers said, they should go to the Divinity School! But Langdell—or at least his students—did believe in justice, including divine justice; he simply believed also that it had nothing to do with contracts. Now it is very different: today if a professor says that contract law has nothing do with justice, neither he nor his students are apt to have any idea of what justice is or whether it exists.

But the changes go much deeper. We still use cases, but since there is not a belief in the ongoing historical development of law over generations and centuries, the doctrine of precedent has grown weaker and weaker, and the law that a case stands for no longer seems to have objectivity. It is taught by some that any case can be decided any way—that law is, basically, an argumentative technique. The judge, it is thought, decides on the basis of his political, economic, or psychological prejudices; legal reasons are merely rationalizations. This used to be called "legal realism." Later it was developed into "policy science." In more sophisticated forms it prevails widely in contemporary American legal education, despite some important qualifications introduced by those who stress inherent limitations imposed by the various aspects of what is called "the legal process."

It is interesting, in this connection, to go back over the introductory sections of law school catalogues through the past eighty-five years. The Harvard Law School catalogue of 1900 says that "the design of this school is to afford such a training in the fundamental principles of English and American law as will constitute the best preparation for the practice of the profession in any place where that system of law prevails." This formula, which was repeated annually in subsequent catalogues, was a reference to the fundamental principles of English and American law as they had developed over many centuries. Legal history provided the transcendent quality by which justice was to be found. The 1930 catalogue—Roscoe Pound was dean—is even more explicit: "The school," it states, "seeks as its primary purpose to prepare for the practice of the legal profession wherever the Common Law prevails. It seeks to train lawyers in the spirit of the common legal heritage of the English-speaking people." More recently, however, this sentence has been omitted and instead in the 1970s and until 1982 we have the following: "The school tries to prepare its graduates to deal with legal problems as they arise wherever the common law prevails." What has happened to the fundamental principles? What has happened to the spirit of the common legal heritage?

Finally, the phrase "Common Law" lost its initial caps, and in the 1983-84 catalogue it disappeared altogether.

"No law school," said the Harvard Law School catalogue of 1970, "can today teach with certainty the law which will be practiced by its graduates throughout their professional lives. The school does seek to provide its students with a solid base of knowledge, analytical skills, and insight which will enable them to perform effectively as laws and legal institutions continue to change around them." There you have the contemporary crisis in American legal education. We are unable to identify a common purpose other than training in the kind of "knowledge, analytical skills, and insight" that are needed to "perform effectively" as lawyers. One who has learned to "perform like a lawyer" will be able, we suppose, to analyze any legal problem that may arise in a world in flux, a world in which law is always a means to other ends, a world in which the concepts of an objective moral law and an ongoing tradition no longer carry great weight.

The triumph of the positivist theory of law—that law is the will of the lawmaker—and the decline of rival theories—the moral theory that law is reason and conscience, and the historical theory that law is an ongoing tradition in which *both* politics *and* morality play important parts—have contributed to the bewilderment of legal education. Skepticism and relativism are widespread. Only a few are sure what has to be taught. We go on using cases as the primary material of instruction, but we hardly even teach the doctrine of precedent. We go on offering basic courses in contracts and torts in the first year, but many teachers of these subjects spend a good deal of time proving that there really is no such thing as a "law of contracts" or a "law of torts."

Meanwhile, after taking "basic" courses in the old "common law" (now in lower case) during the first year, the student is confronted with an enormous array of choices. To give an idea of the nature of change, let me say that when I first came onto the Harvard Law School faculty 36 years ago, *all* courses in the first and second year were required, and at least *one* course in the third year was required. In those days there was something called "law" and people knew what it was! Today the 1983-84 Harvard Law School catalogue lists over 240 different courses and seminars—that is, courses and seminars in 240 different legal subjects! We have moved beyond the legal pragmatism of Justice Holmes, who said that law is a prediction of what courts will do, to the ultimate in legal pragmatism, that law is a prediction of what *lawyers* will do. Someone has said of pragmatism that it is fine in theory but it doesn't work in practice.

Concentration on the instrumental character of law—law as a means, whether a means of social control in the broad sense, or a means of effectuating specific policies, or a means of maintaining power, or whatever, but always as a means, never as an end in itself—has contributed, I believe, to the fragmentation of the law school curriculum. If law is essentially an instrument of politics, there is very little in society to which it is alien, and by the same token there is very little in law that is unique or required. Its nature is shaped by the other ends which it serves. It tends to become, therefore, an infinite series of practical solutions to social problems.

Under these circumstances, it should not be surprising that in recent years a group of law professors has emerged that is demanding a thorough and open "politicization" of law teaching. These critics ask the law schools to devote themselves, on the one hand, to exposing the fundamentally exploitative—and also the inherently self-contradictory—character of all law, and, on the other hand, to transforming our existing legal system into an instrument of rapid social change in the direction of an egalitarian society. Since for them "law is politics"—in the Weberian or Leninist sense—some of them advocate the open use of militant political tactics in order to "seize power" (as they put it) within the law school community. Thus the dominant pragmatist, instrumental, and utilitarian theory of law has paved the way for the emergence of a band of revolutionaries who combine nihilism with utopianism.

It would be a mistake, however, to suppose that the crisis of American legal education consists of this radical attack upon the liberal establishment. The heart of the crisis, in my view, is not in the radical attack but in the liberalism that is being attacked. For two generations liberalism has taught that law is essentially a pragmatic instrument of public policy. The legal process as a whole has been reduced by this to what in reality is only one of its major aspects. Now the pragmatists are being hoist, so to speak, by their own petard.

Obviously, the problems that are being confronted in American legal education today, including the crisis of legal thought, are part of a much larger movement of history. The traditional Western beliefs in the structural integrity of law, its ongoingness, its religious roots, its transcendent qualities, are disappearing not only from the minds of law teachers and law students but also from the consciousness of the vast majority of citizens, the people as a whole; and more than that, they are disappearing from the law itself. The law itself is becoming more fragmented, more subjective, geared more to expediency and less to morality, concerned more with immediate consequences and less with consistency or continuity. The historical soil of the Western legal tradition is being washed away in the twentieth century, and the tradition itself is threatened with collapse.

In part, the crisis of legal education is due to the radical centralization and bureaucratization of economic life, of which socialism in one form or another is an aspect or a consequence. Whole new branches of public law have emerged in areas such as taxation, securities regulation, administrative law of a dozen different kinds. Also the radical changes that have taken place in constitutional law during the past thirty years have had enormous repercussions throughout the law. The center of gravity of the legal system has shifted, and the background of legal ideas, the very style of legal thinking, which was characteristic of previous centuries seems to be increasingly irrelevant. We have moved from an individualistic to a collectivistic age.

If what we are experiencing in the twentieth century—in many countries—were, indeed, only an economic and a technological revolution, or even only a political revolution, we should be able to adapt our legal institutions and our system of legal education to meet the new demands placed upon them, as we have done in revolutionary situations in the past. After the American and French Revolutions of 200 years ago, after the English Revolution of 350 years ago, after the Lutheran and Calvinist Reformations of the early sixteenth century, after the Papal Revolution (the Gregorian Reformation) of the late eleventh and early twelfth centuries, the law eventually caught up with the changes and legal science, legal education, adapted itself to them. Our difficulty, however, is greater than in the past. Today we are threatened by a deep cynicism about the law, which has penetrated all classes of the population. And it is this threat that makes the crisis of legal education so important—and so acute.

The story is told of a man who was hanging on the limb of a tree extending over a canyon. He could not raise himself onto the limb and gradually his grip grew weaker and he looked up to the heavens and called, "If there is anyone up there, please help, help!" A voice came booming out over the canyon, "I am here. I can save you if you have faith." "Yes, yes, I have faith. I will do anything," shouted the man. "If you have faith you will let go of the branch," said the voice. The man looked out over the canyon and then turned again to the heavens and shouted, "Is there anyone *else* up there?"

It may be impossible to restore the ancient Judaic and Christian foundations of our legal tradition. But it is important, first, to recognize that it is the disappearance of those religious foundations that gives power to the convictions of the utopian nihilists—power possibly to overcome the superficial utilitarianism of the liberal establishment. The skeptics, especially, should feel some nostalgia for a time when justice seemed sure and history had meaning. Let them, at least, cry out, "Is there anyone *else* up there?"

Second, we must restore the integrity of our jurisprudential heritage. We must re-combine the separate strands of legal thought that were once wound together: positivism, natural-law theory, and historical jurisprudence. It is a recognition of the historical dimension of law, in my opinion, above all, that we must re-capture in order to restore the creative tensions between politics and morals. We shall not achieve social justice without a strong sense of legality, and we shall not recover a strong sense of legality without an integrative jurisprudence that finds the sources of our law not only in politics but also in history, in human nature, and in the universe itself.

18

IS THERE SUCH A THING—CAN THERE BE SUCH A THING—AS A CHRISTIAN LAW SCHOOL?*

$\mathbb{T}$ here is, of course, at a celebration of this kind, a strong temptation to indulge in the rhetoric of flattery and congratulation. I well remember comparable celebrations at other law schools, when each speaker attempted to surpass the others in paying tribute to the giants of the past who had succeeded in bringing the institution to the glories of the present. Notre Dame, however, as is apparent from the reports to which I have been asked to respond, is not just another law school. Its religious sponsorship and, more particularly, its Christian mission make it necessary, in evaluating its success, to speak with one's whole heart and one's whole mind. That, for me, means that I must speak from a Christian standpoint—indeed, I may honestly say, from a Judaic-Christian standpoint, since I am a Jew, steeped from my early childhood in the Jewish tradition, who at the age of 21 became a follower of Jesus Christ and who has since that time continually and repeatedly attempted to follow him, though usually without success. Such a confession of standpoint would be considered out of place at most other law schools, where public disclosure of one's religious beliefs is taboo; here, however, it seems to me, it is not only appropriate but is even required.

---

* Delivered at a symposium celebrating the sesquicentennial of Notre Dame Law School, September 27, 1991. The author gratefully acknowledges the collaboration of Charles J. Reid, Jr. in the preparation of this talk.

The papers of our principal speakers confirm the view that in the past Notre Dame Law School has attempted to fulfill its special mission in two principal ways. First, it has undertaken to defend a Roman Catholic natural-law theory against the positivist jurisprudence that has prevailed in American legal education generally. Second, it has given persons of Irish-American, Italian-American, Hispanic-American, and other ethnic backgrounds, chiefly Roman Catholic in faith, increased opportunity to become lawyers and to compete with the Anglo-American Protestant elite which at one time dominated the American legal profession and whose traditions are still a decisive element in it.

It must be noted that in fulfilling this twofold mission, Notre Dame Law School has sought to meet—and, indeed, *has* met—the high professional and academic standards that are applicable to other American law schools. Speaking generally, and allowing for exceptions, I have no doubt that a student who goes to Notre Dame Law School can get as good a legal education as he could get at virtually any other law school in the country.

This is admirable. But is it enough? Is it enough for a Roman Catholic law school to be a very good Roman Catholic law school?

My answer to this question starts from my understanding of the word "Catholic." The principal papers use the terms "Catholic" and "Roman Catholic" interchangeably; indeed, there is a marked tendency to omit the word "Roman," while preserving the connotation. Yet other branches of Christianity, namely, the Anglican and the Orthodox Churches, are also Catholic—with a capital "C". Moreover, in a broader sense all Christians, including Protestants, who adhere to the Nicene Creed or the Apostles' Creed confess a belief in the holy catholic church. As a member of the Episcopal Church, which is in the Anglican tradition, I would identify catholicity—universality—with Christianity itself. Nor do I understand it to be an article of the Roman Catholic faith to deny the Christianity, and in that broader sense the catholicity, of other denominations of the Christian church. On the contrary, it is, I believe, an accepted doctrine of Roman Catholicism, articulated by the Second Vatican Council, that in the Church of Christ the Roman Catholic church is "linked" with all baptized Christians and "joined in the Holy Spirit" with all who have received the Gospel.[1] One way, then, of evaluating the role of Notre Dame Law School is to examine the extent to which it

---

[1] See the Dogmatic Constitution on the Church, in *The Documents of Vatican II,* ed. W. M. Abbott (New York, 1966), 33-34. A broadly ecumenical note is sounded as well in other documents of Vatican II, such as the Decree on the Eastern Churches and the Decree on Ecumenism. The Decree on Ecumenism states that "Catholics must joyfully acknowledge and esteem the truly Christian endowments from our common heritage which are to be found among our separated brethren." Ibid., 349.

has been Catholic in a denominational sense, with a capital "C," part of the Church of Rome, and hence non-Orthodox, non-Anglican, and non-Protestant, and, on the other hand, the extent to which it has represented, and served the cause of, universal, or ecumenical, or catholic—with a small "c"— Christianity.

My evaluation will be divided into three parts. The first part addresses the role of Notre Dame in defending a natural-law theory against the positivist jurisprudence that has predominated in American legal education. The second part addresses the question of the relation between a deontological theory of morality, which is concerned with rational moral choice of a universal character, and what I may call an ontological (or better, socio-ontological) morality, which is implicit in the cultural background of Notre Dame law students as members of specific ethnic communities.

I may state my conclusions with respect to these two matters at the outset. I am entirely sympathetic to the attack on legal positivism, but I question the parochialism (as it seems to me) of the neo-Thomist philosophy of law as it has been expounded in the United States at Notre Dame and elsewhere. I believe that the reduction of natural-law theory to a Thomist form has hurt the cause of natural-law theory in the United States. Similarly, although I am entirely sympathetic to the attack on what might be called the deracination of moral judgments that is implicit in conventional discussions of legal ethics as well as in much conventional legal analysis, I am nevertheless critical of the excessive relativism (as it seems to me) of what Professor Thomas Shaffer elsewhere calls an anthropological approach to legal morality.

The third part of my remarks addresses the question of the nature of a law school as a community, and of Notre Dame Law School as a community based primarily on certain theological, philosophical, and socio-cultural bonds. Here, once again, I am of two minds. I appreciate the value of such a community, especially compared with the blandness of most other law school communities, their lack of definite character, their excessive individualism, their lack of close bonds, indeed, their soullessness! Yet here, too, the word "parochialism" seems to me to be appropriate. Has Notre Dame Law School been, *can* it be, a Christian community—catholic with a small "c"—true to its own faith in welcoming into its midst persons of all other faiths, offering its services wholeheartedly to the cause of the poor, the oppressed, and the disfavored, and devoting itself to law—not only in theory but also in practice—both as an instrument of the common good and as a testimony of divine providence?

Natural law theory.—In his paper entitled "The Higher Law Background of Notre Dame Law School," Professor Douglas W. Kmiec has made a powerful case for the faithfulness of Notre Dame Law School to "the Catholic or Natural Law Tradition." "At Notre Dame," he asserts, "moral questions—even very hard moral questions—are asked and discussed within its religious framework."[2] Especially during the long period of Clarence Manion's presence, from 1924 to 1952, but also both before and after, the statutes and decisions of American legislatures and courts have been judged at Notre Dame by standards of a "higher law," a law transcending the State. Derived from this higher law, it is maintained, are the rights that are declared in the United States Constitution and, indeed, the basic principles of positive law generally.

Although Professor Kmiec does not mention Thomas Aquinas by name, it is nevertheless apparent that he identifies the theory of natural law with Roman Catholic jurisprudence, and Roman Catholic jurisprudence with the Thomist principle that, on the one hand, as he puts it, "by reason alone men can arrive at Natural Law"[3] and, on the other hand, that the natural law that is knowable by reason alone is also confirmed by, and itself confirms, divine revelation as understood in Roman Catholic theology.

When I speak of the parochialism of neo-Thomist natural-law theory, as reflected in the writings of many Notre Dame scholars, I have in mind two of its aspects. First is its excessive rationalism, which assumes that the method of reasoning adopted by its adherents is equally valid for all persons at all times and places.[4] Natural law is identified with broad principles, such as the sanctity of life, personal liberty, and private property, leaving aside the elements of circumstance and culture which constitute the historical context in which broad principles are translated into specific decisions; in other words, it is a philosophical jurisprudence, not a historical jurisprudence. It is, to be sure, useful for identifying general propositions of justice, such as the propositions that no one should be condemned without a fair hearing, that there should be no criminal punishment for an act that has not previously been declared to be a crime, that contracts should be kept, and the like. But in

---

[2] Douglas W. Kmiec, "The Higher Law Background of the Notre Dame Law School" (unpublished paper on file with the author), 4.

[3] Ibid., 22.

[4] Anton-Hermann Chroust, who taught law at Notre Dame from 1946 to the 1980s, described this aspect of the natural law in the following terms: "Material natural law is, in the final analysis, *a-historicism* supreme, being but a short ideal code of most worthy general postulates or precepts for 'right and just' action valid for all times and places." (Emphasis in original.) Anton-Hermann Chroust, "On the Nature of Natural Law," in Paul Sayre, ed., *Interpretations of Modern Legal Philosophies* (New York, 1947), 70, 79.

order to explain how such general propositions should be applied in concrete situations something more is needed than a theory of natural law. Thus the insistence upon the supremacy of scholastic reasoning over other methods of reasoning separates adherents of Roman Catholic natural-law theory not only from positivists but also from those who adhere to historical, sociological, and other related schools of legal philosophy.

Second, the postulate that what is accessible to the reason of all men confirms divine revelation as understood in Roman Catholic theology separates Roman Catholic natural-law theory from other schools of natural-law theory. Leading Roman Catholic writers place Thomas Aquinas at the apex of natural law thinking, and treat Protestant, Deist, and humanist natural-law theories of subsequent authors as inevitably and wholly flawed.[5]

In the late 1940s and 1950s, Notre Dame made a splendid effort to emphasize the potential universality of natural law, first in the establishing of the Natural Law Institute and later in creating the *Natural Law Forum* and its successor, the *American Journal of Jurisprudence*. The statement of policy for the *Natural Law Forum*, for instance, disclaimed identity "with any particular school or doctrine of natural law."[6] Nevertheless, non-Roman Catholic legal thinkers who shared the belief that the validity of positive law depends on its conformity to principles of reason and morality—I think of such an outstanding legal philosopher as Lon Fuller—did not flock to the banner raised by Notre Dame Law School and, indeed, often repudiated the term "natural law" for fear that they might be identified with the Roman Catholic theory. One reason for this, I submit, was the claim of at least some Roman Catholic natural-law theorists—including some who advocated a more ecumenical approach—that the same qualities of human reason that require law to be linked with morality and the common good also require that morality and the common good be linked with Roman Catholic theology and ecclesiology.[7]

---

[5] See, e.g., Heinrich Rommen, *The Natural Law*, trans. T. R. Hanley (St. Louis, MO, 1947) and Jacques Maritain, *Three Reformers: Luther, Descartes, Rousseau* (New York, 1947). Rommen's historiography amounts to a polemic against modernity. He sees the history of natural-law theory from Pufendorf onward largely as a story of decline. Maritain asserts an even broader polemic against modernity, which he attributes to the abandonment of Thomism and the adoption of the ideas of Luther, Descartes, and Rousseau. Chroust was a participant in this polemic. Chroust was especially fond of targeting Pufendorf for harsh criticism. See, e.g., Anton-Hermann Chroust, "Some Critical Remarks about Pufendorf and his Contributions to Jurisprudence," *American Journal of Jurisprudence* (1979): 72, and id., "A Note on Samuel Pufendorf," *Vanderbilt Law Review* 1 (1947-48): 47.

[6] "Statement of Policy," *Natural Law Forum* (1956): 3.

[7] Brendan Brown's article "The Natural Law, The Marriage Bond, and Divorce," *Fordham Law Review* 24 (1955): 83, is an example of such reasoning. Drawing heavily on

This claim received support from Pope Leo XIII's call in 1879 for a revival of Thomism and the subsequent declaration that the magisterium of pope and bishops is the supreme authority in the interpretation of Thomist natural law theory.[8] Those who disagree at any point with the authentic interpretation of the magisterium are enjoined to put aside their personal convictions—and, indeed, in the words of a distinguished Roman Catholic theologian, to do so "with joy."[9]

---

ecclesiastical sources, Brown advanced the following "natural law" definition of marriage (ibid., 87): "Hence marriage under the natural law may be defined as a lawful, exclusive, and lifelong contract between a man and a woman, by which is given and accepted a right to those physical functions for the performance of acts which are mutually apt for the generation of children and secondarily for the mutual help of the spouses and the allaying of concupisence." This definition parallels rather closely the definition of marriage found in the then binding 1917 Code of Canon Law (canon 1013): "The primary end of marriage is the procreation and education of children; the secondary ends are the mutual assistance of the spouses and the remedy of concupisence. The essential properties of marriage are unity and indissolubility, which in a Christian marriage obtain special firmness by reason of the sacrament."

[8] Pope Pius XII in a 1954 allocution stated: "The power of the Church is never contained (as they say) within the boundaries of the 'strictly religious', but rather the entire matter, institution, interpretation, and application of natural law is within its power, so far as moral reasoning is concerned. For the observation of natural law belongs, by God's ordaining, to the path by which man is to attain his supernatural end. And the Church is the leader and the guardian (dux et custos) of men on this path to their supernatural end." 46 Acta Apostolicae Sedis, 671-672. It is important to note that when an author like Pius XII speaks of "the Church" he means by it the Roman Catholic hierarchy of pope together with (or even independent of) the college of bishops. Theologians and others may have a consultative role to play in the teaching process, but possess no formal authority. Both of these points, the asserted authority of the Church over the natural law and the equation of the magisterium with the hierarchy, are developed by Joseph R. Lerch, "Teaching Authority of the Church (Magisterium)," New Catholic Encyclopedia (New York, 1967), 13: 959-965.

[9] Josef Fuchs, Natural Law: A Theological Investigation, trans. H. Recker and J. A. Dowling (New York, 1965), 159. In recent work, Fuchs has sharply qualified his earlier dogmatism and certitude. He has recently written concerning the attitude a "believing Catholic" should take toward the magisterium:

A dimension of the spirit of discipleship in the Church is that one opens oneself to the ethical declarations of the magisterium which are meant as a help in the evaluation made by the conscience, and that one attempts—where this seems possible—to give these statements primacy over against other considerations which arise (even one's own); this is required by the responsibility of the conscience.

This, at least, is what is usually the case. This limitation is necessary because the conscience—on the basis of the fundamental conscience—has also the responsibility of not admitting into itself aspects of official statements that are opposed by very important and insurmountable counter-arguments. . . . For the

Ethics and ethnicity.—Professor Thomas L. Shaffer's conference paper, together with his important book, *American Lawyers and Their Communities*,[10] raises the discussion of lawyers' ethics to a new height by focusing on the relationship between lawyers' moral choices and the ethnic, religious, and professional communities whose moral order influences and often determines those choices. Professor Shaffer's paper stresses the tendency of Italian-American law students at Notre Dame to resist assimilation and to maintain their Italian-American identity. Professor Rodolpho Sandoval, in writing about Notre Dame law students of Hispanic background, also stresses the cultural differences between ethnic groups and, in addition, the tension between the morality in which Hispanic-American law students are bred and the morality implicit in the law which they study.[11] For example, the notorious aphorism of Justice Holmes, that when a person makes a contract he agrees either to perform or else to pay damages for its breach, is shocking, Professor Sandoval states, to Hispanic Catholics like himself who are brought up to believe that to break a promise is a breach of faith.

In reading these two papers, I was struck by the opportunity that exists at Notre Dame to compare the morality of American law with the cultural and moral standards of the various ethnic communities represented in the student body. Nevertheless, as I am of two minds with respect to the rationalism of Thomist jurisprudence, so I am also of two minds with respect to the cultural relativism that is described, and perhaps even to some extent endorsed, in the otherwise laudable effort to root professional responsibility in the mores of the diverse communities that make up our common life.

A Christian law school.—Professor Walter F. Pratt, Jr. states that Notre Dame Law School "seems to have followed the national norm without ever taking a distinctive position in legal education"[12] He qualifies this statement,

---

only way the magisterium can attain personal significance is *via* the responsibly formed conscience.

Josef Fuchs, "The Absolute in Morality and the Christian Conscience," *Gregorianum* 71 (1990): 709 (emphasis in original).

[10] The full authorship and title of the book are Thomas L. Shaffer and Mary L. Shaffer, *American Lawyers and Their Communities: Ethics of the Legal Profession* (Notre Dame, IN, and London, 1991). Professor Shaffer's conference paper was a response to Lucy F. Payne's paper entitled "Outsiders in a Catholic Law School" (unpublished paper on file with the author).

[11] Rodolpho Sandoval, "Hispanics at Notre Dame" (unpublished paper on file with the author).

[12] Walter F. Pratt, "Notre Dame Law School: A Catholic Law School in America" (unpublished paper on file with the author).

however, by noting that after the first half-century of its existence, when "the Law School was proudest of its success in preparing graduates for the various bar exams," there was a second period when it did defend natural law against other doctrines, followed by a third period, continuing until today, in which the faculty has emphasized "ethics," in the sense of "a higher value of professionalism against individual selfishness."

Running through the account of all three of these periods, however, is a somewhat unsettling subtext. We are reminded by St. Paul that in Christ Jesus there is neither Greek nor Jew, neither male nor female, neither free nor slave. Bigotry is forbidden to Christians. What is unsettling about the subtext of the Pratt paper is, quite simply, the intimation that in the past bigotry was more than occasionally an intruder at the Notre Dame Law School.

Apparently blacks were not admitted at all to Notre Dame until after World War II and in only quite limited numbers thereafter, at least until the 1960s.[13] In 1922, President Walsh stated that blacks could not be admitted to Notre Dame because they would inevitably be embarrassed by the southerners enrolled in the student body. Apparently it was decided that blacks should be excluded from campus in order to protect them from the insults of bigots.

Other groups were also the subject of exclusion. Women were apparently not allowed into the degree program of the Law School until the academic year 1965-66[14]—decades after their admission to Columbia, Yale, and Harvard law schools. Protestants were admitted from the beginning, but were often made to feel unwelcome. As early as 1858, five Protestant students were expelled from the university for refusing to kneel at chapel. In 1919, an official statement of the university made it clear that all students, Catholic as well as non-Catholic, were expected to attend Mass. As late as 1969, Dean Lawless referred to the organizers of a conference on pornography as a "bunch of shyster Jews from New York."[15]

It would be surprising indeed to find such old-fashioned bigotry at Notre Dame today. Yet, as Lucy S. Payne's paper reveals, an undercurrent of racial and religious animosities belies the Christian character of the School. Judging from her survey, only a minority of students find the School to be a "welcoming" place, and a substantial majority both of non-Roman-Catholics and of inactive Roman Catholics (63 per cent and 68 per cent, respectively) reject the characterization contained in the Notre Dame Law School Bulletin that the Law School community is one where "people of every kind of

---

[13] Ibid., 60.

[14] Ibid., 66.

[15] Ibid., 65-66.

opinion are welcome and valued for the different contributions they have to make[.]"

Such self-criticisms should perhaps be taken with a grain of salt. In any event, the questions are as important as the answers. The questions reflect a deep concern to judge Notre Dame Law School by its calling to be a Christian law school.

This takes me directly to the title of this chapter: "Is there such a thing— can there be such a thing—as a Christian law school?"

Earlier, I referred to a Christian law school as one that remains true to its own faith by welcoming into its midst persons of all other faiths, by offering its services wholeheartedly to the cause of the poor, the oppressed, and the disfavored, and by devoting itself to law, in theory and in practice, both as an instrument of the common good and as a testimony of divine providence. This was not intended as a complete definition of a Christian law school but only as one set of characteristics; and indeed, these may be characteristics of any *religious* law school and, moreover, if the reference to divine providence is omitted, of any *humane* law school. Nevertheless, although it would not be *uniquely* Christian for a law school to constitute an all-inclusive community of universal servanthood, it *would be* Christian; and *not* to do so would, in my view, be *un*Christian and perhaps even *uniquely unChristian*. In other words, I am arguing that it is necessarily incumbent on a Christian law school, although perhaps not necessarily incumbent on a Jewish law school, or a Muslim law school, or a secular law school that strives to be humane in the deepest sense, itself to constitute an all-inclusive community of universal servanthood.

In addition to constituting a distinct type of community, a Christian law school, in approaching law as a testimony of divine providence, would raise two types of questions concerning each of the individual topics of the legal curriculum—contracts, torts, property, criminal law, procedure, constitutional law, corporation law, taxation, administrative law, international law, and all the rest—two types of questions that are largely neglected in those courses in the secular law schools of America. The first type is *philosophical* in nature, and would include, but go beyond, the usual type of philosophical question introduced in Thomistic natural-law theory. More particularly, it would go beyond the question of the moral justification of legal *rules and principles* to the question of the moral justification of legal *decisions*, that is, of the *application* of rules and principles to concrete cases in concrete circumstances. In technical philosophical terms, the questions would go beyond problems of synderesis to problems of conscience. In that way both Roman Catholic and Protestant natural-law theory would be addressed.[16]

The second type of question that would be introduced in every course is *historical*, and, more particularly, it would refer to the historical influence of Christianity on the development of legal doctrine in the particular subject of the course. For example, in contract law students would be introduced to the historical influence upon American contract law of the Roman canon law principle that to break a promise is prima facie a sin, but may be justified where the promisor was not at fault, as in the case of promises induced by fraud or duress or mistake; and also to the influence, at a later stage in the development of the Western legal tradition, of Calvinist concepts of absolute obligation—regardless of the absence of fault—to perform a bargained exchange.[17] I give this as one example of a type of historical inquiry that rests on the premise that American law is a product of the Western legal tradition, which was initially linked not only with Christian theology but also with a Christian historiography. A Christian historical jurisprudence is premised on the belief that history is providential, that it is the fulfillment of a divine plan, and that therefore the past has not only a factual but a normative character. I believe that the historical school of legal philosophy, which has been so woefully neglected by American legal scholars, is a necessary supplement to natural-law theory and a necessary corrective of its unhistorical character.[18]

Finally, in addition to accommodating a particular type of community and in addition to addressing particular types of philosophical and historical questions, a Christian law school must give its students the kind of legal training that will help them to fulfill a Christian vocation as practising lawyers. I would define the Christian vocation of the lawyer—very briefly—as having three aspects. First, it has a *pastoral* aspect: Christian lawyers are called to be genuine counselors to their clients, that is, to devote themselves not only to the protection of their clients' financial interests but also to their total well-being, including their integrity and dignity as persons. A Christian law school should offer courses in legal counseling, just as schools of theology offer courses in pastoral counseling.

The Christian lawyer has not only a pastoral but also a *prophetic* vocation. Lawyers as prophets devote themselves to the cause of social justice and humanity. Certainly, a Christian law school must stress this aspect of the lawyer's calling not only in all its courses but also in its program of student

---

[16] See Chapter 6, above.

[17] See Chapter 7, above.

[18] See Chapter 13, above.

legal services for the poor, for racial equality, for protection of the environment, and for law reform generally.

In addition to a pastoral and a prophetic vocation, Christian lawyers have what I would call a *priestly* vocation, that is, a calling to play a part as responsible leaders in their communities. In the Western political tradition, and especially in that of the United States, the legal profession constitutes a secular priesthood. Lawyers are given a primary role both in proclaiming and in administering the secular ideals and values of their society, especially as those ideals and values are embodied in the legal system itself. The claim upon a lawyer to think and act responsibly *as a lawyer* in helping to maintain unity within the society, resolve conflict, and allocate power—this, too, is a religious claim. In preparing its students to meet this claim, a Christian law school is in most respects no different from any other good law school. But a Christian law school should be aware, first, that in preparing students to meet the challenge of what I have called the priestly vocation of a lawyer, law schools are in fact the beneficiaries of a Christian heritage, however ignorant of that heritage secular law schools may be; and second, that a Christian law school has a special obligation to expose its students to the Christian origin— and here I might properly add the Judaic-Christian origin—of the priestly character of the lawyer's vocation. Nor is that merely an academic obligation; it is also a spiritual obligation, since the priesthood, in the Christian tradition, is called not only to serve but also to serve with humility. The besetting sin of the American legal profession today is commercialization—which is another word for greed; and with it goes the arrogance of power. A Christian law school must teach its apprentice legal priests the sacrificial humility of genuine leadership.

Part Four

RUSSIAN AND SOVIET THEMES

19

ATHEISM AND CHRISTIANITY IN
SOVIET RUSSIA*

When we feel discouraged about our own problems it is comforting to turn our attention to the problems of others, especially if they are our adversaries. Then we can devote our energies to removing the "beam" from their eyes, while treating the obstruction in our own as a mere "mote."

When it becomes painful to face up to our deficiencies—the divisions among us, our lack of a common national purpose, our lack of will and commitment—we try to change the subject. We console ourselves with the thought that things are worse elsewhere, and especially in the Soviet Union. There they lack freedom. If we talk about their deficiency we may be able to forget about our own lack of commitment. We have an abundance of freedom, but on the other hand the Soviet Union has an abundance of commitment, of common purpose and will, an abundance of community spirit, and a strong sense of destiny.

The severe restriction of religious freedom in the Soviet Union stems above all from the deep commitment of the Soviet leadership to atheism as a belief system, and as a militant faith. There are other reasons for Soviet anti-religious policies, but the main one is itself "religious" in a deeper sense of that word than usual. It is the Marxist-Leninist conviction that the belief in

---

* Reprinted from *Freedom and Faith: The Impact of Law on Religious Liberty*, ed. Lynn R. Buzzard (Westchester, IL, 1982), 127-143. Delivered at a conference of the Christian Legal Society held in 1980.

atheism is an essential part of a scientific world-view which is a necessary prerequisite to material and moral progress.

Soviet atheism has deep roots in Russian history. It is also derived from Marxism, which is a characteristically Western philosophy; but whereas for Marx atheism was primarily an intellectual matter, an inference drawn from scientific materialism, for Lenin and his Russian followers atheism was a militant faith, a revolt against God. Lenin could have repeated what the Russian revolutionary Bakunin had said, "If God really existed, He would have to be destroyed." This was not the sentimental sort of atheism that is widespread in America today, especially in universities. On the contrary, Leninist atheism is something to be actively believed in, something to be practiced in one's daily life. It rests in part on Marxian intellectual premises: that the ultimate reality is matter, that man's material conditions and needs ultimately determine his conduct and his beliefs, that the basic fact of human history is the struggle to master these material conditions and needs, and that the natural laws of this struggle lead ultimately to Communism. It rests also on the passionate belief—of which Lenin, not Marx, was the great apostle, and which is more Russian than Western—that man is master of his own destiny and by his own power can construct a paradise on earth. It was Lenin, not Marx, who conceived and created the Communist Party as a dedicated elite vanguard, imbued with "social consciousness," whose mission was to lead mankind into that paradise. For Lenin and the Russian Communist Party, atheism represented man's power to replace God, that is, to do by himself, by his intellect and his will, through collective action, what Christianity—and especially Russian Christianity—had taught that only God can do; namely, create a universal peace in the hearts of men.

Many say that "ideology" is no longer a vital factor in Soviet life, that the Soviet people do not really believe in the Marxian theories upon which the Bolshevik Revolution was based. That may be true, just as it may be true that the American people no longer believe in the Jeffersonian theories of agrarian democracy and individual self-reliance which played such a large part in making the American Revolution. But that does not mean that the Soviets—or we—believe in nothing. What they (and we) believe in are watered-down versions of original revolutionary teachings. No doubt Soviet leaders have lost their excessive optimism about the future, and with it, their excessive pessimism about the past. Their beliefs have become less apocalyptic, less militant, more tired. Nevertheless, they still accept large parts of the Leninist world-view. Leninist atheism, at least, is still a powerful dogma in the Soviet Communist Party, and the Party's campaign against religion is, if anything, stronger than ever.

Unless we see the issue of Communism versus Religion in the Soviet Union, and especially atheism versus Christianity, as a struggle for the minds and hearts of the Soviet people, we shall be led into serious distortions and over-simplifications concerning Soviet policies. We may think in terms of the traditional struggles between Church and State as we have known them in Western history. We shall see only persecutions of the clergy and prohibitions of religious worship. We shall suppose that the Church in Russia has been forced underground. The truth is that tens of millions of Russians openly attend Church services. And while there have been systematic closings of churches and oppression of the clergy, these are not the most significant features of the Soviet struggle against religion; for it is not the churches as such that the Soviet Party leaders or the Soviet people are primarily concerned about, not "organized religion," but religious belief itself.

In pursuing its goal of creating a society dedicated to material and moral progress, as understood in a Marxist-Leninist perspective, the Communist Party of the Soviet Union has for more than sixty years conducted the most massive assault upon Christianity that the Church has experienced since Roman times. I am not speaking primarily of a physical assault or of the closing of churches, although that is part of it. I am speaking of a systematic campaign to remove traditional religious belief from public life and public discourse, and to root it out of the minds of the Soviet people.

The policy of the Soviet government toward religion was laid down in the first law on the subject in January, 1918. It was called "On the Separation of the Church from the State and of the School from the Church." To American ears, the title sounds harmless enough, but when the Soviets say "separation" they really mean it! In principle, the State will give not the slightest support whatsoever to the Church, and the Church is forbidden to engage in activities which are within the sphere of responsibilities of the State. This has a special meaning in a socialist planned economy of the Soviet type. It means, for example, that state publishing houses will not produce religious literature, and that churches may not give to the poor or carry on education. Moreover, schools are not merely to avoid the teaching of religion; they are actively to promote the teaching of atheism. These doctrines were spelled out in a 1929 law that remains the basic legislation on the subject to this day. There is freedom of religious worship, but churches are forbidden to give any material aid to their members or charity of any kind, or to hold any special meetings for children, youth, or women, or general meetings for religious study, recreation, or any similar purpose, or to open libraries or to keep any books other than those necessary for the performance of worship services. The formula of the 1929 law is repeated in the 1936 Constitution and again in the 1977

Constitution: freedom of religious worship and freedom of atheist propaganda—meaning (1) no freedom of religious teaching outside of the worship service itself, plus (2) a vigorous campaign in the schools, in the press, and in special meetings organized by atheist agitators, to convince people of the folly of religious beliefs.

The Criminal Code of the Russian Republic imposes a fine for violating laws of separation of the church from the state and of the school from the church, and for repeated violations, deprivation of freedom for up to three years (Article 142). Such violations include organizing religious assemblies and processions, organizing religious instruction for minors, and preparing written materials calling for such activities. Other types of religious activities are subject to more severe sanctions: thus leaders and active participants in religious groups that cause damage to the health of citizens or violate personal rights, or that try to persuade citizens not to participate in social activities or to perform duties of citizenship, or that draw minors into such a group are punishable by deprivation of freedom for up to five years (Article 227). This provision is directed primarily against Evangelical Baptists, Jehovah's Witnesses, Pentecostals, and other sects whose activities—though illegal—are quite widespread in the Soviet Union.

These laws were enacted as part of the severe anti-religious campaign of Khrushchev in the early 1960s, when an estimated 10,000 Russian Orthodox churches—half the total number—were closed, together with five of the eight institutions for training priests, and the independence of the priesthood was curtailed both nationally and locally. (I speak of the Russian Orthodox Church, which is by far the largest, but the attack was on all religious communities.) This campaign ended with Brezhnev's accession to power in 1964; nevertheless, the rights of believers that were taken away in the Khrushchev period were not restored. The closed churches, monasteries, and seminaries remain closed. Parents who baptize their children must register, and may then be subject to harassment. Practical impediments are placed in the way of church weddings. Sermons are strictly controlled. Since 1959 or 1960 the Soviet leadership has returned to the policy which was criticized in the 1920s by the first Soviet Commissar of Education, Lunacharsky, who said, "Religion is like a nail—the harder you hit it on the head, the deeper it goes into the wood."

Despite this massive effort to suppress traditional religious belief, or perhaps partly because of it, there has been a strengthening of Christian faith. Christianity has not only survived the assault upon it but has been purged and purified by it.

What accounts for the extraordinary vitality of religious faith in the Soviet Union? The vitality of the Russian religious faith must be seen in the context of an atheistic Communist Party of 17 million members which has a virtual monopoly on high governmental and administrative posts. Members who are caught attending church services are subject to expulsion from the Party. Nor can we overlook the fact that the great majority of the youth, though by no means all, are atheists—45 million of them in the two Communist youth organizations, the Komsomol and the Pioneers, which, like the Party, are sworn to atheism. But the striking fact is that despite Soviet official claims to the contrary, and despite the superficial impressions of Western tourists, religion is not dying out in Russia. And it is not only the aged who cling to the church. It is possible, and even likely, that at least among the Russian half of the Soviet population, a majority of the adults are Christian. Also in the past decade there has been a substantial turn to Christianity among students and other young people. Soviet writers themselves have recently estimated the number of believers at twenty percent of the total Soviet population—about 50 million. Competent non-Soviet observers have said forty percent or more.

These are only guesses, since there are no published statistics. Also, there is no satisfactory definition of a "believer" (which is the word generally used in the Soviet Union for one who believes in God).

Certainly, millions of Russians attend church services. I recall a Whitsunday service at the great Trinity Cathedral in Leningrad, where some 12,000 people stood for four hours in rapt devotion, packed together so there was hardly room to breathe. At another Leningrad cathedral every Wednesday night 4,000 people sing a special two-hour service; there is no choir, but the people know the words and music by heart. At a smaller church is Moscow on Easter eve my family and I arrived at 11:30 to find thousands already worshipping, and when we left at almost 4 a.m. we were among the first to go, while there were still people outside the church who had come too late to get in. Of course these large congregations result from the paucity of "working churches" (as they are called) that have been allowed to remain open. On the other hand, for every worshipper there are many more who would attend but for the political pressure not to.

What draws these people to the churches, six decades after the Revolution made it very inconvenient, to say the least, to be religious? Partly, it is the experience of the Russian Orthodox liturgy which has a dramatic appeal of extraordinary power. The liturgy is the principal source of spiritual vitality in the Russian Church; the worship service, including the sacraments, is the heart and soul of Russian religious life. Deprived of religious education, of religious literature, of social activities of all kinds, the Russian Church has drawn its sustenance primarily from the liturgy, whose power has overcome the assaults of atheist propaganda in the minds of tens of millions of Soviet citizens.

The liturgy is, of course, more than mere ritual. It is the story of the Old and New Testaments and of the lives of the saints. It binds believers together in faith, hope, and love. The liturgy also includes the sermon, the word of the priest to his flock. The thirty or forty sermons which I have heard preached during fourteen visits to the Soviet Union in the past twenty-five years (including a twelve month stay in 1961-62) stressed a few closely related themes: love of all men, forgiveness of enemies, unity of all people, joy in suffering.

Each sermon was based on a biblical text, usually a parable or an episode in Jesus' life. The priest would interpret the words of the Gospel and explain their deeper meaning. His message was essentially pastoral, delivered freely without notes, spoken with simplicity but without condescension, usually in beautiful, dignified biblical language which contrasted sharply with the stereotyped slogans of Soviet political speech.

"The kingdom of heaven is within us," one priest told his people. "It consists of love—not just love, but merciful love, inner peace with our neighbor and our enemy. It is said that this is unrealistic, that in fact man struggles to kill his enemy, and it is true that from generation to generation man has behaved that way. But the wickedness of man has not been able to destroy love, which still exists and which man is capable of realizing. But man cannot live a life of merciful love without suffering. That is the meaning of the cross. Christ showed us that through suffering we can manifest merciful love."

"It is a Christian's duty *not* to return evil for evil," said another priest at a church in Moscow which has the wonderful name Church of Joy of All Who Mourn. "We must hate the sin but not the sinner. Though Christians are scorned and offended, they return love. We rejoice in our suffering when we are scorned for Christ's sake—that is the meaning of the name of this Church, Joy of All Who Mourn."

"The most important expression of love for fellowman," said another priest, "is love of homeland—for this means love of our brothers and sisters. Through love of homeland the whole earth can be united in love. All nations are equal in the sight of God."

There are many limitations upon what a Soviet priest can say in a sermon. He is not free to give concrete contemporary examples of the enemies to be loved; he is not free to criticize existing Soviet institutions or policies. Anything which can be called politics is excluded. But there is no doubt in the minds of his hearers of the implications of his words. And the next day his sermon will be reported in detail by his hearers to their neighbors in the communal kitchens of the crowded apartment houses, or at work or elsewhere, and they will draw the implications.

I heard a priest in Leningrad tell his congregation the story of Joseph's interpretation of Pharaoh's dream of the seven fat cows eaten up by the seven lean cows. "We are now living through the lean years," he said, "but we are nourished by all the riches which the Church has accumulated during the past centuries."

These riches are denied, by and large, to Soviet school children, who are taught to scorn them and who have not the experience to appreciate them. But Soviet young people in their late teens and twenties begin to doubt what they have been taught, and in their thirties and forties Soviet men and women often return to the Church, especially if life has been hard for them.

What I have been describing so far is the elemental confrontation of two fundamental faiths, Christianity and atheism, a confrontation that has existed in the Soviet Union for over sixty years. One is a faith in man's power to raise himself, by his own collective will and by disciplined obedience to the Communist Party leadership, to a political order of power and wealth and ultimately to a utopian social order of universal peace and brotherhood. The other is a faith in God's merciful forgiveness of human weakness and selfishness and in His offer of redemption from suffering and death to all who follow the example of Jesus Christ. Both these faiths have shown an extraordinary capacity to survive in the Soviet Union, despite frequent betrayal by their adherents.

That confrontation has, however, reached a new stage in the past twenty years, as many Christians, both individually and in small groups, have defied the Soviet state to live up to its own laws and its own professions of legality—those very laws and that very legality which repress religious activities, but which also offer some protections to freedom of religious worship.

The current struggle for more freedom of worship, and for more freedom to teach religion and to witness to religious faith outside the worship service, is linked with the struggle for legality, and has become increasingly important in the past twenty-five years. The very legal system which the Soviet state has used to contain and subdue religion is now being used by believers as a shield against those who would deprive them of those opportunities to which they are legally entitled.

In the late 1950s and early 1960s, Nikita Khrushchev raised the banner of socialist legality against the past excesses of Stalin's "cult of [his own] personality." This was a period of substantial law reform—which has continued, incidentally, under Leonid Brezhnev. The Stalin terror ended. The KGB itself was subjected to law.

Yet at the same time Khrushchev, starting in 1960, launched a systematic attack on religious belief in which basic principles of Soviet legality were violated. New *unpublished* laws and regulations were adopted—in violation, first, of the new legal requirements concerning publication of laws, and, second, of the fundamental principle of separation of church and state. Under these new unpublished laws the priesthood at the parish level was subjected to agencies of lay control within the church, and political pressures were exerted on those agencies of lay control to close churches, to require registration of baptisms, to divert to the state some of the money derived from contributions of the faithful, and the like. This was true primarily of the Russian Orthodox Church, although repressive measures were also taken against other permitted branches of Christianity (the "official" Baptist, the Lutherans, the Roman Catholics, and others) as well as against non-Christian religious faiths (Islam, Judaism), not to mention many sects that were banned altogether. Also laws confining religious rites to buildings authorized by the state to be houses of worship were invoked with increasing severity, and new religious communities were denied the right to build new houses of worship.

These and other repressions eventually bore unexpected fruit in the form of open opposition on the part of believers. This opposition was sometimes turned against those church leaders who had been co-opted to carry out the state's repressive measures, or who refused to speak out openly against them. Thus a number of independent clergy emerged, who demanded reform within the church itself. Others, both clerics and nonclerics, attacked Party and state policies and practices concerning religion, utilizing secret, though legal, channels to spread their views at home and abroad (so-called *samizdat*). Believers joined the growing number of "dissidents" who, starting mainly in the mid-1960s, risked prosecution for circulating anti-Soviet statements.

Such open opposition would have been impossible under Stalin; also it was more difficult under Khrushchev than it became under Brezhnev. It was connected with the increasing importance of legality in the Soviet Union. Especially after the death of Stalin, the strengthening of law and legality became essential to the Soviet leadership, both as a source of legitimacy and as a means of maintaining control of the Soviet people. At the same time, however, law and legality provided individuals and groups the opportunity to complain against abuses and to press for changes. As that freedom has increased, repressive measures and abuses of legality have also increased; yet the amount of liberalization has increased at a significantly more rapid rate than the amount of repression or abuse. Today there is a genuine ferment beneath the surface of Soviet life, an important part of which is manifested in the demand for further law reform and for stricter observance by the state of its own laws. Included among these laws are those protecting religious worship, making it a crime, for example, to interfere with lawful religious worship, or to discriminate in employment on the basis of religious belief.

Also it is permitted by Soviet law to teach religion to one's children. Yet in 1965 the then President of the Criminal Division of the USSR Supreme Court, G.Z. Anashkin, in an important article, found it necessary to criticize certain lower courts and administrative officials for punishing persons for educating their children in a religious spirit, which he said "does not constitute a crime," but on the contrary is protected by the constitutional freedom of worship. Judge Anashkin's reasoning gives an important clue to the sources of Soviet anti-religious policy: administrative pressure against churches, he stated, "does not serve the struggle against the vestiges of religion. On the contrary, it reinforces religious fanaticism." Moreover, he stated, "It must always be remembered that every unjust or unjustifiably severe sentence can lead only to . . . the embitterment of the religious, and to consolidating and even intensifying their religious prejudices." He added that "The practice of exiling certain sects to other parts of the country . . . sometimes has the consequence that they become propagators of their 'teachings' in new places . . . [and] even . . . recruit individuals among the permanent population into their sect."

Unfortunately, Judge Anashkin's strictures in 1965 did not prevent administrative and even judicial violations from continuing to occur. Such abuses were sometimes based on a provision of the 1968 Family Code that parents have a "duty" to raise their children "in the spirit of the Moral Code of the Builder of Communism." This Moral Code was interpreted to include the Leninist spirit of atheism, and was used especially against those radical sectarians who on religious grounds kept their children out of various school and social activities. In 1979 the Family Code was amended to eliminate this reference to the Moral Code of the Builder of Communism. The provision now reads: "Parents are obligated to bring up their children, care for their physical development and education, prepare them for socially useful work, and raise worthy citizens of the socialist society." This change reaffirms the principles which Judge Anashkin had espoused. It remains to be seen how it will be interpreted.

In reviewing a recent book by Michael Bordeaux and Michael Rowe, John Lawrence has written that "Soviet law is weighted against religious belief of all kinds, but, far worse, those limited rights accorded to believers in theory are denied them in practice. What the believers demand above all is that the law should actually be applied to them." Of particular significance in that statement, in my opinion, is the word "demand." What is new in Soviet Russia during the past fifteen years is that believers now do "demand" their rights under Soviet law, and that one of those rights is precisely the right to make such demands. Unfortunately, that right, too, is sometimes violated, with the result that the Soviet labor colonies now contain such prisoners as Kovalev, Ogorodnikov, Orlov, and other martyrs to their faith whose offense was that they protested too openly and too strongly against the violation of rights of believers. Yet for every person who is arrested, a dozen others rise up to protest.

The struggle for religious freedom—both freedom of worship and the opportunity to bear witness to religious beliefs outside the worship service—is linked with the struggle for legality in a deeper sense, as well. In the West a deep inner connection between law and religion has existed for 900 years. In Russian and Soviet history, law has not played so crucial a role either in political life or in religious life. Traditionally, the Russian Church has been an other-worldly church, and has tended toward antinomianism. Only in recent times has the inner link between religious freedom and legality become apparent to Soviet believers.

A Russian Orthodox priest, Father Dudko, who has been in great difficulty with both Church and Party authorities, recently told of a nine-year-old girl who came to confess her sins. He told her that she was too young to require confession. She then said she had a question. She had been told by her teacher, her classmates, and eventually her parents that she should join the Pioneers, which she did not want to do, because its credo includes opposition to religion. Under pressure, she finally joined, but then she secretly blessed her red Pioneer scarf with holy water. She wanted to know if that was wrong.

I believe this story is a paradigm of the present relationship of Christianity to the Communist Party in the Soviet Union. It is in many ways a paradigm of the relationship of religious faith to legal institutions in the United States as well.

If Christianity in the Soviet Union becomes allied with the struggle for legality, it is conceivable that someday the two together may help to soften the harshness of the Communist system, and to reform it in the direction of greater humaneness.

It is also conceivable that someday the two together—Christianity and respect for legality—may help to overcome the pervasive corruption of Communist society—the widespread bribery, black-marketeering, stealing of state property, drunkenness, and improper use of "influence" (*blat*)—which neither law alone nor law and scientific materialism together can overcome.

For the inner connection between law and faith is much stronger than either Russian Christianity or Soviet Communism has yet realized.

My last point has to do with what we can learn from Soviet experience. We can learn to have a certain respect for militant atheism. The devil is no slob. There is a story of a little old lady who could never speak ill of anyone. She was asked what she thought of the devil. She hesitated and then replied, "Well, he's very hard-working." She could have added that he is very intelligent, that he challenges us where we are most vulnerable. In Christian theology he is a fallen angel. What makes him the devil, as the late Bishop Emrich once said, is not that he lacks virtues, but that he is going in the wrong direction.

We are told that the devil tempted Christ with bread, with power over all the kingdoms of the world, and with miracles. So Soviet scientific materialism offers its adherents economic security, political power, and sensational technological progress—all in return for one thing: absolute subservience to the high priests of these gods, the Party. The challenge of this system *at home* is not that it will fail but that it will succeed—that it will meet its economic, political, and technological ends by means of the very discipline that it demands. For it is a system that, above all, by its means, meets certain real needs of twentieth century man—the need for unity and the need for a common social purpose.

The challenge *to us* is not only in the means but also in the ends. To make it our main purpose to accomplish those ends, but by a different means, is to fall into the danger of trying to serve both Mammon and God. Religion then becomes *our* means for accomplishing the wrong ends.

The Soviets believe what Jesus taught—that no man can serve two masters—no man can be a servant to both God and Mammon. So they have attempted to eliminate the belief in God. We, on the other hand, try to serve both God and Mammon, equally. Indeed, sometimes we think they are one.

The Soviet challenge to us is obvious: we must construct a social order in which the goals of justice, mercy, and good faith—what Jesus called "the weightier matters of the law"—will take precedence over economic security, political power, and technological progress, and we must freely, through voluntary associations, pour into that social order the same spirit of service, self-sacrifice, and common purpose that under the Soviet system is induced by Party discipline.

—————— ✺ 20 ✺ ——————

THE USE OF LAW TO GUIDE PEOPLE
TO VIRTUE: A COMPARISON OF SOVIET
AND U.S. PERSPECTIVES[*]

L aw is usually understood (I would say *mis*understood) as primarily a political phenomenon, an instrument of control by political authorities, which operates chiefly by deterring recalcitrant people from undesired conduct by threat of penalties. The view that law is something more, and something other, than a body of rules enacted by lawmakers and enforced by administrators is not often affirmed today, and even when it is affirmed, it is not often taken as a starting point of analysis.

In contrast to the conventional approach, I begin with the view that law is primarily a psychological phenomenon, that it is primarily rooted in the intellectual, emotional, and spiritual life of the people of a community. Here I follow in the footsteps of the great Polish-Russian jurist of the early twentieth century, L.I. Petrazhitskii, who distinguished between the "official" law of the state and the "unofficial" or "intuitive" law that exists in the consciousness of people.[1]

---

[*] Reprinted from June Louin Tapp and Felice J. Levine, eds., *Law, Justice, and the Individual in Society: Psychological and Legal Issues* (New York, 1977), 75-84.

[1] H. Babb, "Petrazhitskii: Theory of Law," *Boston University Law Review* 18 (1938): 511; Jan Gorecki, *Sociology and Jurisprudence of Leon Petrazhitskii* (Urbana, IL, 1975); Leon I. Petrazhitskii, *Law and Morality* (Cambridge, MA, 1955); Nicholas S. Timasheff, *The Great Retreat; the Decline of Communism in Russia* (New York, 1946).

Law-Consciousness as a Psychological Phenomenon.—Each person, according to Petrazhitskii, has his or her own law-consciousness, own conceptions of rights, duties, privileges, powers, and other legal relations. These derive primarily from the unofficial, intuitive pattern of entitlements and obligations that exists within the family, the school, the church, the neighborhood, the factory or business enterprise, the profession, the city or region or nation. Such legal emotions are distinct from moral sentiments in the Kantian sense. In Kant's theory, moral sentiments are intuitions that people in general have about their moral obligations, that is, about their duties to avoid what is wrong and do what is right. Legal sentiments, on the other hand, as Petrazhitskii saw, are intuitions (or emotions, as he called them) that people in general have about their *rights* and about their duties correlative to rights. A sense that it is right to aid (or not to aid) a person in distress is a moral sentiment; a sense that a person in distress has a right (or does not have a right) to be aided is a legal sentiment.

Legal sentiments include an aversion to inconsistency in the treatment of people ("like cases should be decided alike"), a felt need for an impartial hearing before a judgment is passed on another, an abhorrence of illegality, a commitment to legality. If one person, for example, has taken something belonging to another without justification or excuse, we are outraged not only because the owner has suffered a loss and because the other person has behaved immorally but also because there has been a breach of the legal order. Even if the general moral position of the thief is superior to that of the owner, as it may be in some cases, all concerned are apt to view the matter not in general moral terms but in intuitively recognized legal terms of the violation of rights of ownership. Conversely, the violation of a moral duty to give alms to a beggar offends moral but not legal emotions since the beggar, by definition, does not claim the alms as a matter of right.

If the official law of the state varies significantly from the unofficial law of the people, then officials may be driven to impose their will by a body of rules sanctioned by threat of penalties. This is apt to be both more efficient and more humane than the imposition of their will by naked force. At a time when Soviet jurists tended to view all law solely as an instrument of coercion, N.V. Krylenko, who became a People's Commissar of Justice in the early 1930s, observed, "a club is a primitive weapon, a rifle is a more efficient one, the most efficient is the court."[2] Yet there is another alternative: the state may attempt to persuade and educate people to adapt their intuitive legal ideas and feelings to the official law. In so doing, the state may also find it both

---

[2] Harold J. Berman, *Justice in the U.S.S.R.; An Interpretation of Soviet Law* (Cambridge, MA, 1963), 36.

necessary and desirable to adapt the official law to the unofficial law of the community it is seeking to regulate.

In stable societies, however, the basic values and concepts of the official law will correspond in most respects to the basic values and concepts of the unofficial, intuitive law. From the standpoint of a positivist legal theory, it only remains for the official law to impose its sanctions on violators. Yet even in that case there also remain felt needs—which positivism does not address—to persuade the offender to acknowledge the wrongful character of the offense, to educate him or her not to offend again, and to reassure others of the rightness of their intuitive legal feelings and of the correspondence of such feelings to official legal values.

The Nurturing Role of Soviet Law.—In what has been said thus far there is little to distinguish Soviet from U.S. perspectives. In both societies the predominant legal theory does not recognize that people's ideas, feelings, and attitudes concerning law constitute something that itself can be called law. Yet Krylenko's concept of law as a mere instrument of coercion has been repudiated in the Soviet Union; there, as in the United States, it is asserted that law should also reflect justice. In both societies, too, there are strong efforts on the part of a wide range of social and political agencies to educate citizens to respect the official law and to internalize official legal values.

In the Soviet Union such efforts are valued more highly than in the United States. A conspicuous place is occupied in Soviet public affairs by what is called, in Russian, *pravovoe vospitanie,* literally, "legal nurturing" or "legal upbringing." Also much attention is given to what is called *pravovaia propaganda,* literally, "legal propaganda," that is, the propagandizing of law or the circulation of information about law. Basic codes and statutes are sometimes published in hundreds of thousands of copies. A monthly magazine about law, entitled *Chelovek i Zakon, (Man and the Law)*, contains articles, short stories, pictures, cartoons, and the like. In 1974 it had a circulation of over three million, and a nationwide television show of the same name and purpose is broadcast each week. On the other hand, the U.S. press gives far more detailed and far more objective coverage of court cases and of legislative debates than is given in the Soviet Union, and U.S. television and press reports of such legal events as the 1973 Senate Watergate hearings and the 1974 House Judiciary Committee debate on impeachment of the President constitute a "legal nurturing" and a "legal propaganda" that have no equal in the Soviet Union.

What sharply distinguishes the Soviet from the U.S. concern for the shaping of popular law-consciousness, however, is the heavy Soviet emphasis on using the official law itself for the purpose. This is called, in Russian, *vospitatel 'naia rol' prava*, "the nurturing role of Soviet law." The law itself, through its procedures and substantive provisions, is intended, above all, to educate, guide, and train Soviet citizens in official legal values as well as in Soviet moral and social values generally. The ideas and feelings of Soviet citizens concerning the law are supposed to be fostered not only by the family, the school, the press, the trade unions, and other social and state agencies but also by the courts in the conduct of cases and by legislators and administrators in the performance of their official duties. The purpose of Soviet law itself is not only to make people behave, by threat of sanctions or promise of rewards, according to the official rules. It is also, and more fundamentally, to educate offenders to change their attitudes and to reinforce among nonoffenders their belief in the basic goals of Soviet society. Thus law is intended to help create the "new Soviet person" needed for the building of Communism.

Christian and Communist Parallels.—Perhaps the closest historical parallel to these Soviet concepts is found in sixteenth-century Protestant writings on the use of the law. In both Lutheran and Calvinist thought, law, including both the moral law of scripture and the secular law of the state, had a threefold purpose: first, to deter recalcitrant people from misconduct by threat of penalties; second, to make people repentant of their sins and conscious of their obligations; and third, to guide faithful people in the paths of virtuous living. Of the last purpose, John Calvin wrote:[3]

> The third use of the law, which is the principal one, and which is more nearly connected with the proper end of it, relates to the faithful, in whose hearts the Spirit of God already lives and reigns. For although the law is inscribed and engraven on their hearts by the finger of God—that is, although they are so excited and animated by the direction of the Spirit, that they desire to obey God—yet they derive a twofold advantage from the law. For they find it an excellent instrument to give them, from day to day, a better and more certain understanding of the Divine will to which they aspire and to confirm them in the knowledge of it. As, though a servant be already influenced by the strongest desire of gaining the approbation of his master, yet it is necessary for him carefully to inquire and observe the orders of his master, in order to conform to them. Nor let any one of us exempt himself from this necessity; for no man has already acquired so much wisdom, that he could not by the daily instruction of the law make new advances into a purer knowledge of the Divine will. In the next place, as we need not only instruction, but also exhortation, the servant of God will derive this further advantage from the law; by frequent meditation on it

---

[3] John Calvin, *Institutes of the Christian Religion*, trans. J. Allen (Philadelphia, PA, 1816), 2:176-177.

he will be excited to obedience, he will be confirmed in it, and restrained from
the slippery path of transgressions.[4]

If the language of Christianity in Calvin's statement is replaced by the
language of Leninism—if "Spirit of God" and "finger of God" are replaced by
"vision of communism," "obey God" is replaced by "serve the Party," and
"Divine will" by "will of the Party"—the above passage could be found
duplicated throughout Soviet legal writings today.

In contrast, the prevailing theory of law in the United States not only does
not acknowledge a law "inscribed and engraven on the hearts of the faithful"
but also does not acknowledge that it is a principal purpose of law to bring
people to repentance or guide them to virtue. It is widely recognized that law
does, in fact, influence moral and legal conceptions. However, it is generally
presupposed that this is only a by-product of law, a latent social function of
legal rules and procedures, and not part of their express purpose, not part of
the law itself. The purposes of law, it is said, are to keep the peace, to delimit
interests, to prevent interference by one person in the domain of another, to
enforce rights and obligations established by government or by the voluntary
agreement of individuals, and generally to promote order and justice.
Traditionally, at least, reinforcing or changing people's ideas and attitudes,
including their ideas and attitudes concerning law, is thought to be the task of
the family, the school, the church, the local community, the various informal
associations in which we live and, increasingly, the political system, but not
of the law as such, and especially not of the courts.

The Nature of Legal Man.—These contrasting U.S. and Soviet views of the
role of the official legal system with respect to popular legal ideas and attitudes reflect contrasting assumptions concerning the nature of the person
who is the "subject" of legal rights and duties, that is, of the person to whom
law is addressed, and who participates in legal processes as a litigant or
potential litigant or as a voter or in other ways. The assumption implicit in
the U.S. view is that *legal man* is an independent adult who knows his or her
interests and is capable of asserting them. His sense of law-consciousness has
already been formed. He is a rugged individualist, a "reasonable, prudent
man" who stands or falls by his own claims and defenses and is presumed to
have intended the natural and probable consequences of his acts. The Soviets,
on the other hand, in emphasizing the "nurturing role" of law, assume that
legal man is a person in need of nurturing and capable of being nurtured. In

---

[4] Cf. Harold J. Berman, *The Interaction of Law and Religion* (Nashville, TN, 1974), 94,
166-167.

effect he is a youth, a dependent member of the collective, whom the law must guide and train and discipline. He is treated as a member of a growing, unfinished society that is moving toward a new and higher phase of development.

Some may object that these contrasts are overdrawn. U.S. law is no longer so "bourgeois" as it was fifty or 100 years ago. Soviet law is no longer so "moralistic" or "ideological" as it was in Stalin's time. In both systems a balance has been struck between the use of law, on the one hand, to shape people's moral and legal attitudes and, on the other, to protect their rights and keep the peace. In both systems people are treated for some purposes as mature, independent, right-and-duty-bearing adults and for other purposes as dependent, collective youth. Is there not at least a tendency toward convergence between the two "models"?

To do full justice to this question would require a detailed analysis of many aspects of both legal systems. In certain areas of Soviet law, a person's rights are treated as virtually absolute and no argument based on communist morality and the educational role of law can prevail against them. Conversely, in certain areas of U.S. law, a person's rights are treated as subordinate to considerations of morality and public policy. In fact, a long list of important similarities could be drawn up between Soviet and U.S. law. Yet despite all the particular similarities the ensemble of each legal system is strikingly different from the other. These differences are usually expressed by Western observers in terms of *Rechtssicherheit* and the rule of law; they are usually expressed by Soviet writers in terms of state ownership of the means of production and Marxist-Leninist ideology.[5]

Even more fundamental, in my view, are the differences in concepts of the relationship of the law to the people who are addressed, so to speak, by it. These differences are manifested in the Soviet emphasis on the educational or "nurturing" role of law. Another way of expressing this is by the phrase "parental law," which refers to the role of Soviet law as parent or teacher and to Soviet legal man as a youth to be guided and trained—a phrase that I have used elsewhere and which has incurred the wrath of a Soviet reviewer.[6] A similar concept is expressed by the phrase "legal socialization," or, as

---

[5] V.A. Tumanov, "Failure to Understand or Unwillingness to Understand," *Soviet Law and Government* 4(3) (1965): 3-10.

[6] See Berman, "Reply to Tumanov," *Soviet Law and Government* 4(3) 1965: 11-16; Tumanov, "Failure to Understand."

Petrazhitskii[7] put it, the use of law for "the socialization of the psyche." Such socialization, above all, is the *raison d'àtre* of Soviet legal institutions.

Soviet Techniques of Socialization Through Law.—Soviet legislation furnishes abundant examples of the conscious use of law for the "socialization of the psyche." Thus, Article 3 of the Fundamental Principles of Court Organization of the U.S.S.R. provides:

> By all its activity a court shall educate citizens of the U.S.S.R. in the spirit of devotion to the Motherland and the cause of communism, in the spirit of strict and undeviating execution of Soviet laws, care for socialist property, observance of labor discipline, and honorable attitude toward public and social duty, [and] respect for the rights, honor, and dignity of citizens [and] for rules of socialist community life.[8]

This provision is the foundation stone of Soviet judicial procedure. In implementing it, the Soviet republican codes of criminal procedure require the court not only to determine the guilt or innocence of the accused and to pass sentence but also to "expose the causes and conditions facilitating the commission of the crime and to take measures to eliminate them."[9] A similar provision exists for civil disputes. In order to bring such causes and conditions to light, wide use must be made of the help of the public. Representatives of so-called social organizations—the trade union, the collective of the apartment house, the collective of the institute, and so on—are encouraged to appear in court on one side or the other.[10] In both civil and criminal cases trials are often held in the clubroom of a factory or apartment house or other place where the parties or the accuses live or work or study.[11]

In trying a case, the judges—a professional judge and two law assessors—are supposed to pay special attention to the educational effect of the proceedings not only on the accused or the litigants but also on the courtroom spectators and on the broader public. As stated in Article 243 of the RSFSR

---

[7] L.J. Petrazhitskii, *Law and Morality*, trans. H. W. Babb (Cambridge, MA, 1955), 310-312, 328.

[8] Berman, *Soviet Criminal Law and Procedure; the R.S.F.S.R. Codes*, 2d ed. (Cambridge, MA, 1972), 83.

[9] Harold J. Berman and James W. Spindler, *Criminal Code of the R.S.F.S.R.* (Cambridge, MA, 1972), 259.

[10] See, e.g., 1960 RSFSR Code of Criminal Procedure, Arts. 128, 228, 236, 250, 276, 288, 291, 293-298, & 302 in Berman & Spindler, *Criminal Code*; 1964 RSFSR Code of Civil Procedure, Arts. 141 (6), 147, & 225 in *The Civil Code and the Code of Civil Procedure of the R.S.F.S.R.*, trans. A.K.R. Kiralfy (Atlantic Highlands, N.J., 1966).

[11] Berman & Spindler, *Criminal Code*, 84-87.

Codes of Criminal Procedure, the presiding judge of the court in directing the judicial session "shall [secure] the educational influence of the trial."[12] Indeed, a Soviet book on the legal profession states that the court "is one of the places where . . . people are educated in the spirit of respect for law and for the norms of socialist morality."[13] Therefore, the authors conclude, not only the judges but also counsel for the parties must analyze the social and political aspects of the case and in so doing must attempt to persuade both the court and the spectators.[14]

The Soviet use of law to guide people to virtue is nowhere more evident than in the institution of Comrades' Courts. These are popular laymen's tribunals in factories, apartment houses, educational institutions, and elsewhere, which hear cases of minor offenses and are empowered to issue warnings and reprimands and to impose small fines. In extreme cases they may recommend discharge from jobs or eviction from apartments. Comrades' Courts' sanctions are termed "measures of social pressure."[15] Hundreds of Soviet citizens serve on these "courts" and millions attend their sessions.[16]

Another striking example is the People's Guard, a mass organization of volunteer auxiliary police, which patrols streets, directs traffic, and generally assists in law enforcement. As stated in the 1960 RSFSR Statute on Voluntary People's Patrols, its purpose is "[t]o participate in educational work among the population concerning the observance of the rules of socialist community life and the prevention of anti-social offenses."[17] Some six million young men serve in the People's Guard.

Soviet substantive law also is permeated with provisions intended to induce belief in and conformity to the ideals of civic virtue. The criminal code not only makes punishable—as do non-Soviet criminal codes—immoral acts considered to be socially dangerous but also proscribes the malicious refusal to take an assigned job by a person who "is leading an antisocial way of life" and conducting a "parasitic existence."[18] The civil code expressly declares that private ownership ("personal ownership") is derived from socialist ownership and that rights granted by the code are protected only to the extent

---

[12] Ibid., 351.

[13] Evgenil B. Zaitsev & Arkadii P. Poltorak, *The Soviet Bar*, trans. I. Lasker (Moscow, 1959), 120.

[14] See also George Feifer, *Justice in Moscow* (London, 1964), 104-105.

[15] Berman, *Justice in the U.S.S.R.*, 288-291.

[16] Berman & Spindler, *Criminal Code*; Feifer, *Justice in Moscow*, 115-120.

[17] Berman, *Justice in the U.S.S.R.*, 287.

[18] See Berman & Spindler, *Criminal Code*, Art. 209, 210.

that they are exercised in conformity with the social-economic purpose for which they are granted.[19]

Soviet limitations on rights of private property and private contract have often been viewed both in the West and in the East simply as manifestations of a state that has greatly extended the range of its interests and activities at the expense of individual economic autonomy. However, something more fundamental is also involved, namely, the subordination of *all* individual property and contract rights—however extensive they may be (and they are much more extensive in the Soviet Union than is often supposed)—to the interests of the society as a whole. The same is even more true of rights of speech. What the law intends is to manifest and to instill a sense that individual rights are conferred in trust, so to speak, for the future communist society. A good example is provided by Article 125 of the Soviet Constitution, which provides for freedom of speech, press, and assembly, but only to the extent that it is exercised in "conformity with the interests of the working people and in order to strengthen the socialist system."[20]

The Effect of Positive Law on Popular Law-Consciousness.—Is it possible to change people's beliefs and feelings by law? The eighteenth-century Enlightenment view, which still prevails to a considerable extent in the United States, is that it is not possible and that even if it were possible it would be wrong to try. The law, it is said, should concern itself with people's conduct and their expectations of its consequences, not with their beliefs and feelings. This view of law is built into our legal system, where it survives long after the virtual disappearance of the Enlightenment presuppositions on which it is based.

At least so far as the judicial process is concerned, it would be considered improper, in most cases, for a U.S. court to undertake the kind of broad-ranging inquiry into surrounding circumstances that is required by the Soviet procedural codes. Also it generally would be considered improper for the court to shame litigants or the accused into revealing, and repenting, the sources of their waywardness. The systematic use of representatives of extrajudicial bodies—"the collective" of the factory or neighborhood or institute—as aids to the court in determining the outcome of cases would likewise not be tolerated by legal thought in the United States.

There are, to be sure, some U.S. parallels to the Soviet Comrades' Courts—for example, tenants' councils in low-cost housing projects

---

[19] See *1964 RSFSR Civil Code*, trans. W. Gray and R. Stults, ed. Whitmore Gray (Ann Arbor, MI, 1965), Preamble & Art. 5.

[20] Harold J. Berman & John B. Quigley, *Basic Laws of the Structure of the Soviet State* (Cambridge, MA, 1969), 24.

authorized under guidelines of the Department of Housing and Urban Development.[21] But these are scattered instances and are not integral in the legal system. Similarly, U.S. parallels to the Soviet People's Guards may be found in various volunteer neighborhood law enforcement organizations, especially in big cities; but these, too, are only somewhat comparable to the nationwide mass organization found in the Soviet Union.

Connected with the question of the propriety of attempting to influence beliefs by law is the question of the effectiveness of such an attempt. Here, however, we face insuperable difficulties of proof. On the one hand, a very considerable amount of vice persists in the Soviet Union, including crime, corruption, drunkenness, sloth, and various other kinds of sins; since the Soviets do not publish statistics on these matters, the suspicion is aroused that the rate of vice has in fact increased, rather than decreased, over the years. On the other hand, even assuming that virtue is declining despite all efforts to promote it, it does not necessarily follow that those efforts are in vain, for the rate of decline might possibly have been much greater if such efforts had not been made.

It should also be stressed that not only the law but all social institutions and all forms of social control in the Soviet Union, including the Communist Party, economic organizations, trade unions, the press, the school, the arts, and a host of others, are used to guide people to virtue. If the educational or "parental" role of law were to be abandoned or substantially reduced, the law would become strikingly different from every other official activity of the Soviet social, economic, and political system. Thus, it is impossible to isolate the consequences of moral education through law from those of moral education through social, economic, and political institutions in general.

The experience of the United States seems to be equally inconclusive as to whether law can in fact change people's attitudes and values. Prohibition is often cited to show the ineffectiveness of legal control over morals. Apparent changes in attitudes toward racial equality following court decisions and legislation denouncing racial discrimination are often cited for the contrary position. Again, the multiplicity of factors involved and the "iffiness" of the question make it difficult to test the specific influence of law on beliefs. It is doubtful whether under any circumstances the efficacy of law as an educational instrument—or its inefficacy—can ever be tested by objective criteria.

The Relationship of Legal Theory to Psychological Theory.—Soviet concepts of the educational role of law reflect Soviet concepts of psychology generally

---

[21] See also June Louin Tapp and Felice J. Levine, eds., *Law, Justice, and the Individual in Society: Psychological and Legal Issues* (New York, 1977), 163-182.

and of educational psychology in particular. As is well known, Soviet psychological theory, in comparison with theories such as those of Piaget,[22] which are widely held in Western countries, emphasizes the plasticity of the human psyche and the possibility of influencing attitudes by social conditioning.[23] In part, this Soviet emphasis rests on behaviorist premises that derive historically from the work of the great prerevoluntionary Russian psychologists I.P. Pavlov and V.M. Bekhterev on conditioned reflexes.[24] However, Soviet psychologists have gone far beyond behaviorism in their recognition of the autonomous role of consciousness and their belief that conscious social effort can overcome both hereditary and environmental obstacles to the development of socially desirable beliefs and attitudes.[25] They state that the internalization of social norms is effectuated primarily by communication (especially persuasion and suggestion) and by example within the context of the social group.[26] Thus, Soviet psychology matches Soviet philosophical theories of the perfectibility of human nature and Soviet sociological theories of the ultimate dependence of personal values on social conditions, as well as Soviet legal theories of the educational role of legal institutions.

In conformity with these theories, Soviet educators place great stress, from the earliest years of children's schooling, on collective living, cooperative play and work, and the express goals of Communist morality.[27] Competition among pupils (like competition among state economic enterprises) is "socialist competition"; that is, it is not primarily competition between individuals but rather competition between collectives. In elementary schools, it is competition between rows, between classes, between schools, and so on. According to Urie Bronfenbrenner, in Soviet schools peer

---

[22] See Jean Piaget, *Judgement and Reasoning in the Child* (London, 1928); id., *The Child's Conception of the World* (London, 1929); id., *The Moral Judgement of the Child by J. Piaget with the Assistance of Seven Collaborators* (London, 1932).

[23] See Michael Cole and Irving Maltzman, eds., *Handbook of Soviet Psychology* (New York, 1969); Levy Rahmani, *Soviet Psychology: Philosophical, Theoretical and Experimental Issues* (New York, 1973).

[24] Raymond A. Bauer, *The New Man in Soviet Psychology* (Cambridge, MA, 1952); Jonas Langer, *Theories of Development* (New York, 1969); Ivan Petrovich Pavlov, *Experimental Psychology and other Essays* (New York, 1957).

[25] Aleksei A. Leontiev, Alexsandr R. Luria and Anatolii A. Smirnov, eds., *Psychological Research in the U.S.S.R.* (Moscow, 1966).

[26] A.G. Kovalev, "Vazimovliianie liudei v protsesse obscheniia i formirovanie obshchestvennoi psikhologii," in A.I. Gertsena, ed., *Voprosy psikhologii lichnosti i obshchestvennoi psikhologii* (Leningrad, 1964); A.G. Kovalev, *Psikhologii lichnosti* (Moscow, 1965).

[27] Frederick C. Barghoorn, *Politics in the U.S.S.R.; A Country Study by Frederick C. Baarghoorn*, 2d ed. (Boston, MA, 1972).

evaluation occurs weekly and the "tattletale," as he or she is viewed in other countries, is valued positively as a person who contributes to group achievement. At the same time, Soviet children are taught to be even more sensitive to adult evaluation than to peer evaluation. The most important adult sanction is withdrawal of love, and the ultimate adult sanction is expulsion from the class, from the school, and so forth.[28]

All these characteristics of Soviet educational psychology have important parallels in Soviet legal psychology. The substantive law, as we have already noted, imposes heavy duties of cooperation. The Constitution itself imposes social duties on Soviet citizens, such as the duty, under Article 130, "to respect the rules of socialist community life."[29] Trial procedure, in both criminal and civil cases, is supposed to expose the shame of the offender and to induce him or her to repent.[30] Withdrawal of love is manifested in expulsion to a correctional labor colony, exile to remote regions, or banishment from particular cities or regions.

The psychological presuppostions of both Soviet law and Soviet education bear a considerable resemblance to the social learning theory of child development expounded in the United States by Miller, Dollard, Whiting, Sears, and others.[31] Briefly stated, the social learning theory emphasizes the child's imitation of, and identification with, adults. The child internalizes the norms of behavior due to a desire for approval, which, in turn, reinforces self-confidence. For Western social learning theory, as for Soviet educational and legal theory, the most important negative stimulus to moral development is the withdrawal of love.

What Soviet psychologists add to the social learning theory of Western (and especially U.S.) psychologists is an emphasis on the child's membership in the group. Western psychologists tend to start their analysis by making a division between the consciousness of the individual child and the surrounding environment; the family, the school, the neighborhood, and so on are treated as external factors with which the child interacts. Soviet writers, on the other hand, do not consider the psyche in exclusively individual terms. The child who is influenced by the peer group is not, after all, outside that group: As part of it, his or her interaction with it is also an interaction within the self. Similarly the parent, the teacher, the group, the society are both inside and outside the child and at the same time are both inside and outside

---

[28] Urie Bronfenbrenner, *Two Worlds of Childhood: U.S. and U.S.S.R.* (New York, 1970).

[29] Berman & Quigley, *Basic Laws of the Structure of the Soviet State,* 25.

[30] Feifer, *Justice in Moscow,* 38-44, 147-148.

[31] Jonas Langer, *Theories of Development* (New York, 1969).

the child's environment. This, I believe, is what Soviet writers mean when they speak of "training" as something additional to both heredity and environment.[32] A closely related insight is that of the famous Soviet psychologist L.S. Vygotsky that language forms an important link between the social context and the individual consciousness.[33]

In light of the close connection drawn by Soviet scholars between individual psychology and group psychology, and in light of the emphasis they place upon group persuasion and examples as means of influencing individual attitudes, it is not surprising that in the past decade there has developed a special branch of psychology called "judicial psychology." Indeed, a decree of the Central Committee of the Communist Party (1964) called for the development of judicial psychology as a separate branch of science. In accordance with this decree, articles have appeared and a textbook has been published dealing with psychological aspects of crime, psychological factors in investigative and judicial proceedings, psychological aspects of the re-education of convicted persons, and, more broadly, psychological effects of legal proceedings on the attitudes of people who participate in them, witness them, or are affected by them.[34]

Yet, despite these brave words, an examination of this new literature shows that Soviet judicial psychology is in a very primitive state as both a scholarly discipline and a practical art. An evaluation of its deficiencies would require analysis of Soviet theory and practice with respect to the two primary means of social learning: communication and example. It would also require an analysis of the underlying premise that the official law can best nurture unofficial law-consciousness when it is deliberately used for that purpose.

There is a very great difference between a sociological or psychological generalization concerning the nature and functions of law and an incorporation of that generalization into the legal system. For example, the sociological generalization that in every society law serves the interests of the state may be quite innocent, but a legal principle that law in the given society *must* serve the interests of the state may be quite harmful. It is not accidental that all

---

[32] Raymond A. Bauer, *The New Man in Soviet Psychology* (Cambridge, MA, 1952).

[33] Lev S. Vygotsky, *Thought and Language* (Cambridge, MA, 1962), 1966.

[34] Ateist Vasil'evich Dulov, *Sudebnaia psikhologiia* (Minsk, 1970) wrote this textbook for higher educational institutions. A bibliography on 382 lists 17 items published between 1964 and 1969, chiefly dealing with methods of conducting investigations, methods of examining witnesses, and the like. Several of the articles listed sketch general programs of study of legal psychology. Cf., e.g., O. A. Gavrilo, "O problemakh sovetskoi sudebnoi psikhologii," in Gertsena, ed., *Voprosy*. However, Dulov's book is the first textbook on the subject.

legal *systems*—as contrasted with legal *philosophies*—put themselves forward as embodiments of universal justice.

What the Soviets have added to the legal concept of law as an embodiment of universal justice, and what the United States and other non-Communist societies are coming more and more to add, is the legal concept of law as a *teacher*. The question is what kind of teacher. The Soviet concept implies that the bearer of rights and duties—"legal man"—is a youth to be guided and trained. The socialization of popular law-consciousness is conceived as a process by which the society's unofficial sense of law is raised to the level proclaimed by the official lawmaking authorities. There are obvious dangers in the implicit belief that the movement between official law, with its technical language and professional practitioners, and unofficial law, with its diffuse relationship to custom and morality, may go in only one direction.

——— ⟨⟩ 21 ⟨⟩ ———

THE WEIGHTIER MATTERS OF THE LAW:
A RESPONSE TO SOLZHENITSYN*

To the 10,000 students and alumni assembled at the 1978 Harvard commencement, Solzhenitsyn seemed like a man from Mars. Here was a great prophet from another world. He was known to us primarily as one who, in his writings, had powerfully and brilliantly exposed the evils of the Stalin terror. These are the works not of a philosopher or a sociologist but of a writer, in the traditional Russian sense of that word—a novelist or poet who is at the same time a seer, one who looks into the soul of a people. Using his great literary talent and prophetic insight to tell the story of the sufferings inflicted upon him and millions of fellow prisoners in the "archipelago" of Soviet labor camps, Solzhenitsyn has also portrayed, in a manner that is characteristically Russian, both the tragic and the heroic side of that cataclysmic experience, its diabolical and at the same time its potentially sanctifying character.

Solzhenitsyn's quality as a writer—his short story entitled "Matryona's House," which is not about the labor camps at all, is one of the great literary gems of our time—is measured by his ability to make us share with him the whole experience of the terror. Having been sentenced as a counter-revolutionary because of some veiled derogatory remarks about Stalin that he wrote in a letter to a friend near the end of World War II, Solzhenitsyn used his

---

* Reprinted from Ronald Berman, ed., *Solzhenitsyn at Harvard* (Washington, DC, 1980), 99-113.

mathematical training to devise a mnemonic system for recording in his memory every important detail of life in the camps. To keep even the crudest written report was strictly prohibited; everything had to be committed to memory. The fate of his comrades was impressed like a scar on the tissue of his brain. He swore that he would not let them be forgotten.

His books about the camps are not only, however, a story of those people; they are also a story of the tyranny of the system, especially as that tyranny was manifested in its own inner logic, its internal rationality, indeed, its own perverted legality. We usually think of the camps as being the very opposite of rationality and legality, as the embodiment of arbitrariness. Solzhenitsyn, however, shows us that the arbitrariness of the system was expressed above all in its legalism. Everything was done in the name of the law—some article of the Code, some regulation of the Ministry or of the Chief Administration or of the Director, some rule of the camps that had to be obeyed.

For example, Solzhenitsyn describes the operation of the system of complaints. According to the law, every prisoner was entitled to petition higher authorities if his rights were violated, and all such complaints were to be examined and acted upon. So the prisoner would ask for a pencil and a piece of paper on which to write a complaint. Eventually, he would be given a pencil, but it would hardly write; and a piece of paper, but it was of such a poor quality that it could not be written on, and besides, it was too small. Finally, after tremendous effort, the prisoner wrote out some sort of complaint, which he handed to the investigator or guard—who threw it away, perhaps, or passed it on to someone. Perhaps it eventually disappeared into some file or other. There was never any response. The forms of law were utilized, but in a completely perverse way.

Bureaucratic perversity was connected, in Solzhenitsyn's view, with the emphasis of the system on science and on planning—which was also perverted in practice. The system, by its scientific rationality and by its legalism, "strangles the personality," as he put it in his Harvard address. The only way to overcome the tyranny of rationality and of legalism was to die to oneself, to give up everything, to give up even the desire for anything for oneself. One of the prisoners says to a camp official: "You can tell old you-know-who-up-there that you only have a power over people so long as you don't take *everything* away from them. But when you have robbed a man of everything, he is no longer in your power, he is free again." So Solzhenitsyn, in James Luther Adams' words, "sees in the brutality and dehumanization of the labor camps the consequences of a rationality that wills one thing and one thing only." Yet he believes that the resources of the human spirit are great enough to overcome even this demonic force.

Having been expelled from his country, Solzhenitsyn continued to publish new volumes of *The Gulag Archipelago* and to work for the victims of Soviet repression. At the same time he spoke out for a new Russia in which the old Russia would be restored, a Christian Russia whose leadership might even be Communist but whose people would be free to maintain their Russian Orthodox faith without political interference, and where a strong sense of spiritual togetherness would be combined with humanitarian aspirations and a sense of national mission.

Although he had been in the United States for several years, the Harvard address was to be Solzhenitsyn's first major expression of his views in this country. We looked forward to it eagerly. Most people, no doubt, anticipated that he would now praise America for those strengths and virtues it offers in opposition to the Soviet system: above all, our freedom and our law. Imagine our dismay when, instead, he attacked the things we cherish most, and charged that those very freedoms which we oppose to the brutality of the Stalin terror, those very laws which are genuine laws and not the perverted laws of the Stalin terror, that very humanism, that tolerance, that pluralism, which we suppose to be the very things needed to save us from brutality and dehumanization—that these strengths and virtues, as we conceive them, are in fact the root cause of our decadence, our materialism, our criminality, our superficiality, our spiritual exhaustion, our "loss of civic courage," our breakdown of leadership. And imagine our further dismay when he urged upon us the very values of sacrifice and self-discipline and collective will, of subordination to authority, and of common faith that we in America have long associated with the Communist system.

Ten thousand people cheered and applauded the speech. When they went home and thought about it, however, many of them changed their minds. Soon letters began to appear in the press denouncing the speech and calling the speaker a false prophet. The press itself was not at all pleased that the great man had said it was irresponsible and corrupt and dangerous. The legal profession was not pleased to be told that our laws are cold, hard, and impersonal, and that they are a source of conformism and even corruption. Youth—and ex-youth—were shocked at the assertion that it was lack of civil courage that had induced us to withdraw from the Vietnam war. The clergy was pleased, but the professors were not, to hear a call for a return to faith in a Supreme Being.

A *New York Times* editorial charged Solzhenitsyn with having an "obsessive personality" and a "messianic complex." That newspaper's senior columnist, James Reston, quoted Solzhenitsyn's statement: "A fact which cannot be disputed is the weakening of human beings in the West while in the East [owing to their spiritual training in suffering] they are becoming firmer and stronger. . . . " Reston, who is normally quite calm, responded: "This from the author of the unspeakable tortures of the Soviet prisons and psychiatric wards? This is 'a fact which cannot be disputed?' The hell it can't!" Solzhenitsyn seemed to have touched a raw nerve.

How the West Lost Heart.—When one studies Solzhenitsyn's Harvard address carefully, it turns out to be much more complex and difficult to understand than is generally realized. The spiritual exhaustion of the West, our lack of courage, our decadence, is only one major theme. And it is not a simple one.

Within this theme there are four main points. The first is that modern Western states were founded on a belief in the pursuit of happiness. Here Solzhenitsyn cited, of course, the American Declaration of Independence; however, he mistakenly identified the concept of happiness in that document with the possession of material goods. With regard to the pursuit of happiness (so defined), Solzhenitsyn made two subpoints: that the desire for more material goods does not in fact bring happiness and, more important, that this desire is an obstacle to free spiritual development—more particularly, it is an obstacle to the willingness to risk one's "precious life" in the defense of common values. In a society raised in the cult of material well-being, Solzhenitsyn said, there is little readiness to die to defend one's country.

It may seem like carping to point out that Solzhenitsyn confused eighteenth-century and twentieth-century concepts of happiness, and that what the pursuit of happiness meant to the framers of the Declaration of Independence was really a secular form of blessedness or salvation, namely, an aspiration to the good life. It is by no means unimportant to recognize, however, that the pursuit of material welfare has come to mean something quite different in the twentieth century from what is previously meant. In nineteenth-century America it meant working against heavy odds for a decent standard of living, one that would release time and energy for education and for the improvement of social conditions. Solzhenitsyn neglected to say that the search for material goods may have a spiritual value under conditions of hardship that is entirely lacking under conditions of abundance. Moreover, the notion that there is a necessary conflict between the pursuit of happiness and the willingness to risk one's life for defense is disproved by the example of the framers of the Declaration of Independence, who for the sake of life, liberty, and the pursuit of happiness were willing to pledge their lives, their fortunes, and their sacred honor.

Solzhenitsyn's second main point is that our pursuit of material goods is linked with legalism. In Western society, he stated, "the limits of human rights and justice are determined by a system of laws." A legal solution is considered to be "the supreme solution"—"if a man is proven right by law, nothing more is required." So the selfishness of Western man is closely connected, in Solzhenitsyn's view, with his reverence for law. I shall return later to the concepts of law and legalism implicit in this view.

The third main point is that both the selfishness and the legalism of the West are linked to a larger philosophical concept that Solzhenitsyn called "rationalistic humanism" or "anthropocentrism." Rationalistic humanism, he said—that is, the worship of man and his material needs—which was responsible for the rise of the West in the centuries of the Renaissance and of the Enlightenment, is now the cause of its impending downfall.

Here Solzhenitsyn committed a serious factual error about Western history—one that is widely committed in the West itself, though it has been exposed by virtually all professional historians. He contrasted the materialism of modern Western man from the time of the Renaissance with the spirituality of medieval Western man in the preceding period. He stated that in the Middle Ages spirituality predominated over man's physical nature, and a sense of man's inherent sinfulness and weakness predominated over his self-affirmation and sense of power. The waning of the Middle Ages, according to Solzhenitsyn, was due to exhaustion caused by the despotic oppression of man's physical nature.

In fact, however, it is well known that the High Middle Ages, the period from the late eleventh to the fifteenth century, was a time of great self-confidence and of great energy and expansion. It was a time of dynamic growth in the arts and architecture, in literature and scholarship, as well as in agriculture and industry. Thousands of cities were founded. Commerce flourished. The universities were established. The Gothic cathedrals were built. Sophisticated legal systems were created both in the ecclesiastical and in the secular polity.

Moreover, Solzhenitsyn's notion that it was in the modern period of "rationalistic humanism," dating from the Renaissance, that the existence of intrinsic evil in man was denied, runs into the difficulty that this was the same period in which Protestantism, with its emphasis on man's sinfulness, emerged and flourished. And surely the framers of the United States Constitution, though they were men of the Enlightenment, strongly believed in the intrinsic evil of human nature—indeed, it was to restrain man's natural greed and lust for power that a government of laws, a government of checks and balances, was created.

Solzhenitsyn's fourth main point is quite different from the first three, and even contradictory to them. Two hundred years ago, when American democracy was created, he stated, "all individual human rights were granted on the grounds that man is God's creature." Freedom was then conditioned on religious responsibility. Even fifty years ago, freedom was understood in the context of "the moral heritage of the Christian centuries, with their great reserves of mercy and sacrifice." Today, however, there is a despiritualized and irreligious humanism, both in the East and in the West. We have lost the belief in a "Supreme Complete Entity" that once restrained our passions and our irresponsibility. We have placed too much hope in political and social reform only to find we were being deprived of our spiritual life—in the East by the Communist party and in the West by commercial interests.

This is the real crisis. Solzhenitsyn had started his speech with the words "Our world is divided." He had gone on to say that it was divided among a variety of civilizations—the West, China, India, the Muslim world, Africa, Russia. He had then criticized the West for its "spiritual exhaustion." But near the end of his speech, the splits in the world seemed less terrible than the similarity of the disease plaguing most of its parts. At the end, the speech was not essentially about "The Exhausted West," the title given when it was published in *Harvard Magazine*; nor was it essentially about "A World Split Apart," as it was later entitled when published in book form. It was, instead, a prophetic utterance about the spiritual condition of the whole of mankind, East and West, South and North: a mankind threatened with spiritual suffocation, dehumanized and despiritualized.

In this predicament, mankind's greatest need, Solzhenitsyn said, is voluntary, inspired self-restraint; only this will enable it to rise above the tidal wave of materialism that is engulfing it. His emphasis here on self-restraint is comparable to his earlier emphasis, in his 1970 Nobel Prize speech, on the role of art and poetry and beauty in raising the level of man's spiritual consciousness. At that time he spoke of the need for freedom of the creative arts and literature, quoting the great line that Dostoevsky put in the mouth of Prince Myshkin in *The Idiot*: "The world will be saved by beauty." There is no inconsistency between the two speeches in this respect. An attack on the abuses and excesses of freedom is entirely compatible with a belief in freedom. This is a point missed by many critics of Solzhenitsyn's Harvard address. What is meant by freedom is another matter. For Solzhenitsyn, freedom means primarily moral and spiritual freedom; legal freedoms—legal rights—are seen by him as, at best, a means to that end. This, too, is a matter to which I shall return.

The Harvard address concludes with the prophecy that the world "has reached a historic turning point, equal in importance to the turn from the Middle Ages to the Renaissance." We shall have to rise, Solzhenitsyn states, "to a new, higher vision, to a new level of life, where our physical nature will not be condemned as in the Middle Ages—but, even more important, our spiritual nature will not be trampled upon as in modern times." A new anthropological stage has been reached. "No one on earth has any other way left but—upward."

Two Views of Law.—We can best sort out the paradoxes in Solzhenitsyn's Harvard address, best explain the self-contradictions, by tracing his concept of law to its sources in Russian Orthodox Christianity and in Russian and Soviet experience, and by contrasting that concept with the concept of law embodied in Western Christianity and in the Western legal tradition.

Rare is the commencement speaker who does not pay tribute to our Constitution and to our legal system, or at least to the Supreme Court. Distinctions may be made between the great constitutional principles and the ways in which they have been applied. The Supreme Court may be criticized for departing from values and policies of an earlier period. A call may be sounded for changes in particular laws. But to attack law itself as a value, as a standard, as a bond of our unity—this is unheard of! Yet this is what Solzhenitsyn seemed to be doing. No wonder there was a strong reaction from our "opinion leaders." Some of them even went so far as to see in the speech a defense of totalitarianism. But that, surely, is a misunderstanding. When Solzhenitsyn attacked the sensationalism and irresponsibility of the press, for example, he was by no means suggesting the desirability of censorship or other legal controls. On the contrary, he has little faith in legal controls of any kind. He was calling, rather, for self-restraint. The differences between Solzhenitsyn and most of his critics are subtler and deeper than most of the critics seem to realize.

Solzhenitsyn accuses the West, and especially the United States, of attaching to law a moral value that it does not deserve. He does not deny—on the contrary, he affirms—the necessity of having a legal order for the protection of society against arbitrariness and oppression. "Having spent all my life under a Communist rule," he states, "I can testify that a society with no objective legal scale is terrible indeed." However, "a society with no other scale but the legal one is less than worthy of man." Law belongs, in his view, to a lower order of moral and social life, and the West has given itself over to that lower order. Therefore the West offers no satisfactory model for "us," that is, for the Russians.

Solzhenitsyn's attack on the morality of law, or on law as the embodiment of moral values, reflects a form of antinomianism—"anti-lawism"—whose roots are deep in Russian history and culture. In traditional Russian Orthodox Christianity, law is sharply contrasted with grace, with faith, and with love. Law is thought to be hard, cold, impersonal, formal, intellectual; it is connected only with guilt and with punishment. Such antinomianism does not distinguish between a mechanical "legalism" that proceeds on the basis of technicalities and a creative, purposive "legality" that proceeds from a sense of justice. Indeed, there is no special word for "legalism" or "legalistic" in Russian; the same words must be used for "legalism" and "legality," for "legalistic" and "legal." When Solzhenitsyn speaks of law, he speaks only of the letter of the law, which kills, never of the spirit of the law, which gives life.

An important part of Russian spiritual and cultural tradition has been its stress on informal, spontaneous relations within the group, on togetherness, or what in Russian Christianity is called "*sobornost*" (conciliarity, community spirit). Prior to the latter part of the nineteenth century, this was associated in Russian history with an abhorrence of formal adjudication and, indeed, of all legal relations. The Russian church has always denounced Western Christianity for its legalism. The nineteenth-century Slavophile Ivan Kireevsky wrote scornfully, "In the West, brothers make contracts with brothers." In Russia, on the contrary, there should be no need for contracts at all, since all men should be brothers. Similarly, Dostoevsky's Grand Inquisitor can justify social institutions only as a "correction" of Jesus' work; they necessarily sacrifice the person to society, the unique to the statistical. They necessarily contradict the original Christian faith. Solzhenitsyn follows in Dostoevsky's path when he talks about the spiritual life of the unique person and disparages general rules that apply to large numbers. "Whenever the tissue of life is woven of legalistic [in Russian *iuridiche*, meaning also 'legal' or 'juridical'] relations," Solzhenitsyn states, "there is an atmosphere of moral mediocrity, paralyzing man's noblest impulses."

Certainly Solzhenitsyn was justified in warning us against the dangers of too great a reliance upon law, and especially against the exaltation of our legal system, our beloved Constitution, as an ultimate value, an end in itself, the highest standard of our collective life. This is, indeed, a form of idolatry—to worship a man-made thing, to glorify it for its own sake. Our reverence for law is justified only if law is seen as pointing to something higher than itself.

Perhaps he was also justified in charging that in the West personal morality is too often based upon legal standards. Here, however, his examples were not very satisfactory. One was the example of an oil company that purchases an invention of a new form of energy in order to suppress its use. Solzhenitsyn cited this to illustrate the statement: "One almost never meets with voluntary self-restraint. Everyone tries to go to the very limits of the legal framework." The second example, given to illustrate the same statement, was that of a food manufacturer who poisons his product to make it last longer; "after all, people are free not to buy it." These two examples show that conduct which is legal may nevertheless be immoral (although the word "poisons" suggests that the food manufacturer's conduct was in fact both immoral and illegal). But they are surely not examples of legalism. On the contrary, they suggest the need for more stringent *legal* controls of private economic activity. In England, for example, the law authorizes the government to make an unused patent available to others who are willing and able to exploit it.

Other examples of alleged legalism were supplied by Solzhenitsyn in a letter to the student organizers of a conference on law and religion. One was an example of a false claim for personal injury: a car was barely touched by another, and the driver falsely claimed severe injury to his back. The other was a case of a person who, being in a situation of danger, was rescued by a passerby and who then sued his rescuer on the false charge of having caused the predicament from which in fact the rescuer had saved him. These examples, too, seem to reflect a serious misunderstanding of the nature of legal rules and the differences between personal morality and social morality. Presumably it is socially desirable to have a system of insurance against losses caused by injuries. However, such a system is subject to abuse by unconscionable people who present inflated claims. A person who makes an inflated claim is, of course, committing both an immoral and an illegal act. If what Solzhenitsyn is saying is that many people in the United States think anything is morally justified "provided you can get away with it," then this is a charge against our standards of morality, not against either our legal system or our faith in our legal system.

No doubt there are other better examples, however, to support Solzhenitsyn's contention that we have identified our moral values too closely with legal standards. We say, for instance, that there is nothing *wrong* if an employer pays his workers the minimum wage, even if it is too low and he can afford to pay them more, since he is acting within the law. And many people would say they are entirely justified morally in not paying a debt after the legal time-period has passed within which a claim must be made. Here we are indeed guilty of confusing legality with morality.

Yet it is doubtful that even such examples as these really demonstrate that Americans today are a people who put too much faith in the law and who identify what is legally right with what is morally right. If anything, they show a certain cynicism about the law. And, in fact, Americans increasingly seem to be a people who do not believe in the law, and who are inclined to break the law whenever they can do so with impunity. Judge Lois Forer of the Philadelphia Court of Common Pleas has written that we are a nation of scofflaws—at all levels, rich and poor, old and young, men and women, white and black. If this is so, the message we need to hear is not that we overvalue law but that we undervalue it. We need to recover our sense of the historical rootedness of our law in our moral and religious tradition: this is connected with Solzhenitsyn's fourth point. That recovery would help us reform our legal system in the direction of greater humaneness and greater social justice without making it an object of idolatry.

The Need for Reconciliation of Values.—It is likely, however, that Solzhenitsyn was speaking primarily not to us but rather to his own people. At one point he stated that he does not consider the West as it is today "a model for my country." "I could not recommend your society as an ideal for the transformation of ours. . . . True, a society cannot remain in such an abyss of lawlessness as our country is in. But it also is demeaning for it to remain in a state of such soulless, polished legalism as yours is in. The human soul, which for decades suffered under coercion, longs for things higher, warmer, purer than those offered by today's Western mass existence."

This was not the proper time or place for Solzhenitsyn to present in any detail his vision of the future of his people. Yet whatever that vision may be, it is strange that there is apparently no place in it for a loftier concept of legality than he was willing to suggest. Surely what is needed in the Soviet Union is not just an "objective legal scale," or the elimination of the "abyss of lawlessness." In fact, since Stalin's time the Soviet Union—despite its repression of dissent—has moved far toward establishing a legal regime characterized by objectivity and generality. The terror is gone. People are no longer sentenced merely on the ground that they are "enemies of the people," or convicted without a trial, or tried merely on the basis of denunciations. Permissible areas of criticism of leaders' policies have been greatly expanded. The country has been opened to broad contact with foreigners. Solzhenitsyn is quite wrong in implying that there is still no lawfulness, no objective legal scale, in the Soviet Union.

Yet much is still wrong with the Soviet legal system. There is still severe legal repression of freedom, and there is still much legally sanctioned injustice. Moreover, there are still perversions of legality, though on a greatly reduced scale. Also, outside the law there is much selfishness, arbitrariness, and corruption. What is needed in the Soviet Union, as everywhere, is not only the kind of religious spirit that Solzhenitsyn calls for—the spirit of generosity and of service and sacrifice, the sense of a higher human destiny—but also the kind of political, economic, and social structure, indeed, the kind of legal institutions, in whose soil such a spirit may take root and flourish.

Here Jesus' famous attack upon "the lawyers" is highly relevant. "Woe to you lawyers," he said, "for you tithe mint and anise and cummin and neglect the weightier matters of the law, which are justice and mercy and good faith. These you ought to do, without neglecting the others." Too often the last sentence of this passage is left out. What the whole passage says is first, that the heart of the law is "justice and mercy and good faith," and second, that the lesser matters, the technicalities, the taxes, the "mint and anise and cummin," are also important, although they should be subordinated to the main purpose.

The relation between law, on the one hand, and justice or love, on the other, is not—need not be—one of antagonism. Law is, in fact, a way of translating both justice and love into social situations involving large numbers of people. The individual person who sees a man lying injured by the wayside should be inspired by love of neighbor to help him; a law regulating the provision of medical care and compensation for persons who suffer injuries is a way of generalizing that neighborly spirit. Of course, when society acts, rather than the individual person, the passionate element, the heroic element, the sacrificial element, is to some extent reduced. But it is by no means eliminated. Too sharp a contrast between the personal and the social does a disservice to both. Law is concerned with both, just as religion is concerned with both.

It is no doubt a good thing for Russians, and not only for Americans, to be told that the American way of life is not an appropriate "model" for their future, just as it is good not only for Americans and others but also for the Soviets to hear that the socialist system as practiced in the U.S.S.R. has lost its appeal even for the downtrodden of most other countries of the world. It is good news that the time for such models has passed, and that each country, each culture, must develop its own images of the future. By the same token, however, the perpetuation of the Russian Slavophile dream of an Eastern Christian kingdom in which *sobornost* and spirituality reign and Western "legalism" and "contractualism" have no place—is also anachronistic.

The predominant emphasis on spirituality and other-worldliness that Solzhenitsyn attributes to Western Man in the Middle Ages is a phenomenon of Christianity in the first thousand years of its history, both in the East and in the West, when the monastic life was the only escape from a world seen to be in perpetual decay. Eastern Christianity has to a considerable extent preserved that emphasis, at least in comparison with Western Christianity, which since the Gregorian revolution of the late eleventh century has stressed the mission of the Church to reform the world, not only through faith but also through structures and institutions. Thus the West, together with other parts of the world that have come under its influence, has lived out a second thousand years in which legal and other structural or institutional values have often been raised to a position of predominance.

Both East and West have suffered immeasurably from these dualisms—from the split in values between the eternal and the temporal, grace and law, spirit and matter, passion and reason, the spontaneous and the planned, the sacred and the just. Today we know that to attack one set of these values in the name of the other is to threaten the integrity both of the person and of society. What is required is not a rejection of the positive values either of the East or of the West but rather a new integration of them. Indeed, not only East and West, in the traditional meanings of those names, but all the cultures of the world must draw on one another's resources if mankind is to enter the new stage to which Solzhenitsyn calls us.

～ 22 ～

CHRISTIANITY AND DEMOCRACY
IN SOVIET RUSSIA*

I n opening this conference on Christianity and Democracy, President
Carter said he hoped we would explore the meaning of Christianity and
the meaning of democracy in ways that would give guidance to those who,
like himself, are working to bring the two together in practical ways.

I believe that the experience of the Soviet Union during the past three-
quarters of a century, and up to the present moment, as remote as it is from
our own experience, has much to teach us concerning these matters. I think
that it is a very instructive exercise for us to imagine ourselves to be in the
situation of Christians in Moscow, say, or St. Petersburg, or Kiev, or Vladivos-
tok, today—and to ask ourselves, from their standpoint: What is Christianity?
What is democracy? What is the relationship between the two?

When we have returned from this mental exercise to Atlanta, Georgia,
U.S.A., I hope we will be even more acutely aware that both Christianity and
democracy have quite different meanings in different countries, in different
cultures, among peoples with different historical experience. At the same
time, we will know better than before—perhaps just because the Soviet experience is so remote from our own—what is common to Christianity

---

* Reprinted from *Emory International Law Review* 6 (1992): 23-34. Delivered at the
international conference on "Christianity and Democracy: Past Contributions and Future
Challenges," held at Emory University, November 14-17, 1991.

- 393 -

everywhere, what is common to democracy everywhere, and what is at the heart of their interrelationship.

I would like to explore, first, the meaning of Christianity and democracy in the Soviet Union during the first seventy years of its existence, from 1917 to 1987, and second, their meaning in the present period of extraordinary upheaval and turmoil, a period that was formally inaugurated only three-and-one-half years ago by the 19th Communist Party Conference and whose chief slogans are two Russian words that have now entered world language—*glasnost*, "openness," and *perestroika*, "restructuring"—plus a third Russian word whose root is easily recognized, *demokratizatsiia*, which means, however, not "democracy" but "democratization." These more recent developments, coupled with the transformation of the Union itself, are now being called—both in the Soviet Union and abroad—a revolution. It is now widely believed that the first seventy years of Soviet history constituted a great tragic blunder, to be totally discounted and rejected and, if possible, forgotten. But I assure you that the tremendous changes that are now taking place in the Soviet Union cannot possibly be understood unless one starts from the historical experience of a people that lived for more than two generations, and indeed still lives in many respects, under a political, economic, and social system created by, and until recently dominated by, the leadership of the Communist Party.

One fundamental element of that system was its propagation of a doctrine called Marxism-Leninism, and one fundamental element of that doctrine was militant atheism. Until only a little over three years ago, militant atheism was the official religion, one might say, of the Soviet Union and the Communist Party was the established church in what might be called an atheocratic state.

Leninist atheism rests on the religious—or, if you like, the irreligious—premise that man is master of his own destiny and has the power to construct a paradise on earth. It rests on a conception of man as naturally good and naturally able, by his own intellect and will, to overcome the social forces that exploit and corrupt him. Lenin conceived and created the Communist Party as a dedicated, elite vanguard, whose mission was to lead mankind into this earthly paradise. Man was to replace God; that is, he was to do by himself, through collective action, what previously it had been thought only God could do. Thus the belief that God does not exist is an essential part of the Leninist vision. Leninist atheism is a positive belief about God; that He does not exist—in contrast to agnosticism, which is a belief about man: that man cannot know whether God exists or not.

The Soviet State, led by the Communist Party, had the avowed task of promoting Marxism-Leninism and of rooting all other belief systems out of the minds of the Soviet people. I think it can be said that this was the most massive and the most powerful assault on traditional religious faith—not only on organized theistic religions but on the theistic beliefs of every person— that was ever launched in the history of mankind. Under the doctrine of the separation of church and state, churches in the Soviet Union were forbidden to engage in any activities that were within the sphere of responsibilities of the state. That meant, for example, that churches could not give to the poor or carry on educational activities. They could not publish literature since all publishing was done by state agencies, although after World War II the Russian Orthodox Church was given the right itself to publish church calendars, a very limited number of Bibles, and a monthly journal in a limited number of copies. Churches were forbidden to hold any special meetings for children, youth, or women, or any general meetings for religious study or recreation, or to open libraries or keep any books other than those necessary for the performance of worship services. Severe criminal penalties were imposed for violation of these rules. The formula of the 1936 and 1977 Soviet Constitutions was: freedom of religious worship and freedom of atheist propaganda—meaning, first, no freedom of religious teaching other than the worship service itself, and second, a vigorous campaign in the schools and universities, in the press, and in special meetings organized by atheist so-called "agitators," to convince people of the folly of religious beliefs.

Despite this massive attack, but perhaps also partly because of it, Christianity survived—and not only among a few old people, as our newspapers often reported, and as the Soviet authorities often maintained, but among tens of millions, scores of millions, perhaps, indeed, among the majority of the 150 million Soviet citizens of Russian nationality. (I single out the Russians, and the Russian Orthodox Church, only because of shortage of time. The repressive measures that I have mentioned were applicable also to the several million Russian Baptists, to the Roman Catholics and Lutherans of the Baltic States, and to believing Jews and Muslims, as well as to the Orthodox Churches of Armenia, Georgia, and other nationalities.)

I should make it clear that the figures that I have given are only guesses, since there are no published statistics. Also there is no satisfactory definition of a believer (which is the word generally used in the Soviet Union for a person who believes in God). I remember a dozen or more years ago asking a Moscow taxicab driver who was pointing out churches to me whether he was a believer. He said, "No." I then asked him, "Do you ever go to church?" He answered, "No." I asked, "Never?" He replied, "Well, sometimes when things get very hard, I go." The evidence is very strong, even without statistics, that,

as a Russian Church leader said to me in Moscow—again, many years ago—
"Our people is a believing people, despite Communism."

What accounts for the survival of Christian faith in the Soviet Union
during the pre-Gorbachev era, when religion was repressed so severely, and
indeed, not only its survival, but its extraordinary vitality?

Lenin thought that if the Church were deprived of all its wealth and
power, if it became not a means of social and political advancement but just
the opposite, a bar to all worldly success, then Christianity would die a natural death. In fact, it was purged and strengthened. Left with only its liturgy
and the sacraments, the Church, that is, the community of the faithful, commanded a devotion from its adherents and a respect from most others that the
Communist Party could not match. As Lunacharsky, the head of the Militant
League of Atheists in the 1920s, once said, "Religion is like a nail: the harder
you hit it on the head, the deeper it goes into the wood."

I once asked a leading layman in the Russian Church, "What shall I tell
the American people about the Russian Church?" I had been living in
Moscow for a year, with my wife and four children, and we were about to
return home. We had had close contacts with Russian Christians, including
both clergy and laity. It was in 1962, during Khrushchev's vicious campaign
against Christianity, which had resulted in the closing of 10,000 of the then
20,000 operating Russian Orthodox churches. He said, "Tell the American
people to get down on their knees and thank God for the Russian Church!"
He did not mean primarily the hierarchy; he meant primarily the people of
the Church, the believers. He meant that those people of the Soviet Union
who had remained faithful to God were the seed from which there could
eventually grow the roots, trunks, branches, and fruit of a humane society, a
spiritually creative society. I believe that that is now happening in the Soviet
Union, and in that sense Russian Christianity is a significant factor in what
the Gorbachev leadership in 1987 and 1988 began to call "democratization."

I read the statement in yesterday's issue of the *Atlanta Constitution*,
attributed to Father Georgii Edelshtein, a Russian Orthodox priest from
Moscow who is attending this Conference but who had to be absent this
morning, that "the Church is one of the last strongholds of communism in
the Soviet Union." Presumably he was referring to the hierarchy of the
Church and not to the people of the Church, and especially not to the hundreds of thousands of Russians, including university students and other
young people, who are now flocking to the Church to be baptized.
Presumably he was also not referring to Patriarch Aleksii II, who was on the
ramparts with Yeltsin during the recent coup and who in television appear-
ances and press interviews attacks Marxism-Leninism for the corrupting

effect it has had on the moral and spiritual life of the Soviet people. Father Georgii Edelshtein is right in saying that the hierarchy of the Moscow Patriarchate was, in the past, though it is no longer, under the thumb of the Communist authorities. In a recent interview in a leading Soviet weekly newspaper Patriarch Aleksii defended the hierarchy against the charge of subservience to Communism in the past, saying that the only alternative would have been to expose his flock to the danger of destruction. "The Church," he said, "with its many millions of members cannot descend into the catacombs in a totalitarian state. We sinned. But . . . [f]or the sake of the people, for the sake of preventing [many] millions of people from departing this life for good." In order to save those who have remained faithful, he said, "The hierarchs of the Church took a sin upon their souls, the sin of silence, the sin of nontruth. And we have always done penance before God for this."

He then added something which seems to me to be very significant for our understanding of Russian Orthodox Christianity. "Our refusal to take the Church down into the catacombs," he said, "bore an even more intense spiritual fruit. We members of the Russian Orthodox Church did not cultivate in ourselves hate and a thirst for revenge. I fear that a catacombs psychology would have driven us precisely to this."

It is probably unnecessary for me, in this audience, to say more than a few words about the special features of Russian Orthodox Christianity that distinguish it to a certain extent from both Roman Catholicism and many forms of Protestantism. One of those distinguishing features is its relative passivity with respect to politics. This passivity bears on the Patriarch's remarks which I have just quoted. The hierarchy of the Russian Church under Soviet rule preached not only love of neighbor but also love of enemy. It preached the providential nature even of persecution. I heard many sermons to this effect in Russian churches in the 1960s, 1970s, and 1980s.

The traditional political passivity of the Russian Church is associated with its strong sense of the transcendence of the heavenly kingdom. Western Christians often call this "otherworldliness," but to the Russian it is a world that is not "other" but rather "present"—present especially in the togetherness of the faithful in worship and especially in the beauty of the worship service. I am sure that most of you know that the Russian liturgy has a dramatic appeal of extraordinary power. The music carries you indeed into another world. Time stands still. One's heart soars as the priest, the deacons, and the choirs sing prayers of praise, thanksgiving, suffering, penitence, forgiveness, and grace. The faces of the worshipers shine with devotion. The eyes of the priest burn with passion. The triumphant beauty of the singing is matched by the splendor and the pathos of the ikons. The priest and deacons in resplendent robes of gold, green, blue, and white march in and out of the bema, carrying the Bible, chanting and enacting the drama of the mass. Yet this is not merely an aesthetic experience. Once when I was looking up at the ikons on the ceiling of the St. Sophia Cathedral in Kiev, a young man behind me tapped my shoulder and said, "You are disturbing the worship; this is not a museum."

The appeal of the Church to the Russian is that it offers an answer to his deepest need, the need for an alternative to the hatred, sin, and violence of this world, an alternative to its drabness and ugliness—his need to find a connection with other worlds, so that suffering and death will have a positive meaning.

You may ask, but what has this to do with democracy? My answer is Dostoevsky's. You will recall that in *The Idiot*, Prince Myshkin says *mir spasiot krasota*—"the world will be saved by beauty." Incidentally, Solzhenitsyn used this as the text of his Nobel Prize address.

It is not, of course, only an aesthetic beauty. It is also a spiritual beauty. It is the beauty of what President Carter called for in his keynote address to this conference—the beauty of sharing and alleviating suffering, the beauty of compassion, the beauty of the interaction of divine and human love.

I have given some impressions of Russian Christianity that will help, perhaps, to explain its survival and its power. I have also suggested that one important reason for the collapse of the Marxist-Leninist conception of socialism in the Soviet Union in the past three or four years was the survival of Christian faith in the hearts and minds of the Russian people. In the struggle between atheism and Christianity, atheism went under. And I have implied, at least, that atheism lost because it deprived Russians of the spiritual beauty and power, and the element of transcendence and of personal salvation that they crave. Also I have suggested that the persistence of that craving, and its expression in the surviving Christian faith of millions of Russians, against great odds, was an important factor in the introduction of Gorbachev's policy of democratization.

It is to that last point, and to the meaning of democracy in the Soviet Union, that I now turn.

Why did the power of the Communist Party leadership collapse in 1989-91? Of course there were many causes, but at least two were the introduction in 1987 and 1988—by that same leadership—first, of freedom of speech and second, of relatively free elections with competing candidates to the supreme legislative bodies of the USSR and of the various republics.

Why were *glasnost* and *demokratizatsiia* introduced? One reason, and probably the most immediate one, was the rapidly deteriorating economy and the need to carry out the drastic economic reform called *perestroika*.

But the search for causes must go still deeper: *Why* were economic conditions rapidly deteriorating? The answer usually given is that a planned economy is inherently inefficient, that it does not and cannot work. But with all its faults the Soviet planned economy did work in the past—from the 1930s to the 1970s. It worked badly, but it did succeed in making the Soviet Union the second greatest military and industrial power in the world and as late as the 1960s and 1970s, it produced substantial growth rates and also substantial improvements in the standard of living of the Soviet people. I know not only from statistics but from personal observation that Soviet citizens—with respect to consumer goods, automobiles, housing, dress, food—lived better in 1965 than in 1955 and better in 1975 than in 1965. The improvement was not substantial enough, to be sure, to meet rising expectations as the Soviet people were able for the first time to get a true picture of the economies of Europe, Japan, and the United States. Moreover, in the 1970s and early 1980s rates of growth and, above all, productivity steadily declined. It was the prospect of continued and drastically increased decline that constituted the economic crisis which Gorbachev faced when he came to power in 1985 and which drove him to introduce revolutionary changes.

The right question is, why did the planned economy stop working nearly as well in the late 1970s and early 1980s as it had worked previously?

One important reason—and one that brings me back to Marxism-Leninism, and thence to Christianity, and thence to the relationship of Christianity to democracy—was the increasing corruption, the increasing incidence of fraud, embezzlement, and stealing of state property, the expansion of the black market, the increasing dishonesty at all levels of Soviet society, and eventually, the refusal to work. In other words, at the core of the economic crisis of Soviet society was a moral crisis.

Of course there were also fundamental economic causes, but those economic causes were also closely related to the moral causes. Socialism itself, to succeed, requires a moral commitment to the collective, a spirit of collaboration, a certain altruism, a certain patriotism. Gorbachev's first efforts to meet the economic crisis that confronted him in 1985 were directed primarily to raising discipline, to fighting corruption and the black market, and to taking drastic measures to limit the consumption of alcohol. But he soon found out that the causes of the demoralization of the Soviet people were deeper.

In 1987 and 1988, when the Soviet people were given the first opportunity in their entire history to say publicly what for many years they had been saying to each other privately, their resentment, alienation, anger, surfaced—and increased. And when in 1989 they were given for the first time in their entire history the opportunity freely to elect relatively independent and authentic supreme legislative and executive bodies, they chose, for the most part, people who opposed the Communist Party, who opposed the planned economy, and who opposed Marxist-Leninist ideology—the three main pillars of the Soviet system.

The revolution began. But thus far it is a revolution without a clear vision of the future other than the rejection of the past. That is why, I believe, it is dissolving into nationalism. No one knows what kinds of political parties will replace the Communist Party monopoly. Nobody knows what kinds of economic enterprise will replace the planned economy. Nobody knows what kinds of belief will replace Marxist-Leninist ideology.

There is, indeed, a kind of democracy in the Soviet Union. People can elect their leaders and there is freedom of speech and of assembly. But there is a great fear that, as in the former Soviet Republic of Georgia, for example, the people they elect will be dictators. Already Yeltsin has been given, and is exercising, the power as President of the Russian Republic unilaterally to issue edicts that have the force of law.

It is still unclear whether the Russian people or the various other peoples of the republics *want* democracy. Is it democracy if a people has the power to rule through freely elected representatives yet chooses not to exercise that power? Or if it consents, by majority vote, to be ruled by a dictator? There is something wrong, I submit, with our definitions of democracy.

The best hope, I am convinced, for genuine constitutional governments in the republics of the Soviet Union, and at the center, is the revival of Christian faith that is now taking place. Some 6000 Russian Orthodox churches have been opened in the past two years. Christianity is being taught in some of the elementary and secondary schools and in the universities. There are religious broadcasts on television and radio. There is a massive wave of baptisms. The churches have undertaken charitable activities, including sending people to help in the hospitals and opening soup kitchens and other facilities for the poor.

The religious revival is of crucial importance, in my opinion, if the morale of the people, their hope, their willingness to work, their trust in each other, are to be raised to the level necessary for a constitutional government to operate and, for that matter, for a market economy to work.

The collapse of Communism was primarily a moral collapse, a spiritual collapse. Soviet socialism preached altruism, social responsibility, honesty—but it practiced self-seeking, corruption, and deception. A primary reason for that failure, it seems to me, was its doctrine of the fundamental goodness, and consequently the self-sufficiency of man and its lack of belief in a transcendent order, personal salvation, and an eternal life. If honesty is only a virtue and not a divine commandment, it lacks the necessary element of sanctity, and it will be discarded when it becomes inexpedient.

Today at relatively high levels of government and among scholars and opinion leaders there is a strong belief that religious faith is essential to the process of democratization in Russia. I was told a few days ago that the Minister of Justice of the Russian Republic at a talk given recently in Washington to a large gathering of prominent persons opened his remarks by saying that Russia needs to rebuild its legal system "with God as the backbone."

I said at the outset of these remarks that I hope that after examining sympathetically what Christianity and democracy mean in the Soviet Union we will be better able to say what is common to Christianity everywhere, what is common to democracy everywhere, and what is at the heart of their interrelationship.

In concluding, I would only say that by thinking about Christianity in the Soviet Union we can better understand that Christianity is not a given, it is not something that is just there, which you have or you do not have; rather it is something to be struggled for, fought for, always against great odds.

Second, democracy means not just free elections and a government based on public opinion, or even a government in which the people themselves participate. This may be its literal meaning: rule by the people—as contrasted with aristocracy, which is rule of the few, and monarchy, which is rule of the one. But we should understand democracy in a deeper sense. After the despots have been overthrown, after the oligarchy's powers and privileges have been taken away, and the will of people—in some sense of that word—has made itself felt, there comes the problem of leadership (in our system, the presidency) and the problem of wise and responsible representation (in our system, the Congress and the judiciary). In other words, every nation must find its own proper balance between the Aristotelian categories of monarchy, aristocracy, and democracy—the rule of the one, the rule of the few, and the rule of the many.

We might call this, as the Russians do "democratization." It is a process, not a fact. It is ultimately what we Americans call constitutionalism. In the tradition of Western Christianity, it is the rule of law, with "God as the backbone."

ACKNOWLEDGMENTS

The author wishes to thank the following parties for permission to reprint copyrighted material herein:

Association for the Sociology of Religion for "Law and Religion in the Development of a World Order," *Sociological Analysis: A Journal in the Sociology of Religion* 52(1) (Spring, 1991): 27-36.

Board of Trustees of the University of Illinois for "Why the History of Western Law is Not Written," *University of Illinois Law Review* (1984): 511-520.

Boston College Law Review for "The Crisis of Legal Education in America," *Boston College Law Review* 26 (1985): 347-352.

Ethics and Public Policy Center for "The Weightier Matters of the Law," in Ronald Berman, ed., *Solzhenitsyn at Harvard* (Washington, DC, 1980), 99-113.

Good News Publishers/Crossway Books for "Atheism and Christianity in the Soviet Union," in Lynn Buzzard, ed., *Freedom and Faith: The Impact of Law on Religious Liberty* (Westchester, IL 1982), 127-143.

Journal of Law and Religion for "The Religious Sources of General Contract Law," *Journal of Law and Religion* 4 (1986): 103-124.

The University of California Press Journals Department for "Toward an Integrative Jurisprudence: Politics, Morality, History," *California Law Review* 76 (1988): 779-801.

Washington University Law Quarterly for "Some False Premises of Max Weber's Sociology of Law," *Washington University Law Ouarterly* 65 (1987): 758-770.

INDEX